Traditional Leaders
in a Democracy

Traditional Leaders in a Democracy

Resources, Respect and Resistance

EDITORS

Mbongiseni Buthelezi, Dineo Skosana
& Beth Vale

MAPUNGUBWE
INSTITUTE FOR STRATEGIC REFLECTION (MISTRA)

First published by the Mapungubwe Institute for Strategic Reflection (MISTRA) in 2019
142 Western Service Rd
Woodmead
Johannesburg, 2191

ISBN 978-0-6399238-3-3

© MISTRA, 2018
Production and design by Jacana Media, 2019
Text editors: Terry Shakinovsky, Susan Booysen
Editorial assistance: Nqobile Mangena, Njabulo Zwane
Copy editor: Linda Da Nova
Proofreader: Megan Mance
Designer: Shawn Paikin
Set in Sabon 10.5/15pt
Printed and bound by CTP Printers, Cape Town
Job no. 003413

Contents

Preface

In October 2018, as this book was going to print, South Africa's apex court made a ruling on the Bakgatla community in the Northwest Province that has been described as ground-breaking. It rejected the power of traditional leaders to enter into agreements with mining companies without consulting residents occupying the affected land. In the same period, communities in Melmoth, KwaZulu-Natal, were opposing an attempt by the traditional Ingonyama Trust to assume custodianship of farms that they had got through land restitution.

These developments underline the three basic elements that typify relationships in South Africa's communal areas: supremacy of the country's constitution across the length and breadth of the republic; control over resources; and the continuum of respect and resistance.

It is precisely these issues that this edited volume of the Mapungubwe Institute for Strategic Reflection (MISTRA), *Traditional Leaders in a Democracy: Resources, Respect and Resistance* seeks to address.

The role of traditional authority in a democratic dispensation is highly contested. While the constitution acknowledges this system, the formulations are vague, and they are a source of much frustration among traditional leaders, who clamour for more power and authority. Legislation aimed at regulating traditional institutions has sought to democratise the system. Yet, in many areas, these laws are observed in the breach. Other statutes, which have tended to tilt the balance in favour of traditional leaders, have either failed to pass muster in the courts or crumpled in the face of civil protest.

Public discourse on traditional leadership has been deeply divided. Centred on a dichotomy between democracy and chieftaincy and between continuities and discontinuities in the system of traditional governance, the divisiveness of these debates has meant that nuances in the lived experience are often missed.

In this volume, the authors seek to capture these nuances by delving into such questions as: whether reference to a historically frozen traditional system is not pretentious given how that system itself was continually shaped and reshaped before and during colonial rule; how constitutional democracy and traditional leadership are influencing each other in ways that are not immediately obvious; and how people living under traditional authorities combine conformity and resistance to shape these institutions in new ways under new conditions.

As they take their journey through history, document development and distributive struggles, and examine the fraught question of authority and legitimacy, the authors add complexity to many salient debates. Using conceptual frameworks and rich ethnography, they reflect on the processes of appointment of traditional leaders; the assertion of popular sentiment including the historical flux of ethnic fusion and fission that helped keep chiefly arrogance in check; the jackboot of patriarchy and the tenuous influence of women in traditional settings; and the distortions that colonial rule imposed on the essence and praxis of traditional leadership.

As with all management of social relations, the issue of resources plays a critical role in determining levels of social cohesion or anomie in traditional communities. Against the backdrop of the mode of economic production in today's South Africa, 'custodianship' easily transmutes into 'ownership' as greedy leaders pursue personal accumulation of wealth. Confrontation around land and mining resources then becomes the stock-in-trade. In the recent period, the opening of platinum and other mines in some communal areas has generated tensions variously between the traditional leaders, municipal governments, private companies and local communities.

In examining issues of legality and legitimacy, some of the authors illustrate how, after colonial conquest, legislation served to freeze and distort traditional leadership in ways that benefitted the political and economic elites. Although under circumstances of professed good intentions on the part of government, this is now playing out in the paradoxes and inconsistencies of the post-apartheid dispensation. At the same time, both the law and the courts have been mobilised in the struggles against the abuse of power.

This book argues that it is not traditional leadership as such that poses problems for democracy – or even the inverse – but rather the ways in which the system has been distorted. It posits approaches to the resolution of these paradoxes in a manner that eschews rigidity.

MISTRA wishes to thank all the contributors, and to encourage all sectors of society to reflect on these issues as we continue shaping South Africa's democracy. Our gratitude also goes to all the partners, including the funders, who make such independent and dispassionate inquiry possible.

Joel Netshitenzhe
Executive Director

Acknowledgements

The Mapungubwe Institute for Strategic Reflection (MISTRA) would like to express its deepest gratitude to the project leaders and co-editors of this book, Mbongiseni Buthelezi, Dineo Skosana and Beth Vale, who was also the project coordinator. All three of them provided invaluable oversight of, and editorial contributions to, this book. We also owe our thanks to the contributing authors for the time and energy dedicated to producing these chapters.

Appreciation is extended to the subject specialists who provided invaluable comment and feedback, strengthening the book's analysis: Cynthia Kros, John Wright, Andrew Ainslie, Sheila Meintjies, Sarah Godsell, Noor Nieftagodien and Inkosi Sbonelo Mkhize. Members of the History Workshop (University of the Witwatersrand) not only gave invaluable feedback on content and analysis, but also co-hosted the colloquium at which these chapters were workshopped. Thanks go to Antonette Gouws for her logistical support in this regard.

A number of MISTRA staff also contributed to the successful completion of this project: Lorraine Pillay, who expedited contracts and invoices; Thabang Moerane, Dzunisani Mathonsi, Duduetsang Mokoele and Towela Ng'ambi for their substantive logistical support; Xolelwa Kashe-Katiya for guidance on project planning; Barry Gilder for facilitating the operational activities necessary for publication; Njabulo Zwane and Nqobile Mangena for assisting with technical edits. Appreciation also goes to Susan Booysen, Terry Shakinovsky and Joel Netshitenzhe for their close reading and editing of the manuscript.

Final thanks go to the Jacana Media publishing team who copy-edited, designed and produced the publication, and to MISTRA's donors who make it possible to do this work.

Project Funders

Intellectual endeavours of this magnitude are not possible without financial resources. The National Institute for the Humanities and Social Sciences (NIHSS) deserve special thanks for their support of this project.

MISTRA Funders

MISTRA would also like to acknowledge the donors who were not directly involved with this particular research project but who support the Institute and make its work possible. They include:

- ABSA
- Airports Company of South Africa Limited (ACSA)
- Albertinah Kekana
- Anglo American
- Anglo Coal
- AngloGold Ashanti
- Anglo Platinum
- Aspen Pharmacare
- Batho Batho Trust
- Belelani Group
- Brimstone Investment Corporation Limited
- Chancellor House
- Discovery
- FirstRand Foundation
- Friedrich-Ebert-Stiftung (FES)

- Goldman Sachs
- Harith General Partners
- Jackie Mphafudi
- Kumba Iron Ore
- Mitochondria
- National Institute for the Humanities and Social Sciences (NIHSS)
- National Lotteries Commission (NLC)
- Oppenheimer Memorial Trust (OMT)
- Open Society Initiative for Southern Africa (OSISA)
- Phembani Group
- Power Lumens Africa
- Royal Bafokeng Holdings
- South African Breweries (SAB)
- Safika Holdings
- Shell South Africa
- Simeka Holdings
- Standard Bank
- The Department of Science and Technology (DST)
- Vhonani Mufamadi
- Yellowwoods

Contributors

Mbongiseni Buthelezi

Mbongiseni Buthelezi holds a PhD in English and Comparative Literature from Columbia University, New York, where he also obtained a Master of Philosophy in English and Comparative Literature. A dedicated scholar, he graduated cum laude from both the University of KwaZulu-Natal and the University of Natal, earning a Master of Arts in English Studies and Bachelor of Arts (Hons.) in English and Drama, respectively. Working in various academic and activist capacities, Mbongiseni has been interested in how the state interfaces with citizens in areas that include land restitution, the role of traditional leaders in governance, heritage and public archives. With various collaborators he has researched and written on the state's constructions of the identities of citizens in KwaZulu-Natal through heritage discourse and commemorative events. He has also written on land and citizenship rights in rural areas and the role of traditional leaders in the realisation of these rights, as well as the dire state of public archives and its implications for accountable government.

Aninka Claassens

Aninka Claassens is Director of the Land & Accountability Research Centre (LARC) in the Faculty of Law at the University of Cape Town. She has been a land activist in South Africa for many years. She worked with communities who were resisting forced removals and farm evictions during the 1980s as part of the Transvaal Rural Action Committee (TRAC), a project of the Black Sash. She was a senior researcher at the Centre for Applied Legal Studies at the University of the Witwatersrand from 1990–1996, during which time she was a technical advisor (land rights) to the Constitutional Assembly. She was an advisor to the Ministry of Land Affairs from 1996–1999. Between 1999 and 2009 she worked with the Programme for Land and Agrarian Studies (PLAAS) at the University of the Western Cape and for the Legal Resources Centre. Aninka was a member of the High-Level Panel on the Assessment of Key Legislation and the Acceleration of Fundamental Change chaired by Kgalema Motlanthe during 2016 and 2017. Aninka holds a PhD in Development Studies.

Peter Delius

Peter Delius retired as Professor and Head of the Department of History, University of the Witwatersrand, in 2016. His research has focused on the history of the Pedi kingdom and his books include: *The Land Belongs to Us* (1983), *A Lion Amongst the Cattle* (1997), *Mpumalanga: An Illustrated History* (with Michelle Hay, 2009) and *Forgotten World: The Stone-Walled Settlements of the Mpumalanga Escarpment* (with Tim Maggs and Alex Schoeman, 2014). He has written extensively on rural issues and migrant labour, and in recent years has been deeply involved in research on land restitution and tenure reform. His most recent book, co-authored with William Beinart and Michelle Hay, is *Rights to Land* (2017).

William Ellis

William Ellis is a lecturer in the Department of Anthropology and Sociology at the University of the Western Cape. For the past eight years he has served as a lecturer and tutorial programme coordinator in the department. Prior to this (1999–2003), he worked as a research fellow at the Programme for Land and Agrarian Studies (PLAAS), during which he conducted fieldwork among the Khomani San of the southern Kalahari. This research served as the basis for his PhD dissertation, titled 'Genealogies and Narratives of San Authenticities'.

Nkosi Phathekile Holomisa (Ah! Dilizintaba)

Nkosi Phathekile Holomisa (Ah! Dilizintaba) is a traditional leader of amaGebe (aka amaHegebe) Clan of Mqanduli, Thembuland. He is former Chairperson and member of a number of Parliamentary Committees, including the Joint Constitutional Review Committee, Agriculture and Land Affairs and Provincial and Local Government. He was President of the Congress of Traditional Leaders of South Africa (Contralesa) from 1990 until 2013. During his tenure as President of Contralesa, Dilizintaba sought to gain meaningful recognition for the institution of traditional leaders in South Africa. In 2011, he published a book entitled *A Double-Edged Sword*, which outlines the history and formation of Contralesa, which was followed the next year by another entitled *According to Tradition*.

Sonwabile Mnwana

Sonwabile Mnwana is Associate Professor and Head of Department of Sociology at the University of Fort Hare, East London. He is the former deputy director of the Society, Work and Development Institute (SWOP), University of the Witwatersrand (Wits), Johannesburg. He is currently a research associate at SWOP (Wits). Sonwabile's research focuses on the meanings of land, extractives and rural social change.

He has published widely in reputable scholarly and public platforms. He is also Project Leader for the research project: 'Mineral Wealth and Politics of Distribution on the Platinum Belt'. This research project is funded by the Open Society Foundation for South Africa. Some of the work in Sonwabile's chapter has been produced under this project. Sonwabile is also the former president of the South African Sociological Association (2016–2017).

Sindiso Mnisi Weeks

Sindiso Mnisi Weeks is Assistant Professor, Public Policy of Excluded Populations, in the School for Global Inclusion and Social Development at the University of Massachusetts, Boston. She is also Adjunct Associate Professor in the Department of Public Law at the University of Cape Town (UCT), where she was previously a senior researcher in the Rural Women's Action Research Programme at the Centre for Law and Society, combining research, advocacy and policy work on women, property, governance and participation under customary law and the South African Constitution. Dr Mnisi Weeks received her DPhil in Law from the University of Oxford, where she was a Rhodes Scholar based at the Centre for Socio-Legal Studies. Prior to Oxford, she clerked for then Deputy Chief Justice of the Constitutional Court of South Africa, Dikgang Moseneke.

Tlhabane Mokhine 'Dan' Motaung

Tlhabane Mokhine 'Dan' Motaung worked for the South African government for 15 years as a speechwriter for former presidents Thabo Mbeki and Kgalema Motlanthe. His general areas of interest include world history, African history, classical philosophy and African philosophy as well as political economy. His particular area of research is South African history. He is a senior researcher at MISTRA.

Fani Ncapayi

Fani Ncapayi holds a PhD (2013) in Sociology from the University of Cape Town (UCT), and is currently an honorary research associate of the Centre for African Studies (CAS), UCT. His passion for poor rural people has linked him to the land-based non-governmental organisation (NGO) Cala University Students Association (CALUSA) in Cala, Eastern Cape. He is currently a senior researcher for the Trust for Community Outreach and Education (TCOE) – a national NGO. His work combines research with organising and supporting rural residents in their struggles for socio-economic justice. Ncapayi's research interests are land and agrarian issues, as well as rural governance.

Nkosi Mwelo Nonkonyana (Zanemvula)

Nkosi Mwelo Nonkonyana (Zanemvula) is Head of the Ama-Bahla clan. Presently, in 2018, he serves as Chairman of the Congress of Traditional Leaders of South Africa (Contralesa) in the Eastern Cape, as well as Chairman of the Eastern Cape House of Traditional Leaders. Trained as a lawyer, Nonkonyana is also an advocate of the High Court of South Africa.

Dineo Skosana

Dineo Skosana is a PhD candidate in the Department of Political Studies, Wits University and a lecturer at North-West University, Vaal Triangle Campus. She is a Wits History Workshop and City Institute affiliate. Her doctoral project investigates the contestations over African grave site removals in a coal mined area in Tweefontein, Mpumalanga. She holds a Master of Arts in Political Studies and has expertise in traditional leadership disputes and local governance in South Africa. Her broad range of research interests includes indigenous politics, governance, policy, heritage, religion, as well as land restitution in South Africa.

Beth Vale

Beth Vale is a researcher in the Humanity Faculty at the Mapungubwe Institute for Strategic Reflection (MISTRA). Her research interests span health and illness, body politics and everyday configurations of power and privilege in South African society. Her PhD (from the University of Oxford) and her master's (from the University of Cape Town) theses produced ethnographic work on the ways that HIV treatment is delivered, used and appropriated in South Africa's Western and Eastern Cape. Before joining MISTRA, she worked as a postdoctoral fellow of the Wits History Workshop. In her long-standing effort to bridge research and policy, Beth has worked with a range of NGOs and advocacy groups, and often consults on matters of health policy.

Sithandiwe Yeni

Sithandiwe Yeni is the national coordinator of Tshintsha Amakhaya, a civil society alliance for land and food justice in rural South Africa. She is the former Rural Transformation project manager at Oxfam South Africa, researcher at the Land and Accountability Research Centre at the University of Cape Town and development facilitator at Surplus People Project. She received her master's in Land and Agrarian Studies at the University of the Western Cape and her master's in Development Studies at Erasmus University in the Netherlands. She is an inaugural fellow for the Atlantic Fellowship for Racial Equity hosted by the Nelson Mandela Foundation and Columbia University in New York.

ONE

Collisions, collusions and coalescences

New takes on traditional leadership in democratic South Africa – an introduction

MBONGISENI BUTHELEZI
& BETH VALE

In January 2018, the newly elected African National Congress (ANC) president, Cyril Ramaphosa, and his executive team paid two courtesy visits: the first to Zulu King Goodwill Zwelithini kaBhekuzulu (Mthethwa, 2018), and a second, later visit to Xhosa King Zwelonke Sigcawu (eNCA, 2018). Both visits formed part of a well-publicised trip to KwaZulu-Natal and the Eastern Cape provinces, following Ramaphosa's highly contested election as president of the ANC at the party's December 2017 Nasrec conference.

Strikingly, this newly elected ANC leadership chose to meet traditional leaders as one of the first political statements of its incumbency. These visits were integrated into a wider tour of places of historical significance to the ANC, including the graves of former party presidents John Langalibalele Dube, Josiah Gumede, Pixley ka Isaka Seme and Albert Luthuli (Matiwane, 2018). The meetings

1

between the new ANC president and traditional leaders raised a number of questions: what kinds of relationships could be expected between government and traditional leaders under Ramaphosa, given the rapprochement between the two institutions under President Jacob Zuma? Would state institutions be reorganised once again to reposition traditional authorities vis-à-vis local governments and rural communities?[1] And would we finally see clarity in policy and legislation on the role of traditional leaders in land administration and rural governance?

The chapters in this book bring fresh eyes to questions surrounding the evolution of traditional leadership in democratic South Africa. The volume investigates traditional leadership across the country, from KwaZulu-Natal and North West, to the Eastern Cape, Northern Cape and Gauteng, drawing from the disciplines of history, anthropology, political science and legal studies. Indeed, the book is unique in its geographic, historical and disciplinary scope. Yet this has not diminished its depth, with many authors offering detailed and complex case studies of traditional leadership in flux.

At the core of the book is an exploration of two types of governance – traditional and democratic. They remain discernibly distinct in contemporary South Africa but have also mutually transformed one another to look nothing like the institutions envisaged in formal legislation. The recognition of traditional leaders post-1994 – whether as custodians of land, mediators of disputes or champions of local development – has changed the very nature of constitutionally prescribed democracy. In this volume, Peter Delius's chapter draws on pre-colonial history to show how the relationship between traditional leaders and land has been distorted in the democratic period, favouring static and imposed formulations of the institution instead. Taking this argument further, Aninka Claassens's chapter describes how the laws of the new South Africa have entrenched colonial and apartheid formulations of traditional leadership, and so have robbed rural people of their land rights in profoundly undemocratic ways. Her chapter tracks the effect of post-apartheid legislative interventions in the wake of the report of the High Level Panel on the Assessment of Key Legislation and the Acceleration of Fundamental

Change released in November 2017.[2] Claassens's intervention shows that legislation passed since 2002 has favoured the interests of elites, including traditional and political party leaders, at the expense of the people living in the former homelands. What's more, the space for holding leaders accountable has remained limited and in some cases has even narrowed.

In Sindiso Mnisi Weeks's chapter, we learn that post-apartheid approaches to traditional leadership have (ironically) eroded forms of democratic participation inherent in customary communities. The state's approach has favoured senior traditional leaders – chiefs – at the expense of lower-level leaders – headmen. Her chapter demonstrates that it is in fact at the lower levels of traditional leadership, below the chieftaincy, where the most extensive dispute resolution and community building takes place. Similarly, Fani Ncapayi's chapter draws on a case study from the Eastern Cape's Cala Reserve, in which traditional leaders were imposed in ways that were contrary to the (far more democratic) customary practice of electing lower-level traditional leadership.

In these and other ways, the incorporation of traditional leadership into post-apartheid governance has had a profound effect on how democracy has (or has not) unfolded. Indeed, the ongoing role of traditional leaders in local governance has led some authors to argue that South Africa's democracy has been distinctly uneven, benefitting urban but not rural citizens (see Claassens's chapter 3; Ntsebeza, 2004).

But while traditional leadership has had an indelible impact on the shape of South African democracy, so too has post-1994 democracy imprinted itself on traditional leadership. To return to the Cala Reserve: rural residents used democratic legal institutions to assert their right to elect local headmen, which had been custom in their community for some time. As Ncapayi's chapter illustrates, these residents leveraged *democracy* to retain ownership over the forms of *traditional* leadership they held dear. Similarly, in the KwaZulu-Natal village of Makhasaneni, the local headman, along with his constituents, drew in legal counsel to launch a campaign against mining on the community's land, premised on the land rights accorded them in a democracy (see Sithandiwe Yeni's chapter 5).

Similarly, the October 2018 landmark judgment of the Constitutional Court upheld the land tenure rights of the Lesetlheng community over and above mining rights that had been obtained in collaboration with traditional leaders. Here, it is quite explicitly a democratic constitution that serves to delimit the powers of traditional leaders, thereby disrupting prior practices which had positioned Bakgatla Ba Kgafela traditional leaders as primary custodians of the land.

South Africa's new dispensation, along with the democratic government's attempts at redress, have also created the context for the KhoiSan revival movement explored in William Ellis's chapter. The diverse KhoiSan community who, under colonial and apartheid administrations, had their land, identity and languages stripped from them is now leveraging both democratic and traditional institutions to campaign for recognition. They have leveraged the South African parliamentary process and rights-based discourse, alongside post-1994 traditional leadership legislation, in their attempts to claim territory and recognition as a customary community in a modern democracy.

Indeed, what both democratic and traditional institutions seem to share, at least in theory, is a mandate to restore the dignity of African and 'indigenous' peoples. Calls for cooperation between elected and traditional leaders have often been premised on this principle. The contributions by Dineo Skosana, Nkosi Holomisa and Nkosi Nonkonyana bear witness to this.

The chapters presented here show that there continues to be astonishing fluidity and heterogeneity in the practice of traditional leadership, despite legislative attempts to homogenise the roles and functions of the institution. In this regard, traditional leadership has remained true to its form: ever changing and contextually rooted. This will have implications for the future of both traditional leadership and democracy, as the two institutions continue to rub against and remould each other.

A political history

One argument used to explain the persistent relevance of traditional leaders in a democracy is that the ANC makes advances to traditional leaders at election time, in keeping with the untested assumption that 'chiefs bring the rural vote' (Oomen, 2005; Claassens, 2014; Bendile, 2018). In the context of renewed political fervour around land reform in South Africa, even the opposition party, the Economic Freedom Fighters (EFF), is beginning to form its own relationship with the Congress of Traditional Leaders of South Africa (Contralesa); this was illustrated by a recent joint media conference on 5 July 2018 (*Polity*, 2018). Traditional leaders, too, are cognisant of political parties drawing closer to them in order to vie for rural votes. Following a meeting with EFF officials, Contralesa General Secretary Zolani Mkiva is reported to have said, 'We [Contralesa] need to be advising political parties on what to do and actually, sometimes, command them on what they have to do. And that thing of people agreeing with you simply because they want your vote ... We're not going to take that anymore. We will tie political parties to their word' (Bendile, 2018).

The question remains: to what extent does the nature of a political party's relationship with traditional leaders influence how voters vote at election time? It's a question that cries out for fuller examination. Recently, Aninka Claassens (2016) has called for an interrogation of the assumption that aligning with traditional leaders will deliver the rural vote. Classens argues that this assumption has been discredited by increasingly vigorous protests by rural citizens at traditional leaders' lack of consultation in negotiating and profiting from mining deals.

Many of the chapters in this book describe the contests and contradictions of traditional leadership in democratic South Africa. In this introduction, we offer a historical reflection on the crafting of South Africa's democratic constitution to understand how the roles and powers of traditional leaders were negotiated, as well as the effect of these negotiations on contemporary instantiations of traditional leadership.

South Africa's democratic transition and the formal establishment of a precarious balance

The negotiators at the Convention for a Democratic South Africa (CODESA I and II) and then the Multi-Party Negotiation Process (MPNP) (1991–1993) arrived at a precarious compromise on the future roles and powers of customary leaders who, to all intents and purposes, had formed local government in the homelands of apartheid South Africa. As Michael Williams (2010: 82) notes, chiefs were adamant that they should continue to exercise authority at local level as representatives of the people. Williams (2010: 85) explains that when the first round of negotiations took place in 1991, traditional leaders were not invited. They were only included in the second round of negotiations in 1993 (Williams, 2010: 85). The Inkatha Freedom Party (IFP), which was the ruling party in the KwaZulu homeland, refused to take part in these CODESA II negotiations in protest at what they deemed a slight to King Goodwill Zwelithini.[3] Inkatha also doggedly refused to commit to participation in the elections until quite late in the process, pursuing a policy of brinksmanship and violence. Williams (2010: 86) notes: 'It was not until the ANC and the National Party [NP] agreed to a constitutional principle that guaranteed the Zulu monarchy would be recognised and protected in the newly formed KwaZulu-Natal province, that the IFP agreed to participate in the elections.' At about the same time, the Ingonyama Trust Act No. 3KZ of 1994 was rushed through the KwaZulu legislature and was eventually signed into law by FW de Klerk in the last days before the first democratic elections. Traditional leaders in former homelands across the country became beneficiaries of the IFP's brinksmanship and Contralesa's engagement in the negotiations. A settlement with the IFP and Contralesa was conditional on traditional leaders being granted constitutional recognition. This, in turn, would be used to give legitimacy to the powers of traditional leaders over rural land and citizens, well into South Africa's new dispensation. And so it was that chieftaincy – a hereditary, largely patrilineal institution – was entrenched at the very birth of the South African democratic state.

Before the transition to democracy

Long before the negotiations and transition of the early 1990s, ANC intellectuals such as Govan Mbeki in the 1950s and subsequently Jabulani 'Mzala' Nxumalo as late as 1988, had seen chieftaincy as a 'backward' institution that would be abolished once democracy had been achieved (Van Kessel & Oomen, 1997: 565). The emergence of Contralesa in 1987 took the ANC by surprise and forced a change of stance (Van Kessel & Oomen, 1997: 568).

The position of chiefs in relation to the state and to liberation politics had undergone major changes in the preceding century, as traced by Ineke van Kessel and Barbara Oomen (1997). Despite representing the concerns of the small, urban, black middle class, the early ANC had maintained a connection with the rural aristocracy. It had created an Upper House for traditional leaders who joined the organisation.[4]

However, the organisation was radicalised by the growth of its working-class membership in the 1940s and 1950s when South Africa's industrialisation process accelerated, the National Party gaining power in 1948 (Van Kessel and Oomen, 1997: 562–563). From the 1950s onward, the apartheid government restructured rural society, making chiefs responsible for the recruitment of labour for the mines, commercial agriculture and industry; implementing land 'betterment' schemes, which involved culling livestock and demarcating land, and trying minor cases such as family disputes and disputes over livestock.[5] Chiefs became accountable to the state and not the people they led, leading to despotism and deep unpopularity (Mamdani, 1996: 122). Hereditary chiefs were deposed if they resisted state policies and new chiefs were installed. New chiefdoms were also created in the drive to re-tribalise Africans, and chiefs were imposed on communities that previously had no institution of chieftainship (Van Kessel & Oomen, 1997: 563).

From about 1950, the ANC had turned the focus of its mobilisation to urban areas, and by 1960 it no longer perceived chiefs as potential allies (Van Kessel & Oomen, 1997: 564). In the 1980s, youths aligned to the United Democratic Front (UDF) revolted against the authority of these chiefs. By then, chiefs in the bantustans had, for the most part, become functionaries of the state with little popular legitimacy.[6] In the 1980s, many of them collaborated with the apartheid state's security forces to try to suppress the youth revolts, organising vigilante groups – armed by the South African Defence Force – that fought bloody battles against members of civic organisations (Van Kessel & Oomen, 1997: 567–568).

Contralesa emerged out of this maelstrom as an alliance of progressive chiefs who were resisting the creation of a new bantustan for the Ndebele Ndzundza people in the then northern Transvaal, which is part of the Limpopo province today. The organisation quickly aligned itself with liberation movements. The ensuing debate about what the place of chiefs should be in an anti-apartheid alliance was resolved when the ANC shifted focus to a negotiated settlement, as a military victory seemed less and less likely. Thus, '[w]ith the promise of delivering the "block vote", chiefs assumed a new role: no longer relics of a feudal past, but strategic allies in the conquest of state power' (Van Kessel & Oomen, 1997: 571).

Extending the South African state: Entrenching the chieftaincy after 1994

Borrowing Richard Sklar's concept, Williams (2010: 30, 86) correctly maintains that South Africa established a 'mixed polity' when accommodating the chieftaincy in the Interim Constitution of 1993. However, there was a significant shift in how customary authorities were to be accommodated from the initial agreements reached in the negotiations and formalised in the Interim Constitution Act 200 of 1993, and the final form that was incorporated into the post-apartheid state, defined in the Constitution of the Republic of South Africa (Act 108 of 1996). Williams (2010: 87) usefully draws out the change: firstly, whereas in the Interim Constitution chiefs were entitled to be members of local government and were eligible to be elected to any office in local government, in the final Constitution the president, at his or her discretion, decides the status of traditional leaders in local government. Secondly, the Interim Constitution 'provided that provincial legislation must establish Provincial Houses of Traditional Leaders to deal with matters relating to the chieftaincy or customary law' (Williams, 2010: 87) whereas the final Constitution watered down this provision, stating that provincial legislation 'may' create such houses. Finally, in the Interim Constitution, a Council of Traditional Leaders was to have 'the authority to review national legislation that affected the chieftaincy' (in Williams, 2010: 88). In 1996, this was revised to say national government 'may' establish such a body (Williams, 2010: 88). Ultimately, the final Constitution rendered the powers and roles of customary leaders hollow. Chapter 12 of the Constitution merely recognises the institution of traditional leadership as subject to the Constitution itself and to customary law. The chiefs, their positions voiced by Contralesa and the Inkatha Freedom Party, were unhappy (Williams, 2010: 88).

Things were to get worse for traditional authorities when the Local Government White Paper was published in 1998. The White Paper proposed the creation of wall-to-wall municipalities, superimposing new institutions over apartheid-era tribal and regional authorities that were legislated by the 1951 Bantu Authorities Act No. 68 and had been established in the 1970s in most homelands (Williams, 2010: 91–92). Institutional plurality at local level was firmly established to continue the mixed polity established in 1993. The White Paper was soon followed by the Municipal Structures Act No. 117 of 1998 that formalised many of the proposals in the White Paper. Effectively, this meant legislation that established a system of governance that retained apartheid-era structures (now defended by customary leaders in an attempt to retain the authority given to them by the apartheid state) and superimposed on them another structure to be elected through the ballot, as Aninka Claassens and Brendan Boyle have argued (2015: 2). It also meant two different systems of governance: one for areas previously designated as homelands for black South Africans, and another for urban areas and rural areas previously demarcated for white people. In effect then, this legislation retained the demarcations laid down in the 1913 Natives Land Act No. 27, which had formalised and legalised black South Africans' dispossession from the land by white settlers.

It took until 2004 for the state to define and legislate the place of traditional leaders in the democratic dispensation. By 1997 in KwaZulu-Natal, at the IFP's unbending insistence, traditional leaders still formed part of local government (Van Kessel & Oomen, 1997: 576). The ANC attempted to loosen Inkatha's grip on traditional leaders and their rural support base by transferring the responsibility for paying the chiefs from the provincial to the national government in 1996. The IFP challenged this move in court and won (Van Kessel & Oomen, 1997: 577). According to Jo Beall, Sibongiseni Mkhize and Shahid Vawda (2004: 763), with the rushing through Parliament of the Traditional Leadership and Governance Framework Act (TLGFA) No. 41 of 2003 ahead of the election in 2004, the state finally validated the role of chiefs in local government. They would be leaders of 'traditional councils' in the rural areas of South Africa where they would work alongside elected representatives. Beall, Mkhize and Vadwa (2004: 763) see the effect of this law as '... significantly entrench[ing] the authority of traditional leaders', meaning, 'in effect, that legislation introduced in the 21st century will give perpetual life to a system of "indirect rule" dating back to the colonial era and ossified under apartheid'. This is because these 'traditional councils' were a continuation of apartheid-era tribal authorities. The former were never discontinued.

The 2009 TLGFA also established the Nhlapo Commission, which was set up to investigate, among other things:

- a case where there is doubt as to whether a kingship, principal traditional leadership, senior traditional leadership or headmanship was established in accordance with customary law and customs,
- a traditional leadership position where the title or right of the incumbent is contested,
- all traditional leadership claims and disputes dating from 1 September 1927 to the adoption of provincial legislation dealing with traditional leadership and governance matters.

As Dineo Skosana and I have written elsewhere,

The Commission received 1322 submissions, conducted many problematic investigations and hearings, and published a report on paramountcies in its five-year life span. By the end of its term, it had not resolved all claims and disputes before it, leading one claimant, Melizwe Dlamini of the Nhlangwini in southern KwaZulu-Natal, to challenge the President of South Africa in court to extend the Commission's term so that his claim could be resolved. The result was the establishment of a new Commission in 2011 (Buthelezi & Skosana, 2018).

While it took until 2003 for legislation attempting to clarify the powers and roles of chiefs to be passed, customary leaders, as Williams (2010: 2–3) shows, did not sit around and wait for their roles, functions and powers to be legislated. The chieftaincy was now compelled to share its authority with a new set of institutions based on norms, rules and processes that differed from its own. Consequently the chieftaincy set to work, negotiating a way to accommodate itself to the new institutions. The result has been 'the mutual transformation of both the state institutions and the chieftaincy, and the blending together of the different political norms, rules and processes associated with each' (Williams, 2010: 2–3). In other words, we have observed the development of vernacular forms of democracy or, in Lucia Michelutti's (2007: 1) formulation, 'the vernacularisation of democracy'. By this, Michelutti (2007: 1) means 'the ways in which values and practices of democracy become embedded in particular cultural and social practices, and in the process become entrenched in the consciousness of ordinary people'.

Williams (2010: 80) describes how 'the post-apartheid South African government has sought to simultaneously accommodate and transform the chieftaincy as it has attempted to introduce democratic norms, processes and institutions into the former bantustan areas'. The ruling ANC's policy of 'incrementalism' (Williams, 2010: 83), which saw the TLGFA passed almost 10 years into the democratic era, meant that 'at the local level there were important informal relationships being formed' while the formalisation of the chieftaincy was being negotiated. After they had lost the battle to be local government, chiefs had to compete with the new local government institutions. They thus set about establishing 'accommodations' with these local government institutions 'with the goal of controlling them as much as possible' (Williams, 2010: 143). Mutual transformation of both institutions thus took place in several ways:

- Local government councillors have to accommodate themselves into pre-existing local rules, procedures and norms. 'They cannot simply claim that their authority [is] the result of democratic elections and begin working directly with rural communities' (Williams, 2010: 153). They thus have to work with chiefs and their deputies such that they end up appearing to work with, or even under, chiefs.

- In some places, chiefs and elected councillors work together on matters of development to best serve the interests of members of rural communities (Williams, 2010: 132–3). This sometimes extends to the co-option of councillors by chiefs, some of whom have their own independent access to power which allows them to bypass local elected councillors.

- At the same time, whereas the positions of chiefs (*amakhosi*), their deputies (*izinduna*) and assistants have historically been hereditary, with the introduction of democratic norms and processes in post-apartheid South Africa, internal reforms have been increasingly adopted. This has meant that greater participation and choice have become possible. Williams (2010: 225) cites the case of village-level elections introduced to choose the chief's councillors.

It is clear, therefore, that following the end of the transition negotiations in 1993, tribal authorities were left in place to accommodate the regional Inkatha Freedom Party, which was waging political violence that could have ended in a protracted civil war (Traniello, 2008: 36). In 1998, elected local government was then superimposed onto this institution in the hope that the chieftaincy would be overridden by this new democratic institution. Subsequently, an attempt was made to 'democratise' the chieftaincy. This attempt took the form of introducing legislation in 2003 that laid down rules for representation on the tribal councils, which were then renamed 'traditional councils'.

The regulations stipulated that women should hold at least 30 per cent of the seats on the council, and that 40 per cent of representatives on the council should be elected rather than appointed. By 2018, that formal democratic transformation had failed. Meanwhile, at local level, informal, contingent transformation has proceeded apace – and not necessarily in directions that enhance democracy. This has yielded hybrid vernacular practices, norms and rules.

The two types of institutions – the chieftaincy and local government – have mutually transformed each other. Away from the eyes of national authorities, both traditional leaders and their constituents work out institutional forms, norms and rules that suit their needs. There is evidence of a trend towards chiefs using their hereditary positions to negotiate with mining and agricultural capital on behalf of communities, becoming business partners in mining and farming initiatives ostensibly on behalf of these communities and then pocketing the communities' share of the money. Sonwabile Mnwana's chapter gives the historical context for these dynamics in the Bakgatla area of the North West. Mnwana illustrates how the relationship between traditional leaders and land has instantiated over time, contributing to the present-day centrality of traditional leaders in struggles over the distribution of resources. The chapter demonstrates that, at least in some instances, chiefly power over land precedes post-apartheid legislation, and is instead located in a much longer history. Similarly, in his chapter, Tlhabane Motaung delves into a chieftaincy dispute near Hammanskraal, with roots that date back to the 1800s. The cases explored by Mnwana and Motaung are two of many in which the legitimacy of the chieftaincy – in the eyes of either other members of their chiefly family or the wider community – is fiercely disputed. The interventions of the Nhlapo and similar provincial commissions, have been unable to resolve these disputes.

In fact, it appears impossible to resolve disputes for all time. As Peter Delius's chapter shows, leadership positions are almost – by definition – fluid. Legitimacy, therefore, is not an indefinite given. Legitimation of chiefly authority is a repetitious process through which the right to govern is earned. Contestation and challenges to leadership, either from the ruled or from contenders to the throne, are a common feature of leadership systems, be they democratic or hereditary (Comaroff & Comaroff, 1974; Hamilton, 1998). Both Sithandiwe Yeni's and William Ellis's chapters show us how processes of contestation are playing out. In Sithandiwe Yeni's chapter, we see unaccountable power being challenged from below in Makhasaneni. In this case, a lower-level traditional leader (headman) collaborates with constituents to challenge the royal council. Similar contests over legitimacy are described in William Ellis's chapter. He explores how KhoiSan groups have seized opportunities opened up by the state in their ongoing attempts to resolve vexed questions of traditional leadership. This is after more than two decades of the state focusing on traditional leadership in black African groups, and KhoiSan groups being giving little consideration. Historically, the KhoiSan have had an ad hoc leadership structure. However, the recognition afforded traditional leaders in South Africa's democratic dispensation has encouraged some KhoiSan revivalists to define and leverage 'authentic' KhoiSan leadership.

Finally, Fani Ncapayi's chapter explores how people in the Cala Reserve have resisted the imposition of traditional leaders, which is in contravention of established local practices of electing headmen. This led to the imposed laws being subverted or resisted by the community. In instances like these, it takes adjudication by a court to avert confrontations that have the potential to turn violent. To be sure, violence in the contests over traditional leadership has manifested in various parts of the country over the years. It has especially been driven by contestation over land rights in relation to mining operations, as touched on by Mwana and Yeni.[7]

To offer a different perspective from the critical takes by academics and activists who dominate this volume, Nkosi Phathekile Holomisa and Nkosi Mwelo Nonkonyana trace a history of traditional leaders becoming progressive activists in the struggles against colonial and apartheid authorities. They offer their personal experiences to demonstrate a side of the institution that is often considered only in passing in public debates. Taken together with the other chapters, their contributions reinforce the complexity of traditional leadership and the ways in which it interfaces with democratic institutions in post-apartheid South Africa. This interface is not only a South African phenomenon, but one that is acutely visible in other contemporary African societies. Contributions to *The Politics of Custom: Chiefship, Capital and the State in Contemporary Africa*, edited by John and Jean Comaroff (2018), show just how complex these matters are in countries including Mozambique, Zambia, Cameroon, Ghana, Sierra Leone and Burkina Faso. The Comaroffs (2018: 7) put these complexities down to

> … the changing character of the global economy as it has worked its way into Africa, the political effects of which include the greater or lesser decentring of the state and the outsourcing of many of its functions; the deregulation of markets and, with it, the circumventing of national administrations by corporations, NGOs, and donor and development agencies; the pluralisation of sovereignties, jurisdictions, and modes of legitimation; the privatisation of public life and the empowerment of parochial authorities, communities, cultures, and identities; forces that play out diversely in their encounter with micro-ecologies of the local.

What remains unresolved

Many matters remain unresolved as multiple interests – including those of various arms of the state, traditional leaders, activists, citizens, academics, mining and international bodies – sometimes violently collide, sometimes cooperate and, at all times, remain in ongoing negotiation with one another. Some long-standing questions remain relevant:

- What is the source of traditional leaders' authority today?
- Can there ever be a resolution to the impasse about whether support for traditional authorities means replicating colonial and apartheid formulations of African political power?
- Can drawing on precolonial thinking about, and frameworks for, systems of governance help to resolve this impasse? In other

words, what should African pasts mean in postcolonial presents as new modes of existence are being worked out?

- How are the boundaries of contemporary 'customary communities' determined and on what basis is one a member?
- How do residents in these communities accommodate a life as both traditional 'subjects' and democratic citizens? Why do only some South Africans grapple with this dual governance, while others do not?
- How do we accommodate the fluidity and heterogeneity of traditional leadership, while still regulating its roles and functions?
- Can the hereditary nature of traditional leadership ever coexist comfortably with a democratic system of election to office? Answers to this question need to take into account the fact that previous means of contesting succession, including violent usurpation, are no longer open to those wishing to take office, as they may have been prior to colonial and apartheid legislation.
- And, ultimately, what should be the place of traditional leaders in democratic dispensations?

This volume offers us routes to engaging with these complex questions. In historically and contextually grounded chapters, authors help readers to navigate some of the most contested questions of South Africa's democracy. The debates they raise, and enter into, will rage on as the balance of forces changes and changes again over the coming years. As South Africa continues to negotiate what is a protracted and messy democratic transition, it would do well to understand the trade-offs, power structures and high social stakes entailed in the future of traditional leadership.

A note on terminology

The English terms 'chief' and the more palatable 'traditional leader' remain contentious and conceptually imprecise. In most indigenous South African languages, there are extensive lexicons describing rulership and relationships between various levels of authority.

Across the various languages, the terms do not name or describe the same offices or relationships, making translation or description in another language a difficult, if not impossible, task. Consequently, it was left up to each author to choose the terms used in his or her contribution. Hence authors have employed different vocabularies to name institutions and office holders, anchoring these terms in the specificities and context of their work.

References

Beall, J., Mkhize, S. & Vawda, S. 2005. 'Emergent democracy and "resurgent" tradition: Institutions, chieftaincy and transition in KwaZulu-Natal'. *Journal of Southern African Studies*, 31 (4), 755–771.

Beall, J. 2006. 'Cultural weapons: Traditions, inventions and the transition to democratic governance in metropolitan Durban'. *Journal of Southern African Studies,* 31 (2), 457–473.

Bendile, D. 13 July 2018. 'Contralesa out shopping for allies'. *Mail & Guardian*, https://mg.co.za/article/2018-07-13-00-contralesa-out-shopping-for-allies, accessed 2 October 2018.

Buthelezi, M. & Skosana, D. 2018. 'The salience of chiefs in post apartheid South Africa: Reflections on the Nhlapo Commission', in Comaroff, J. L. and Comaroff, J. (eds.) *The Politics of Custom: Chiefship, capital and the state in contemporary Africa.* Chicago: University of Chicago Press, pp. 100–135.

Carnie, T. 2018. 'Chaos on the Wild Coast after attorney arrested following fracas with Mantashe'. *Times Live*, https://www.timeslive.co.za/news/south-africa/2018-09-24-watch--chaos-on-the-wild-coast-after-attorney-arrested-following-fracas-with-gwede-mantashe/, accessed 24 September 2018.

Claassens, A. & Boyle, B. 2015. 'A promise betrayed: Policies and practice renew the rural dispossession of land, rights and prospects'. Johannesburg: South African Institute of International Affairs.

Claassens, A. 13 May 2014. 'Haste over land rights bill not just in aid of buying votes'. *LARC* website, http://www.customcontested.co.za/haste-land-rights-bill-just-aid-buying-votes/, accessed 2 October 2018.

Comaroff, J. & Comaroff, J. 1974. 'Chiefship in a South African homeland: A case study of the Tshidi chiefdom of Bophuthatswana'. *Journal of Southern African Studies*, 1 (1), 36–51.

Comaroff, J. & Comaroff, J. 2018. *The Politics of Custom: Chiefship, capital and the state in contemporary Africa*. Chicago: University of Chicago Press.

eNCA. 9 January 2018. 'ANC visits amaXhosa king'. eNCA, https://www. enca.com/south-africa/ramaphosa-visits-amaxhosa-king, accessed 24 September 2018.

Hamilton, C. 1998. *Terrific Majesty: The powers of Shaka and the limits of historical invention*. Cambridge: Harvard University Press.

Land and Accountability Research Centre (LARC). 2018. 'Traditional and Khoi-San Leadership Bill ('TKLB')', http://www.customcontested.co.za/ laws-and-policies/national-traditional-affairs-bill/, accessed 24 September 2018.

Mamdani, M. 1996. *Citizen and Subject: Contemporary Africa and the legacy of late colonialism*. Princeton: Princeton University Press.

Matiwane, Z. 2018. 'Ramaphosa's KwaZulu-Natal visit seen as bid to consolidate ANC support'. *IOL*, https://www.iol.co.za/dailynews/ pics-ramaphosas-kwazulu-natal-visit-seen-as-bid-to-consolidate-anc-support-12659462, accessed 24 September 2018.

Michelutti, L. 2007. 'The vernacularization of democracy: Political participation and popular politics in Northern India'. *Journal of the Royal Anthropological Society*, 13 (3), 639–656.

Mthethwa, B. 7 January 2018. 'ANC's top leadership pay homage to Zulu monarch'. *Times Live*, https://www.timeslive.co.za/politics/2018-01-07-ancs-top-leadership-pay-homage-to-zulu-monarch/, accessed 24 September 2018.

Ngqulunga, B. 2017. *The Man Who Founded the ANC: A biography of Pixley ka Isaka Seme*. Johannesburg: Penguin.

Ntsebeza, L. 2004. 'Rural governance in post-1994 South Africa: Has the question of citizenship for rural inhabitants been settled 10 years in South Africa's democracy?', Indiana University website, https://dlc.dlib. indiana.edu/dlc/bitstream/handle/10535/2319/Ntsebeza_Rural_040512_ Paper033a.pdf?sequence=1&isAllowed=y, accessed 2 October 2018.

Ntsebeza, L. 2005. *Democracy Compromised: Chiefs and the politics of the land in South Africa*. Leiden: Brill.

Oomen, B. 2005. *Chiefs in South Africa: Law, culture, and power in the post-apartheid era*. New York: Palgrave Macmillan Press.

Parliament of South Africa. 2017. 'Report of the High Level Panel on the assessment of key legislation and the acceleration of fundamental change', https://www.parliament.gov.za/storage/app/media/Pages/2017/october/ High_Level_Panel/HLP_Report/HLP_report.pdf, accessed 24 September 2018.

Polity. 6 July 2018. 'EFF, Contralesa defend Zulu King's special land imbizo.' *Polity*, http://www.polity.org.za/article/eff-contralesa-defend-zulu-kings-special-land-imbizo-2018-07-06, accessed 24 September 2018.

Traniello, M. 2008. 'Power-sharing: Lessons from South Africa and Rwanda'. *International Public Policy Review*, 3 (2), 28–43.

Van Kessel, I. & Oomen, B. 1997. '"One Chief, One Vote": The revival of traditional authorities in democratic South Africa'. *African Affairs*, 96 (385), 561–585.

Williams, J. M. 2010. *Chieftaincy, the State and Democracy: Political legitimacy in post-apartheid South Africa*. Bloomington: Indiana University Press.

Endnotes

1 Traditional Affairs was elevated into a national department alongside Cooperative Governance in 2014.

2 The Panel was tasked by the Speakers' Forum in Parliament with reviewing the effects of key legislation passed since the dawn of democracy on the triple challenge of poverty, unemployment and inequality; wealth creation and distribution; land reform; and social cohesion and nation building.

3 See https://www.sahistory.org.za/dated-event/codesa-ii-talks-end-deadlock.

4 See Ngqulunga (2017) on Pixley ka Isaka Seme and his relationship with chiefs. As with a British House of Lords, this Upper House would serve as a review and advisory board for elected officials (the Lower House), but would have lesser powers and functions.

5 This is the function of maintaining order that Williams (2009) argues gives the chieftaincy legitimacy, having been exercised by chiefs since pre-colonial times and been continuous even as it was elaborated by colonial and apartheid authorities.

6 It is a moot point that legitimacy was uneven. Scholars like Oomen (2005) and Mamdani (1996) argue stridently that chiefs had such little popular legitimacy that this effaces the nuances that existed.

7 At the time of writing this introduction, media carried news of a confrontation in the Eastern Cape between the Minister of Mineral Resources accompanied by some chiefs on the one hand, the Amadiba Crisis Committee, other people opposed to mining on the Wild Coast and their lawyers during a public consultation (Carnie, 2018).

SECTION ONE

A History Of 'Traditional' Leadership

In the former Ciskei, the people were opposed to the traditional leadership system. And yet this government is imposing the system on the people. This situation exposes that we are divided, there are people in urban areas that are governed by human rights and democracy, and there are people in rural areas who are governed by traditional leaders.

NTSIKA DAPHO, HIGH-LEVEL PANEL EASTERN CAPE PUBLIC HEARINGS, 16 AUGUST 2016, P. 50

They [the government] [...] forget that the fathers of the anticolonialism struggle, for two thirds of the period of that struggle, were traditional kings and leaders like Adam McKock the Fifth, Moshoeshoe, Hinta, Shaka ... and others.

CHIEF PIENAAR, HIGH-LEVEL PANEL NORTH-WEST PUBLIC HEARINGS, 1–2 MARCH 2017, P. 14

Chairperson, let me take you back to the first electoral victory for the ANC government: you said you would respect the traditional leadership. Even Walter Sisulu, during his rally in KwaMhlanga, said traditional leaders [...] will never be slaves. It seems like traditional leadership has been turned into slaves, used by municipalities to rubber stamp their decisions ... please, just like pre-1994, make sure that traditional leadership are part of government, and they do not play second fiddle to [the] premier and councillors. Please restore the dignity [of] the institution of traditional leadership.

MAHLASELA, BAKGAGA BA MOTHAPO TRADITIONAL COUNCIL, HIGH-LEVEL PANEL LIMPOPO PUBLIC HEARINGS, 14–15 MARCH 2017, P. 66

The introductory chapters in this section offer a broad, critical history of traditional leadership in South Africa, spanning the pre-conquest, apartheid and democratic periods. Each also serves to highlight the volume's central themes: land, leadership and law. First, drawing on precolonial history, Peter Delius unsettles a number of key assumptions at work in post-1994 constructions of chieftaincy, including that chiefs are 'owners' of land. Dineo Skosana's chapter then investigates questions of leadership, looking particularly at the relationship between chiefly authority, party politics and state power over time. Using the historical record, Skosana argues that, although many have viewed present-day chieftaincy as being dependent on the African National Congress (ANC)-led government, there have in fact been interdependent relationships between traditional leaders and the ANC dating back to the Congress's formation. More so, relations between liberation, political and traditional leadership have been historically tied to struggles over land. Finally, Aninka Claassens's chapter attends to the post-1994 period, interrogating the role of legislation in characterising traditional leadership in contemporary South Africa. History is also salient here: Claassens argues that new laws have, ironically, defaulted to apartheid borders, and indeed apartheid constructions of chieftaincy, rather than upholding more inclusive customary law. All these chapters point to the heterogeneity and fluidity of traditional leadership. Indeed, traditional institutions have been shaped, and reshaped, along with relationships of power, capital and dispossession. What might contemporary struggles over traditional leadership tell us about the present moment? How might we read the landscape – and indeed the book – as a reflection of how power is configured, reconfigured and fought for in democratic South Africa?

TWO

Mistaking form for substance

Reflections on the key dynamics of pre-colonial polities and their implications for the role of chiefs in contemporary South Africa

PETER DELIUS

The question of how best to accommodate traditional leadership within a framework created by a democratic constitution dogged South Africa's negotiation process in the early 1990s and has cast a shadow over our society ever since (Ntsebeza, 2006; 2008). Part of the difficulty is that the Constitution prescribed that traditional leaders should be recognised, but also stipulated that this endorsement should not impinge on the equality rights clauses inscribed in the Bill of Rights.[1] These debates, as well as the practices and legislation that flowed from them, were all underpinned by assumptions about the nature of traditional authority in pre-colonial times and the ways it was reshaped by conquest and colonial rule.[2]

This chapter challenges three key assumptions that have bedevilled the discussion of pre-colonial chieftainship. The first of these is that it is possible to comprehend key political dynamics through examining rules and norms outside of historical processes. The second is that political centralisation was either unilinear, or necessarily a form of progress. And the third is that chiefs were the owners of the land. My key argument in relation to all of these themes is that since conquest, and post-1994, a colonially defined form of chieftainship has been entrenched at the expense of the pre-colonial substance of the institution. This substitution has made the institution far less compatible with a democratic order than might have been the case if pre-colonial practice had informed policy formation and practice.

My focus in this chapter will be limited to the dynamics of chieftainship prior to the formal incorporation of African societies into a colonial system of administration. I don't spell out in any detail processes of transformation in the 20th century – topics I have dealt with elsewhere (Delius, 1996; 2008). As it is, this essay traverses a vast sweep of history and speeds across a variety of political systems, each with its own special features. It plays fast and loose with questions of periodisation and skates over salient forms of change. In short, it will dismay specialists who have laboured long and hard to illuminate dimensions that are poorly lit in this account. But I beg the indulgence of both general readers and experts in the belief that some of the cross-cutting patterns and issues that emerge from a broad focus can make a significant contribution to the debate about traditional leadership in the past and the present.

Some terminological issues first need to be addressed. The term 'traditional leader' is extremely broad but is widely used nowadays. Its appeal is that it has a less colonial ring to it than the term 'chief', which was previously the name commonly given to forms of political leadership in southern African societies. The term 'chief' has the advantage of being somewhat more specific, but it has been deployed, usually by outsiders, in relation to so many different societies across the globe that it carries a multitude of potential meanings. I use it in this paper as an overarching translation of the terms *inkosi, kgoši, hosi, khosi*, which are used in southern Bantu languages and are derived from the common root *kosi* (Landau, 2010b: 397). This term is also used with suffixes that indicate rank and scale. In Sepedi, for example, *košikgolo* refers to a paramount chief or king while *kgošana* refers to a small or subordinate chief or headman. Exactly which of these forms was used, and by whom, was shaped by struggles over, and perceptions of, power and rank.

Chieftainship: Deeply rooted and responsive

One thing that is clear is that chieftainship was an institution of considerable historical depth within African societies. Core elements probably arrived with the earliest farmers around 300 AD. It seems highly unlikely, as some writers have assumed, that the institution emerged *in situ* out of systems previously organised primarily on the basis of kinship groups (Hammond-Tooke, 1985; Bonner, 1980). Part of what distinguished chiefly forms of rule was the absence of overarching, common kinship. Particular chiefdoms were defined by the recognition of a particular chief. This individual was usually drawn from a dominant or royal lineage.[3] Although some of the subjects of chiefs belonged to related lineages, others had no kinship connection at all to the royal group. Some of the chief's subjects were descended from groups who had lived in the area prior to the arrival of the chiefly lineage. Others had arrived later and sought permission to settle in the area. If you start to unpick the composition of particular chiefdoms, for example, as Krige did in the Lowveld in the 1930s, what is revealed is a sometimes bewildering diversity of origins and histories of the subject groups (Krige, 1937). What this complexity reflects is the very high levels of mobility that existed between different chiefly foci. Individuals, families and groups came and went on a considerable scale.

A crucial factor that allowed for high levels of mobility and more broadly shaped the nature of the political system was the availability of land. It is now a clichéd comment on African history, but one that I believe provides important insights, that in pre-colonial Africa there was a relative abundance of land. Population densities were generally sparse. Africa was a relatively under-populated continent and, in many areas, including South Africa, there was more land available than people to work it (Iliffe, 1995; Delius, 2010). Power and wealth as a result depended on being able to build up large followings. Chiefs needed to attract and retain subjects. Those who could offer material and military security and effective leadership gained followers. But capricious and incompetent rulers lost followers. Leaders who were able to accumulate large numbers of cattle and/or control high value trade goods, including imports of beads, cloth, iron and brass, were able to attract and reward subjects and clients.

The fact that land was relatively easily available made it relatively easy for groups to move between chiefdoms (Iliffe, 1995; Delius, 1983, 2010). The richer seams of evidence that are available for 17th-, 18th- and 19th-century South Africa suggest that there was considerable movement between chiefdoms (Krige, 1937). This process and possibility placed significant restraints on the chiefly abuse of power. But in case we imagine that this process was always or essentially benign, we should recall that the capture and forced incorporation of women and children was an aspect of this competition for followers, which at times became a central theme in politics in the region (Delius, 2010). It would also be wrong to assume that these possibilities entirely prevented chiefs from treating their subjects violently, greedily or unfairly in the short term. It took long periods of time before the checks on abusive rule became effective (Morton, 2017). In some societies, certain strata were locked into servile relationships (Morton, 1994).

The importance of control over people rather than land meant that territorial boundaries were not as sharply defined as in more land-based systems. The perimeter of a political unit was defined by the location of families who recognised the authority of a particular ruler. It was by no means uncommon for the subjects of different rulers to live in intermingled and overlapping settlements (Delius, 1983). Some households recognised and so paid tribute to more than one chief, while others used these rather messy realities to retain effective independence.

An equally significant result of pervasive mobility and fluid boundaries was cultural heterogeneity and adaptation within and between chiefdoms. In some instances, an initially dominant language gave way to another. The population of Bokoni provides a good example. Over three centuries, the dominant language shifted from being Nguni to Sotho. Among the neighbouring southern Ndebele, a Nguni dialect remained dominant (though not exclusive) from the 17–19th centuries. But these groups become famous for wall art that drew heavily on northern Sotho patterns (Delius, 1989; Delius et al., 2014). Cultural elements were also far from coterminous with political and language boundaries. Even pottery styles, which have often been regarded as key ethnic markers, can cut across linguistic boundaries and take their cue from regional systems of trade and interaction (Delius et al., 2014).

The widely held belief that tribes – consisting of culturally homogenous groups with clear political, social and geographic boundaries – held sway across the land completely fails to capture the realities of chiefly rule and pre-colonial society in South Africa. In fact, the concept of the tribe is rooted in Eurocentric misconceptions and colonial manipulation (Iliffe, 1979; Vail, 1989; Delius, 1989; Landau, 2010a: 1–2; Hamilton & Liebhammer, 2017). It is a major impediment to understanding pre-colonial African societies.

Chiefly control had considerable historical depth and geographical coverage. But it was not as pervasive as many historians and officials have assumed. Part of the blame for this rests with historians who, blinkered by an interest in state formation and the biases in their sources, focused their research on kingdoms and centres of political power. They were less concerned with the areas that lay between states where very much weaker forms of overarching political authority often existed. In these zones, individual homesteads could more or less run their own affairs (Hay, 2014; 2015).

The extent and populations of these areas of autonomy expanded and contracted in relation to levels of insecurity and degrees of access to key resources. The conquest of African kingdoms in the last decades of the 19th century, along with the existence of large areas of land controlled by absentee landlords – especially in the north of the country – also allowed for an accelerated process of dispersal of homesteads. The white officials who constructed the new systems of native administration had to deal with the reality of decentralisation and dispersal. But most remained wedded to the idea that chieftainship had been the dominant institution prior to colonial rule and should play a central role in the future (Hay, 2014; 2015).

Fission, fusion, succession and transformation

There were a number of recurring political tendencies within chieftainship (Hall, 1987:63–64):

> One of these was an ongoing tension between the forces of centralisation, which allow individuals to build up political and economic power and competition for authority by rivals. Thus, through time chiefdoms are constantly fragmenting and reforming as factions gain power, build up strength and subsequently lose control to other groups.

These processes are called fusion and fission. This description captures repetitive processes, but it can also convey a sense of randomness of outcomes. It does not explain the changing substance of the conflicts that fuelled competition and shaped longer-term trajectories of change. In short, while it underscores that chieftainship is a dynamic institution, it is less effective at laying bare the underlying forces at play.

The available evidence suggests that a recurring point of conflict and fission in chiefly political systems was succession to office (Delius, 1983; Comaroff, 1974; Morton, 1994). Rule-based accounts of the institution, which were compiled largely in and after the period of colonial conquest, came to frame the understanding of succession. In this view, clear rules were laid down as to who should become chief. The expectation was that the eldest son of the chief's wife would become chief on the death of his father. There were also a number of subsidiary rules stipulating what should be done if the heir was a minor or if no heir had been born at the death of the chief.

The belief that these rules had determined succession to office in pre-colonial South Africa played a very important part in shaping the nature of chieftainship after African societies had been conquered in the 19th century. Officials and some anthropologists believed that succession disputes could be properly and effectively dealt with by turning to the rules of succession and genealogies for guidance. Dealing with succession became one of the principal preoccupations of the Department of Native (later Bantu) Affairs. An ethnography section set up in the department in 1925 busied itself with collecting genealogies and determining who were the legitimate heirs – unless one of the contenders was seen as being rebellious and/or uncooperative, in which case a more controllable individual was appointed. In this world, pliability trumped rank or popular legitimacy (Comaroff, 1974; Delius, 1983; 1996).

But the idea that rules determined who succeeded to office in pre-colonial South Africa was fundamentally flawed. As is copiously detailed in almost all collections of oral traditions, succession was as much a flashpoint for conflict in pre-colonial African societies as it was in the 20th century (Ellenberger, 1912; Hunt, 1931; Molema, 1920; Peires, 1981; Soga, 1930; Webb & Wright, 1976; Winter, 1912). At the most extreme, these disputes resulted in violence with the most militarily powerful contender taking office after having defeated his rival or rivals. Defeated contenders often moved away with their followers and established their own settlements and chiefdoms (Comaroff, 1974; Delius, 1983; Morton, 2017).

There are numerous examples of the most genealogically senior contender being defeated by a more junior rival. Some of South Africa's best-known and most celebrated leaders – Tshawe, Shaka, Thulare and Sekhukhune, to name but a few – rose to power in spite of, rather than because of, the formal rules of succession. They became rulers because they commanded popular and/or military support which allowed them to defeat their rivals.

These outcomes were often shaped by the respective popularity of the contenders rather than their relative seniority. Military strength after all depended in part on popular support, as reflected in the number of individuals prepared to fight on your behalf. Historian Jeff Peires (1989) has pointed out that people often supported contenders of relatively low rank against harsh or greedy rivals of higher rank. But it was not only in instances of open conflict between rival contenders that the rules could be overturned. As John

Comaroff (1974) has illustrated, there is ample evidence of the rules being manipulated to replace unpopular rulers. Conversely, there are many instances of individuals who started as regents, but then asserted their own claim to the throne and were succeeded by their own sons.

Councillors often played a crucial role in the process of appointing a new chief, or even in replacing an existing one, and this could be achieved by manipulating genealogies or using the concept of regency (Comaroff, 1974). A chief who had taken office but then fallen out with his councillors and lost the support of his subjects might find that it was argued with increasing force and conviction that he had in fact never been appointed as a chief. It might be asserted that he was no more than a regent who had a caretaker role until a minor heir was of age and should therefore step aside. Issues of biological, rather than sociological, parentage were also raised. An heir might, for example, find that his mother's status as chief wife starts to be questioned – perhaps on the basis that bride wealth payments had not really been concluded. A popular candidate would be able to muster popular support to resist such an interpretation, but an unpopular candidate might find that such assertions gathered force and undermined his claim to office.

As a result, accession to high office was no guarantee of security of tenure. As an informant of Tshidi Barolong observed (Comaroff, 1974: 50): 'Many are born and some are robed with the leopard skin [installed], but few die as chiefs.' Furthermore, particular office holders' rights to rule were under constant review (Comaroff, 1974: 51):

> The Tshidi ... have a clearly defined model in relation to the incumbency of a chiefship – it suggests that the rights and duties of an incumbent are not immutably fixed: the chief and his subjects are thought to be in a perpetual transactional process in which the former discharges obligations and, in return, receives the accepted right to influence policy and command people. The degree to which his performance is evaluated as being satisfactory is held to determine his legitimacy, as expressed in the willingness of the Tshidi to execute his decisions.

This is not to suggest that rules of succession had no effect at all. It was very rare – though by no means unknown – for an individual who was not of royal blood to become a chief in an established chiefdom. And being of low rank was clearly an impediment to succession unless the heir apparent was particularly incompetent or unpopular. While commoners often reminded rulers that, '*Kgoši ke kgoši ka batho*' (a chief is a chief by the people), those of royal blood and others could retort, '*Kgoši ke kgoši ka madi a bogoši*' (a chief is a chief by the blood of chieftainship) (Pitje, 1950: 47). But it is clear that the idea that rules determined succession in these societies is a considerable oversimplification of a more complex and interesting reality. The practice of turning to rule books and genealogies to determine succession was a product of colonial administration and conceptions of customary law.[4] What is remarkable is that such a crude understanding of *bogoši* (chieftainship) and pre-colonial politics has survived the advent of democracy. It has, among other things, loomed large in chiefly appointments and in the deliberations and recommendations of the Nhlapo Commission (2004–2010) and the Commission on Traditional Leadership Disputes and Claims (2011–) (Peires, 2014; Wicomb & De Souza, 2013).

But there is another equally important set of issues about the nature of pre-colonial societies and chieftainship that we need to address. Thus far, I have discussed chieftainship in a way that is timeless and stresses a broad uniformity. This, of course, skates over the issues of diversity and change. While there were broad similarities between African societies, there were also considerable differences of scale, culture and political form. For example, settlements could vary from a handful of people to villages of thousands of inhabitants. In the 19th century, some societies stopped the practice of initiating men and women, while others placed even greater emphasis on it. Political systems fell along a continuum of degrees of centralisation, from isolated clusters of homesteads to overarching kingdoms encompassing entire regions. It is impossible to even attempt to itemise the range of diversity in this context. But one dimension of this process was that certain chiefdoms established their dominance over other chiefdoms. In some instances, this consisted of little more than recognition of a loose political and ritual superiority, expressed in limited payments of tribute by subordinate chiefdoms. But in some areas, more centralised political control and systematic forms of administration were established (Delius, 1983). There has been a tendency in the literature on South Africa, and African societies more broadly, to see political centralisation as a key indicator of 'progress', modernisation and development. This perspective has proved to be deeply tenacious, despite having been subject to a number of telling critiques (Neale, 1985). It tends towards teleology with the nation state representing a crucial navigational point. It also assumes that European history should be the template for evaluating changes in the rest of the world and that models of development derived largely from European experience have universal application (Neale, 1985). Most recently, it has figured in debates about the pre-colonial roots of African poverty (Acemoglu & Robinson, 2010: 21–50).[5] One of the problems with this approach is that it does not adequately consider the complex and innovative arrangements that have emerged in different African contexts.

In South Africa, for example, the Bokoni settlements that dominated the Mpumalanga escarpment in the 17th and 18th centuries had a relatively decentralised political system. Yet these societies established particularly intensive and innovative forms of agriculture. Equally in the Phalaborwa area, major centres of iron and copper production were established, which were not the product of political centralisation (Delius et al., 2014).

There was not a unilinear pattern of political evolution in which relatively decentralised political systems, with limited economic dynamism, evolved towards more stable, centralised, economically innovative systems. Powerful states expanded and contracted, fractured and fell. In the northern area of South Africa, for example, the Mapungubwe kingdom dominated politics, as well as trade in gold in the Limpopo Valley in the 12th and 13th centuries, but then lost power, allowing more decentralised systems to prevail for several centuries (Hall, 1987: 75–80). From the 17th century, trade-important new kingdoms emerged in the region, with the Venda and Pedi kingdoms providing particularly significant examples. But the power of both polities fluctuated, and in the Pedi case collapsed, for a period in the 1820s. The Ndwandwe state in northern Natal, which seemed set to dominate the region in the 1810s, had entirely disintegrated by the end of the 1820s (Delius, 1983; Delius et al., 2014).

Regiments and raiders

In the late 18th century, there was a significant change in the balance of power in some chiefdoms. One important constraint on the power of rulers had been the absence of standing armies or established police forces. A political leader who wished to use physical force against his critics or enemies depended on being able to mobilise his subjects to take up arms. The gathering of an army could be a slow process and also provided ample opportunity for resistance. Those who disapproved of the chief's actions could simply not arrive when called upon or take their time to respond. As a result, an unpopular or incompetent chief might find that his ability to use physical coercion against his enemies or recalcitrant subjects was profoundly circumscribed. In some societies, regimental systems had developed directly under the control of chiefs, which provided them with some additional coercive capacity. But these regiments were established on a localised basis and were only mobilised at times of particular need. There were still significant possibilities for resisting a call to arms (Delius, 1983).

In the late 18th century in the hinterland of Delagoa Bay, a major upswing in the demand for ivory, and later slaves, stimulated hunting and raiding, which in turn led to innovations in the organisation of regiments. Over time, standing regiments were created, which consisted of concentrations of mobilised men that stayed together for long periods and which fell more directly under the control of rulers. There, regiments also drew on male subjects from a range of chiefdoms, as well as incorporating young captives. Men living in military barracks for many years, and regularly depending on each other in battle, developed a strong sense of common identity and achieved a much higher level of battle readiness and effectiveness than occasional soldiers. Their training and structures of leadership were also designed to deepen their loyalty to kings and paramounts, rather than local-level leaders (Chewins, 2017; Wright, 2010; Omer-Cooper, 1966).

These rulers, as a result, had relatively high levels of coercive capacity and were far less dependent on cooperation from subordinate rulers or their broader body of subjects than had previously been the case. The Zulu kingdom is the state most commonly associated with this new regimental system and is seen by some as a radical new departure from previous political systems (Omer-Cooper, 1966). But this view ignores the fact that these shifts drew on much deeper and wider processes of change and patterns of innovation in the region over the 100 years and more prior to Shaka's rise to power (Wright, 2010; Delius 2010).

The concentration of power in rulers' hands that resulted from processes of political and economic centralisation diminished the effectiveness of the checks against despotic rule that existed within more devolved polities. These processes also coincided with a period of intensified military activity, when raiding for captives on a large scale by African, Boer and Portuguese forces created a generalised condition of insecurity. In this context, for many, the advantage of being under the protection of a powerful leader outweighed the costs of onerous or capricious rule (Delius et al., 2014; Chewins, 2017; Delius, 2010).

In troubled times, restless subjects had to weigh the ease of mobility that came with a relative abundance of land against the vulnerability that went with living in isolated settlements with limited military capacity. The fate of the prosperous, populous and innovative Bokoni settlements in the 1820s provides a telling illustration of potential risks. With a decentralised political and military system and a focus on production rather than war and extraction, these settlements suffered massive defeats at the hands of the regiments of Ndwandwe, Ndebele and other raiding states, which collided with the societies of the Mpumalanga escarpment. Their attackers carried off vast numbers of women, children and cattle. The Koni settlements never recovered from these hammer blows and the stone-walled homesteads and terraced fields that had dominated the region for hundreds of years thenceforth stood empty (Delius et al., 2014). The destruction of the highly productive and innovative Bokoni system by relatively militarised raiding states, and the triumph of extraction over production, is hard, for this writer at least, to characterise as progress!

As noted above, the power of the rulers of the most centralised states also waxed, waned and collapsed. In consequence, the tendency to assume, for example, that the high point of Shaka's rule of the Zulu state represents the norm within that society is more than a little displaced – especially given the fact that he was murdered in office, as was his brother Dingane. These events rather show that the processes of political competition for office were neither constrained by rules of succession nor subdued in the Zulu kingdom. Some depictions of the Zulu state also tend to exaggerate the extent to which the new political and military system displaced previous patterns, in which political power was contested but to a significant extent located in the hands of subordinate chiefdoms in polities. While the Shakan system certainly modified this underlying system, it did not replace it; in the decades that followed Shaka's death, the power of constituent chiefdoms of the kingdoms was strongly reasserted (Guy, 1979).

The power of kings or paramounts in relation to subordinate chiefdoms was in a constant state of flux, with the centripetal forces in tension with centrifugal ones. The competence, popularity and age of an incumbent could impact on the extent of his power and the same was true of the strength of subordinate rulers. Uneven patterns of drought also played their part in the distribution of power, as did the location of resources and the direction of trade routes. The relationships between different levels of leadership were dynamic and variable, as was the relationship between rulers and subjects. In the Pedi kingdom, for example, in theory all the chiefdoms within the kingdom were equally subordinate to the king. In reality, at times of weakness, the king was little more than first among equals with very tenuous overall control. Even when the centre was relatively strong, powerful chiefdoms acted as regional foci of power that mediated and profited from flows of labour and produce to the king (Delius, 1983).

Consultation rules

These dangers and challenges helped to ensure that processes of consultation to establish the views of both royals and commoners, and to garner support for potentially divisive initiatives, were a fundamental part of political systems. The more fundamental and divisive the issue, the more in-depth these processes of consultation were likely to be. The extent to which rulers consulted with followers was no doubt affected by how secure they felt in their hold on power. But very few indeed would have taken potentially divisive and unpopular decisions without in-depth processes of consultation (Delius, 1983).

Chiefs also did not act alone. They were advised by councillors, who were men highly regarded by their peers, drawn both from the ruling lineage and from subordinate groups in the chiefdom. The influence of these councillors varied. A young man who had recently assumed office could easily be dominated by his councillors. An older, more established chief often exercised considerable power over his councillors and could remove those who he fell out with – an accusation of witchcraft being one method. Councillors kept chiefs informed of popular opinion on the key issues of the day and chiefs rarely acted without seeking their advice. On particularly contentious and important issues, the process of consultation went even further. In many chiefdoms, gatherings of all the adult men in the community were held from time to time. These were partly used to inform the community of important developments, but they also provided subjects an opportunity to talk back to their rulers and sometimes even to force them to change their policies. These public meetings are particularly well described for the Sotho Tswana chiefdoms, but they also occurred in Nguni communities. In the Pedi kingdom (Delius, 1983; 57–58):

> Meetings of various degrees of exclusivity also played a key role in the political processes within both the paramountcy and subordinate chiefdoms ... the historical evidence is that participation in these meetings was fluid and incident-specific.

A broad distinction can nevertheless be made between meetings in the *lapa* (courtyard) of the chief, and *pitšo*. The former typically comprised the ruler and his closest aides, but also clients possessed of specials skills and information. These meetings could be broadened to include a wider set of royals and even all the heads of subordinate *kgoro*, and they played a central role in the formulation of policy and the administration of the polity.

The still more broadly based *pitšo* were attended by all the initiated men of the chiefdom and, in the case of the paramountcy, surrounding groups. Major and contentious issues were discussed in this forum. This allowed the weight of popular opinion to be brought to bear on the royals. The paramountcy was able to gauge the strength of and divisions within popular feeling and to moderate or even reverse policy in its light. My book (Delius, 1983) provides a number of important examples of the nature and impact of popular consultation, which show that *pitšo* were called when important decisions had to be made, including vital choices about whether or not to go to war (Delius, 1983; 57–58, 121, 241).

After 1652, imperial power and colonial expansion created additional change and contestation. From early on in the Cape Colony, KhoiSan communities found themselves under new pressures and were subordinated and dispossessed. But when pastoralist Trekboers encountered Bantu mixed farming communities in the Eastern Cape, they proved much harder to displace. The establishment of British control at the Cape after 1895 helped swing the balance of power against African societies in the longer term. British control and restructuring of economic and administrative systems – including the abolition of slavery in 1834 – led some groups of Boers to trek northwards. From the 1830s, a protracted struggle over land and labour took place in the interior, resulting in the foundation of independent Boer republics. Conflicts were largely fuelled by settlers' demands for additional land and labour for their expansive system of farming. The discovery first of diamonds and later gold in the interiors exacerbated these conflicts, and contributed to the pressure on African polities. In the main, this mounting threat contributed to processes of centralisation and militarisation of African polities. In an increasingly dangerous world, the protection of a powerful ruler was appealing – although some groups saw colonial power as offering the best security in the long term. But colonial pressures also fuelled fission and division in some instances.

The long process of colonial conquest of African polities was substantially complete by the 1880s, largely as a result of the new phase of British imperial expansion in response to the mineral discoveries. It was concluded by the end of the 19th century and allowed for significant shifts of power within African polities. Especially in the north of the country, centrifugal forces reasserted themselves. Relative peace, inadequate reserves, relatively sparse settlement by whites and large holdings by absentee landlords allowed for a considerable dispersal of homesteads.

Many Africans preferred to live on land owned by the state or absentee landlords, where taxes were lower than in the reserves where, if they paid rent, it was in cash rather than labour and where existing forms of social control and production could be maintained. Others moved from chief to chief or farm to farm in an attempt to better their living conditions (Harries, 1989: 93).

This process, along with the initially very limited recognition of chiefly power by the colonial state, undermined chiefly authority and further enhanced the autonomy of homesteads in many areas. It was only with the systematic and pervasive reassertion of chiefly power as a result of the Bantu Authorities Act of 1951, and the mass eviction of African families from white-owned land in the 1950s, that chiefly control was revived (Delius, 1996; Hay, 2014; 2015).

Land rights and chiefs

One particularly important strand in the colonial and post-1994 debates is the nature and extent of the power chiefs exercised over land in the pre-colonial period. Once the military threat posed by independent chiefs was snuffed out, colonial officials were prone to exaggerate the power of chiefs in earlier decades – often drawing on the Zulu kingdom under Shaka as their key template. This rendition of all-powerful chiefs was not initially because they had any intention of restoring chiefly power. Quite the reverse: its appeal lay in the fact that colonial rulers regarded themselves as the heirs of chiefly power and thus welcomed inflated versions of their power. Especially attractive was the idea that chiefs held ultimate authority over land, and that with the coming of colonial conquest, this control had legitimately been transferred to the colonial state (Chanock, 2001).

The description and interpretation of rights in land within African communities was also influenced by a powerful strand of Social Darwinism in British 19th-century official and legal thinking, which saw indigenous communities as being at a lower level of social evolution. According to this view, private property was the mark of civilisation, while less evolved societies were believed to have weak communal rights. The presumed absence of more 'advanced' individual rights of ownership within African societies also provided a convenient justification for seizing the land of colonised peoples (Chanock, 1991; 1996).

These perspectives led towards an exaggeration of chiefly power, especially over land, and to an understatement of the rights of their subjects and the occupants and users of the land. The 1883 Native Laws Commission (40), for example, concluded:

> the land occupied by a tribe is regarded theoretically as the property of the paramount chief; in relation to the tribe he is the trustee holding it for the people who use it in subordination to him on communistic principles (Cape of Good Hope, 1883).

This conclusion represented a very selective reading of the already partial evidence at its disposal, but it has often played an influential part in debates over whether or not chiefs were the owners and/or trustees of the land in pre-colonial South Africa.

As noted above, the relatively easy availability of land in pre-colonial Africa placed checks on the power of chiefs. But land was nonetheless a vital resource for communities whose economies depended on various combinations of farming, gathering, hunting and trading. The system of land holding in these societies is often described as a system of communal tenure. This characterisation stemmed in part from the idea that land was held within these communities on a communistic or communal basis. A corollary of this view was that chiefs were owners of the land and/or held it as trustees for their subjects. But these characterisations are misleading and partly reflect the difficulties experienced by outsiders in understanding or naming African systems (Chanock, 2001). Failures of cultural translation resulted in the use of inappropriate comparison with terminology often derived from European rather than African history. While this terminology has endured over time, a much fuller picture of systems of land tenure has emerged from both historical and social anthropological research.

The first point to make is that not all African families and small groups that settled in South Africa, particularly in the 19th and early 20th century, accessed land through a chief and within an established system of customary law. There was a lot of mobility in this period due to war, drought and economic changes. Some families, sometimes fleeing war, separated from larger groups, settled on land independently and by, opening it up and establishing their fields and gardens, made it their own. In more established African communities, rights to land came from membership of a localised kinship/residential group and a political unit – usually a chiefdom. When a group settled in a new, unpopulated area, the chief along with his councillors would grant particular areas of land to subordinate leaders, who would in turn allocate land to ward heads, who in turn would allocate areas of land to household heads on which to build and cultivate (Beinart, 2001; Delius, 2008). Plots were normally only given to married men, and men who had more than one wife would allocate each spouse her own field to work. Every married man expected to be given land, although the quantity and quality of land controlled by different households varied significantly.

When households needed additional land, they would approach local leaders to request extra land. Local leaders who required additional land would in turn approach the chief. When new groups entered an area, they had to approach the chief to ask for land.

Once land had been granted, it was usually passed on to the next generation within the same household. As a result, in settled societies most individuals received land not directly from the chief but through inheritance and allocation through households and within localised groups formed around a core of kin. New chieftainships were also as likely to be established over pre-existing populations as over vacant land, and oral traditions suggest that a common practice was to recognise the existing rights of such groups and even to acknowledge their prior relationship to the land in key rituals within chiefdoms (Delius, 1983).

Grazing land which formed the bulk of the areas of most chiefdoms was not as tightly controlled or clearly allocated as farming land. Grazing land was open to all who had livestock and there was no limitation on the number of animals that a household could put out to pasture. Chiefs and lower-level political leaders did, however, play a significant role in establishing the boundaries between grazing and arable land (Delius, 2008).

The historical evidence suggests that once land was allocated to households, it was very unusual for it to be reclaimed by a chief or local leader. Land was normally only taken away from households in the case of individuals being found guilty of witchcraft or as punishment for revolt against the chief.

A chief who denied his subjects additional land or attempted to take away lands already allocated ran the risk that he would quickly lose support and followers. It is thus clear that, while chiefs played a significant part in administering land, there were very real limits on their powers. Hunter (1936: 112–113) made the point in relation to the Pondo: 'a chief had jurisdiction over people ... [and] over land ... All of this implies political power over lordship (including small economic rights) not ownership in the European sense.'

Schapera is also very clear that chiefs could not be described as owning the land (1970: 196):

Except for the portions reserved for him and his family, on more or less the same basis as everybody else, none of the land is his property: nor can he dispose of it except gratuitously and to members of his own tribe. All members of the tribe are entitled to use as much of the land as they need; and the tribal authorities must see to it that their claims are gratuitously satisfied.

Hunter's (1936: 113) suggestion that household rights over arable land approached more nearly the European conception of ownership has been taken further by Kerr (1990) in an analysis of customary law. He points out that chiefs' key role in allotting unoccupied land has often been mistaken for ownership, and he challenges the notion that individuals acquired usufruct over arable land, but not ownership (Kerr, 1990: 61–62).

> The right to the use and enjoyment of allotted land vests in non-statutory customary law in the individual and not the chief. One must guard against the danger of assuming that a term used to describe a right in one system of law can only be used in another system if all the incidents of the right in the first system are to be found in the second. In customary law, it is necessary to reiterate that the [individual's] right is exclusive; and that it may be enforced against anyone who has taken the possession of the land; that it is inheritable and that it is alienable... it is a right which is 'good against the world', which is the definition of a real right in South African common law.

The formulation of his conclusion has been challenged by other scholars of customary law, but there is general agreement that the strongest rights to arable and residential land in pre-colonial systems were located at the level of the homestead/household (Bennet, 2004: 379).

Conclusion

The key point of this chapter is that in pre-colonial political systems competition for followers was fundamental to the survival and expansion of polities. Rulers who ignored or went against popular sentiment were likely to lose followers and/or face popular resistance, which often took the form of rallying to the cause of rival contenders to chiefly office. It was not uncommon for ruling chiefs to be deposed and killed by disgruntled rivals and subjects. Chiefdoms rose and fell, some prospered for long periods of time, others flared briefly and died. The subjects of fading centres of power often relocated to find those who could offer better protection and access to richer resources. Boundaries were porous and culture was not static and homogenous, but adaptive and heterogeneous. As a result, the concept of 'the tribe' comprehensively fails to capture the essential dynamics of pre-colonial societies. Change had cyclical elements, but was also caught up with and shaped by broader processes of transformation in the region. Colonial conquest and rule did not capture static societies long set in their ways, but incorporated dynamic and changing societies and in (some cases) quite recently established political and social systems.

Colonial rule was not informed by this rich history. Instead, as the threat of revolt receded, it saw chiefs as a useful instrument of control over land, people and labour. In this new system of administration, authority and power were seen as flowing downwards from the Governor General, who in the colonial order doubled as the imagined 'Supreme Chief' in the system of native administration. The Supreme Chief was vested with huge powers sometimes loosely justified in terms of the despotic rendition of the Zulu kingdom, but in fact far exceeding the powers of the most dominant African rulers. Issues of succession were not dealt with through the competitive political processes and tests of ability and delivery that were features of the pre-colonial polities. Instead, they were resolved by white officials armed with a simplistic understanding of the rules of succession, poring over genealogies, while bearing in mind which of the candidates for office were most likely to do the government's bidding.

In the first decades of colonial control, no more than a handful of chiefs received official recognition. This official disinterest meant that many chiefs had to maintain a significant degree of popular respect and support if they wished to survive. The extent to which chiefs remained responsive to the views of their subjects moderated the corrosive impact of colonial control. But the introduction of the Bantu Authorities Act in the 1950s and the crushing of opposition on the part of migrant workers, rural residents and a handful of chiefs further diminished the pressures on chiefs to be chiefs by the people. Instead, in the main, they became chiefs by virtue of the state (Delius, 1996). The Bantu Administration Department set about defining the boundaries of the newly proclaimed Tribal Authorities in a way designed to freeze once-porous and shifting boundaries. It was an intervention designed to reward those who cooperated with the apartheid state and to punish those who did or had not. African polities were being reshaped into the rule-based, culturally homogenous tribes of colonial imagining and distanced from the dynamic, competitive, fluid and culturally heterogeneous societies that had in fact existed in the years prior to conquest.

The dramatic political transition in the years after 1990 provided an opportunity to fundamentally rethink the nature of chieftainship and its potential role in a constitutional democracy. This was an opportunity that was far from fully exploited, for reasons which are elaborated elsewhere in this edited volume. In practice, the ways in which chiefs have been incorporated into the new South Africa show clear continuities with the colonial conceptions of chieftainship as a top-down, hereditary, rule-based, patriarchal and tribal institution. Ineffectual attempts have been made to tweak the institution through notional elections and rules about the gender composition of tribal councils. But there has been a failure to recognise the existence of a dynamic, competitive, pre-colonial institution in which the idea that a leader was a leader by the people influenced practice. Incompetent, unpopular and corrupt rulers could be blocked (or removed) from office by a wide variety of means. Subjects could make choices about whether or not they wished to be ruled by particular chiefs or indeed by any chief.

Surely in a fledgling democracy, the reality of legitimacy conferred at least in part from below should have been one starting point for defining a postcolonial role for chiefs? Instead, a co-opted institution reconstituted to serve as an instrument of colonial control, and formed by fantasies about primitive and tribal Africa, has served as the primary template for chieftainship in post-colonial South Africa.

References

Acemoglu, D. & Robinson, J. A. 2010. 'Why is Africa poor?'. *Economic History of Developing Regions*, 25 (1), 21–50.

Beinart, W. 2001. *Twentieth Century South Africa*. Oxford: Oxford University Press.

Bennet, T. W. 2004. *Customary Law in South Africa*. Johannesburg: Juta.

Bonner, P. 1980. 'Classes, the mode of production and the state in pre-colonial Swaziland', in Marks, S. & Atmore, A. (eds.) *Economy and Society in Pre-industrial South Africa*. London: Longman, pp. 31–41.

Cape of Good Hope. 1883. *Report and proceedings with Appendices, of the Government Commission on Native Laws and Customs*. Cape Town: W.A. Richards and Sons, p. 40.

Chanock, M. 1991. 'Paradigms, policies and property: A review of the customary law of land tenure', in Mann, K. & Roberts, R. (eds.) *Law and Colonial Society*. London: James Currey, pp. 61–84.

Chanock, M. 1996. 'Making and unmaking a segregated land regime', in Arnfed, S. (ed.) *Legal Change in North South Perspective*. Occasional Paper No. 18, International Development Studies, Roskilde University, pp. 18–44.

Chanock, M. 2001. *The Making of South African Legal Culture 1902–1936: Fear, favour and prejudice*. Cambridge: Cambridge University Press.

Chewins, L. 2017. 'The exclusive ivory commercial company of Inhambane and Lourenço Marques: Re-evaluating slavery out of Delagoa Bay during the early 19th century'. Unpublished seminar paper.

Comaroff, J. 1974. 'Chiefship in a South African homeland: A case study of the Tshidi chiefdom of Bophuthatswana'. *Journal of Southern African Studies*, 1 (1), 36–51.

Delius, P. 1983. *The Land Belongs to Us*. Berkeley: University of California Press.

Delius, P. 1989. 'The Ndzundza Ndebele: Indenture and the making of ethnic identity', in Bonner, P. I., Hofmeyr, I., James, D. & Lodge, T. (eds.) *Holding Their Ground*. Johannesburg: Witwatersrand University Press, pp. 227–258.

Delius, P. 1996. *A Lion Amongst the Cattle*. London: Heinemann.

Delius, P. 2008. 'Contested terrain: Land rights and chiefly power in historical perspective', in Claasens, A. & Cousins, B. (eds.) *Land Power and Custom*. Cape Town: UCT Press, pp. 211–237.

Delius, P. 2010. 'Recapturing captives and conversations with cannibals: In pursuit of a neglected stratum in South African History'. *Journal of Southern African Studies, 36* (1), 7–23. Delius, P., Maggs, T. &

Schoeman, A. 2014. *Forgotten World: The stone walled settlements of the Mpumalanga escarpment*. Johannesburg: Wits University Press.

Ellenberger, D. F. 1912. *A History of the Basutu*. London: Caxton.

Guy, J. 1979. *The Destruction of the Zulu Kingdom*. London: Longman.

Hall, M. 1987. *The Changing Past: Farmers, kings and traders in Southern Africa*. Cape Town: David Phillip Publishers.

Hamilton, C. & Liebhammer, N. (eds.) 2017. *Tribing and Untribing the Archive*: 1 & 2. Durban: UKZN Press.

Hammond-Tooke, W. D. 1985. 'Descent groups, chiefdoms and South African historiography'. *Journal of Southern African Studies*, 11 (2), 305–319.

Harries, P. 1989. 'Exclusion, classification and internal colonialism: The emergence of ethnicity among Tsonga-speakers of South Africa', in Vail, L. (ed.) *The Creation of Tribalism in Southern Africa*. Berkeley: University of California Press, pp. 82–117.

Hay, M. 2014. 'A tangled past: Land settlement, removals and restitution in Letaba District, 1900–2013'. *Journal of Southern African Studies*, 40 (4), 745–760.

Hay, M. 2015. 'South Africa's land reform in historical perspective: Land settlement and agriculture in Mopani District, Limpopo, 19th century to 2015'. Unpublished PhD, University of the Witwatersrand.

Hunt, D. R. 1931. 'An account of the Bapedi'. *Bantu Studies*, 5 (1), 275–326.

Hunter, M. 1936. *Reaction to Conquest*. Oxford: Oxford University Press.

Iliffe, J. 1979. *A Modern History of Tanganyika*. Cambridge: Cambridge University Press.

Iliffe, J. 1995. *Africans: The history of a continent*. Cambridge: Cambridge University Press.

Kerr, A. 1990. *The Customary Law of Removable Property of Succession*. Grahamstown: Rhodes University.

Krige, J. D. 1937. 'Traditional origins and tribal relationships of the Sotho of the Northern Transvaal'. *Bantu Studies*, 11 (1), 321–356.

Landau, P. 2010a. *Popular Politics in the History of South Africa: 1400–1948*. Cambridge: Cambridge University Press.

Landau, P. 2010b. 'Transformations in consciousness', in Hamilton, C., Mbenga, B. & Ross, R. (eds.) *The Cambridge History of South Africa*, Vol 1. Cambridge: Cambridge University Press, pp. 397–398.

Molema, S. M. 1920. *The Bantu Past and Present*. Edinburgh: W. Green & Son.

Morton, B. 1994. 'Servitude, slave trading and slavery in the Kalahari', in Eldredge, E. A & Morton, F. (eds.) *Slavery in South Africa*. Boulder: Westview Press, pp. 251–269.

Morton, F. 2017. 'To die for: Inherited chieftainship (Bogoši) among the

Tswana before 1885'. *Journal of Southern African Studies*, 43 (4), 699–714.

Neale, C. 1985. *Writing Independent History: African historiography, 1960–1980*. Westport: Greenwood.

Ntsebeza, L. 2006. *Democracy Compromised: Chiefs and the politics of land in South Africa*. Pretoria: HSRC Press.

Ntsebeza, L. 2008. 'Chiefs and the ANC in South Africa: The reconstruction of tradition', in Claassens, A. & Cousins, B. (eds.) *Land Power and Custom*. Cape Town: UCT Press, pp. 238–260.

Omer-Cooper, J.D. 1966. *The Zulu Aftermath*. Evanston: Northwestern University Press.

Peires, J. 1981. *House of Phalo*. Johannesburg: Ravan.

Peires, J. 1989. 'Were chiefs democratic?', in Bonner, P. (ed.) *New Nation New History*. Johannesburg: History Workshop.

Peires, J. 2014. 'History versus customary law'. *SA Crime Quarterly*, 49, 7–20.

Pitje, G. 1950. 'Traditional systems of male education among the Pedi and Cognate tribes'. *African Studies*, 9 (2), 53–76.

Schapera, I. 1970. *A Handbook of Tswana Law and Custom*. London: F. Cass.

Soga, J.H. 1930. *The South-Eastern Bantu*. Cambridge: Cambridge University Press.

Vail, L. 1989. *The Creation of Tribalism in Southern Africa*. Berkeley: University of California Press.

Webb, C. & Wright, J. (eds.) 1976. *The James Stuart Archive:* Vol. 6. Durban: University of Natal Press.

Wright, J. 2010. 'Thinking beyond "tribal traditions": Reflections on the precolonial archive'. *South African Historical Journal*, 62 (2), 268–286.

Wicomb, W & De Souza, M. 21 June 2013. 'An urgent rethink on customary law is needed'. *Mail & Guardian,* https://mg.co.za/article/2013-06-21-00-urgent-rethink-on-customary-law-neede, accessed 3 August 2018.

Winter, J. A. 1912. 'The tradition of Ra'lolo'. *South African Journal of Science*, IX, 1–14.

Endnotes

1 There is general agreement that pre-colonial political systems were patriarchal and strongly discriminatory in relation to gender. In many respects these tendencies intensified in the colonial period. Court rulings have had some effect in reforming some of the most blatantly

discriminatory aspects of customary law. But a great deal needs to change before women living under chiefly rule and in other rural societies will enjoy equal rights. In my view our current failure to live up to the values imbedded in the Constitution should be at the forefront of any discussion of the recognition and reform of traditional leadership.

2   While the debates about the nature of chieftainship in pre-conquest South Africa have intensified since 1994, there was already a considerable body of scholarship relevant to this issue available at the time of the transition to democracy that could have informed the debates more fully. Some of this material is reflected in the references for this chapter.

3   The term lineage refers to a group of people defined by descent from a common-named ancestor.

4   With the proviso that the individual was acceptable to the colonial state.

5   They also, in a somewhat contradictory fashion, point to the existence of centralised states that became too inflexible and extractive as a further cause of Africa's poverty.

THREE

Traditional leadership and the African National Congress in South Africa

Reflections on a symbiotic relationship

DINEO SKOSANA

Chieftaincy has a chequered history in South Africa. Apartheid and colonial rule were accomplished in some part through traditional leadership, producing interesting speculations about the sustainability of this leadership in a post-apartheid era. Democracy's requirement to determine leadership through elections seemed incompatible with traditional leadership's ascendency through heredity lines. One of the more remarkable features of South Africa's transition to democracy was the crafting of a political structure that incorporated traditional leadership into the post-apartheid, democratic state. In this way, traditional leadership proved itself resilient and flexible.

Research has insightfully explored the dynamics described above. Two schools of thought have emerged. The one argues that chieftainship should not be given recognition within a democratic system because it undermines the values and principles espoused in the South African Constitution No. 108 of 1996. The second view is presented by scholars who believe that certain aspects of traditional leadership are not as contradictory to democratic principles as conventionally comprehended. Therefore, there is an opportunity for the coexistence of both institutions.

I am particularly interested in the first school of thought, because the argument to do away with traditional leaders is often premised on the notion that they are parasites to the African National Congress (ANC)-led, democratic government. In this chapter, I suggest that, contrary to popular belief, traditional leaders and the ANC-led government are co-dependent. This symbiosis has historical roots that reach back to the time of the formation of the African liberation movement. The ANC and its antecedent organisation, the South African Native National Congress, needed to draw support from the rural parts of South Africa and chiefs needed a relatively organised structure to challenge the land dispossession that took place soon after the formation of the Congress. This chapter highlights the complexities of this historically interdependent relationship. In this analysis I introduce into current debates about traditional leadership elements that have not been sufficiently considered in scholarship to date, namely the intricacies of the relationship between the government and chiefs, and how this relationship is historically grounded. In order to highlight these dimensions, this chapter draws from two different case studies.

I therefore review a normative assumption among scholars that the relationship between traditional leaders and government is parasitic; that traditional leadership survived because of its historical dependence on colonial and apartheid administrations (Ntsebeza, 2005). There is a further assumption that, post-1994, traditional leaders continue to benefit from a relationship with the ANC-led government, because the legitimacy conferred on them by the state brings with it socio-economic and political benefits (Skosana, 2012). Although the latter is accurate, I suggest, on the contrary, that the relationship between the ANC and traditional leaders was historically – and remains – symbiotic. The two institutions rely on each other for much of their political legitimacy. The interdependence of traditional leaders and the ANC government was partly evident in the years leading to the formation of the Congress and, more so, after the enactment of a series of notorious pieces of land legislation, which was a concern for both the new liberation movement and for traditional leaders.

Drawing on case studies of the Eastern Cape district of Xhalanga and the Vaaltyn area of Mokopane, Limpopo, this chapter highlights the complex yet interdependent relationship between traditional leaders and the ANC-controlled government. My case study of Vaaltyn, located within the Mogalakwena municipality of Limpopo province, illustrates the intricate relationships between traditional leadership, local government and capital. This is evidenced in relation to municipal and provincial government, as well as to the Platreef mine (operating provincially) and the Kekana royal family. In this case study, government officials legitimised the Kekana claim to chieftaincy, while the recognised *kgosi*,[1] Kekana, made material gains from being the middleman between Platreef mine, the Mogalakwena local government and the Limpopo provincial government. With the help of Kgosi Kekana, the municipality was able to shift some of its service delivery responsibilities and costs to the mine.

My contention about this symbiotic relationship between the ANC government and traditional leaders deviates from Lungisile Ntsebeza's analysis, which perceives this relationship as one sided and beneficial only to the institution of traditional leadership. In his study, Ntsebeza (2005) investigates the survival of traditional leaders pre- and post-1994, through a case study of Xhalanga district in the Eastern Cape province. He focuses on questions about how traditional leaders historically obtained their legitimacy and authority. He submits that land is fundamental to understanding how traditional leaders have remained relevant throughout the colonial, apartheid and democratic dispensations.

Drawing from Mamdani's (1996) ideas, Ntsebeza maintains that 'the powers that traditional leaders possessed during the colonial and the apartheid era forced communities to abide by tyrannical chiefs, otherwise, they would stand little chance to acquire land' (Ntsebeza, 2005: 20). He argues that, as a result, traditional leadership through-out its existence has been dependent on the state for survival and that 'chiefs derived their authority from being involved in the land allocation process rather than support from their subjects' (Ntsebeza, 2005: 20–22). In Xhalanga, he argues, land issues such as 'the struggle of landholders against apartheid's engineered "re-tribalisation" gave traditional leadership in this area a specific trajectory' (Ntsebeza, 2005: 22).

Additionally, he argues that the ability of people to choose their own leaders is central to the concept of liberal democracy. For this reason, and those above, Ntsebeza argues against the continuance of chieftainship in a democratic dispensation. Even so, Ntsebeza's suggestion to do away with chiefs is, in my opinion, overstated. His argument is based on a case study in which traditional leaders have never been favoured by people (Ntsebeza, 2005). In contrast, Barbra Oomen's study (2003) in Sekhukhune illustrates a long-standing relationship between the communities in the area and traditional leaders. I draw from both Ntsebeza's and Oomen's arguments, and my case study of Vaaltyn, to show the varying complexities of the relationship between traditional leaders and the state. In doing so, I aim to establish a platform for scholars to begin to think about a comparative history of rural communities under the authority of traditional leaders. In Sekhukhune, for example, some traditional leaders did not collaborate with the colonial and apartheid governments but formed part of the broader national liberation struggle to challenge the colonial and apartheid policies. I elaborate on this later in the chapter.

To make the point about the interdependence of the institution of traditional leadership and the ANC, this chapter first traces this relationship in the context of the Union of South Africa. This is followed by a consideration of colonial land policies and legislation and the effect of these on the nature of rural society, traditional leadership and ANC leadership. A close look at historical developments at the time of the formation of the ANC reveals that traditional leaders were a major component of the opposition to the creation of the Union of South Africa, as well as land dispossession. For these reasons, traditional leaders worked closely with the liberation movement. Traditional leaders maintained a relationship with the ANC, a connection that stretches to the post-1994 political dispensation, in which the ANC-led government became more sympathetic to the institution of traditional leadership. The ANC's 'empathy' towards traditional leaders is evident in recent laws, namely, the Traditional Leadership and Governance Framework Act No. 41 of 2003; the Communal Land Rights Act of 2004 and the Traditional Courts Bill of 2012. These were passed to define and strengthen the role of the institution of traditional leadership.

Traditional leaders and the formation of the ANC

In 1909, the British parliament drafted a new constitution for its colonies in South Africa that facilitated the formation of the Union of South Africa in 1910. The Constitution paved the way for what Thompson (1971: 325) describes as 'the institutionalisation of white supremacy', defending, among other things, the colour bar, while denying suffrage and membership to Parliament to the majority of South Africans. To provide an overview of this context, Francis Meli (1998: 34) notes that:

> When translated into practice, [the South Africa Act 1909], meant the repression of all blacks in every conceivable form; it was used to curtail African freedom of movement; to deny blacks the rights of trading in their (or any other) areas; to cripple their education and generally to deny them basic human rights and chances of equality of opportunity in economic development, cultural welfare, and social advancement.

Although resistance began in the early days of the conquest, the draft constitution and later the Union of South Africa was met with intensified resistance and mobilisation. Groups of urban-based Africans and coloureds, as well as chiefs and their rural constituencies, sought ways to protect their interests. As a result, the period was marked by an increase in national and international delegations to oppose the imminent Union. This resistance was paved by intellectuals, activists and organisations from the 1860s onwards

(Odendaal, 2012). Most notable from the activists of this era, and the early 1900s, are chiefly families who 'articulated a new model for "race relations" and political participation in South Africa' (Odendaal, 2012: 10). Despite its intent to break African paganism, or 'uncivilised tribes', by subjecting the children of chiefs to British education, elite missionary education gave rise to a cohort of militant black intellectuals. The unintended social consequence of the mission schools was that they 'became the breeding grounds for twentieth-century African nationalism' (Odendaal, 2012: 13). This was the beginning of a complex relationship between the embryonic ANC and chiefs, in which members of chiefly families straddled traditional and national politics, and where nationalism flowed into chiefly realms.[2]

To challenge the proposed Union of South Africa, members of different chiefly families, such as the Soga, Kama and Ntsikana, joined the South African Native Congress (SANC),[3] which called for unity and a more organised political structure. The Congress and traditional leaders opposed the discriminatory provisions of the South Africa Act of 1909 and Britain's position regarding its protectorates by various methods. For example, Paramount Letsie Moshoeshoe of the Sotho, Sebele Sechele of Bechuanaland and the Queen Regent of Swaziland raised their apprehensions with the British government and Letsie sent a delegation that would convey the grievances to King Edward VII (Odendaal, 2012: 370). Also concerned about the implications of the impending union on chiefly authority, the *kgosi* of the Rolong appointed a delegation to attend an upcoming Bloemfontein convention. The delegation consisted of Kgosi Lekoko Montsioa, Silas Molema and Stephen Lefenya (Odendaal, 2012: 386). In the wake of several failed attempts to negotiate with the British government at conventions, Pixley ka Isaka Seme (recognised founder of the ANC) sent circulars to African leaders, communities and newspapers, outlining the need for unity and for a South African Native Congress to be formalised (Odendaal, 2012: 139–144). A large number of traditional leaders, their representatives and the leaders of local and regional political organisations converged on Bloemfontein on 8 January 1912 to attend the historic conference convened by Pixley Seme to witness the formation of a new national organisation for the African people. Traditional leaders who could not attend, such as Dalindyebo of the abaThembu, sent donations – a herd of 100 oxen – to the founding conference (Odendaal, 2012: 467).

At the launch of the South African Native National Congress (SANNC) in 1912, Seme (1912) made a call for unity when he said:

> Chiefs of royal blood and gentlemen of our race, we have ... discovered that in the land of their birth, Africans are treated as hewers of wood and drawers of water. The white people of this country have formed what is known as the Union of South Africa – a union in which we have no voice in the making of laws and no part in their administration. We have called you, therefore, to this Conference so that we can together devise ways and means of forming our national union for the purpose of creating national unity and defending our rights and privileges (cited in Rive & Couzens, 1993: 89).

Seme therefore declared the Congress's intention of honouring traditional leaders and of establishing them in the upper house. George Montsioa, grandson of the Barolong chief and in charge of setting up an ANC office in Pietersburg, suggested that

> ... seven paramount chiefs and the Zulu king, Dinizulu, be adopted as honorary presidents of the ANC. These included Dalindyebo of the Tembus, Montsioa of the Barolong, Lewanika of Barotseland (Zambia), and Letsie II of Basutholand who were elected 'Leaders of the Nobles' of what was to be an upper house in which membership was to be for life (Meli, 1988: 38).

When the upper house of the new native Parliament was formed, 22 traditional leaders served as an advisory body of the 'Executive Commoners'. The 'elected' honorary presidents (traditional leaders) represented the rural masses that would later be affected by land dispossession.

This is evidence that, prior to the formation of the Union of South Africa and the subsequent founding of the ANC, there was already an intricate coalition between traditional leaders and members of the ANC – who, if not born within chiefly families, worked and served these families. The Congress, during this time, was arguably an elitist organisation which – in collaboration with traditional leaders – was gradually able to draw membership from the countryside. While it may seem that the oppression of African people was the common enemy and a uniting factor for traditional leaders and the Congress, the major concern for traditional leaders was in fact the threat that the British government posed to their authority. The Congress was more concerned about the unjust exclusion of African people in national politics, whereas traditional leaders were apprehensive about a possible loss of power and independence in the rural parts of South Africa. However, the existence of a common enemy allowed for all the concerns to be encompassed under the banner of a struggle for African emancipation. This alliance would also be apparent in the struggle against land dispossession.

Chiefs, the ANC and the Natives Land Act of 1913

Another issue that brought the newly formed Congress, traditional leaders and different communities together was the passing of the Natives Land Act of 1913 and its effects on the rural and urban populations. This by no means implies that land dispossession only began in this period. In fact, scholars emphasise that the alienation of land from KhoiSan and Africans has a long history pre-dating 1913 (Beinart & Delius, 2014). The authors point out that alienation 'resulted from conquests between the seventeenth and nineteenth centuries, as settlers and colonial states expanded their authority into the interior' through violence and legal measures (Beinart & Delius, 2014: 669). In addition, Beinart and Delius argue that the impact of the Natives Land Act of 1913 as an instrument of land dispossession and agrarian transformation has been exaggerated, and that the Act was primarily the result of a long-term drive towards agrarian capitalism, executed through the extension of legislative measures already in place in the Cape, Natal and the Boer republics.

However, the catastrophic results of the Act – the first uniform law facilitating land expropriation across the Union of South Africa – should not be understated. It must be emphasised that the Land Act paved the way for various atrocious forms of dispossession. The Act, as Beinart and Delius (2014) identify, was passed to curtail the growing number of Africans in the Cape and Natal who had been able to purchase land through both legal and unlawful measures. The now-legalised land expropriation forced many Africans into towns, suppressing the emerging African peasantry and creating the proletarianisation of Africans. For this reason, land dispossession once more became a burning issue for Congress and traditional leaders, alongside the problem of segregation.

To challenge the 1913 Act, the Congress, which then comprised religious ministers, traditional leaders and lawyers, mounted a national campaign against native administration. Recording the history of the ANC, Meli notes that although the Congress leadership was rurally based it was not yet popular among the working class and, as a result, the movement lacked the necessary strength to challenge white power directly. Meli says this is why it opted to use tactics such as deputations and appeals (Meli, 1988). In March 1913, the Annual Conference of the SANNC appointed a deputation to present African objections to the proposed Act to the government in London (Meli, 1988). While the great challenge for the ANC was the broad struggle for equal citizenship rights – including the right to own property – for traditional leaders, the Land Act undermined their authority, which had always been asserted through their role in land administration.

The changing nature of chieftaincy

Retribalisation[4] in the 1920s and 1930s changed the dynamics of the relationship between traditional leaders, their followers and the ways in which they engaged with politics. In this period, there was a discourse shift in the state's practice of indirect rule: this was now articulated as the governance of cultural difference, rather than a practice of exclusion (Mamdani, 2013: 44). The management of difference was done through the race-tribe divide, where non-natives were labelled 'races' and natives were classified as 'tribes' (Mamdani, 2013: 44). Mamdani observes that the race-tribe divide determined the law that people would be subject to: races were governed through civil law, whereas tribes were subject to different kinds of customary law. Parts of South Africa were divided into tribal homelands, and each homeland was identified with a tribe, which was given the administrative tag of 'native' (Mamdani, 2013: 51). The administration of the homelands (indirect rule) was employed through the anthropological model of chiefs. In cases where British authorities could not find a ready-made traditional leader they manufactured one, creating a chieftaincy where none had existed before. In other instances where hereditary elites actually appeared to exist, deeper problems arose. Here, the difficulty was not in locating a traditional leader, but controlling the institution of chieftaincy. This began to taint the relationship between traditional leaders and the ANC (now renamed from the SANNC), while fostering a connection between some traditional leaders and the native administration. In other words, the handpicked chiefs who were prepared to collaborate with the native administration's governor general began to detach from the liberation movement's vision of a free South Africa.

The manufacturing and manipulation of traditional leaders had, however, already been common in the 1840s (Meyers, 2008: 2). Meyers's observation is that traditional leaders in this period assumed economic functions. For example, in Natal the British Colony established hut taxes, which were meant to be collected by chiefs, and later forced labour was also organised through chiefs. Traditional leaders who disobeyed the British authorities were expelled (Meyers, 2008: 2). As such, traditional leaders lay at the centre of the segregationist state's strategy for gaining legitimacy. State authorities and traditional leaders existed side by side, with the latter in an unresolved oscillation between being the leaders of their people and of the broader liberation struggle and being an extension of the native administration.

The extension of chieftaincy's legal foundation during the 1920s makes clear the presumption on the part of South Africa's segregationist leaders that indirect rule was far more than a temporary colonial expedient. The segregationist strategy of differentiation became law with the 1927 Native Administration Act No. 38. The Act gave traditional leaders the responsibility of carrying out all orders and instructions given to them by the local native commissioner. The legislation also made them responsible for the registration of taxpayers, the collection of taxes and population statistics, the allocation of land, the prevention of illegal occupation and squatting, the detection and punishment of offences and the supply of labour when required (Meyers, 2008: 17).

Traditional leaders and the ANC post-1948: A growing but chequered relationship

At the time of its formation, the ANC represented the concerns of a small professional middle class that maintained close links with the African aristocracy, namely the rural chieftaincy.[5] However, Ntsebeza (2005: 258–259) notes that from the 1940s onwards, the ANC became a radical movement and that, under pressure from its Youth League as well as its communist allies, it began to bifurcate between those who supported traditional leadership and those who argued that the institution of traditional leadership belonged to a feudal era. In their work about the survival of traditional leaders in post-apartheid South Africa, Van Kessel and Oomen (1997: 562) observe that South Africa's industrial revolution of the 1940s and 1950s transformed the ANC into a mass movement, with a following located mainly in the industrial centres. They further argue that the National Party's rearrangement of the countryside in the 1950s fundamentally altered the relationship between the ANC and the rural aristocracy, with the reserves being the centres of labour supply for the government (Van Kessel & Oomen, 1997: 562).

One of the central features of apartheid policies in the 1950s and 1960s was the restructuring of segregation. This entailed ending the oscillation between liberalism and traditionalism with regard to black South Africans and fusing the two tendencies into a new paradigm of so-called 'separate development'. Traditionalist ideological apparatuses were enhanced and revitalised. The 1950s saw the reinforcement of tribal tradition. The Bantu Authorities Act No. 68 of 1951 introduced the homelands system, in which Africans were to 'develop separately' under tribal authorities. The Act made provision for the establishment of regional and territorial authorities for each specific ethnic group in the homelands. This did not mean that chieftaincy was exercised in isolation from the state. Rather chieftaincy became a subordinate function of the apartheid state.

Traditional leaders were given the powers to administer the affairs of a 'tribe', to assist the government in its administration of areas and to maintain a treasury into which judicial fines collected by the chief – or fees taken in accordance with 'recognised customs' – were paid (Davenport, 1977). Similar to the native administration, traditional authorities were appointed from above and were protected by the apartheid government so long as they continued to be cooperative. Davenport (1977: 383) maintains that appointed chiefs were 'well rewarded for their preparedness to enforce government policy at the expense of their own popularity'. Copelyn elaborates on the concessions granted to those chiefs who were willing to collaborate. His research reveals that:

> Paramount Botha Sigcau had his salary increased from 700 pounds to 1 500 pounds per annum upon accepting the Bantu Authorities system. Whatever the price, it remained a fact that chiefs could not be relied upon to represent Mpondo interests to the government, but rather had turned around in their stools and were prepared to implement state interests independently of general Mpondo sentiments (Copelyn, 1974: 10).

The dual loyalty that traditional leaders held towards their subjects and to the colonial and subsequently the apartheid state has led some scholars such as Mamdani (1996), Ntsebeza (2005) and Van Kessel and Oomen (1997) to conclude that chiefs were accomplices in the oppression of their rural subjects. Although this argument is to some extent accurate, it falls short because in some areas, such as Sekhukhune, chieftaincy survived in part because of its historical and cultural legitimacy and popularity within communities. This is evidenced by the fact that while the colonial administrations attempted in various ways to influence the polity of Sekhukhune, their efforts were counteracted by resistance from Sekhukhune leaders and their subjects (Delius, 1983).[6] For example, to defend his chiefdom from European colonisation, Chief Sekhukhune sent young men to work on white farms and on diamond mines (Delius, 1983). The money earned by the young men was used to buy guns from the Portuguese and cattle to increase the wealth of the Marota people. For the chiefs of Sekhukhune and their subjects, the 1800s were years of war and resistance, against the Boers and later the British. This resistance would continue into the 20th century in the area of Sekhukhune. In the 1950s, following the passing of the Bantu Authorities Act, people in Sekhukhune resisted the authorities through organisations such as Fetakgomo – a predominantly migrant worker organisation aligned to the ANC (Delius, 1983).

However, Sekhukhune should not be romanticised as a chiefdom that has been without internal disputes, nor has it been without those who collaborated with the colonial administration. Certainly, there were individuals who were prepared to accept disputed pieces of legislation and proposals such as the so-called 'Betterment' schemes.[7] What is striking about the area of Sekhukhune is that, despite the inducements offered by colonial administrations, chiefs in the area resisted becoming part of the colonial administration, and later of the apartheid government, in one form or another.

However, the legitimacy of chiefs, as perceived by the general population, waned in many parts of the former homelands, particularly over the 1950s and 1960s. The changing nature of traditional leadership kindled resistance in various parts of rural South Africa, including Sekhukhune, Tembu and Mpondoland (Delius, 1983; Mbeki, 1964). Van Kessel (1993: 562) concludes that the rural struggles over this period indicate that 'the ANC, although now a banned organisation, was finally establishing an effective presence amongst the peasants'. She observes that for nearly 25 years subsequently, 'the bantustans would remain largely quiescent, while

African urban areas exploded periodically in waves of open protest' (Van Kessel, 1993: 562). Oomen (2002: 6) suggests that traditional leaders initiated their comeback from the late 1980s as a result of broader global developments, including the fragmentation of nation states; the emergence of alternative politics that operated locally, transnationally and internationally; and a reliance on group rights and culture as a means of engaging with modernity. Van Kessel and Oomen (2002: 565) submit that in the late 1980s, those traditional leaders – including those who were an appendage of the colonial state – who were seeking to secure their future in a post-apartheid South Africa also evoked the history of resistance. In doing so, they drew on examples of resistance, rather than the mainstream pattern of chiefly compliance (Van Kessel and Oomen: ibid). Notably, by the late 1980s the formation of the Congress of Traditional Leaders of South Africa (Contralesa) was an instance of the resuscitation of the relationship between traditional leaders and the ANC (Oomen, 1996: 49). Contralesa 'emerged on the political scene couched in the discourse of liberation politics' (Oomen, 1996: 49).[8] This has not yet been the subject of serious study. However, at a minimum, it suggests the growing connection between traditional leaders and the ANC.

Towards the transition

After the unbanning of the ANC in 1990, Contralesa's membership increased dramatically (Van Kessel & Oomen, 1996: 571). Traditional leaders perceived Contralesa as the best forum to safeguard their interests under a future ANC-led government and the ANC's view was that wooing chiefs made political sense. After the 1994 elections, the ANC government was, for some time, conflicted about the actual role of traditional leaders in a democracy (Oomen, 2002). Following pressure from Contralesa to clarify the role of traditional leaders in the post-apartheid dispensation, the South African parliament finally proposed the Traditional Leadership and Governance Framework of 2003 (Van Kessel & Oomen, 1996). The Framework, like the Bantu Authorities Act passed under apartheid, and the Native Administration

Act passed under colonial rule, established traditional councils that would play an advisory role in the local government.

The continuous pressures from traditional leaders and Contralesa for a clear, active role in a democratic dispensation led, once again, to legislation, this time the Communal Land Rights Act No. 11 of 2004. The Act came about as an attempt to compensate those who were dispossessed of land during the apartheid era, through legalisation of security of tenure in South Africa's former homelands, as proclaimed in Section 25 (6) of the Constitution of South Africa. This Act repositioned traditional leaders as the custodians of land. Thus, scholars such as Meer (1997) and Ntsebeza (2005) argue that the responsibility for land administration given to traditional leaders (mostly men) reinforced inequalities and hindered the development of the conditions necessary for a transformation in the socio-economic position of women.

Another attempt to redefine and enhance the role of traditional leaders was the recent, notorious Traditional Courts Bill (B1 of 2017). This was originally submitted to parliament in 2008 and later withdrawn after uproar from civil society organisations and the rural populace (Land and Accountability Research Centre, 2012). Towards the end of 2011 the bill was reintroduced with no major amendments. It met with the same public outcry, compelling its instigators to resubmit it to the National Council of Provinces for review. Traditional leaders who favoured the bill supported Phathekile Holomisa's (2011) view that the bill was an extension of South Africa's justice system to the countryside, and that traditional courts are more accessible than those in a more formal judicial system. The opponents of the bill argued that it reinforced old colonial and apartheid divides between urbanised citizens and rural subjects, and that it inhibited the latter from enjoying the same economic, political and legal benefits as the former (Gasa, 2011; Mnisi Weeks, 2011). Feminists argued, in line with Gasa (2011), that the bill would undermine the rights of women, as the institution of traditional leadership does not allow for women to represent themselves in traditional courts. Other critics were concerned that traditional leaders would gain absolute powers should the bill become law (Gasa, 2011; Claassens, 2013). For these reasons, the bill was deemed unconstitutional.

Many scholars have argued that post-apartheid policies on traditional leadership resemble similar policy frameworks adopted during colonial and apartheid administrations (Claassens & Cousins, 2008; Ntsebeza, 2005; Skosana, 2009). However, an overview of the existing legislation reveals concerted efforts by the democratic government to accommodate traditional leaders. This relationship is not parasitic, as scholars often argue (see Ntsebeza, 2005: 20; Bank & Southall, 1996; Ray, 1996: 37–38), but is rather interdependent, as my case study of Vaaltyn illustrates below. The reasons for this interdependence are complex but they relate as much to the continued salience of traditional leaders as they do to the need of the democratic state to acquire the support of traditional leaders and to integrate chiefdoms into government structures.

Vaaltyn: A case study

To illustrate my argument about the interdependence of traditional leaders and the ANC government, I examine Vaaltyn[9] and surrounding villages under Kgosi Kekana, in the Limpopo province, in the post-apartheid period. My study offers valuable insight into a community with a different composition from the one researched by Ntsebeza. In his case study of Xhalanga in the Eastern Cape, the institution of chieftaincy was never truly embraced by its residents. Vaaltyn also illustrates how the alliance between the state and traditional leaders in the new dispensation is not a new phenomenon, but rather the continuation of a relationship that dates back to colonial and apartheid South Africa.

The Kekana chiefdom is located approximately 280 km northeast of Johannesburg and 8 km northwest of the town of Mokopane[10] (formerly known as Potgietersrus). Vaaltyn is administered under the Mogalakwena local municipality. The municipality is 6 166 km^2 in size and consists of 38 proclaimed townships and 109 villages (Mogalakwena Local Municipality, 2006).[11] The municipal area is mostly rural, consisting of agricultural land with several small settlements dotted about. Mokopane has been identified as an area for economic development and service provision within the provincial context, as well as at a district and local municipal level (Mogalakwena Local Municipality, 2018/2019).

Like many African chiefdoms, the Kekana chiefdom has been affected by political changes that altered and to some extent fragmented the structure of its chieftaincy.[12] Although there have been turbulent succession conflicts in the pre-colonial era and again throughout the colonial and apartheid eras, the Kekana chieftaincy remained resilient and popular among the northern Ndebele. As Ntsebeza shows, this is not the case in Xhalanga where chieftainship had been challenged and undermined by the state and the people. Ntsebeza points towards the particular nature of his case when he writes that in Xhalanga, 'unlike KwaZulu, Pondoland and Tshezi, chieftainship never entrenched itself' (Ntsebeza, 2005: 37). He gives two reasons behind the failure of traditional leaders to establish themselves in the Xhalanga district. First, Ntsebeza points to the multi-faceted class and ethnic divisions among the educated 'school people' as well as the traditional 'red people' (reference to red earth). Ntsebeza identifies a second factor, namely that 'the colonial state tarnished the institution before abolishing it' in the area. This has not been the case in Vaaltyn; both Esterhuysen's and Hofmeyr's studies demonstrate the resistance of traditional leaders against colonial administrations, which eventually led to the siege of the Kekana northern Ndebele in Makapan's Caves. This does not mean that the Kekana traditional leaders never cooperated with the colonial and apartheid administrations; some leaders after Mokopane's reign did, but the history of resistance by the chiefly institution in the area would, in later years, resurrect the popularity of traditional leadership, unlike in Xhalanga.

The complexity of the relationship between the Kekana royal family and the state is reflected in the negotiations between the Kekana traditional council and one of the biggest platinum mining companies in South Africa, Platreef Resources. Platreef is a subsidiary of the Canadian Ivanplats Limited, which holds 64 per cent ownership of the mine in Mokopane (Ivanhoe Mines, 2015). Platreef began negotiations with the Kekana traditional council in 1988 (Kekana

Traditional Council's minute book, 1993–2007). These negotiations were affected by the constant amendment of mineral rights legislation in South Africa and the dawn of the politically unpredictable democratic era. The mining dialogue between the Kekana chiefly family and Platreef was on hold until 2000, when the Department of Land Affairs enjoined the mine to enter prospecting negotiations with the Kekana (Kekana Traditional Council's minute book, 1993–2007). During this time, the then regent of the Kekana chieftaincy, Chief Alfred Kekana, died. His death ignited a chieftaincy dispute between what I call the Vaaltyn I camp and Vaaltyn II camp, as well as their respective traditional councils. This dispute has profoundly shaped the local politics of the area.

The Mogalakwena local municipality and the Limpopo provincial government arbitrated the dispute and awarded the chieftaincy to Vaaltyn II, son of the late Chief Alfred Kekana's uncle, Molalakgori. Tracing the Kekana genealogy, De Beer (1986) suggests that Molalakgori was not the rightful regent when he stood in briefly in the 1980s for Chief Alfred Kekana, who at the time was declared medically unfit to hold the position of chief. Vaaltyn I's traditional council also reasoned that Molalakgori had relations with the apartheid administration, as well as the Transitional Local Council (TLC), which made it possible for his son, Vaaltyn II, to become chief. Since 2000, the unrecognised traditional council has made several attempts to reverse the ruling which made Vaaltyn II *kgosi,* all in vain. This failure can be attributed mainly to Vaaltyn I's lack of political connections in government, as well as a lack of financial means to challenge the status quo (Mocks, 2014).

On the other hand, Vaaltyn II's relationship with Platreef and the government has matured. A confidential agreement between the *kgosi* and the mine records that he received a monthly sum of R30 000 from the mine during the prospecting phase, which Platreef deemed to be 'reasonable remuneration for time spent on company activities' (Kings, 2014). During this prospecting period, residents of the villages under the authority of *Kgosi* Kekana handed several memorandums to Platreef and the Mogalakwena local municipality. Resistance from the local community was prompted by the mine's tactics of securing prospecting and mining rights, as well as the chief's failure to include communities in the deals negotiated. Pensioner Margaret Makgabo recounts the mine's as well as one of kgosi Kekana's headmen's scare strategies, when she relates that 'their representatives threatened to withdraw my monthly pension if I didn't sign an agreement to let them prospect on my piece of farm. They also promised to compensate us the amount of R5 250 a year for entering our farms. That is why I signed, I was scared' (Makgabo, 2014).

At the height of these events Kgosi Vaaltyn II encouraged those who were present at a meeting held at the traditional council's offices to welcome the change that mining would bring to the area, saying 'we want development in our area; the mine will bring us water, roads, electricity and many more' (Address by Chief Vaaltyn Kekana, at Vaaltyn traditional offices, 30 July 2014). He said this despite the provision of such infrastructure being the responsibility of the South African government. However, it would seem that if the development of infrastructure is undertaken or financed by a mine instead, it would relieve local government of the burden. Noteworthy are Mogalakwena municipal records from 2000 which record meetings, proposals and agreements to construct grids for water supplies and road constructions, not only on the mining sites but also in the surrounding villages, through various projects involving different mining houses.[13] Municipal and provincial governments, therefore, seem to promote and encourage mining companies seeking to negotiate with traditional leaders. The role of these leaders, according to both local and national law, is not entirely clear (Local Government: Municipal Systems Act No. 32 of 2000). Nonetheless traditional leaders are often positioned at the centre of local economies because of their historical connection to land.[14]

Conclusion

In this chapter, I show that the ANC-led government has always, in some form or another, been sympathetic to traditional leaders. This relationship has its roots in the historic development of the party. From the early days of the Congress's inception, it realised its limitations resulting from a lack of support in the rural parts of South Africa. Consequently, it turned to traditional leaders to generate support for the party in their constituencies. This resulted in traditional leaders becoming, in effect, a rural extension of the liberation movement, akin to colonial and apartheid conceptions of the role of traditional leaders. For their part, traditional leaders were keen to develop ties with the liberation movement as they sought to challenge threats to their authority from colonial and apartheid powers. Land dispossession further strengthened the relationship between traditional leaders and the ANC because historically land has been central to the legitimacy of traditional leadership. For the Congress, lack of land rights threatened citizenship rights. A coalition between the liberation movement and traditional leaders was relatively unchallenging, as traditional and national politics, as well as membership to traditional institutions and nationalist movements, have always been blended. As a result of the factors described above, traditional leaders became involved in challenging the Natives Land Act of 1913 and subsequent related laws.

The interdependence between the two institutions has continued into post-apartheid South Africa. However, scholars such as Ntsebeza tend to analyse this relationship as one sided, as only beneficial to the institution of traditional leadership. I have argued here, through a review of the case studies of Xhalanga and Vaaltyn, that the relationship between chieftaincy, the ANC and an ANC-led government is more complex than we comprehend. Traditional leaders have positioned themselves at the centre of local economies because of their historical role in land administration. As a result, mining houses who approach municipal government for prospecting and mining permit negotiations are encouraged by the government to avoid sidelining local traditional leaders. The government here assumes the position of a political mediator because if the proposed mining deals go through, then traditional leaders (and not so much their constituencies) stand to benefit. In addition, the municipality benefits from having some of its responsibilities and costs borne by the mine. This mutual dependence is often overlooked by scholars who tend to focus on the tarnished credibility of traditional leaders and therefore conclude that both systems cannot coexist. Although the case of Vaaltyn, like that of Xhalanga, should not be over-generalised, it provides a lens through which to question the historical role of traditional leaders in South Africa, and in turn to help explain why they remain favoured by post-apartheid laws.

References

Bank, L. & Southall, R. 1996. 'Traditional Leaders in South Africa's New Democracy'. *The Journal of Legal Pluralism and Unofficial Law,* 28 (37– 38), 407– 430.

Beinart, W. & Delius, P. 2014. 'The historical context and legacy of the Natives Land Act of 1913'. *Journal of Southern African Studies*, 40 (4), 667–688.

Claassens, A. & Cousins B. 2008. *Land, Power and Customs: Controversies generated by the Communal Land Rights Act.* Cape Town: UCT Press.

Claassens, A. 2013. 'Recent changes in women's land rights and contested customary law in South Africa'. *Journal of Agrarian Change*, 13 (1), 71–92.

Comaroff, J. & Comaroff, J. 2018. *The Politics of Custom: Chiefship, capital, and the state in contemporary Africa.* Johannesburg: Wits University Press.

Copelyn, J. 1974. 'The Mpondo revolts, 1960'. Honours thesis. Johannesburg: University of the Witwatersrand.

Davenport, T. R. H. 1977. *South Africa: A modern history.* Toronto: University Press.

De Beer, F. 1986. 'Groepsgebondenheid in die familie-, opvolgings- en erfreg van die Noord Ndebele'. PhD thesis. Pretoria: University of Pretoria.

Delius, P. 1983. *The Land Belongs to Us: The Pedi polity, the Boers, and the British in the nineteenth-century Transvaal.* Cape Town: Ravan Press.

Esterhuysen, A. B. 2010. 'Excavation at historic cave, Makapan's valley, Limpopo: 2001–2005'. *South African Archaeological Bulletin*, 65 (191), 67–83.

Hofmeyr, I. 1993. *We Spend Our Years as a Tale That is Untold.* Johannesburg: Wits University Press.

Holomisa, P. 2011. 'Balancing law and tradition: The TCB and its relation to African systems of justice administration'. *SA Crime Quarterly,* 35, 17–22.

Ivanhoe Mines. 13 March 2015. 'Platreef Project'. *Ivanhoe Mines* website: http://www.ivanhoemines.com/s/platreef.asp, accessed 7 September 2018.

Kekana Traditional Council. 1993–2007. Meeting minutes.

Kekana, V. 30 July 2014. Address observed by author, Vaaltyn traditional offices.

Kings, M. 5 December 2014. 'No mining in our backyard, villagers say'. *Mail and Guardian*, https://mg.co.za/article/2014-12-04-no-mining-in-our-backyard-villagers-say, accessed 7 September 2018.

Land and Accountability Research Centre. 2012. 'Submissions: Traditional Courts Bill [B1-2012].' *LARC* website: http://www.larc.uct.ac.za/submissions, accessed 7 September 2018.

Local Government Municipal Systems Act No. 32 of 2000. 14 November 2000, http://extwprlegs1.fao.org/docs/pdf/saf93030.pdf, accessed 4 August 2017.

Makgabo, M. 14 November 2014. Interview with author and Geoffrey York, Magongoa.

Mamdani, M. 1996. *Citizen and Subject: Contemporary Africa and the legacy of late colonialism*. Cape Town: David Phillip Publishers.

Mamdani, M. 2013. *Define and Rule: Native as political identity*. Johannesburg: Wits University Press.

Mbeki, G. 1964. *The Peasants' Revolt*. London: Penguin.

Meer, S. 1997. *Women, Land and Authority: Perspectives from South Africa*. Cape Town: David Phillip Publishers.

Meli, F. 1988. *A History of the ANC: South Africa belongs to all of us*. Harare: Zimbabwe Publishing Press.

Meyers, J. C. 2008. *Indirect Rule in South Africa: Tradition, modernity and the costuming of political power*. Rochester: The University of Rochester Press.

Mnisi Weeks, S. 2011. 'The Traditional Courts Bill: Controversy around process, substance and implications'. *South African Crime Quarterly*, 35, 3.

Mocks, M. 30 July 2014. Interview with author, Vaaltyn.

Mogalakwena Local Municipality. 2006. 'Local Economic Development Strategy'. *Mogalakwena Municipality* website: http://www.mogalakwena.gov.za/mogalakwena-admin/pages/sites/mogalakwena/documents/otherdocs/LED%20STRATEGY%20compressed.pdf

Mogalakwena Local Municipality. 2018/19. 'Integrated Development Plan Review'. *Mogalakwena Municipality* website: http://www.mogalakwena.gov.za/mogalakwena-admin/pages/sites/mogalakwena/documents/idp/2018-2019%20Final%20IDP1.pdf, accessed 7 September 2018.

Ntsebeza, L. 2005. *Democracy Compromised: Chiefs and the politics of land in South Africa*. Leiden: Brill.

Odendaal, A. 2012. *The Founders: The origins of the ANC and the struggle for democracy in South Africa*. Johannesburg: Jacana.

Oomen, B. 1996. 'Talking tradition: The position and portrayal of traditional leaders in present-day South Africa'. MA thesis. Leiden: University of Leiden.

Oomen, B. 2002. *Chiefs! Law, power and culture in contemporary South Africa*. Leiden: University of Leiden.

Oomen, B. 2003. '"Walking in the middle of the road": People's perspectives on the legitimacy of traditional leadership in Sekhukhune', in Vaughan, O. (ed.) *Indigenous Political Structures and Governance in Africa*. Ibadan: Sefer Press, pp. 127–174.

Ray, D. 1996. 'Divided sovereignty: Traditional authority and the state in Ghana'. *Journal of Legal Pluralism*, 37–38, 181–202.

Rive, R. & Couzens, T. 1993. *Seme: The founder of the ANC*. Trenton: Africa World Press.

Skosana, D. 2009. 'Traditional authority in the context of democratic governance: A case study of a dynastic dispute in Vaaltyn'. Honours paper. Johannesburg: The University of the Witwatersrand.

Skosana, D. 2012. 'Why are chiefs recognised in South Africa's new democracy? Issues of legitimacy and contestation in local politics: A case study of chiefly and local government in Vaaltyn'. MA thesis. Johannesburg: University of the Witwatersrand.

Thompson, L. 1971. 'The compromise of the Union', in Wilson, M. & Thompson, L. (eds.) *The Oxford History of South Africa: South Africa 1870–1966*. Oxford: Clarendon Press, pp. 325–64.

Van Kessel, I. & Oomen, B. 1997. 'One chief, one vote: The revival of traditional authorities in post-apartheid South Africa'. *African Affairs*, 96, 561–585.

Van Kessel, I. 1993. 'From confusion to Lusaka: The youth revolt in Sekhukhuneland'. *Journal of Southern African Studies*, 19 (4), 593–614.

Notes

1 Setswana term for 'king' or 'chief'

2 Odendaal (2012) identifies, for example, some of the political activists from chiefly families who attended mission schools such as 'the Dubes of Inanda, Luthulis of Groutville, the Kumalos and Msane of Edendale, the Morokas of Thaba Nchu, the Moshoeshoes of Lesotho, the Molemas of Mafikeng, and the Sandiles, Sogas and Umhallas of Mgwali and St Mark's'.

3   Founded in 1891, and later fed into the formation of the South African Native National Congress in 1912.

4   The organisation of black people into 'tribes' under tribal authorities

5   Moreover, further debate emerged in the 1960s among the ANC leadership on Robben Island about whether the Congress should be working with chiefs like Mangosuthu Buthelezi of the Inkatha Freedom Party (IFP) who were operating within the apartheid system.

6   In the Eastern Cape, Ineke van Kessel in '"From Confusion to Lusaka": The youth revolt in Sekhukhuneland' illustrates that 'Paramount Chief Sabata Dalindyebo headed the revolt in Tembu-land. He was sidelined and later deposed by his rival Kaiser Matanzima, who as the more compliant chief profited from government patronage to become prime minister and subsequently president of the Transkei. Later Dalindyebo went into exile where he linked up with the ANC. He died in exile, but his reburial in the Transkei in 1989 turned into a massive demonstration of support for the ANC in the countryside' (Van Kessel, 1993: 562).

7   'Betterment' schemes during the apartheid era included the removal of people to homelands under the disguise of 'Rural Development Planning'.

8   According to its Constitution, Contralesa aims to unite all traditional leaders in the country, to fight for the eradication of the bantustan system, to 'school the traditional leaders about the aims of the South African liberation struggle and their role in it', to win back 'the land of our forefathers and share it among those who work it in order to banish famine and land hunger', and to fight for a unitary, non-racial and democratic South Africa (Van Kessel & Oomen, 1997: 574).

9   The area is named after Vaaltyn (Likxhobo) who was chief in 1910. It is also referred to as Moshate, 'the chiefly kraal'. Both the contending chiefs have been named Vaaltyn after the earlier chief. In order to avoid confusion, I have named the contending chiefs Vaaltyn I (born in 1964) and Vaaltyn II (born in 1974). The former is largely recognised by the people as the legitimate chief and the latter is the government-recognised chief. The distinction between the two chiefs as Vaaltyn I and Vaaltyn II is mine and is based on their age differences.

10 Adopted in 2003 in commemoration of the chief Mokopane who is said to have killed Piet Potgieter during the 1854 siege in which the northern Ndebele were besieged by the Boers.

11 During this study, which commenced in 2009 until 2013, the ANC held more seats in the Mogalakwena municipality.

12 Information about the changes in the Kekana polity and the aftermath of the conquest can be found in Esterhuysen's (2010) study about archaeological excavations of Makapan's Caves (named after the early

chief of the Kekana, Mokopane, after the northern Ndebele were besieged in 1854) and in Hofmeyr's (1993) work about the construction of historical narratives in the Kekana chiefdom.

13 See Appendix 1 and 2, Mogalakwena Records, file: January to April 2001 or the Traditional Leadership and Governance Framework Act 41 of 2003, as well as other legislations at a local and national level.

14 This idea is also articulated by Capps, G. 2012. in 'Victim of its own success? The platinum mining industry and the apartheid mineral property system in South Africa's political transition', *Review of African Political Economy*, 39 (131), 63–84, p. 70; Mnwana, S. 2013. 'Are communities benefitting from mining? Bafokeng and Bakgatla cases. South Africa', *Labour Bulletin*, 37 (3), and in Mnwana, S. 2014. 'Chief's Justice? Mining, accountability and the law in the Bakgatla-ba-Kgafela Traditional Authority Area, North West Province'. *South African Crime Quarterly*, 49, 21–29.

FOUR

Mining magnates and traditional leaders

The role of law in elevating elite interests and deepening exclusion, 2002–2018

ANINKA CLAASSENS

'To use the [Bantu] Authorities Act of 1951 as a platform for land reform in 2004 is simply incredible.'

– DEPUTY CHIEF JUSTICE DIKGANG MOSENEKE, 2010[1]

Introduction

This chapter details how the law has been used to entrench structural inequality in post-apartheid South Africa. I argue that laws analysed here advance the interests of a small elite at the expense of the property and citizenship rights of 17 million South Africans living in the former homelands. A key and enduring driver of inequality is the legacy of the colonial 'reserves' that became apartheid 'homelands' and which remain zones of desperate poverty and exclusion. Another fundamental driver of inequality in South Africa has been the mining industry. The discovery of precious metals such as platinum, chrome, iron and coal in former homeland areas moved the epicentre of the mining boom to land that is owned and occupied by the poorest South Africans (see Parliament of South Africa 2017: 445; 447). This has resulted in brutal evictions and dispossession. The scale of the problem is ever-increasing. Millions, if not billions, of rand due in mining revenues are unaccounted for; increasingly violent protests have led to regular shaft closures and an entire mountaintop of chrome has been illegally mined and driven off to the docks for export, in plain sight of the many people traversing the major road in Limpopo on which it was transported (Saba, 2016a).

The pivotal laws at play are the Mineral and Petroleum Resources Development Act 28 of 2002 (MPRDA) and the Traditional Leadership and Governance Framework Act 41 of 2003 (TLGFA). These laws, I argue, were developed in concert with each other to enable politically connected business and traditional leaders to use their homeland antecedents, as well as their political connections, to cut themselves into South Africa's most significant source of wealth, the mining industry, on terms that exclude the poor black people who own the land on which mining takes place.

Other laws were intended to bolster the TLGFA but did not survive sustained opposition. The Communal Land Rights Act 11 of 2004 (CLRA) would have given traditional leaders and councils control over all the land in the former homelands but was struck down by the Constitutional Court in 2010. The Traditional Courts Bill (TCB) of 2008 and 2012 would have provided traditional leaders with far-reaching punitive powers over those living within their tribal jurisdictions. The TCB failed to garner the support of the majority of provinces in Parliament and was withdrawn.

The TLGFA confirms the tribal boundaries put in place by the Bantu Authorities Act of 1951 and the official status of traditional leaders recognised under apartheid. It does not, however, provide traditional leaders with specific powers or the legal authority to sign agreements binding on the land or the rights of those living within the leaders' disputed tribal boundaries. The CLRA and the TCB would have done that. Despite the fact that these laws did not come into effect, government has treated traditional leaders as landowners with the sole authority to represent the rural people residing within the apartheid boundaries that the TLGFA reinstated. Both the Department of Mineral Resources and the Department of Rural Development and Land Reform have been complicit in traditional leaders signing surface leases with mining companies in contravention of the consultation and consent requirements of the Interim Protection of Informal Land Rights Act 31 of 1996 (IPILRA) (Parliament of South Africa, 2017: 266; South African Human Rights Commission, 2018: 90).

This has resulted in many legally precarious mining deals in which hundreds of millions of rands have gone missing from tribal accounts[2] supervised by government (Bloom, 2016; Bloom & Wales-Smith, 2018). These deals are shrouded in secrecy and have been strenuously opposed by rural communities through petitions to government, legal challenges and violent protests (Claassens & Matlala, 2014). Government has played an active role in enabling unlawful transactions to proceed and in shielding the perpetrators from efforts to hold them accountable (Parliament of South Africa, 2017: 264).

A slew of bills presented before Parliament in mid-2018 seeks to provide a veneer of legality to the shadowy land of unlawful mining deals involving traditional leaders and senior African National Congress (ANC) officials and politicians. The key bill is the Traditional and Khoi-San Leadership Bill (TKLB) which would repeal and replace the TLGFA of 2003. It states in clause 24 that traditional leaders can sign deals with third parties that apply to land within their apartheid-era tribal jurisdictions without obtaining the consent of those whose land rights are undermined or eliminated by such deals.

In order to justify defaulting to contested tribal boundaries and apartheid-era appointments, the initial TLGFA of 2003 had included 'transformation' mechanisms, such as a commission to investigate the legitimacy of disputed apartheid-era traditional leadership appointments and tribal boundaries. This has failed spectacularly, as has the requirement that traditional councils must include women and elected members. Unlike the TLGFA, the TKLB makes explicit its bias in favour of apartheid-era appointments. It criminalises assertions of traditional leadership by those who are not officially recognised despite numerous outstanding disputes and legal challenges, and removes the legal consequence of invalidity for councils that fail to include women and elected members. It denies the decision-making authority of ordinary South Africans with respect to their homes, fields and grazing lands throughout the former homelands.

Former President Kgalema Motlanthe chaired the High Level Panel (HLP) on the Assessment of Key Legislation and the Acceleration of Fundamental Change during 2016 and 2017.[3] The Panel had three focus areas, namely poverty and inequality, land, and social cohesion. The panellists unanimously recommended that the TKLB, and – among others – a bill to amend the MPRDA, be withdrawn from Parliament and reconsidered in light of the Panel's findings and its report about the abrogation of constitutional rights in former homeland areas. The Panel made detailed recommendations about how these and other bills could be amended to deal with the problems identified. The Panel's report (Parliament of South Africa, 2017), which included numerous recommendations for both immediate and longer-term measures to address the urgent crisis in land reform, has been put on the back burner.[4]

Instead, the processing of the 2018 bills, like their predecessors in 2003 and 2004, has been expedited during the build-up to national elections in 2019. This has contributed to the view that favouring the interests of traditional leaders are about electoral politics – that appeasing traditional leaders will 'deliver the rural vote'. This detracts attention from the role of the bills in providing a veneer of legality to mining and other third-party transactions that are legally precarious because they were signed by traditional leaders without the legal authority to do so, in contravention of the right to tenure security contained in section 25(6) of the Constitution. The bills also flout other constitutional rights, such as equality, freedom of association, language and culture and just administrative action.

Opposition to the bills has been dismissed as 'anti-traditional leadership' and 'anti-custom' in meetings of the Justice portfolio committee, which is processing the TCB, and the Cooperative Governance portfolio committee, which is processing the TKLB (see PMG minutes of meetings). I argue, rather, that the opposition stems from resistance to the autocratic apartheid distortions that the legislation seeks to entrench, and not to opposition to customary law or the institution of traditional leadership per se (Claassens, 2011a). In many instances, current opposition builds on past opposition to the apartheid laws and policies that shaped the current bills. People who opposed forced removals and the bantustans have been at the forefront of struggles against the bills (Thipe, 2013; Luwaya, 2013). The long history of struggles over land and identity is an important factor in opposition to the bills, as are opposing constructs about the nature of customary law (Delius, 2018). Time and again rural people reference the inclusive and consensual nature of customary law as the standard against which they reject the provisions of the laws and bills. Many written and oral submissions criticise the laws for undercutting customary land rights and indigenous accountability mechanisms (Thipe et al., 2015–2016). In contrast, the laws entrench the institutions and disputed tribal boundaries that were created by the much-resisted Bantu Authorities Act of 1951, used to bed down apartheid-era forced removals (De Souza & Jara, 2010).

The inclusive and participatory version of customary law described by rural people has been upheld in several judgments of the Constitutional Court,[5] which warns about the dangers of past distortions inherited from the apartheid version of 'official' customary law. It points to the 'living' version of customary law, which is constantly reshaped by changes in society and practices on the ground.

There is thus a fundamental divergence between the interpretation of customary law advanced by rural people in fora such as the High Level Panel (HLP) public hearings (Parliament of South Africa, 2017: 467–509); other public hearings (Luwaya, 2013; Thipe, 2013; De Souza & Jara, 2010) and the Constitutional Court on the one hand, and that of the executive, endorsed in the bills approved by the Cabinet and introduced to Parliament, on the other. A striking feature of legislation, such as the TCB, the TLGFA and the TKLB, is the explicit focus on the powers and status of traditional leaders, as opposed to the content and development of customary law. I will illustrate in this paper that this is the result of a strong lobby of some (not all) traditional leaders, especially those who were officially recognised during the apartheid era.[6]

The basic premise of the traditional-leader lobby, which includes the Congress of Traditional Leaders of South Africa (Contralesa) and the national and provincial houses of traditional leaders, is that these leaders should be recognised as the sole representatives of 'their' communities (which exist wall-to-wall[7] within the former homelands), backed by laws that provide them with governmental powers and power over communal land and traditional courts (Cogta, 2017). This is not to say that all traditional leaders who were recognised during the apartheid period support or practise the approach of the traditional-leader lobby.

I argue that the content of the bills portrays their autocratic intent, despite attempts by the traditional-leadership lobby to justify them as upholding idealised and participatory versions of African tradition (Holomisa, 2011). The laws rename the 'tribes' created by the Native Administration Act and the Bantu Authorities Act as 'traditional communities', but they retain the boundaries put in place during colonialism and apartheid.

A key theme of this chapter is how the creation of Bantu authorities, and the consolidation of the bantustans, were both predicated on the forced removal of over three-and-a-half million South Africans between 1960 and 1983 (see Platzky & Walker, 1985). Many among the current traditional-leadership lobby were involved in, or benefitted from, that process.

Another theme explored here concerns the role of the law in both eliciting and obscuring illegal transactions. This chapter describes the unlawful processes of looting the residual assets of the poorest South Africans. Had the CLRA made it into operation, these processes would have had the appearance of legality. But legislation such as the CLRA and the TCB would have been unconstitutional in denying property and basic citizenship rights to rural South Africans. However, the government's (failed) attempts to pass the laws has been sufficient to convince major players that they have government backing, which has led them to act with reckless impunity. In the run up to 2019 elections, they are again reaching for law, particularly the TKLB, to protect themselves from increasing legal scrutiny as court challenges work their way up to the Constitutional Court. At the same time, violent intimidation and assassination of mining activists is on the increase as protests by mining communities become increasingly desperate (Ntongana, 2018; Morare, 2016; Bloom & Wales-Smith, 2018).

This chapter is divided into four parts based on the context given above. I start by asking how it came about that a mere 10 years after rural people rebelled against the bantustans and voted overwhelmingly for a united South Africa, the ruling party introduced laws (the TLGFA of 2003 and the CLRA of 2004) that defaulted to bantustan boundaries and to the very stereotypes used to deny black people property and citizenship rights under colonialism and apartheid. I suggest that this has more to do with shoring up the short-term interests of key constituencies within the ANC, including business and mining interests and some traditional leaders, than with concern for rural people and how they are likely to vote. This section includes examples of mining deals involving senior ANC politicians and their close allies.

The second part examines how the laws have been interpreted and applied in some (but not all) areas. It describes processes of systematic exclusion, extortion, dispossession and intimidation that are very similar to the bantustan excesses of the apartheid era.

In the third and fourth sections I retrace the events that culminated in this situation. The third section focuses on the emergence of the traditional-leader lobby from the early 1990s. It places this lobby in the context of the anti-bantustan struggles that contributed to the 1994 transition to democracy. The fourth part examines key elements of the 2002/3 laws, the 2018 TKLB and TLGFA amendment bills and the Communal Land Tenure Bill to make the case that the laws introduced from 2002, and the phalanx of proposals before Parliament in 2018, embody apartheid distortions, as opposed to customary law. It describes how the bills cement the violence and division that were a product of forced removals and bantustan consolidation, particularly in the former province of Transvaal where six 'homelands' were created after 1960.

Part 1: The ruling party's constituency?

When the deputy minister of the Department of Cooperative Governance and Traditional Affairs, Obed Bapela, debates and defends the bills on television, he is often accompanied by Kgosi Nyalala Pilane of the Bakgatla Ba Kgafela and deputy chair of Contralesa, whose actions have been the subject of three stinging Constitutional Court judgments, and are currently the subject of the Baloyi Commission of Inquiry in the North West.[8] On 24 May 2018 an appeal, this time against an eviction order for villagers displaced by mining within the Bakgatla Ba Kgafela boundaries, was argued in the Constitutional Court. In their questions, the judges indicated their disapproval of an interpretation of the law that holds that black people, who in this case bought their land one hundred years ago, could be evicted without their rights being formally terminated, or having any compensation quantified and offered to them before mining activities started on their land. In October the Constitutional Court set aside the eviction order in the far-reaching judgment of *Maledu and Others v Itereleng Bakgatla Mineral Resources (Pty) Limited and Another* [2018] ZACC 41.

The judgment states at para 5 (footnote omitted):

> Mining is one of the major contributors to the national economy. But there is a constitutional imperative that should not be lost from sight, which imposes an obligation on Parliament to ensure that persons or communities whose tenure of land is legally insecure as a result of past racially discriminatory laws or practices are entitled either to tenure which is legally secure or to comparable redress. Accordingly, this case implicates the right to engage in economic activity on the one hand and the right to security of tenure on the other.

The judgment provides that the MPRDA must be read concurrently with the Interim Protection of Informal Land Rights Act of 1996, and that the compensation provisions of the MPRDA contained in section 54 must be complied with before mining can commence, and before people can be evicted. Unilateral deals with traditional leaders are therefore unlawful unless those directly affected by mining have provided their consent, or been expropriated. This is a fundamental game changer in relation to how both business and government have used the MPRDA and TLGFA to justify signing mining deals with traditional leaders. Last-minute amendments have been proposed to the pending TKLB that attempt to override the implications of the judgment. These will be discussed below.

South Africa's ruling party, the ANC, is not homogenous and has taken different positions about traditional leadership at various times, but as Lungisile Ntsebeza (2005) documents, it has been ambivalent about the institution of traditional leadership from its inception. Steven Friedman (2017) argues that the draconian content of the current bills is a product of the Jacob Zuma era, in that they seek to legalise looting processes that flourished during his presidency.

This does not, however, explain the timing of the TLGFA in 2003 and the CLRA in 2004, which emerged in concert with the MPRDA of 2002. While the rhetoric of the MPRDA was about a significant dilution of white domination in favour of a state acting in the public interest, it was common knowledge by 2002 that the locus of mining had swung away from depleted gold reserves along the Witwatersrand and in the Free State to rich reserves of platinum, chrome, iron and coal in former homeland areas (Capps, 2012). The Lebowa Mineral Trust and former Bophuthatswana homeland leader Lucas Mangope had long monopolised profits from chrome and platinum mining in Lebowa and Bophuthatswana, and homeland leaders had insider knowledge about the location of rich reserves of platinum on 'tribal land' (Capps, 2012).

At the same time, Black Economic Empowerment (BEE) was widely deemed to be in crisis, resulting in the far-reaching report of the BEE Commission of 2001, which recommended greater state regulation of industry to support black ownership of key assets. The sector most directly and immediately affected by the introduction of the MPRDA and the Mining Charter was the mining industry. A number of major deals were quickly brokered, for example between Harmony Gold and Patrice Motsepe's African Rainbow Minerals, and between Gold Fields and Tokyo Sexwale's Mvelaphanda (Southall, 2004). Roger Southall suggests that the policy decision to support the aggressive expansion of a class of black capitalists would inevitably lead to class conflict between ANC-sponsored black capitalists and the working class (Southall, 2004: 16).

My argument is that the legislative agenda of the early 2000s went further than supporting specific class interests in struggles between bosses and workers. It was, and is, about processes of primary accumulation and dispossession that undercut the ability of rural communities in the platinum belt to hold traditional leaders, government or mining houses to account. The legislation created a regime that has enabled the confiscation of black surface rights without consent or compensation. The MPRDA, read in conjunction with the TLGFA, CLRA and the TKLB, denies that customary land rights constitute property rights for ordinary people, and elevates the unilateral decision-making power of traditional leaders over the basic citizenship rights of rural South Africans.

More research needs to be conducted into the mining interests, and homeland antecedents, of those who drafted and supported both the MPRDA and the traditional leadership bills. We know, for example, that discredited former lawyer[9] Seth Nthai was a key player in the conceptualisation of the approach adopted by the MPRDA in concert with the TLGFA and laws like the CLRA and the TCB. Nthai was the first Safety and Security Member of the Executive Committee (MEC) in Limpopo province and a close associate of Ngoako Ramatlhodi, then premier of Limpopo. Media reports indicate that Ramatlhodi benefited from the purchase and subsequent resale of a farm adjacent to the richest platinum deposit in the world at Mokopane in Limpopo. The farm was registered in the name of Ngoako Properties at the time that Ramatlhodi was premier of Limpopo (Brümmer & Sole, 2009). Mokopane fell within Seth Nthai's constituency while he was an ANC member of the provincial executive.

Nthai acted for both sides in the expansion of platinum mining by Anglo Platinum in the Mokopane area. He was retained by Anglo Platinum to represent villages that were to be displaced by mining and relocated to other land. He did this by establishing 'representative' companies in terms of Section 21 of the Companies Act. Anglo, also represented by Nthai, then negotiated the terms of the resettlement with the Section 21 companies. Within a short space of time, the Section 21 companies were discredited and became defunct. At the time of the main negotiations about mining and resettlement, the Mapela community, on whose land the mine lies, was represented by Queen Mother Athalia Langa, who was also an ANC member of the provincial legislature (Rutledge, 2014).

The grave relocations and removals that took place to enable mining in Mokopane have created a legacy of serious mistrust in the community, which, in 2015, exploded into particularly violent protests (Boyle, 2016a). The then *kgosi*, David Langa (son of Athalia), had agreed with Anglo Platinum that a community school would be closed down for re-use by the mining company. The protests turned violent when young adults torched the *kgosi's* unoccupied house and an unoccupied old age home built by Anglo Platinum. The youths who led the protests in 2015 blamed their parents for allowing the destruction of their previously agricultural economy, without obtaining fair compensation or guarantees of employment at the mines.

Rural people and restitution claimants assumed that black-owned groups would control the revenue generated from their land after 1994, because the stranglehold on mining revenue by homeland leaders would end with the demise of the homeland system. The introduction of the MPRDA in 2002 put paid to that hope, transferring control over mining in communal areas from bantustan presidents to national government, particularly the minister of Mineral Resources.

This has allowed for extraordinary continuities between the role of mining-rich chiefly dynasties during and after apartheid, as Professor Freddy Khunou (2017) spelled out in an affidavit for the Baloyi Commission about the Bakgatla Ba Kgafela chieftainship in North West province. Former Bophuthatswana president Lucas Mangope had centralised all revenue from mining to accounts within his office. These accounts remained in place after the transition to democracy and became the accounts from which R600 million belonging to the Bapo ba Mogale disappeared under the watch of post-apartheid premiers (Public Protector, 2017/2018). Mangope, and families closely associated with him, such as the Motsepe family (Masilela, 2015) had insider knowledge of where the platinum deposits were, which groups occupied that land and on what terms. Further investigation is needed into media reports of how the farms of the Moiletswane land buyers, and the land of the Mmakau community, came to bolster the mining interests of the Motsepe family at the time that Jeff Radebe was minister of Mineral Affairs (Brümmer, 2000; Yende, 2017).[10] Patrice Motsepe is a generous donor to both Contralesa and the ANC, and styles himself as prince of Mmakau (Barnard, 2015; Moatshe, 2017).

The mining interests of prominent ANC politicians, such as Mathews Phosa, are in the public domain. Journalist Athandiwe Saba (2016b) places Phosa at a 2007 meeting of the Department of Mineral Resources (DMR) to discuss prospecting rights to mineral-rich land in Sekhukhuneland. At the time, the acting king of Sekhukhuneland was Kgagudi Kenneth Sekhukhune. For decades, there has been a kingship dispute between the families of KK Sekhukhune and Rhyne Thulare Sekhukhune. Phosa had been advising and representing Rhyne and his family in this dispute (Saba, 2016b).

Somehow Rhyne Thulare was awarded prospecting rights 'on behalf of the Bapedi nation' in 2006, behind the back of the official acting king. However, a DMR official told Saba that the rights were vested not in the Bapedi nation, but in Rhyne Thulare. When Rhyne died he was succeeded by his son Victor Thulare, who signed over about 10 prospecting rights to Bauba Platinum, a company in which he was a shareholder and Phosa was a non-executive director (Saba, 2016b). The plot thickens in that in 2010, then President Jacob Zuma recommended that Victor's father, Rhyne Thulare, be posthumously recognised as rightful king in the place of Kgagudi Kenneth Sekhukhune. This example of the interplay between mining interests and royal appointments has played out in other provinces as well.

Part 2: The on-the-ground impact of the TLGFA and the 2017/18 bills

The two laws that had been intended to provide specific powers to traditional leaders, namely the CLRA and TCB, did not make it into operation. Only the TLGFA of 2003 survived. As its name indicates, it is a framework act, and so was complemented by provincial traditional leadership laws enacted during 2005. These provincial laws are remarkably similar to the homeland laws they replace. The North West Traditional Leadership and Governance Act of 2005, for example, has much of the same wording as the Bophuthatswana Traditional Authorities Act of 1978.

Despite the fact that these laws are confined to issues of status, recognition and financial accountability and do not provide traditional leaders with explicit powers, they have deliberately been misinterpreted to suppress opposition to mining deals (Claassens & Matlala, 2014; Boyle, 2016b) and to undermine attempts to hold traditional leaders, mining houses and government to account. They have led to a resurgence of the practices that fuelled the widespread anti-bantustan rebellions of the 1980s and early 1990s (as is discussed below).

The resurgence of levies, interdicts and costs orders

One such practice is the extortion of 'tribal levies' across the former bantustans. Traditional leaders demand levies for a range of purposes, including contributions to the royal bride price, *khonza* (tribute) fees for land and for permission for burials. In addition, people are required to pay annual levies that are recorded by the traditional secretary (Maurice Webb Race Relations Unit, 2009). If a rural person's levies are not up to date, he or she will not be given the 'proof of address' letter that is required when applying for an ID book, a social grant, a driver's licence, or to get on the voter's roll (Claassens, 2011b).

Another bantustan practice that has resumed since the TLGFA of 2003 is the banning of community meetings. Traditional leaders claim to have the sole authority to call meetings within their territories, as delineated in Government Gazette notices after 1951. When people defy such bans, traditional leaders routinely go to court to interdict the meetings from taking place (Claassens & Matlala, 2014). Despite a Constitutional Court judgment – *Pilane & Another v Pilane & Another* (28 February 2013) CC 431, which strikes down such an interdict and asserts the right of freedom of association – magistrates continue to issue such interdicts (Pickering & Motala, forthcoming).

The allocating of legal costs to activists who try to demand accountability from traditional leaders in the lower courts is also reminiscent of bantustan days. Activists almost invariably lose their cases and are left without the resources to appeal to higher courts, where they would be likely to win.[11] Sonwabile Mnwana (2014) has documented how this practice was used historically, and is still being used today to bankrupt activists who demand financial accountability in the Bakgatla Ba Kgafela area. This is particularly galling because the legal costs incurred by the traditional authority come from the very revenue that is unaccounted for, and in principle should belong to all members of the 'traditional community'.

Despite the *Pilane v Pilane* judgment, traditional leaders and mining houses continue to act as though officially recognised traditional leaders are the only people authorised to represent rural people in mining and investment deals. They have received a boost from clause 7(9) of the Traditional and Khoi-San Leadership Bill that, in November 2018, was in the final stages of its enactment. It provides that:

Any person who is not a recognised leader as contemplated in subsection (1) but purports to be such a leader, is guilty of an offence and liable upon conviction to a fine or imprisonment not exceeding three years.

The clause is startling for at least three reasons. Firstly, it ignores the colonial and apartheid manipulation of leadership positions and levels. NJ van Warmelo, a government ethnologist from the 1930s to the 1960s, foregrounded the arbitrary nature of the pegging of leaders at different levels by government officials in 1936 (Van Warmelo as cited in Claassens & Hathorn, 2008: 346):

[T]he distinctions that the authorities made between chiefs and headmen appears, to one who looks at the actual facts, a very superficial one, for while there are appointed chiefs who have no hereditary right, there are actual chiefs of rank who are not recognised in any way whatever. There are, further, so-called 'independent headmen' ... who are regarded as chiefs amongst natives.

The second reason is that a key mechanism for accountability among indigenous communities is the interplay of power between different levels of traditional authority. Historically, rural people could align themselves with leaders who challenged the authority of unpopular incumbents:

Whoever currently wielded power would invariably be challenged by rivals, who in their turn would gain power and consolidate their strength, but would eventually lose control to new competitors. These tensions explain why the African ruler's power was never in the past absolute. Anyone who attempted tyrannical rule would soon face revolt or secession (Bennett, 1995: 67; see also Schapera, 1956: 207).

The third reason that the clause is extraordinary is that it illustrates how closely the legislative agenda is tied to shoring up the authority of traditional leaders who were recognised during apartheid, by foreclosing possible counter claims by others who were sidelined during apartheid.

There are numerous, hotly contested disputes about the validity of the tribal boundaries entrenched by the TLGFA and the legitimacy of incumbent traditional leaders (Peires, 2014). The TLGFA of 2003 set up a commission, the Commission on Traditional Leadership Disputes and Claims, to investigate and make findings about such disputes. However, the Act was amended in 2009 to downgrade the Commission's findings to recommendations to the president regarding kingship disputes and to provincial premiers regarding disputes at the level of senior traditional leaders and 'traditional community' boundaries. Faced with the possibility of findings that might undermine apartheid-era power structures, the amendment made acting on the Commission's recommendation subject to the discretion of senior officials. In North West and other provinces, people have had to go to court to get these recommendations made public, despite having spent days providing testimony to the commissions.

This follows an established pattern of colonial and apartheid governments appointing traditional leaders whose interests align with those of powerful figures in government, rather than appointing leaders on the basis of legitimacy and history (Peires, 2014).[12]

Invalid traditional councils and legally precarious mining deals

The transformative provisions of the TLGFA, namely that 40 per cent of the members of a traditional council must be elected and that one-third must be women, have been routinely flouted,[13] as has the legal requirement that books of tribal account must be audited annually. This, together with the fact that traditional councils have been exercising powers beyond their legal mandate, means that many of the deals they have signed with mining houses and other investors are legally precarious (Business Leadership South Africa and Business Unity South Africa, 2017: 42–46). The Department of Traditional Affairs cites this so-called 'failure to transform' as the reason for a 2018 amendment to the TLGFA. Rather than ensure that the failure is rectified, the amendment removes the consequence of legal invalidity for non-compliant traditional councils. Preserving mining deals thus takes precedence over democratisation and gender transformation.

The dual application of the MPRDA and the TLGFA has stripped rural people of the capacity to hold their leaders to account, and to ensure that compensation and mining royalties are properly reported and fairly distributed. Recent investigations (Human Rights Commission, 2018; Bloom & Wales-Smith, 2018) have laid bare the scale at which poor rural people are losing out through mining deals (Noble et al., 2014). It is massive. In 2017, the Public Protector reported on the R600 million missing from the 'tribal account' of the Bapo ba Mogale in North West province (Public Protector, 2017/2018). More recently, the Baloyi Commission sitting in Rustenburg heard evidence of how the Bakgatla Ba Kgafela community lost billions of rands in mining revenue through secret deals negotiated between Kgosi Nyalala Pilane and veteran South African mining magnate Brian Gilbertson's Pallinghurst Resources Ltd, among others (Bloom & Wales-Smith, 2018).

Government is deeply implicated. The account from which the R600 million of the Bapo ba Mogale went missing is held in the North West premier's office and supervised by officials of the Department of Traditional Affairs (Bloom, 2016). The office of the auditor-general has confirmed in public hearings that the account has not been audited since 1994, despite this being a requirement of the TLGFA. In 2016, when the funds were reported missing, then North West Premier Supra Mahumapelo refused to depose either the Pilane or Mogale traditional leaders, who were implicated in these serious financial irregularities, despite the recommendation for their replacement by the TLGFA commission, set up to investigate the legitimacy of traditional leaders (De Souza Louw, 2016).

The bills before the National Council of Provinces (NCOP) – the TLGFA amendment and the new TKLB – aim to deal with the fact that traditional leaders do not have the legal standing to contract with mining houses and external investors in relation to communal land. Only the minister of Rural Development and Land Reform, as nominal owner of the land on behalf of the people who live on it, has this authority. And he or she is bound by the Interim Protection of Informal Land Rights Act (IPILRA) to obtain the consent of those whose informal rights (as defined in the IPILRA) to occupy, use or access land would be affected.[14] If residents do not consent, then their rights must be expropriated and duly compensated. This has now been confirmed by the *Maledu* judgment of the Constitutional Court.

The role of government

The previous minister of Rural Development and Land Reform, Gugile Nkwinti, ignored his legal and fiduciary responsibilities and ceded his authority to authorise mining deals in former homeland areas to traditional leaders. The TKLB attempts to legalise this abrogation of state accountability by, for the first time, explicitly empowering traditional leaders to sign such deals.

Section 24(2) of the TKLB explains:

> Kingship or queenship councils, principal traditional councils, traditional councils, Khoi-San councils and traditional sub-councils may enter into partnerships and agreements with each other, and with—
> (a) municipalities;
> (b) government departments; and
> (c) any other person, body or institution.

The agreement

> ... is subject to a prior consultation with the relevant community represented by such council and a prior decision of such council indicating in writing the support of the council for the particular partnership or agreement (clause 24(3)(c)).

The consultation sub-clause was added only after sustained objections by civil society and at public hearings. However, unlike IPILRA, the clause does not require that the people whose rights would be directly affected must consent to changes to their land rights. Instead the clause is opaque about whom the traditional council must consult, how and under what circumstances.

In late October the Department of Traditional Affairs put forward another amendment that attempts to head off the far-reaching consequences of the *Maledu* judgment. The proposed amendments are to 24(3):

> (3) Any partnership or agreement entered into by any of the councils contemplated in subsection (2) must be in writing and, notwithstanding the provisions of any other national or provincial law –

(c) is subject to –
  (i) a prior consultation with the relevant community represented by such council;
  (ii) a decision in support of the partnership or agreement taken by a majority of the relevant community members present at the consultation contemplated in subparagraph (i) ...

Far from solving the problem of inadequate consultation, this amendment seeks to oust IPILRA by using the word 'notwithstanding' as opposed to 'subject to' or 'in addition to'. The TKLB, as more recent legislation, would thereby trump the older IPILRA.

The new reference to 'a majority of relevant community members' takes us nowhere because it operates within the framework of the TKLB. This does not start with rights holders as IPILRA does. It starts with councils and traditional leaders who represent the 'traditional communities' formerly named 'tribes'. The relevant community is that represented by the council, according to old Bantu Authorities Act delineations. This would trump IPILRA's focus on the people directly affected by mining who are never whole 'tribes' but always families and sub-groups whose homes, fields and grazing land are targeted for mining activities.

The only way for the TKLB to be consistent with the *Maledu* judgment is for it to state that it is subject to the Constitutional rights that IPILRA was enacted to protect and secure.

The late October proposed amendments indicate that government and Parliament remain hell-bent on entrenching the current practice of traditional councils authorising deals after nominal processes of consultation, notwithstanding the *Maledu* judgment. Issues of scale are crucial here. The Mapela traditional council in Limpopo has jurisdiction over 42 far-flung villages. The Bakgatla Ba Kgafela traditional council has jurisdiction over 32 villages. Mining shafts typically impact directly on the land of one or two villages, as opposed to that of the entire 'tribe'. Traditional council members may come from villages that are over 50 km away from where the mining takes place. When the traditional council authorises mining deals that generate revenue for the council, there is no direct correlation between the council that reaps the benefits and the people whose rural livelihoods are destroyed by mining (Mnwana & Capps, 2015).

Why would mining houses with expert lawyers and onerous responsibilities to their shareholders take such extraordinary risks in signing deals with traditional leaders? According to the then Chamber of Mines (now Minerals Council of South Africa as of 2018), the Department of Mineral Resources (DMR) routinely advises potential investors to deal directly with traditional leaders (Chamber of Mines, 2017). Mining companies have privileged the DMR's advice over the law, in much the same way as many of them accepted DMR officials' advice about linking with politically connected Black Empowerment Equity partners, rather than including affected communities as BEE shareholders (Burgess, 2010: 12–13; Anonymous, 2013). This collusion between mining houses and parts of government has seen the consent and compensation requirements in IPILRA flouted with impunity and the absence of effective financial oversight to guard against the theft of mining revenue, as experienced by the Bapo ba Mogale, Bakgatla Ba Kgafela and many other communities (Manson, 2013).

A local land activist, speaking at the October 2016 KwaZulu-Natal public hearing of the High-Level Panel led by Kgalema Motlanthe, explained it thus:

> Investment deals are concluded by the traditional leader without consulting with, or even informing, the community, who simply see bulldozers and trucks on the job. Dynamiting operations crack the walls of houses; coal dust covers roofs so that it becomes impossible to harvest rain water; the same soot covers grass and renders it unfit for grazing. The traditional leader does not want to account, refuses to attend meetings (High Level Panel, 2016).

Another person from a mining-affected community in KwaZulu-Natal said:

> We live in great hardship in South Africa. We are dispossessed of our land by development, by the mines, and we get no

compensation or benefits out of the so-called development on our ancestral land. We are not consulted. We have turned into non-entities with nothing, and yet we are the rightful owners of the land (High Level Panel Public Hearings, 2016).

The broader political climate of seeking rent and having legal impunity under former President Zuma appears to have emboldened senior politicians and officials, along with some traditional leaders, to brazenly ignore the law and use violence to subdue opposition (Bloom, 2016). Now they are backing legislation intended to cover their tracks. These bills cannot legalise current practices, let alone create retrospective immunity for what has already happened, because they flout basic constitutional rights. But they can do a massive amount of damage on the ground by signalling that the state remains solidly behind mining deals with traditional leaders and will not uphold the land rights of the poor, even if it has to disregard its own laws, like IPILRA, in the process.

The demands of the traditional-leader lobby

In making the case for these laws, the traditional-leader lobby has not been shy to say that its members want the same powers they had under apartheid.

As early as 2006, Inkosi Mtirara of the Eastern Cape is quoted as saying (Mtirara as cited in Bentley et al., 2006: 59–60):

> In the new democratic government, people no longer [obey the tribal authority] because there are no laws to compel people to heed what the tribal authority says. An example is the Transkei Authorities Act 4 of 1965, which was against illegal gatherings, but now people do as they wish or please. People hold meetings at schools, churches, even in open areas.

The lobby is explicit in insisting that the kind of authority they want is coercive. The content of the bills confirms this.

The lobby also wants immunity from prosecution, as illustrated by the February 2016 Contralesa application to the Cape High Court[15] to be granted an interdict to stop the president from removing Inkosi Buyelekhaya Dalindyebo from his position as traditional leader. Dalindyebo had been found guilty of arson and kidnapping as well as concealing the death of Saziso Wofa.[16] His initial sentence of 15 years was reduced to 12 years on appeal in 2015. In their court application at paragraph 67, Contralesa argued that had the Traditional Courts Bill been expedited by Parliament, Dalindyebo would not have suffered the fate he did:

> Plainly put, if the TCB had been in operation at the time it would have lent statutory authority to some of King Dalindyebo's actions. In terms of the TCB, anyone within the traditional leader's jurisdiction may be ordered to come before him (as presiding officer), where s/he may be fined and stripped of customary entitlements (Mnisi Weeks, 2011: 4).

This was despite the fact that the actions for which Dalindyebo was found guilty did not arise from judgments from his traditional court, but from violent actions against villagers before they appeared in court.[17] This sort of narrative provides scant pretence that the legitimacy of traditional leaders derives from popular support by the people – indeed, Contralesa insists that without state law to back them up, they are 'out in the cold' (High Level Panel, 2017).

Speaking at a press briefing by the National House of Traditional Leaders in Durban on 28 June 2018, Inkosi Mwelo Nonkonyana, the chair of the Eastern Cape branch of the National House, stated that: 'We want to make it clear that chapters 7 and 12, and section 25 of the country's Constitution should be amended before the elections in 2019' (see Mngadi, 2018). Chapter 7 is about the status and powers of local government, chapter 12 is about the status of traditional leaders and section 25 governs property rights.

Senior ministers appear to support the demands of traditional leaders. Early in 2018, the minister of Co-op gov and Trad affairs, Dr Zweli Mkhize, went on record as saying that he supported the demands being made by traditional leaders. Mkhize said traditional leaders 'have a vital role to play within the South African governance system.' (Saxby, 2018).

The decision to give traditional leaders control over communal land and governmental powers is in direct conflict with the Bill of Rights contained in the Constitution. People living in the former homelands are full citizens with the same rights as other South Africans. These laws therefore cannot pass constitutional muster. The legal battles ahead are one issue. Far starker, however, is the symbolism of the choices being made by the ruling party, and the question of whose interests the ANC is seen to prioritise over the basic rights of poor South Africans.

Part 3: The emergence of the traditional-leader lobby in the context of countervailing histories and identities

This section takes us back to the early 1990s to retrace the events that have led to the current contradictions between the claims of the traditional-leadership lobby and the Bill of Rights. The Congress for a Democratic South Africa (CODESA) negotiations in the early 1990s between the newly unbanned ANC and other political organisations sought agreement on the terms of the anticipated transition to democracy. A lobby of traditional leaders, including the Inkatha Freedom Party, Bophuthatswana homeland leader Lucas Mangope (backed by right-wing Afrikaners) and other homeland leaders, vociferously opposed the re-incorporation of the bantustans or homelands into a unitary South Africa with a common voters' roll. This was against the backdrop of the massacre at Bisho where anti-bantustan protestors had been shot down, the Bophuthatswana coup of 1988 and subsequent violence in Mmabatho. The period also saw severe repression of the surge of anti-bantustan rebellions in Lebowa, KwaNdebele and other former homelands. These rural rebellions were an important component of the struggle by the United Democratic Front (UDF) to make South Africa 'ungovernable' (South

African History Online, 2011). The UDF had played a key role in precipitating the unbanning of the ANC and in the negotiations at CODESA. In that context, it was inevitable that the ANC would support the dismantling of the bantustans and equal citizenship for all South Africans. The traditional-leader lobby thus lost the first round at CODESA when the bantustans were reincorporated into South Africa.

The next round played out during the constitutional negotiations (1994–1996) when Contralesa and others argued that the Bill of Rights, and particularly the right to equality, should be subject to customary law. This precipitated a major stand-off between Contralesa and organisations representing women (Albertyn, 1994; Murray, 2001). Again, the traditional-leader lobby lost the battle, at least partly because of extraordinary statements about the place of women under customary law. Thereafter, Contralesa and Inkatha challenged the Constitution for failing to provide explicit powers to traditional leaders, but lost in the Certification judgment of 1996.[18]

The phalanx of laws and bills before Parliament in 2018 seeks to recover lost ground by giving traditional leaders the exclusive power to represent people living within the boundaries of the former bantustans, and ownership and control over all the land within them. The problem the bills confront is that other people already have countervailing rights to this land and countervailing forms of identity and representation, many of which derive from customary law and from prior histories of resistance to colonial dispossession and Bantu authorities.

Opposition to the laws is built, in many places, on decades of resistance to the impact of the colonial and apartheid policies and laws that went before them. Rural resistance to dispossession and indirect rule took many forms, which resulted in forms of property and identity that contradict the apartheid vision of neatly abutting 'tribes', existing in a separate legal sphere where land ownership is not allowed and the court system is segregated from the rest of South Africa.

That history of opposition cannot be airbrushed away. It is engraved on the land in very material ways, which differ from province to province. For example, thousands of people clubbed together and bought land with title deeds between the 1860s and 1936,[19] which their descendants still have (Feinberg, 2015; Mnwana & Capps, 2015). People also went to court, repeatedly arguing from the 1860s onwards that they, not traditional leaders, owned the land. They challenged the authority of traditional leaders to make decisions binding on their land rights (Chanock, 2001; Klug, 1995: 35). Some joined mission settlements on church land. Many thousands resisted the apartheid policy known as 'Betterment' and the imposition of Bantu authorities (Mbeki, 1964; Luthuli, 1962: 200). Some formed community authorities instead, some formed civic associations, some simply ignored the leaders and tribal identities imposed on them during apartheid and elected local leaders instead (Ntsebeza, 2005). Groups of labour tenants who had resisted eviction over decades continue to live independently on South African Development Trust (SADT)[20] land that had been expropriated from white farmers (Harries, 1989; Claassens, 2001). Traditional leaders and tribal identities superimposed on communities faded from relevance over time in various places.

These various forms of resistance culminated in the anti-chief and anti-bantustan rebellions of the late 1980s and early 1990s, which played a significant role in the 1994 transition to democracy (Delius, 1996: 112–118; Maloka & Gordon, 1996).

Part 4: The early laws, the TLGFA, the CLRA, the TCB and the MPRDA

This section discusses the legislation in the context of prior opposition to previous laws passed with similar intent, for example the Native Administration Act of 1927 and the Bantu Authorities Act of 1951, and in relation to contemporary opposition to the TLGFA, the CLRA, the TCB and the MPRDA after 2002 and until 2014. It ends by discussing the damaging effects of the legislation on the legitimacy of the institution of traditional leadership and to the political and economic stability of mining in communal areas.

The Traditional Leadership and Governance Framework Act of 2003

Thuto Thipe (2014) has analysed the 2000 TLGFA Discussion Document generated by the then Department of Provincial and Local Government, the draft white paper on traditional leadership of 2002 and the final white paper that culminated in the TLGFA of 2003. These documents show a remarkable about-turn in policy direction at the same time as the MPRDA was being drafted and enacted. The initial discussion document of 2000 concedes the distortions created by the implementation of the Bantu Authorities Act (Government of the Republic of South Africa, 2000: 36):

> [N]o 'chief' who held views contrary to those of government was confirmed in his position as 'chief' ... traditional leaders became important tools in the government's strategy of extending its control over Africans in the countryside, through the establishment of 'reserves', 'self-governing states', 'homelands' and later 'independent states'.

Thipe (2014: 8) traces how this analysis is turned on its head during the evolution of the draft and final white papers, which advocate for the recognition of untainted, pre-colonial forms of traditional authority, and ultimately posit that the leaders recognised in terms of the Bantu Authorities Act, and the tribal boundaries delineated by it, embody just such pre-colonial formations.

Rural groups who made submissions to Parliament opposing the TLGFA in 2002 rejected the assertion that Bantu Authorities reflected legitimate tribal boundaries, and that traditional leaders inherited from apartheid had pre-colonial legitimacy. They pointed out the serious material consequences for groups who had been subsumed under the 'wrong' tribal authority jurisdictions after the enactment of the Bantu Authorities Act in 1951. The Act provided that as, and when, Bantu Authorities were delineated, notices would be published in the Government Gazette establishing each Bantu Authority, naming the traditional leader and his council and describing the extent of the land over which the authority had jurisdiction.

The legacy of this history is very close to the surface in the former Transvaal where black people were separated by language and forcibly removed from previously multi-ethnic settlements to create the six separate homelands of Bophuthatswana, Lebowa, KaNgwane, Venda, Gazankulu and KwaNdebele. Leaders who resisted establishing Bantu Authorities were either given tiny jurisdictional areas or put within the tribal jurisdictions created for chiefs who cooperated with the bantustan agenda. Many cooperative chiefs became ministers within the homeland legislative assemblies.

During the two states of emergency between 1985 and 1990, the Black Sash conveyed a request for help from the multi-ethnic Driefontein and KwaNgema communities in the Eastern Transvaal, who were fiercely resisting pending forced removal. The Zulu-speaking people in these communities were to have been moved to Babanango, adjacent to KwaZulu; the Swati-speaking people to Oshoek, adjacent to KaNgwane and the Sotho-speaking people to land adjacent to QwaQwa. Only Enos Mabuza of KaNgwane refused to accept the additional people and land that were gifted to the homelands through forced removals (Claassens, 1990).

In the Transvaal, unlike parts of the Eastern Cape and KwaZulu, many traditional leaders were appointed only after the Bantu Authorities Act was enacted in 1951 – and some as late as the 1980s. Their disputed authority and tribal boundaries have since been set in stone by the TLGFA. One example is that of the Tsonga-speaking Makuleke community of Limpopo, who were brutally removed from their land in the Kruger Park to resettlement camps at Ntlhaveni. These camps were established on land that had been purchased or expropriated from white farmers by the South African Development Trust for ultimate inclusion in the Gazankulu bantustan. Unbeknown to the Makuleke community, the land was included in the newly delineated Mhinga Bantu Authority. Successive waves of other Tsonga-speaking people were also removed to the same area, all of whom Chief Adolf Mhinga claimed as his subjects despite their furious denials. At the time, Mhinga was Minister of Justice in Gazankulu (Claassens & Hathorn, 2008).

As Thipe argues (2014: 2), 'the TLGFA reproduces many of the violences and material inequalities … that its predecessors set in place'.

The Communal Land Rights Act (CLRA)

The problems created by the TLGFA were exacerbated by the proposed powers of the CLRA.[21] While the TLGFA re-instituted and renamed tribal authorities[22] as traditional councils, the CLRA sought to give traditional councils the power to administer 'communal land'. As many authorities have pointed out, the term 'communal land' is a misnomer (Chanock, 1991; Gluckman, 1965: 76–108; Mamdani, 1996; Bennett, 2008). Within so-called communal areas, families have ownership of their homes and fields. Only grazing, woodlands and access to other shared resources such as thatching grass and medicinal herbs are 'communal'. Moreover, these resources are often shared by discrete user groups, rather than the large overarching 'tribes', which the TLGFA renames 'traditional communities' and superimposes over all other forms of community and identity within the former bantustans.

The CLRA empowered the minister of Rural Development and Land Affairs to transfer (by endorsement) the hard-won title deeds of historical land buyers and new land reform beneficiaries to the superimposed tribes that had been delineated under the Bantu Authorities Act. This would have meant that title deeds belonging to specific small groups of people, who had fought for and obtained ownership for themselves, could become the property of much larger tribes within which they would be structural minorities.

The problems the CLRA would have created were not restricted to the descendants of black, land-buying syndicates. In a 2012 judgment, the KwaZulu-Natal High Court upheld the argument of the Ingonyama Trust, namely that because a Hlubi traditional leader (BG Radebe) was consigned under apartheid to a small community authority[23] shared with three other groups, the amaHlubi in the Newcastle area have no rights to land outside that small shared community authority. This is despite strong historical evidence to the contrary and ongoing occupation of the land in question.[24]

In 1981, multi-ethnic land-buying syndicates who had bought land northeast of Pretoria before 1936, through exemptions from the Land Act, found their land subsumed under tribal authorities that had been imposed on them when the KwaNdebele homeland was created (Claassens & Gilfillan, 2008). Overnight, their title deeds meant nothing anymore. They became tribal subjects of superimposed Ndebele traditional leaders. This led to serious and violent conflicts in many areas (Claassens & Gilfillan, 2008).

KwaNdebele was the site of particularly well-organised anti-bantustan mobilisation during the apartheid years, with the entire civil service going on strike at times and the army stationed in rural villages to guard the palaces of traditional leaders and to quell protests (Yawitch, 1986). The 1994 transition was hailed as a victory over those dark days, only for the TLGFA and CLRA to subsequently reinstate the control ceded to Ndebele traditional leaders who had been recognised as late as the 1970s and 1980s. Most were members of the KwaNdebele Legislative Assembly that was targeted during the anti-bantustan revolts.

The CLRA was also rejected by members of customary communities headed by traditional leaders, who argued that decision-making power over land is layered and decentralised, starting at family level and then referred upwards to user-group or village level. They argued that vesting ownership and control at the tribal level would undermine the accountability inherent in the interactions and trade-offs within and between lower, village-level and clan-based systems of customary decision making (Claassens, 2011a).

Four rural communities brought a legal challenge to the constitutionality of the CLRA in the North Gauteng High Court in 2006, arguing that by vesting control over their land exclusively in traditional councils, the Act rendered their tenure less rather than more secure.

Section 25(6) of the Constitution promises legally secure tenure to those whose current insecurity is the result of past discriminatory laws and practices. The High Court ruled in 2009 that sections of the CLRA were in conflict with the Constitution because they undermined the right to tenure security. The judgment was appealed in the Constitutional Court, which struck down the CLRA in its entirety in 2010, but this time on procedural grounds. The Act had been rushed through Parliament with great haste during the build-up to the 2004 national elections, despite vocal opposition.

Because the Act was declared unconstitutional on procedural grounds, the Constitutional Court did not rule on the substantive issue of tenure security. The 2010 judgment did however warn that:

> [T]he field that CLARA now seeks to cover is not unoccupied. There is at present a system of law that regulates the use, occupation and administration of communal land. This system also regulates the powers and functions of traditional leaders in relation to communal land. It is this system which CLARA will repeal, replace or amend. [...] Indeed all the parties approached the matter on the footing that the land which the four applicant communities occupy is regulated by indigenous law' (*Tongoane & Others v National Minister for Agriculture & Land Affairs & Others*, 2010, para 79).

This is a powerful indication that 'communal' land is not the government's gift to bestow on traditional leaders, unless it does so in accordance with pre-existing indigenous law and customary land rights. The Constitution recognises rights derived from customary law in section 39(3) of the Bill of Rights.

During the hearing of the case, then Deputy Chief Justice Dikgang Moseneke remarked that 'to use the (Bantu) Authorities Act of 1951 as a platform for land reform in 2004 is simply incredible'.

These statements go to the heart of the issue that this paper addresses, which is that while most land in the former bantustans may be registered as state owned, it is subject to pre-existing, countervailing property rights, whether derived from customary law, common law (the land buyers) or statutory law (for example the holders of Permission to Occupy certificates).[25] The government would have to expropriate these land rights before it could transfer title deeds to superimposed tribes. Any claim that leaders whose boundaries were delineated after 1951 in terms of the Bantu Authorities Act have 'indigenous ownership' of all the land in the former bantustans would not survive legal or historical scrutiny.

The Traditional Courts Bill

The next traditional leadership bill to be introduced to Parliament was the Traditional Courts Bill in 2008. The memo accompanying the bill stated that it had been drafted in conjunction with the National House of Traditional Leaders (NHTL). This was after the NHTL had rejected the South African Law Commission's (2003) recommendations and draft bill concerning customary courts. The Law Commission had conducted public consultation about the reform of customary courts, including a special set of large consultation meetings with rural women.

The sticking point was the Law Commission's recommendation that people must be allowed to opt into, or out of, using customary courts. The NHTL, on the other hand, insisted that it should be a criminal offence for anyone living within delineated tribal territories to opt out of using traditional courts.[26] By this stage the TLGFA had been enacted and made it clear that the territories of traditional leaders coincided with the tribal boundaries gazetted in terms of the Bantu Authorities Act.

The bill was predicated on the model presented by the Native Administration Act of 1927, with traditional leaders as presiding officers and no role for councillors or the lower-level village forums where most disputes are heard. Though the traditional-leader lobby valorised traditional justice systems as 'restorative' of good community relations, rather than punitive like Western courts (Holomisa, 2011), the TCB included extraordinary punishments such as forced labour to be ordered on anyone in the 'traditional community', no matter whether they were before the court or not. It enabled the traditional leader, as presiding officer, to strip people of customary rights (land rights are one such right) and made it a criminal offence not to appear when summoned. Judgments by traditional leaders had the same status as judgments made by Magistrates' Courts.

Rural people feared that the bill would enable traditional leaders with disputed authority to deal comprehensively with anyone who challenged them, including other traditional leaders who disputed their status or legitimacy. There are fewer than 900 senior traditional leaders in South Africa, yet around 1 244 disputes had been lodged with the Commission on Traditional Leadership Claims and Disputes[27] by 2013.[28]

The people who spoke out eloquently against the bill in public hearings included village-level headmen who complained that it ignored the crucial role they play in dispute resolution, and traditional leaders who were not recognised during apartheid and so are not recognised in terms of the TLGFA. They disputed the superimposed jurisdictions of the TLGFA, pointing to the fact that people flock to their courts – in recognition of their authority – and the bill would instead force them and their supporters to appear before TLGFA-recognised leaders with draconian powers.

The strongest opposition to the bill came from women. Instead of nudging along the processes of change that are underway in many areas by providing a quota of women members for customary courts, as recommended by the South African Law Commission, the TCB failed even to provide that women must be allowed to attend, and if they choose, represent themselves in traditional courts. Many of the women opposing the bill said that this failure to create a framework for substantive equality for women in the legislative process is indicative of the derogatory attitudes towards women that prevail in many traditional courts (Mnisi Weeks, 2011).

The Constitution provides that the NCOP can only pass bills that affect provinces with the support of a majority of the nine provinces, which the TCB failed to attract. The provinces that opposed it did so not because of opposition to customary law or to traditional leadership, but because it undermined *existing* customary dispute resolution processes. Many said that the bill reflected skewed power relations and would enable TLGFA-recognised traditional leaders to flout important customary accountability mechanisms (Thipe et al., 2015–16: 532).

Ultimately the TCB of 2008, which was reintroduced unchanged in 2012, failed in Parliament in 2014. A reworked version, which addresses some of the key challenges, was introduced in 2017, but by mid-2018 was still bogged down by disputes over the opting-out issue. The traditional-leader lobby seems to be of the view that people will not use their courts unless they are forced to do so by law.

The Mineral and Petroleum Resources Development Act

The TLGFA, CLRA and TCB emerged in concert with the Mineral and Petroleum Resources Development Act (MPRDA) of 2002. The MPRDA effectively nationalised mineral rights and allowed for the Department of Mineral Resources to issue mining licences. To soften the blow for the prior (overwhelmingly white) holders of mineral rights, the Act included a process to convert their existing mineral rights to new-order mining licences.

At face value, the MPRDA attempts to break the stranglehold of white capitalists in the mining sector by requiring that black capitalists be cut into the sector. But in combination with the TLGFA, it goes much further than that. It reinstates the very mechanisms that were used to exclude and subjugate the black majority during colonialism and apartheid and to reserve key assets for a small elite. These mechanisms were, and are, justified on the basis that customary land rights do not qualify as property rights and that rural black people do not have independent decision-making power in respect of their land. They are primarily tribal subjects, bound by decisions taken by traditional leaders. Their consent is not required. Their rights are not even worthy of expropriation according to this logic.

The Act has been interpreted to provide licence holders with the unconditional right to access the land needed to undertake mining, without any requirement for agreed levels of compensation for those whose surface rights to the land are affected or destroyed by mining (Dale et al., 2005: 155). In elevating mining rights over surface rights, the MPRDA has ridden roughshod over the land rights and livelihoods of poor black people living in the former homelands.

The Interim Protection of Informal Land Rights Act (IPILRA) of 1996

All of the laws described above exist in tension with an early post-apartheid law that was enacted to implement the security of tenure promised by section 25(6) of the Constitution. As its name implies, IPILRA, which consists of only two pages, was put in place to secure land rights until more comprehensive legislation could be enacted. IPILRA states that no one can be deprived of an informal right to land without their consent, except by expropriation. Most people in the former homelands qualify as the holders of informal land rights, though some also have formal rights. IPILRA recognises three types of land rights: occupation, use (e.g. fields) and access (e.g. grazing). It requires that the people whose rights are directly affected must be consulted and must consent to any changes affecting their access to land. If they refuse to consent, their rights must be expropriated and compensation paid to them. IPILRA makes it binding on the minister of Rural Development and Land Reform, as the nominal owner of most communal land, to obtain the consent of those directly affected before signing surface leases with mining companies.

The minister has abrogated this responsibility, and the Department of Mineral Resources has encouraged mining companies to enter into mining deals directly with traditional leaders. At face value the MPRDA and the TLGFA are subject to IPILRA, which is a constitutionally mandated law. The *Maledu* judgment has now confirmed that the MPRDA must be read concurrently with IPILRA, but there is not yet a similar ruling in relation to the TLGFA. As discussed recent proposed amendments to the pending TKLB seek to oust IPILRA. The problem these amendments will run into go deeper than IPILRA, however. They must confront the constitutional right to tenure security in section 25(6) of the Constitution.

Legitimacy and instability – the damage done

The view that traditional leadership is a legitimate and important institution was reiterated in all the HLP public hearings. What people objected to was the behaviour of certain leaders, for which government was squarely blamed. A man in Limpopo lamented that government had corrupted 'our leaders' by giving them unaccountable powers. In fact, traditional leaders are generally small players in a larger web of Black Empowerment Equity deals and kickbacks for politicians. They are the mechanism that has been used to deny the land and mineral rights vested in the people whose land is directly affected by mining, and to exclude these people from consultation, compensation and oversight of the profits generated from their land.

The nub of the laws is in their content, interpretation and practical application. The ways in which these laws are being interpreted and practised is generating opposition at a scale that cannot be ignored. Mining companies indicated in October 2017 that protests involving road blocks, vehicle stoning and assaults on people going to work had caused a significant reduction in platinum production at Mogalakwena, the world's largest open-pit platinum mine, and Impala Platinum's Marula mine (Stoddard, 2017). Impala has said that it may soon have to close Marula, which would be the first such shutdown in South Africa linked purely to social upheaval. Chris Griffith, Chief Executive of Anglo American Platinum, told Reuters that 'what we are trying to do is get away from some of the previous structures where we felt obliged to pay the money over to the Kgoshi [chief]' (Stoddard, 2017).

In a written submission to the HLP about problems confronting mining-affected communities, the Minerals Council South Africa wrote (Chamber of Mines, 28 July 2017):

We are conscious that the legitimacy of traditional leaders is disputed by some community members in some jurisdictions, and that this can be the source of negative relationships between mines and adjacent communities ... There have also been cases where the proceeds of these transactions have been mismanaged. None of this is satisfactory for the mines and the companies that own them ... However, the industry's interest is in greater stability and a reduction of social conflict both within those communities and between disaffected members of those communities and the mines. That would need to include acceptance of greater accountability by traditional leaders.

Yet mining companies continue to enter into agreements with traditional leaders and insist that the consent or expropriation provisions of IPILRA do not apply when people's surface rights to land are destroyed by mining. Government and Parliament continue to support legislation that would effectively empower traditional leaders to control the land rights of all those living within apartheid tribal boundaries, without requiring the consent of, or accountability to, the community.

This suggests strongly that the ruling party, government and the mining industry have no alternative vision for how to go about mining in a way that upholds constitutional rights and secures the rural livelihoods of communities whose land is destroyed by mining. Instead, they have defaulted to the same mechanisms of exclusion enacted by white governments to secure the interests of white capital in the past, and have resorted to using the law as a mechanism to deny black property rights and to re-assert indirect rule by chiefs to subdue opposition. Mining deals are made in secret, in order to avoid legal scrutiny, especially by those whom they systematically exclude. This secrecy veils the use of transfer pricing by multinational companies to ensure that their real profits do not reflect in South Africa (Radebe, 2015). The profits from mining, and indeed large volumes of raw minerals, are ending up offshore, rather than benefitting South Africa as a nation, contrary to the narrative used to justify the MPRDA.

Minister Gwede Mantashe has reiterated in the context of the 2018 draft of the Mining Charter that 'communities' should benefit from mining through a portion of mining revenue being deposited to 'community trusts'. Given that the laws discussed in this paper define community to mean 'tribe', this means that revenue will continue to be deposited into tribal accounts, rather than compensation being paid to those directly affected. The law governing trust property in South Africa, the Trust Property Control Act of 1988, was not designed for trusts with hundreds of thousands of beneficiaries and the complex interface with laws such as the TLGFA. The Trust Property Control Act is notorious for failing to include effective oversight and mechanisms to address breaches and internal disputes.

I argue that a key driver of these laws has been the wealth to be extracted from the mineral-rich northern provinces of South Africa and the bantustan legacies and continuities that benefitted particular leaders and their politically connected investment partners. This does not imply that the traditional-leader lobbies in the Eastern Cape and KwaZulu-Natal are not implicated in similar deals about natural resources, including less valuable minerals and tourism land. They too have lobbied fiercely for laws to bolster the power and authority of traditional leaders.

Conclusion

As someone who witnessed the rural land struggles of the 1980s, and to some extent participated in them, it has been hard to come to terms with the legislative agenda of the ruling party of South Africa, the ANC. In the 1980s, young people were risking their lives to challenge tribal levies and to confront traditional leaders and their tribal police who went around collecting levies from poor women. Many activists ended up fleeing their homes and sleeping in our Transvaal Rural Action Committee (TRAC)[29] offices at Khotso House in central Johannesburg. It was a heady time of UDF alliances and people desperately trying to connect with the leadership in exile. But the passion and the bravery were home-grown and irrepressible, notwithstanding the violence and oppression of the 1985–1990 states of emergency.

People were convinced that even if they were not in contact with the 'Congress', what they were doing followed in the footsteps of Govan Mbeki, Albert Luthuli and Nelson Mandela in voicing opposition to the bantustan system. When rural people voted overwhelmingly for the ANC in 1994, they voted for equality within a reunited South Africa.

The bills referred to in this paper fundamentally betray the promise of a unitary democratic South Africa, and seem to be an extraordinary risk for the ruling party to take during the run-up to the national elections in 2019. Having heard the sense of betrayal and bitter disillusionment expressed by thousands of people during the provincial public hearings of the Motlanthe HLP, one wonders whether senior officials and politicians are oblivious to this anger because they speak only to traditional leaders, as opposed to the people affected by the laws.

Opposition to the proposed traditional leadership bills discussed in this chapter does not reject the legitimacy of the institution of traditional leadership, but rather the colonial and apartheid distortions of customary law that the bills embody. This opposition builds on decades of resistance to the apartheid laws and practices that went before these bills. That resistance resulted in multiple, different forms of property and identity in rural areas, which the new bills seek to deny and to subjugate.

How has it come about that the ruling party would ram these bills through Parliament, given the ANC's commitment to the democratic transition and the ideal of equal citizenship in a unitary South Africa? Many of the people who oppose these bills risked their lives in anti-apartheid and anti-bantustan struggles. The answer appears to be that senior politicians are deeply implicated in and profit from, the ways in which the traditional leadership laws interact with the MPRDA to deny the property and citizenship rights of rural citizens.

Far from bringing a new dawn for local communities, mining has been a curse that has destroyed many rural livelihoods, divided communities and seen billions siphoned out of South Africa through deals which, because they are secret, are easy for mining magnates to manipulate.

Judged by the actions and policy choices that have been analysed in this paper, the ANC has chosen mining magnates and traditional leaders over the poorest and most vulnerable of South Africans. This reflects dominant class interests within the ANC, but also puts those class interests under the spotlight in relation to the Constitution and elections. We know from history (and South Africa's in particular) that capitalists and aspirant capitalists use the state to pass laws that favour their interests. The problem, from their point of view, is that

South Africa now has a Constitution, and these laws cannot withstand constitutional scrutiny because they abrogate basic political rights.

The South African state, in concert with apartheid-era traditional leaders, has therefore resorted to a 'shadow land' of traditional powers and functions that do not actually exist in law, backed by violent forms of repression that are seemingly invisible to the police. Protective laws such as IPILRA are abrogated and the financial accountability mechanisms in the TLGFA are ignored while 'tribal' funds disappear under the watch of some provincial premiers. The scale of illegality is now coming back to bite the mining companies and traditional leaders who are implicated, hence the attempt by the 2018 bills to provide a veneer of legality for mining deals signed by traditional leaders. But all the TKLB can do is buy time, because it too will be struck down for abrogating constitutional rights. In the meantime, dispossession continues and fertile land is irrevocably destroyed. Kgalema Motlanthe told the ANC's May 2018 Land Conference about the scale and nature of the problems his panel had witnessed in former homeland areas, in relation to the failure of land reform throughout the country. He pointed to the panel's detailed legislative recommendations about how the situation could be turned around to protect the poor and the marginal, who he insisted must remain the ANC's primary constituency. In response he was effectively rebuked for having 'insulted' traditional leaders by pointing to examples where specific leaders had acted dictatorially (Zungu, 2018).

Not only do the laws and bills discussed in this paper enable dispossession, they also conflict with the ANC's own history of opposition to the Bantu Authorities Act. They reaffirm the denial of basic citizen rights of the 17 million South Africans living in the former homelands, denials that the bantustan system had justified. They also deny – and trump – the forms of identity and land rights that people created in opposition to the Land Acts, the Native Administration Act, the Bantu Authorities Act and the bantustans themselves. These land rights and identities were hard-won, over many decades. The bills subsume them all within tribal overlordship. Rural people are watching the passage of the TKLB and the TCB in Parliament closely. At stake is not just the reputation of the ANC, but the long-term legitimacy of the South African state, the Constitution of South Africa and the rule of law in South Africa.

References

Albertyn, C. 1994. 'Women and the transition to democracy in South Africa'. *Acta Juridica*, 1, 39–63.

Anonymous. 23 September 2013. 'BEE deal not forced on Gold Fields'. *Mining Mx* website: http://www.miningmx.com/news/off-the-wires/17633-bee-deal-not-forced-on-gold-fields/, accessed 7 July 2018.

Barnard, M. 2015. 'The Motsepe ethic: An exploration of the BEE power elite'. MA thesis. Johannesburg: University of the Witwatersrand.

Bennett, T. 2008. '"Official" v "living" customary law: Dilemmas of description and recognition', in Claassens, A. & Cousins, B. (eds.) *Land, Power and Custom*. Cape Town: UCT Press, pp. 138–153.

Bennett, T. W. 1995. *Human Rights and African Customary Law: Under the South African constitution*. Johannesburg: Juta.

Bentley, K., Cherry, J., George, K., Mafundityala, U., Maphunye, K., Mbhanyele, E., Mulaudzi, T., Ngomane, N., Ngqulunga, B., Nxumalo, T. & Yarbrough, M. 2006. 'Longitudinal study: The effect of the legislated powers of traditional authorities on rural women's rights in South Africa'. Pretoria: Baseline Report of Human Science Research Council and Centre for Applied Legal Studies.

Bloom, K. 2016. 'What's mine is mine: How the Bapo Ba Mogale got robbed of R800 million'. *Daily Maverick*, https://www.dailymaverick.co.za/article/2016-10-26-whats-mine-is-mine-how-the-bapo-ba-mogale-got-robbed-of-r800-million/#.W03rVGAzaM9, accessed 7 July 2018.

Bloom, K. & Wales-Smith, S. 2018. 'Stealing the crust: How the Bakgatla Ba Kgafela were robbed of their inheritance'. *Daily Maverick*, https://www.dailymaverick.co.za/article/2018-02-01-stealing-the-crust-how-the-baktatla-ba-kgafela-were-robbed-of-their-inheritance/#.W03okmAzaM, accessed 7 July 2018.

Boyle, B. 2016a. 'Mining communities out in the cold over compensation'. *Custom Contested* website: http://www.customcontested.co.za/mining-communities-out-in-the-cold-over-compensation/, accessed 23 August 2018.

Boyle, B. 2016b. 'From undemocratic laws to violence: How South Africa's mine-hosting communities are silenced'. *Heinrich Böl Stiftung Perspectives*, (3), 20–24.

Brümmer, S. & Sole, S. 27 June 2009. 'Behind Ramatlhodi's front'. *Mail & Guardian*, https://mg.co.za/article/2009-06-27-behind-ramatlhodisfront, accessed 7 July 2018.

Brümmer, S. 28 January 2000. 'Granite mining scars Bakgatla village'. *Mail & Guardian*, https://allafrica.com/stories/200001280205.html, accessed 7 July 2018.

Burgess, S. 2010. 'Sustainability of strategic minerals in Southern Africa and potential conflicts and partnerships,' DTIC website: http://www.dtic.mil/dtic/tr/fulltext/u2/a535875.pdf, accessed 7 July 2018.

Business Leadership South Africa and Business Unity South Africa. 16 March 2017. 'A review of regulatory challenges & policy uncertainty impeding investment & employment in South Africa'. Johannesburg: BUSA.

Capps, G. 2012. 'Victim of its own success? The platinum mining industry and the apartheid mineral property system in South Africa's political transition'. *Review of African Political Economy,* 39 (131), 63–84.

Chamber of Mines. 28 July 2017. 'Responses to the issues raised by the HLP'. Letter addressed to chairperson of HLP.

Chanock, M. 1991. 'Paradigms, policies, and property: A review of the customary law of tenure', in Mann, K. & Roberts, R. (eds.) *Law in Colonial Africa*. London: Heinemann.

Chanock, M. 2001. *The Making of South African Legal Culture 1902–1936: Fear, favour and prejudice*. Cambridge: Cambridge University Press.

Claassens, A. 1990. 'Rural land struggles in the Transvaal in the 1980s', in Murray, C. & O'Regan, C. (eds.) *No Place to Rest: Forced removals and the law in South Africa*. Cape Town: Oxford University Press, pp. 27–53.

Claassens, A. 2001. '"It's not aasy to challenge a chief": Lessons from Rakwadi'. *PLAAS Research Report 9*. University of the Western Cape: PLAAS.

Claassens, A. 2011a. 'Contested power and apartheid tribal boundaries: The implications of "living customary law" for indigenous accountability mechanisms'. *Acta Juridica*, 1, 174–209.

Claassens, A. 2011b. 'The resurgence of tribal taxes in the context of recent traditional leadership laws in South Africa', *South African Journal on Human Rights*, 27 (3), 522–545.

Claassens, A. & Gilfillan, D. 2008. 'The Kalkfontein land purchases: Eighty years on and still struggling for ownership', in Claassens, A. and Cousins, B. (eds.) *Land, Power and Custom: Controversies generated by South Africa's Communal Land Rights Act*, Cape Town: Juta, pp. 295–314.

Claassens, A. & Hathorn, M. 2008. 'Stealing restitution and selling land allocations: Dixie, Mayaeyane and Makuleke', in Claassens, A. & Cousins, B. (eds.) *Land, Power and Custom: Controversies generated by South Africa's Communal Land Rights Act*. Cape Town: Juta, pp. 315–352.

Claassens, A. & Matlala, B. 2014. 'Platinum, poverty, and princes in post-apartheid South Africa: New laws, old repertoires'. *New South African Review*, 4, 117–139.

Cogta 2017. 'Commission reports from the Traditional Leader Indaba 2017'. *CoGTA* website: http://www.cogta.gov.za/?page_id=2239 (in general); http://www.cogta.gov.za/cgta_2016/wp-content/uploads/2017/05/ Commission-On- Communal Land Rights Act No. 11 of 2004. 20 July 2004, http://www.saflii.org/za/legis/num_act/clra2004207.pdf.

Constitutional-and-Legislative-Mandate-.pdf (in particular), accessed 22 August 2018.

Dale, M., Bekker, L., Bashall, F., Chaskalson, M., Dixon, C., Grobler, G., Loxton, L., Ash, M. & Cox, A. 2005. *South African Mineral and Petroleum Law.* New York: Lexi Nexis.

De Kadt, D. & Larreguy, H. 2014. 'Agents of the Regime? Traditional Leaders and Electoral Politics in South Africa'. *The Journal of Politics*, 80 (2).

Delius, P. 1996. *A Lion Amongst the Cattle: Reconstruction and resistance in the Northern Transvaal.* London: James Currey.

Delius, P. 2018. *Mistaking Form for Substance: Reflections on the key dynamics of pre-colonial polities and their implications for the role of chiefs in contemporary South Africa.* MISTRA working paper 1. Johannesburg: Mapungubwe Institute for Strategic Reflection.

De Souza, M. & Jara, B. (eds.) 2010. *Custom, citizenship and rights: Community voices and the repeal of the Black Administration Act.* Cape Town: Law, Race and Gender Research Unit, University of Cape Town.

De Souza Louw, M. 26 January 2016. 'Will North West premier depose tainted tribal leader and challenge the status quo?', *Daily Maverick,* https://www.dailymaverick.co.za/article/2016-01-26-groundup-will-north-west-premier-depose-tainted-tribal-leader-and-challenge-the-status-quo/, accessed 23 August 2018.

Feinberg, H. 2015. *Our Land, Our Life, Our Future: Black South African challenges to territorial segregation, 1913–1948.* Pretoria: UNISA Press.

Friedman, S. June/July 2017. 'The fate of the land: Rural power and the battle to shape South Africa's polity'. 7th European Conference on African Studies, Basel.

Gluckman, M. 1965. *The Ideas in Barotse Jurisprudence.* New Haven: Yale University Press.

Government of the Republic of South Africa, Department of Provincial and Local Government. 2000. 'A discussion document towards a white paper on traditional leadership', https://www.gov.za/sites/default/files/trad_0. pdf, accessed 7 July 2018.

Harries, P. 1989. 'Exclusion, classification and internal colonialism: The emergence of ethnicity among Tsonga-speakers of South Africa', in Vail, L. (ed.) *The Creation of Tribalism in Southern Africa*. Berkeley: University of California Press.

High Level Panel (HLP) 2016. Public Hearings, http://www.parliament.gov. za/high-level-panel, accessed 28 November 2018.

High Level Panel (HLP). 31 May 2017. Contralesa Round Table With HLP, Cape Town, https://www.parliament.gov.za/storage/app/media/ Pages/2017/october/High_Level_Panel/Roundtable-Land_reform/ Contralesa_round_table_with_HLP.pdf, accessed 28 November 2018.

Holomisa, P. 2011. 'Balancing law and tradition: The TCB and its relation to African systems of justice administration'. *South African Crime Quarterly*, 35, 17–22.

Interim Protection of Informal Land Rights Act 31 of 1996. 26 June 1996, http://www.ruraldevelopment.gov.za/phocadownload/Acts/interim%20 protection%20of%20informal%20land%20rights%20act%2031%20 of%201996.pdf, accessed 20 November 2018.

Klug, H. 1995. 'Defining the property rights of others: Political power, indigenous tenure and the construction of customary land law'. *The Journal of Legal Pluralism & Unofficial Law*, 27 (35), 119–148.

Khunou, F. 2017. 'Makgale-Chwaro-Khunou Supp 2-Genealogy'. Affidavit for the Baloyi Commission, https://www.evernote.com/l/AZo-IgBb5O1O DpiVjIIUMZqUZuhFapVbySw, accessed 7 July 2018.

Luthuli, A. 1962. *Let My People Go: An autobiography*. London: Collins.

Luwaya, N. 2013. 'Report on the provincial Traditional Courts Bill hearings'. Cape Town: Centre for Law and Society.

Maloka, E. & Gordon, R. 1996. 'Chieftainship, civil society and the political transition in South Africa'. *Critical Sociology*, 22 (3), 37–55.

Mamdani, M. 1996. *Citizen and Subject: Contemporary Africa and the legacy of colonialism*. Princeton: Princeton University Press.

Manson, A. 2013. 'Mining and "traditional communities" in South Africa's "platinum belt": Contestations over land, leadership and assets in North-West Province c. 1996–2012', *Journal of Southern African Studies*, 39 (2), 409–423.

Maurice Webb Race Relations Unit, University of KwaZulu-Natal. 2009. 'Draft report on the consultative process on communal contributions paid in traditional communities within KwaZulu-Natal'. Unpublished report.

Masilela, J. 13 December 2015. 'Memories of a village boy named Tlhopane'. *Sunday Independent,* https://www.iol.co.za/sundayindependent/memories-of-village-boy-called-tlhopane-1959581, accessed 23 August 2017.

Mbeki, G. 1964. *South Africa: The peasants' revolt*. London: Penguin Books.

Mineral and Petroleum Resources Development Act 28 of 2002. 10 October 2002, http://www.eisourcebook.org/cms/South%20Africa%20 Mineral%20&%20Petroleum%20Resources%20Development%20 Act%202002.pdf.

Mngadi, M. 28 June 2018. '"It's the beginning of war", warn traditional leaders on whoever takes land forcefully'. News24, http://www.news24. com/SouthAfrica/News/its-the-beginning-of-war-warn-traditional-leaders-on-whoever-takes-land-forcefully-20180628, accessed 28 November 2018.

Mnisi Weeks, S. 2011. 'The traditional courts bill: Controversy about process, substance and implications'. *SA Crime Quarterly*, 35, 3–11.

Mnwana, S. & Capps, G. March 2015. '"No Chief ever bought a piece of land"': Struggles over property, community and mining in the Bakgatla-ba-Kgafela Traditional Authority Area, North West Province'. Society, Work and Development Institute. Johannesburg: University of the Witwatersrand.

Mnwana, S. 2014. 'Chief's justice?' *South African Crime Quarterly,* 49, 21–29.

Moatshe, R. 13 September 2017. 'Protestors claim Motsepes use cash to get control of tribe'. *Pretoria News*, https://www.iol.co.za/pretoria-news/ protesters-claim-motsepes-use-cash-to-get-control-of-tribe-11194748, accessed 7 July 2018.

Morare, M. 2016. 'Mining wars, the people versus the leaders'. *Catholics Bishops Conference,* Briefing Paper *415,* http://www.cplo.org.za/wp-content/uploads/2016/02/BP-415-Mining-Wars-The-people-vs-The-Leaders-Oct-2016.pdf, accessed 23 August 2018.

Murray, C. 2001. 'Negotiating beyond deadlock: From the constitutional assembly to the court', in Andrews P. & Ellmann, S. (eds.) *The Post-Apartheid Constitutions: Perspectives on the new South Africa's basic law.* Johannesburg: Witwatersrand University Press, pp. 103–127.

Noble, Z., Zembe, W. & Wright, J. 2014. 'Poverty may have declined, but poverty and deprivation are still worst in the former homelands'. Southern African Social Policy Research Institute (SASPRI), http://www. econ3x3.org/sites/default/files/articles/Noble%20et%20al%202014%20 Former%20homelands%20FINAL.pdf, accessed 23 August 2018.

Ntongana, T. 2018 'Battle over mining rights in remote Eastern Cape villages'. *Ground Up* website: https://www.groundup.org.za/article/ xolobeni-villagers-fight-be-heard-minister/, accessed 22 August 2018.

Ntsebeza, L. 2005. *Democracy Compromised: Chiefs and the politics of land in South Africa.* Leiden: Brill.

Parliament of South Africa. 2017. 'High-level panel on the assessment of key legislation and the acceleration of fundamental change'. *South African Parliament* website: https://www.parliament.gov.za/storage/app/media/Pages/2017/october/High_Level_Panel/HLP_Report/HLP_report.pdf, accessed 23 August 2018.

Peires, J. 2014. 'History versus customary law: Commission on Traditional Leadership Disputes and Claims'. *Crime Quarterly*, 49, 7–20.

Pickering, J. & Motala, A. Forthcoming. *The Abuse of Interdicts by Traditional leaders in South Africa: Silencing dissenting voices and undermining customary law.* Johannesburg: Witwatersrand University Press.

Platzky, L. & Walker, C. 1985. *The Surplus People: Forced removals in South Africa.* Johannesburg: Ravan Press.

Public Protector of South Africa. 2017/2018. 'Allegations of maladministration in the Bapo baMogale Administration'. *PPSA* website: http://www.pprotect.org/sites/default/files/legislation_report/SKMBT_C55417061916570.pdf, accessed 7 July 2017.

Radebe, B. August 2015. 'Transfer pricing to blame for many of SA's woes'. *Mining Weekly*, http://www.miningweekly.com/article/transfer-pricing-to-blame-for-many-of-sas-woes-2015-09-18, accessed 7 July 2018.

Rutledge, C. 17 June 2014. 'Ramathlodi more of the same?' *The Con* website: http://www.theconmag.co.za/2014/06/17/ramatlhodi-more-of-the-same/, accessed 23 August.

Saba, A. 23 September 2016(a). 'Illegal Limpopo chrome mining – digging deep for empty promises'. *Mail & Guardian*, https://mg.co.za/article/2016-09-23-00-illegal-limpopo-chrome-mining-digging-deep-for-empty-promises, accessed 7 July 2018.

Saba, A. 30 September 2016(b). 'Phosa, mining and a royal battle'. *Mail & Guardian*, https://mg.co.za/article/2016-09-30-00-phosa-mining-and-a-royal-battle, accessed 7 July 2018.

Saxby, P. 10 April, 2018. 'More clout for traditional leadership in local government'. Legalbrief Policy Watch.

Schapera, I. 1956. *Government and Politics in Tribal Societies.* New York: Schocken Books. South African History Online. 2011. 'Turning the tide: A chapter from the UDF: A history of the United Democratic Front in South Africa'. *South African History Online* website: https://www.sahistory.org.za/articles/turning-tide-chapter-udf-history-united-democratic-front-south-africa, accessed 23 August 2019.

South African Human Rights Commission. 2018. National Hearing on the underlying socio-economic challenges of mining-affected communities in South Africa'. SAHRC website: https://www.sahrc.org.za/home/21/files/SAHRC%20Mining%20communities%20report%20FINAL.pdf, accessed 23 August 2018.

South African Law Commission. 21 January 2003. 'Project 90 Report on Traditional Courts and the Judicial Function of Traditional Leaders'. *DOJ* website: http://www.justice.gov.za/salrc/reports/r_prj90_tradlead_2003jan.pdf, accessed 7 July 2018.

Southall, R. 2004. 'The ANC and black capitalism in South Africa'. *Review of African Political Economy*, 31 (100), 313–328.

Stoddard, E. October 2017. 'Protests test tribal authority on South Africa's platinum belt'. *Reuters* website: https://www.reuters.com/article/us-safrica-platinum-insight/protests-test-tribal-authority-on-south-africas-platinum-belt-idUSKBN1CD06E, accessed on 12 May 2018.

Thipe, T. 2013. 'Voices in the legislative process: A report of public submissions on the Traditional Courts Bill (2008 and 2012)'. Centre for Law and Society, Cape Town.

Thipe, T. 2014. 'The boundaries of tradition: An examination of the Traditional Leadership and Governance Framework Act'. *Harvard Human Rights Journal*, 29, Online Symposium, http://harvardhrj.com/2014/11/the-boundaries-of-tradition-an-examination-of-the-traditional-leadership-and-governance-framework-act/, accessed 23 August 2018.

Thipe, T., De Souza, M. & Luwaya, N. 2015–2016. 'The advert was put up yesterday: Public participation in the Traditional Courts Bill Legislative Process'. *New York Law School Law Review*, 60, 519–551.

Tongoane & Others v National Minister for Agriculture & Land Affairs & Others (CCT100/09) [2010] ZACC 10; 2010 (6) SA 214 (CC); 2010 (8) BCLR 741 (CC) (11 May 2010), www. saflii.org/za/cases/ZACC/2010/10.html, accessed 25 November 2018.

Traditional and Khoi-San Leadership Bill B23-2015. 18 September 2016, http://www.cogta.gov.za/cgta_2016/wp-content/uploads/2016/06/TRADITIONAL-AND-KHOI-SAN-LEADERSHIP-BILL.pdf.

Traditional Courts Bill of 2008 [B15-2008]. Gazette 30902. 27 March 2008, https://www.gov.za/sites/default/files/b15-08.pdf

Traditional Courts Bill of 2012 [B1-2012]. Gazette 34850. 13 December 2011, http://www.customcontested.co.za/wp-content/uploads/2013/03/TCB_B001-2012.pdf

Traditional Courts Bill of 2017 [B1-2017]. Gazette 40487. 9 December 2016, http://www.justice.gov.za/legislation/bills/2017-TraditionalCourtsBill.pdf.

Traditional Leadership and Governance Framework Act No. 41 of 2003. 11 December 2003, http://www.cogta.gov.za/cgta_2016/wp-content/uploads/2016/06/TLGFA-Traditional-Leadership-and-Governance-Framework-Act-2003-Act-No-41-of-2003.pdf

Yawitch, J. August 1986. 'Kwa-Ndebele: A rural Trojan horse'. *The Black Sash* website: http://disa.ukzn.ac.za/sites/default/files/pdf_files/BSAug86.0036.4843.029.002.Aug1986.14.pdf, accessed 23 August 2018.

Yende, S. 15 January 2017. 'Motsepe's ARM finally pays up'. *City Press*, https://www.fin24.com/Companies/Mining/motsepes-arm-finally-pays-up-20170115-2, accessed 7 July 2018.

Zungu, L. 27 May 2018. 'Traditional leaders accuse Motlanthe of stirring a war'. *IOL*, https://www.iol.co.za/news/south-africa/kwazulu-natal/traditional-leaders-accuse-motlanthe-of-stirring-a-war-15183834, accessed 23 August 2018.

Notes

1 Comment made by then Deputy Chief Justice Dikgang Moseneke in 2010 during the hearing of the Tongoane case in the Constitutional Court – see note 27.

2 These are accounts or trusts registered in the name of a particular tribe but administered by the government.

3 The author was one of 14 members of the High-Level Panel.

4 The ANC appears to have distanced itself from former President Motlanthe after he urged it to address the vested interests of those complicit in dispossession, including some traditional leaders, at its land summit in May 2018.

5 *Alexkor Ltd & Another v Richtersveld Community & Others* (2003) 12 BCLR 1301 (CC); *Bhe & Others v Magistrate, Khayelitsha & Others* (2005) 10 SA 580 (CC); *Shilubana and Others v Nwamitwa* (2009) (2) SA 66 (CC)

6 As discussed later the TKLB criminalises unrecognised traditional leaders who claim they are legitimate leaders.

7 'Wall-to-wall' denotes that the areas over which traditional leaders govern are determined by old homeland boundaries, regardless of whether all the communities 'within the walls' recognise these boundaries or not, or whether there is ethnic homogeneity within the boundaries.

8 Previously named the Maluleke Commission until the passing of Judge George Maluleke in August 2017. The Commission continued, chaired by former co-commissioner Adv Sesi Baloyi. It finished hearing evidence in June 2018 and the findings are expected to be delivered in early 2019.

9 Nthai was struck off the roll of advocates after the North Gauteng High Court found that he had acted disgracefully by suggesting that his opponents bribe him while representing the South African government

in a matter concerning mining rights. Another charge was the amount that he was claiming from Anglo Platinum for legal services over and above the monthly retainer that he received of R330,000.

10 The sisters of Patrice Motsepe, Dr Tshepo Motsepe and Mrs Bridgette Radebe, are the wives of President Cyril Ramaphosa and Energy Minister Jeff Radebe, respectively.

11 Lower courts tend to default to the existing legal precedents set during apartheid. It is in the nature of courts to be precedent based and therefore backward looking. It is mainly in the higher courts, and in the Constitutional Court particularly, that lawyers have challenged the constitutionality of apartheid precedents and where judgments have struck these down. It takes time for new precedents set in the Constitutional Court to filter down to the lower courts, especially if local lawyers do not bring them to the attention of the lower courts.

12 The specific example of the suppression of the explosive records of the 1990 Mushasha and 1998 Ralushai Commissions of Inquiry into Venda and Limpopo apartheid manipulation of historical chieftainship disputes has been omitted here because of space constraints but will be discussed in a forthcoming publication by the author.

13 The written reply by Cogta on 4 September 2015 to parliamentary question 3378 posed in the National Assembly indicates that no traditional councils in Mpumalanga or Limpopo met the composition requirements in relation to women and elected members. Only 14 traditional councils in North West met the composition requirements, while 28 failed to do so. In Northern Cape, KwaZulu-Natal and Free State all traditional councils met the composition requirements. No information was available in relation to traditional councils in the Eastern Cape.

14 IPILRA is discussed further in part 4.

15 *Congress of Traditional Leaders of South Africa v the Speaker of the National House of Assembly & Others* (2016) 16 WCC 2474

16 Saziso Wofa was beaten to death as punishment for breaching tribal rules. The murder was allegedly committed by subjects of Dalindyebo, on his instruction.

17 The record of violent actions committed by Dalindyebo include setting three villagers' homes alight as a means to evict them, and publicly assaulting two young men.

18 *Ex parte Chairperson of the Constitutional Assembly: In re Certification of the Constitution of the Republic of South Africa*, 1996 (4) SA 744 (CC)

19 Many exemptions to the Land Act's prohibition of African purchase were

granted between 1913 and 1936 as Feinberg and others document.

20 Created in terms of the South African Native Trust and Land Act of 1936. The trust was initially named the South African Native Trust (SANT), but was subsequently renamed the South African Development Trust (SADT).

21 The CLRA was never brought into operation because of pending litigation about its constitutionality.

22 Formerly named Bantu Authorities.

23 An amendment to the Bantu Authorities Act in 1964 provided for the establishment of community authorities alongside tribal authorities. In some instances, groups who rejected or had no tribal identity were made community authorities as opposed to tribal authorities. But community authorities were also used to 'downgrade' the status of separate historical groups by lumping three different 'tribes' into one community authority, rather than each group being separately recognised. This was particularly common in Limpopo when mixed Venda- and Tsonga-speaking communities were separated and forcibly removed in order to create the Venda and Gazankulu homelands.

24 *Ingonyama Trust v Radebe & Others* (2012) ZAKZPHC 2

25 A PTO or a Permission to Occupy certificate is issued most commonly in terms of Bantu Land Regulation R180 of 1969, although there are also much older forms of PTOs in various provinces. PTOs are upgradable to ownership in terms of the Upgrading of Land Tenure Rights Act of 1991.

26 In this respect, the NHTL's position echoes the Native Administration Act of 1927, which did away with various provincial provisions that had allowed Africans to apply for exemptions to chiefly jurisdiction (Chanock 2001: 342–345).

27 Established by Chapter 6 of the TLGFA of 2003.

28 Answer to Parliamentary question 697 posed to the Minster of CoGTA in March 2013 and answered in May 2013

29 I worked for the Transvaal Rural Action Committee (TRAC), a project of the Black Sash, which supported people resisting forced removals and farm evictions from 1983–1990.

SECTION TWO

'Development' and Distributive Struggles

The quarries come and go without consulting the people about the piece of land that is being utilised. We would like that this be paid attention to, especially that word 'community' – that doesn't mean to be 'represented'. 'Community' is the homes that are in that area where the quarry is going to be opened, not a representative, nor a councillor or traditional leader, but the land belongs to the people.

– BORDER RURAL COMMUNITY, HIGH-LEVEL PANEL EASTERN CAPE PUBLIC HEARINGS, 16 AUGUST 2016, P. 43

There are two traditional councils in Babanango that have coexisted for many years. When COGTA imposed councils that process development, a lot of problems and strife started. Even the regent was stripped of her powers.

– THOKOZANI NDAWO FROM BABANANGO, HIGH-LEVEL PANEL KWAZULU-NATAL PUBLIC HEARINGS, 20 OCTOBER 2016, P. 28

Where I stay is 45 km away from Rustenburg. When you go look for a job, for example, we are surrounded by mines, mines that are in royal villages. I am not a Mofokeng unfortunately. When I went to go look for a job at Impala mine, they told me to go and get a letter from the chief. I then went to see the headman. The headman asked me from which kutla am I from. I do not even know what kutla is Mr Motlanthe. Now like a child from Rustenburg I have a right to minerals in Rustenburg Mr Motlanthe. I can't work anywhere because I am not of any kutla.

– KAIZER MOEME, HIGH-LEVEL PANEL NORTH-WEST PUBLIC HEARINGS, 1–2 MARCH 2017, P. 97

The next two chapters consider the role of traditional leaders in contemporary struggles over land and resources – particularly mining. Post-1994 government policy offers traditional leaders a central role in local development, in which land and mining revenues are seen as important instruments of wealth redistribution and economic growth. Each of the quotations above deal with the role of traditional leaders in 'development' – serving as gatekeepers of minerals and economic opportunity, but also having to work with (and sometimes for) state institutions. Contemporary chiefs are often positioned as custodians of mineral-led development, premised on their 'historical' role in land administration.

Drawing on a case study of the Bakgatla Ba Kgafela, Sonwabile Mnwana's chapter explores the historical processes that have entrenched chiefs' control over land, making them central figures in these distributive struggles. In doing so, he illustrates that the Bakgatla's power over land long precedes post-apartheid legislation and new mining interests. Sithandiwe Yeni's chapter then offers a detailed case study of a group of residents in Makhasaneni, KwaZulu-Natal, who resisted collusion between senior traditional leaders and mining companies. The story of activists in Makhasaneni resonates with struggles recorded in other parts of the country, which have seen rural people suffer losses rather than gain benefits from mining, and some traditional leaders collaborating with elites to override local participation. It is worth highlighting that, in the Makhasaneni case, the local headman performed a powerful role in representing community interests, even at his own risk. Indeed, as this case shows, a rejection of certain instantiations of traditional leadership need not amount to a wholesale rejection of the institution or its role in a contemporary democracy; while the people of Makhasaneni may have resisted the actions of their senior traditional leaders, they also drew on the institution of traditional leadership in their struggle, attributing significant import to the role of their headman.

With land being such a vexed question for a South African democracy, this is likely to be the issue on which the future role of the country's traditional leaders is tested, contested and re-invented.

FIVE

Chiefs, land and distributive struggles on the platinum belt, South Africa[1]

SONWABILE MNWANA

Introduction

Recent studies have shown that South Africa's post-apartheid state has – through several pieces of legislation – increased the power of local chiefs in rural areas, particularly in the former 'homeland' areas (Mnwana & Capps, 2015; Mnwana, 2016). This is contributing to new struggles on the platinum belt, where mining expands largely on 'communal' land. This chapter argues that while many studies report land-related conflicts across Africa, there have been limited attempts to understand the historical processes that shape the structure of power at a local level, and how these processes connect to distributive struggles.

The resilience of traditional leaders (chiefs) in postcolonial Africa has largely been attributed to chiefs' authority over customary land. There have been intense debates about whether communal (customary) land is better protected (legally secure) when left under the custodianship of chiefs, as opposed to the titling and privatisation of communal land (World Bank, 1989). Here, privatisation comes attendant with the risks of promoting inequality and land grabbing, while also falling short of government's rhetorical promises to legally empower the rural poor, encourage 'market-promotion' and advance sustainable economic growth through rural peasant agriculture (Boone, 2017). Scholars have also reported new forms of exclusion, inequality, competition and intensified conflict over land, fuelled by the increased scarcity and consequently increased value of land in different regions of Africa (Peters, 2004; Chimhowu & Woodhouse, 2006; Mnwana, 2015b). Chiefs are at the centre of these struggles because land struggles are also about the meanings of property – particularly among local political authorities regulating it and the social institutions that shape relations over it (Lund, 2008). Power and legitimacy of property-governing authorities – mainly traditional leaders in this case – are mobilised and defined in terms of custom (Mamdani, 1996). The dominant notion of 'communal' ownership of all land held under customary systems of tenure in Africa tends to enhance the chiefs' power over land (Mnwana, 2016). Moreover, this idea promotes the problematic perception that Africans in the countryside exist exclusively within, and act as, homogenous groups (or 'communities') and can be expected to respond to economic shifts (or even pursue development) as these collectives, under the authority and control of chiefs. The latter are often (also problematically) seen 'as the most culturally appropriate guardians of community' and 'assumed to embody communal norms' (Grischow, 2008: 64). As such, they are deemed suitable to act 'as trustees' in development projects (Grischow, 2008: 64).

In post-apartheid South Africa, debates about the resurgence and resilience of chiefly power have grown over the past two decades. Among others, dominant arguments include questions of whether chieftaincy is a hindrance to democratic principles and progress, given that some of its elements still resonate with the character of the erstwhile colonial indirect rule (Mamdani, 1996; Ntsebeza, 2005). To add to this is the ever-dominant question of political legitimacy – state and chiefs competing for power and legitimacy in the countryside (Krämer, 2016).

Anthropologists John Comaroff and Jean Comaroff (2009: 7) observe that, to a great extent, the ability of chiefs to survive in the post-apartheid era can be attributed to the increasing commoditisation of the politics of ethnic identity, culture and tradition. These authors (2009: 21) describe this process as 'incorporation of identity, the rendering of ethnicised populations into corporations of one kind or another'. The Bakgatla, Bafokeng and other traditional communities who are involved in the mining industry on South Africa's platinum belt fit into this analysis well. Manson and Mbenga (2012: 109) have argued that struggles in South Africa's former homeland areas, especially on the rural platinum belt, epitomise a revival of those ethnic identities suppressed under the former Bophuthatswana homeland, thus 'leading to forms of a better-defined ethnic sense'.

All these processes are strongly rooted in the ability of chiefs, through collusion with the state (and capital, at times) to successfully position themselves as custodians of communal land (Mnwana, 2016). But the resilience of traditional leadership remains less understood at the micro level, particularly how regional and local land, as well as political histories, shaped the status and influence of certain powerful chiefdoms in South Africa. This chapter attempts to narrow this gap by drawing on empirical findings from a detailed case study (conducted mainly through archives and oral histories) of the Bakgatla Ba Kgafela traditional authority in North West province to demonstrate some less-reported historical processes that enhanced the power of chiefs over rural land. The analysis shows how such processes connect to contemporary distributive struggles over land and mining revenues.

The arguments in this chapter are divided into two main sections: The first, shorter section maps out the resurgence of chiefly power in post-apartheid South Africa, particularly chiefs' control (or assumed custodianship) over land and mining revenues. The second details the case of the Bakgatla chieftaincy.

As this manuscript was going to print (in late 2018), the Constitutional Court of South Africa passed a significant judgment in favour of the Lesetlheng land-claiming group in the Bakgatla area. The judgment upheld the Lesetlheng community's land tenure rights, overturning an eviction order awarded to Itereleng Bakgatla Mineral Resources (IBMR) and Pilanesberg Platinum Mines (PPM), which would have seen the community removed from their land. This land had been bought by the community in 1919, registered in the name of the native commissioner and held in trust for the leader of the Bakgatla Ba Kgafela. In 2008, IBMR and PPM were granted a mining licence and a surface lease agreement was signed with the Bakgatla Ba Kgafela traditional authority. In October 2018, the Constitutional Court ruled that the land tenure rights of the Lesetlheng community trumped these mining rights. The judgment sets an important precedent, by asserting that communities themselves, and not simply traditional leaders, must have a role in deciding whether mining can proceed. The implications of the judgment for future legislation and land disputes remains to be seen. However, by tracing the historical relationship between the Bakgatla Ba Kgafela, the land, and its resources, this chapter articulates the significance of this judgment and the configurations of power that will continue to shape how land rights are negotiated in the North West.

Chiefs in post-apartheid South Africa

One of the 'holy cows' at the centre of South Africa's political landscape is the institution of traditional leadership (kings and chiefs of various ranks). This has become increasingly evident in the manner in which the major political party leaders have competed for the attention of traditional leaders, and the latter for greater state recognition.

Chiefs in South Africa currently enjoy an advantageous position, especially on the platinum belt, where they control and distribute vast mining revenues and act as custodians of community property, including land and mining revenues, and rural development. This is in the face of democratically elected local government officials and administrators (Mnwana, 2015a).

Chiefly control over land and mineral wealth is often attributed to two processes: The first critical process is the attempt by the ruling African National Congress (ANC) government to define residents in rural areas, through legislation, as subjects of 'traditional communities' (or 'tribes') under chiefs. The ANC has, since the early 2000s, introduced and passed laws that not only gave chiefs a secure position in the post-apartheid political scene, but significantly enhanced their powers over rural land and local governance. This move came after almost a decade of doubt and oscillation by the ANC about what the roles and functions of traditional leaders would be under the new democratic dispensation. Some argue that the ANC's shift towards recognising and empowering chiefs was informed by the Inkatha Freedom Party's historically entrenched dominance over chiefs, as well as local politics in KwaZulu-Natal (Van Kessel & Oomen, 1997). However, it is becoming increasingly evident that politicians believe that chiefs in post-apartheid South Africa have a significant role in controlling and mobilising rural votes. For Beinart (2014:1):

> The ANC has come to see chiefs as able to deliver a block rural vote. The movement has consistently gained its highest percentage vote in rural provinces such as Limpopo and Mpumalanga, as well as parts of the Eastern Cape, not in the cities.

However, it remains highly contested whether chiefs have the ability to deliver rural votes, or whether the good fortunes of the ruling ANC, and its dominance in the former homeland areas, have a direct connection to the party's close ties with, and placation of, local chiefs (Beinart, 2014; Buthelezi & Yeni, 2016). What remains clear is that the post-apartheid government has increased the powers of chiefs, legitimising both their control over land and their mediation of relations between mines and communities (Mnwana, 2016).

The Traditional Leadership and Governance Framework Act No. 41 of 2003 (TLGFA) re-enacts traditional (tribal) authorities to preside over precisely the same geographic areas that were defined by the apartheid government (Claassens, 2011: 14; Mnwana, 2014b). Among other things, the Act enables chiefs and their traditional councils to be granted powers over the administration and control of communal land and natural resources, economic development, health and welfare, and to administer justice. As such, not only does this Act impose the former colonial tribal authority's demarcations on rural citizens, it also promotes a controversial governance role for chiefs. Other controversial laws that have so far been successfully resisted by rural citizens include the Communal Land Rights Act No. 11 of 2004, the Traditional Courts Bill [B-2008, B-2012 and B-2017] and the Traditional and Khoi-San Leadership Bill [B-2015].

Rural communities and civil society organisations have strongly resisted these laws, mainly because they give traditional leaders disproportionate and illegitimate powers, and because of the poor consultative and top-down processes with which the state has introduced them. However, the government has in most instances gone ahead, regardless of the limited participation and marginalisation of rural citizens, who are directly affected by these laws. Communities have, at times, sought relief from the courts of law. This is often an arduous and expensive exercise, which does not always yield success. Nevertheless, there have been a few remarkable successes for rural communities in resisting some of these policies. For instance, in 2010, the Constitutional Court struck down the Communal Land Rights Act.[2]

The laws highlighted above epitomise a paradox of state-led 'retribalisation' of African people in a democratic dispensation (Mnwana, 2016). The post-apartheid laws regulating and governing traditional leadership and mining reform have been criticised for promoting exclusion and corruption by using 'distorted constructs of custom' to 'impose contested identities', thereby 'undermining [rural residents'] capacity to protect their land and ... mineral rights' (Claassens & Matlala, 2014: 116).

The second critical process is the post-1994 state attempts to redistribute wealth through the minerals policy reform. In an effort to redress past injustices, the post-apartheid government has introduced some legislative measures in the mining sector, particularly with regard to the historical racial exclusion of Africans from mine-ownership structures and the relationships between mining companies and local communities (Mnwana & Capps, 2015). The Minerals and

Petroleum Resources Development Act No. 28 of 2002 (MPRDA) is the key piece of legislation in this regard. Through this legislation, the state has promoted a range of measures, including black economic empowerment (BEE), mine-community partnerships, continued royalty payments and social labour plans, as requirements for mining companies (Mnwana, 2015b). Communities that previously received royalty payments for mineral rights on their land have been encouraged by the state to convert their royalties into equity shares (Mnwana, 2014a). Several communities on the platinum belt have converted their royalty payments into equity stakes and entered into other complex deals with mining companies who operate on their land. Local chiefs, as assumed custodians of communal resources, have become mediators of mineral-led development and mining deals. As such, chiefs control mining revenues and also champion mining-led community development. Such a phenomenon renders the state's attempt to redistribute the country's mineral wealth to local communities, and historically disadvantaged social categories, highly problematic.

The model of mediation and control of mining revenues by the local elite (mainly chiefs) has produced significant tensions and conflict in the villages that host mining operations on the platinum belt (Mnwana 2015a). Not only have distributive struggles over mining revenues led to unrelenting chieftaincy (power) disputes among the local elite in the North West and Limpopo provinces, but ordinary villagers have laid strong claims over some of the mineral-rich farms, where some of the large mining operations occur. They assert that these farms were bought by their forefathers as private properties and should never have become 'tribal' land in the first place. As such, they dispute and resist the role of local chiefs as signatories of the mining deals and assumed custodians of mining revenues on behalf of local communities (see Mnwana & Capps, 2015; Mnwana, 2016).

The mounting resistance to local chiefs is also rooted in the lack of transparency in their corporate dealings and serious allegations of corruption that are levelled against them by ordinary community members (Mnwana, 2014b). The paucity of tangible benefits epitomises this challenge. Moreover, mining, especially in rural areas, tends to exacerbate conflict and power struggles (Mnwana, 2015a). Detailed research in several areas/villages/communities has shown that these transformations have not led to economic benefits for the majority of ordinary residents, since most benefits that accrue from the community BEE equity deals tend to be captured by the local elite, who occupy high positions in traditional leadership structures (Mnwana, 2015a; Mtero & Hay, 2016).

Although the processes highlighted above are fairly well reported and recent, it is not accurate to suggest that the upsurge of chiefly power over land and mineral resources is purely a post-apartheid phenomenon. The following section describes the historical processes that conjured up the powerful position of the Bakgatla chieftaincy in the North West province.

Chiefs and their power over property in the Bakgatla area: A brief history

The Bakgatla Ba Kgafela 'tribe' ('community') is one of at least five Setswana-speaking African groups that share the name 'Bakgatla', and can be found in both South Africa and Botswana. Two groups in Botswana (Mochudi) and South Africa (North West) share both the Bakgatla Ba Kgafela (henceforth 'Bakgatla') name, and a similar historical origin. (For the sake of space, this chapter will not deal with this aspect of pre-colonial history, which dates back to the 16th century; see Makgala, 2009.)

The early history of Bakgatla is not well recorded. There are gaps and diversions in various accounts from different sources. What is clear is that Bakgatla, like other African groups, have been subjected to a turbulent history, characterised by cessations, wars, colonial conquest, land dispossession and multi-ethnic integration. As such, the Bakgatla chiefdom has not always been fully functional as a political unit, and it cannot be described as a purely homogenous ethnic community. Having noted this, the historical formation of the Bakgatla Ba Kgafela 'tribe'[3] can be summarised in relation to five critical historical moments, which the rest of this section addresses.

The first significant historical moment in the formation of the current Bakgatla tribe was in the first half of the 19th century (1820s–1850s). This period began after the death of Kgosi (chief) Phetho, early in the second decade of the 19th century. During the first half of the 19th century, the Bakgatla chiefdom experienced great social and political instability. Such instability emanated from a number of factors, including inter-tribal wars, internal power struggles, cessations, colonial invasion and increasingly ruthless land dispossession by colonial invaders (Boers). The tribe, during this period, was already settled in what the Boers would call the Pilanesberg region, north of the present-day town of Rustenburg (Schapera, 1942).

A critical figure during this period was Kgosi Pilane, Pheto's son from his second house, the progenitor of the current ruling dynasty of the Bakgatla tribe both in Pilanesberg (South Africa) and Mochudi (Botswana). Most accounts about the settlement of Bakgatla in the Pilanesberg point to the leadership of Kgosi Pilane, after whom the Pilanesberg mountains were named. Kgosi Pilane is thought to have ruled between 1825 and 1850 (Schapera, 1942).

When Pilane came into power around 1825, he consolidated the tribe in Pilanesberg. There was some stability during the early days of Pilane's rule, until the arrival of Mzilikazi (also called Moselekatse by the Tswana people) and his Ndebele (Matebele in Setswana) raiding fugitive warriors, in the late 1820s. The entry of the Ndebele marked the Bakgatla's first direct experience of the vicissitudes and devastating impact of the Difaqane Wars. The already-weakened Bakgatla were no match to Mzilikazi's powerful Ndebele fugitive armies, and did not pose any resistance to Mzilikazi. To keep the latter placated, at least for a while, the Bakgatla paid tribute in the form of 'skins, corn and ivory' to the Ndebele (Schapera, 1942: 8).

The fortunes of Mzilikazi and his Ndebele warriors were soon to diminish with the 1836 arrival of the Voortrekkers (Afrikaners) in the Highveld. In 1837, after a series of attacks by Boers in alliance with some Tswana regiments (including Pilane's Bakgatla) and another fierce attack by the Zulus under King Dingane, Mzilikazi's Ndebele were forced to flee northwards across the Crocodile River, until they finally settled in the Matopo Hills in Zimbabwe (Schapera, 1942: 9).

Kgosi Pilane died around 1850 and was succeeded by his eldest son from the first house, Kgamanyane Pilane (1850–1874).

The arrival, in the late 1830s, of the Voortrekkers in the Highveld, especially in the area north of Rustenburg (Pilanesberg area), marked the first experience of colonial invasion and land dispossession for the Bakgatla and other African polities in the area. This was the dawn of a new era in the history of the agro-pastoralist African communities in the western Transvaal – the earliest encounter with white colonial rule and ruthless alienation of all land belonging to Africans. When the Transvaal (Zuid-Afrikaansche Republiek, ZAR) was formed, all land belonging to Africans was demarcated into white-owned private farms. So ravaging were the exigencies of the colonial conquest that, according to Capps (2010: 159), 'the entire African population was converted into a tenantry, living on formally demarcated farms and subject to the rentier demands of their new white landlords'.

By virtue of 'conquest', the Afrikaners regarded and asserted themselves as the owners of both the land and labour of African communities on it. The process of colonial dispossession was soon to be followed by new relationships between the white 'masters' and African landless 'servants'.

The second important moment in the history of the formation of the Bakgatla tribe was the period of multi-ethnic integration of the tribe after colonial conquest. This era (which was roughly the second half of the 19th century) was distinguished by the 'patron-client' relationships between the Bakgatla *dikgosi* (plural of *kgosi*) and the Afrikaner leading figures of the ZAR. Kgosi Kgamanyane of Bakgatla was one of the prominent chiefs in the Western Transvaal, and displayed extraordinary compliance with Boer demands. His allegiance to local white leaders was evidenced in his consistent provision of labour regiments (*mephato*), reinforcing hunting expeditions, assisting the Boers in horrific slave-raiding operations on other African communities and supporting the Boers in battle with other indigenous groups that attempted to resist colonial domination (Morton, 1998: 83; Morton, 2005: 201). With much-needed communal labour under their command, Kgamanyane and other prominent African chiefs in the Transvaal accumulated vast amounts of material wealth and enormous recognition from the Transvaal colonial authorities in exchange for their loyalty – a phenomenon which researcher Gavin Capps (2010: 150) regards as 'new forms of accumulation'.

Kgamanyane accumulated significant benefits from his allegiance to the white colonial state officials. His relationship with the Rustenburg field cornet, Paul Kruger, was the epitome of this (Bergh, 2005: 97). Loyalty to the Boers earned Kgamanyane and his Bakgatla people many privileges, including being accommodated on Paul Kruger's farm, Saulspoort (the present Moruleng village) along the north-eastern foothill of the Pilanesberg mountains (Manson & Mbenga, 1997). As Morton (1992: 108) puts it '[w]ealth and power belonged to *dikgosi* who served the Boers' – the wealth of Kgosi Kgamanyane of Bakgatla rose in tandem with his political status. Morton (1992: 108) continues, 'In addition to wagons, houses, horses, cattle, and guns, Kgamanyane maintained 48 separate households, one for each of his wives ... Kgamanyane ... traded in ivory north of the Limpopo.'

The patron-client relationship also helped Kgamanyane to forcibly absorb smaller and weaker African groups into his Bakgatla chiefdom (Morton, 1992: 108). This phenomenon was prevalent in some powerful polities in the Transvaal and was also made possible through the 'politico-military' support and reinforcement from the Boer authorities in the Rustenburg region (Capps, 2010: 141). During the mid-1820s, several small African groups displaced by the Difaqane Wars settled in the Magaliesberg (Rustenburg) region. Some of these groups successfully absorbed smaller and weaker groups into their polities, while others were asylum seekers, who were integrated into bigger and stronger tribes without cohesion (Capps, 2010: 141–142). These small groups of raiders and asylum seekers later became known as *bafaladi* (alien ethnic immigrants) (Schapera & Comaroff, 1991: 30). Some of the smaller and weaker of these were absorbed into the more powerful groups, who were already in the area north of Rustenburg. As suggested above, *Kgosi* Pilane and Kgamanyane (his successor) formed an allegiance with Boer leaders, such as Potgieter and later Paul Kruger. Together they successfully warded off the devastating attacks by Mzilikazi's Ndebele warriors and launched severe attacks on other African communities who were not willing to accept colonial rule in the Transvaal region (Morton, 1992: 107). Some of the defeated groups were integrated into the Bakgatla tribe.

It is against this background of the post-Difaqane political power surge, which was a result of colonial patron-client relations and the integration of smaller groups, that the Bakgatla 'tribe' could no longer be accurately described as a purely homogenous ethnic group. However, such multi-ethnic integration was by no means a new phenomenon – it predates colonialism and continues well beyond colonial conquest.

Not all groups that joined Bakgatla were constituted as tribes at their point of entry. At different historical moments, groups of diverse sizes, political status and ethnic origins joined the Bakgatla chiefdom, some out of choice and others by coercion. The Bakgatla *dikgosi* also gained significant power and status when they became the main 'recognised chiefs' through whom Africans could purchase and register the land in the 'scheduled areas' around Pilanesberg.

The third significant moment was a period of political instability and division of the Bakgatla 'tribe', which resulted in the colonial evolution of the contested seat of 'paramountcy' in Botswana and further disintegration of the tribe in South Africa. This period began with the colonial separation in 1870 of the 'tribe' into two groups: one in Botswana and the other in South Africa. This separation was a result of an incident in 1869, when Kgosi Kgamanyane's relationship with the powerful 'patron' Paul Kruger took a drastic turn. Facing internal resistance from his followers, Kgamanyane could no longer keep up with Kruger's insatiable demands for forced labour from the Bakgatla people in Saulspoort. This failure led to Kgamanyane being tied against 'a wheel of a wagon' and publicly flogged by Kruger, in full view of his followers and other chiefs from the neighbouring Tswana groups (Makgala, 2009: 91). So unbearable was the humiliation caused by this incident that Kgamanyane and approximately half his followers decided to leave the Pilanesberg area and trekked northwards, until they finally settled in Mochudi in Bechuanaland (Botswana) (Mbenga & Morton, 1997: 157). Kgamanyane died around 1874 and was brought back and buried at Mabule hill, in Pilanesberg. The historical separation of the Bakgatla Ba Kgafela tribe into two groups, residing in what were to become two different countries, has a significant bearing on the 'tribe's' contemporary battles over political power and communal property.

It should be noted that the white colonial state in South Africa (1910 onwards) and the post-1994 democratic government at different historical moments recognised the superiority of the Bakgatla group in Botswana over the one in South Africa, hence the Bakgatla chiefs in Botswana are referred to as the 'paramount chiefs'. The courts in South Africa have upheld this view, even during moments when the Botswana-based paramountcy was seriously contested by different sections of the Bakgatla group in South Africa.

The fourth period worth highlighting was the period between 1910 and the late 1930s, which was marked by the intensification of the racially segregative 'Native Land Policy' under the Union government in South Africa. Of critical importance are the second and third decades of the 20th century, which marked a period of the highest increase ever in the history of land buying by Africans in the Bakgatla area. This period, according to Mbenga (1996: 203), marked the 'golden years' of the Bakgatla chieftaincy:

> The first two decades of this century were their 'golden years' in terms of the resources with which to buy land. The Bakgatla's major resource of cattle was then relatively plentiful due to their large-scale looting of Boer cattle during the South African War. Consequently, the Bakgatla, who had far more cattle than any other group in the Pilanesberg region, were better able to buy more land than anyone else.

The increase in wealth in terms of cattle numbers during the post-war period may have contributed towards the Bakgatla's increased capacity to buy land. However, there is evidence that land was not always purchased on a tribal basis in the Bakgatla area, but quite often on a private basis. Recent research on contemporary land disputes in the Bakgatla area points towards a history significantly dominated by private groups of Africans buying land (Mnwana &

Capps, 2015). Indeed, this was a common phenomenon in the colonial Transvaal Republic. The land purchased in this fashion would then be transferred to a white state official who held the property 'in trust' for the tribe or 'chief'.

When the whites in the Transvaal Republic established their legal and administrative systems of ownership and registration of land, they debarred Africans from owning land (Bergh & Feinberg, 2004). Despite this prohibition, groups of Africans in the Transvaal managed to purchase land anyway. African land-buying syndicates purchased land through white intermediaries, mainly missionaries residing among them. After the first British occupation of the Transvaal, the notion of trusteeship was formalised through the declarations of the Pretoria Convention of 1881, which was replaced by the London Convention in 1884. These provisions later formally granted a right to purchase land, but the land purchased by Africans was to be formally registered under the name of a white state official 'in trust' for the African purchasers, thus establishing a legalised (formalised) form of trusteeship which Capps (2010) terms 'state trusteeship'. The main policy shift introduced by the London Convention was that, instead of registering the land acquired by Africans 'in the name of the Native Location Commission' (as stated under Article 13 of the Pretoria Convention), it was to be registered 'in the name of an officer of the South African republic' (Delius & Chaskalson, 1997: 29). Bergh and Feinberg (2004: 170) summarise the informal and formal trusteeship as follows:

> Trusteeship meant that although Africans might have paid for land, they could register the transfer of the property from the previous owner in the name of a white person only, especially a missionary [informal] or, after 1880, a public official [formal], who would hold it 'in trust' for the real buyers. Only registration could give legal validity to the transaction.

The formalisation of the institution of trusteeship as a tenure system for Africans in the Transvaal began with radical colonial-state bureaucratic and policy measures for controlling and limiting the land rights of the 'native' population. It was immediately after the British annexation of the Transvaal Republic and during the short-term rule of the British colonial government (1877–1880) that the latter began the formalisation of the institution of 'state-trusteeship' by curbing the then dominant informal institution of missionary intermediation by 'declaring the new Secretary of Native Affairs as *ex officio* trustee of all lands purchased by or for the natives' (Capps, 2010: 173; see also Berg & Feinberg, 2004: 178–179). Despite the fleeting tenure of British rule, this initial step by the colonial state was to be confirmed and enforced by the major clauses of the Pretoria and London Conventions in the retrocession Transvaal.[4] Further, 'trusteeship' was to become a formal institution of land tenure for Africans not only in the Transvaal (and Natal), but throughout colonial South Africa. Through these processes, all African land acquisitions would follow a detailed administration process that would culminate in a precarious form of ownership for the purchasers and in another form of dispossession through the custodianship of the chiefs (in whose 'tribal' group the land was registered). This tenural regime, although legally ambivalent and administratively laborious, was kept intact and sustained through colonial declarations as well as the two major Natives Land Acts of 1913 and 1936.[5] There is insufficient space here to describe various forms of trusteeship.

A significant portion of power and control over the purchased land was in the domain of the tribal trustees – the chiefs, who were assumed to be custodians of tribal properties. Mnwana and Capps (2015: 13) summarise how this historical process unfolded in the Transvaal during the late colonial and segregation periods:

> [Since] The colonial authorities worked within an ideological framework that presumed all Africans to be members of tribes, they would only sanction new group land purchases if they were tribally based. This in turn encouraged such groups to seek out the nearest chief, or simply reconstitute themselves as a 'tribe', in order to enter the land market.

Subsequently, chiefs had enormous leverage to define and impose customary rights on their subjects who occupied the purchased land.

Therefore, it is no exaggeration to say that the powerful political status and control over 'tribal' landed property that is enjoyed by the Bakgatla *dikgosi* is rooted in the 'tribal-trusteeship' institution. As will be seen in the next section, various chiefs of the Bakgatla, including Lenchwe, Ramono, Isang, Ofentse and Tidimane Pilane, mediated land purchases in the Bakgatla area at different times.

The fifth moment which bears noting is the moment of constitution of the Bakgatla 'tribe' as a tribal authority under the Bantu Authorities Act No. 68 of 1951 (BAA). Tribal authorities were established as part of the apartheid state policy of racial separation. The Bakgatla Tribal Authority was established in 1953 in line with the said policy (Breutz, 1989: 278, 339). During the first half of the 20th century, 27 farms were purchased by Africans in the Bakgatla area, of which four were privately owned (Breutz, 1989: 339). All the farms were generally regarded as 'tribally owned farms' (Breutz, 1989: 339) and in 1953 these farms, together with eight 'Trust' farms in the Pilanesberg, were amalgamated to constitute the newly established Bakgatla Ba Kgafela Tribal Authority in terms of the BAA. As such, the current boundaries of the Bakgatla Tribal Authority were established and formalised in terms of the BAA. Like other tribal authorities that were incorporated into the Bophuthatswana 'homeland' in 1977, the Bakgatla chieftaincy had farms registered with the state in trust for the chief and his tribe. Remarkably, beneath these farms – unbeknownst to many at the time – spanned some of the world's richest platinum group metals.

During apartheid, the minister of Bantu Affairs mediated the contracts between mining companies and tribal authorities. The powers of 'state trusteeship' regarding mineral and surface rights on tribal land were to be transferred to the Office of the President of Bophuthatswana when the latter gained its 'independence' (Capps, 2012: 72) from South Africa in 1977. It was during the time of the Bophuthatswana regime that the Bakgatla chieftaincy began to receive mining royalties from Anglo American Platinum (Amplats) Union Mine in 1982 (Mnwana, 2015). These royalties were deposited into Bophuthatswana state accounts, called development accounts (D-accounts), held by the Office of the Bophuthatswana President.

Due to the global upsurge in platinum demand in the 1980s and 1990s, income from platinum mining, and thus the royalties payable, rose significantly. From time to time, the chiefs would request funds from these accounts for various community development projects. After 1994 and South Africa's first democratic elections, the D-accounts fell under the administration of the North West province's Department of Finance. Since then, significant amounts of money have mysteriously disappeared from these accounts (*City Press*, 2012). Since it took over the administration of these funds, the North West provincial government has been neither transparent nor accountable to the relevant communities (Mnwana, 2015a).

Bakgatla chiefs as African intermediaries in the colonial land markets

Due to the colonial policies, particularly the Pretoria and London Conventions, that forbade formal registration of land privately purchased by independent African syndicates, most land purchased by independent groups in the Pilanesberg area had to be registered and managed through the 'recognised' chiefs of Bakgatla (Mnwana & Capps, 2015). In fact, archival documents confirm that during the period when the contested farms were acquired, the Department of Native Affairs demanded that at least three essential bureaucratic requirements be met without fail by African land buyers when acquiring landed property.[6] First, the local commissioner in Pilanesberg had to produce a certificate of recognition which confirmed that the land-buying group was constituted as a tribe under a recognised chief. Second, a copy of a Tribal Resolution had to be produced which confirmed that the purchase of the farm was authorised by a tribe in a tribal meeting. The Tribal Resolution had to contain the signatures of the chief, tribal council members and some local state officials. Third, before a land transfer was done, the sub-commissioner in Pilanesberg had to produce the original Deed of Sale, which would show, among other details, the name of the chief who was (supposedly) buying the land on behalf of his tribe. The transfer of the purchased land could only be registered once the buyers had paid the full price, including the bond interest.

Another requirement, which was a hindrance to African group buyers, was that it was not just any chief or tribe that could secure a mortgage bond and have easy access to the legal expertise required in the highly technical process of acquiring land. Correspondence between the secretary of Native Affairs and local state officials reveal that, for the state to approve the sale, the chief and his tribe had to enjoy a reputation of being capable of meeting the purchase price. The Bakgatla chiefs, having purchased 27 farms during the first half of the 20th century on behalf of the tribe and several other farms for their own private use, were ostensibly held in high esteem by the colonial state in South Africa when it came to land markets.[7] Therefore, it was highly possible that many independent land-buying syndicates had to depend on the Bakgatla *dikgosi* for land purchases and registration of the purchased land. Consequently, the Bakgatla chieftaincy grew significantly in size and political stature, since this process meant that independent land buyers could only retain their rights to land if they remained loyal and submissive to the authority of the Bakgatla chiefs. Even in cases where the buyers were somehow affiliated to the Bakgatla chief, their private land rights vanished as soon as their land was registered under a state official 'in trust' for the Bakgatla chief and his tribe.

Despite the already mentioned highly bureaucratic process of entry by African groups into the colonial land markets in the early 20th century, oral traditions in the selected villages revealed that African land buyers were especially vulnerable to manipulation by chiefs and European land sellers. Moreover, the process of entry into the colonial land market was economically and emotionally challenging for African land buyers; there is evidence that some of the farms may have been overpriced by European land-owning companies, who seem to have been determined to make a fortune out of the land-dispossessed Africans. The purchasers had to raise vast amounts to meet the purchase price. They had to find a 'recognised chief', and not just any chief, but a chief with a reputation for buying land – an essential requirement for securing a mortgage bond.

Very few people were more strategically positioned to benefit from this arrangement than the Bakgatla *dikgosi*. In Pilanesberg, many individual Europeans and speculating companies that owned farms in areas that were reserved for African occupation were poised to make a quick fortune out of the land-hungry, dispossessed and (at times) fugitive African groups. As rulers of the most powerful chiefdom in the Pilanesberg area at that time, the Bakgatla chiefs became the main land intermediaries in the land-buying processes. As such, not only did they enjoy rapid expansion of their territory and political stature, they also amassed significant personal wealth in the process.

Another factor, which not only inhibited written records about farm purchases at the level of the land-buyer groups but also made the buyers even more vulnerable, was the fact that very few among them were literate and numerate. Quite often, buyers did not fully understand the process of buying land, including the price of the land and how much they still had to pay. They relied on the chiefs (who were often literate) to tell them what to pay and when. It is evident that such a position benefitted the chiefs. It is common knowledge that several Bakgatla chiefs purchased many farms in the Rustenburg region in their own personal names. For instance, Kgosi Isang Pilane (Kgosi Lenchwe's son), who died in 1941 at the age of 56, owned more than 300 cattle, a significant number of small stock (sheep and goats), three large farms in Rustenburg and two lots in the township of Lady Selborne in Pretoria. In Transvaal alone, Isang's landed property was worth £4,522.[8] Isang's estate was divided among his heirs (his wife and children) after his death.[9]

Unsurprisingly, chiefs were not always transparent about their farm purchases, especially with regard to the funds that were raised for purchasing farms. For example, during the rule of Chief Tidimane Pilane, there were a number of instances where complaints would surface, particularly about his lack of transparency about the tribal levies collected for buying farms. One particular instance was a court application filed by a certain Mr Jacob Pilane against Chief Tidimane in June 1956. Chief Tidimane Pilane had, in 1953, imposed a levy of one ox per person on every male adult member of his tribe for the purchase of the farms Middelkuil No. 564 and Cyferkuil No. 372.

These farms were purchased from Chief Molefe Pilane who was the Bakgatla 'paramount chief' based in Botswana. The combined price for the two farms was £14,000. Those who could not pay the levy were obliged to pay £15 per person. The main contention of Jacob and his group of dissenters was that Chief Tidimane never reported how much money was collected in total and how many people (tax payers) contributed, and they were never given receipts or told how much their oxen were sold for. Furthermore, Jacob wanted Tidimane to account for how the tribal funds were being utilised, and if there were funds that the chief utilised without first securing a tribal resolution to do so (Mnwana, 2014b).[10]

Jacob lost his court application against the chief. However, the findings of the court were revealing. The court dismissed Jacob's application based mainly on the arguments that the chief has no responsibility to account 'to any one of his individual subjects' concerning the tribal accounts. The court also accepted the argument that Jacob, although a member of the tribe, did not have *locus standi* to present a petition against the chief who, according to the court, was accountable only to the tribe and not to individual subjects. This negative verdict was not the last of Jacob's troubles. His family was constantly harassed by the chief's loyalists in Moruleng. The ultimate punishment that Jacob received from the chief was to have his cattle and agricultural tools taken by force and sold to a neighbouring white farmer. Having lost the court application, he had nowhere else to turn, and his fellow 'rebels' had learned their lesson – never to challenge the chief again (Mnwana 2015b).

The question of abuse of power by the Bakgatla chiefs is inextricably linked to a distinctive history of group land buying and policy, which regulated African land purchase in the colonial Transvaal. It was this history which placed the Bakgatla *dikgosi* at a political and economic advantage as custodians ('trustees') over significant portions of land that were (reportedly) acquired privately by diverse African syndicates in the Bakgatla area during the first half of the 20th century. It is against the backdrop of this history that modern contestations over land in the Bakgatla area have taken the form of distinctive group land histories that function to assert group-exclusive entitlements – and disentitlements – to the benefits that accrue from mining.

Conclusion

Through the empirical material drawn from detailed research conducted in the Bakgatla traditional authority, this contribution has attempted to demonstrate how the entrenchment of chiefly power over rural land is not exclusively a product of post-apartheid legislation, nor the product of ethnic commodification, nor a revival of previously suppressed ethnic identities, as scholarly contributions (highlighted earlier) seem to suggest. Although colonial processes of dispossession and alienation of Africans from landed property had clear variations between different regions, the case of the Bakgatla chieftaincy sheds important light on some of the historical processes that produced the powerful and pre-eminent position that the Bakgatla chiefs enjoy today over land and mining revenues. To fully understand the roots of present-day mining and land-related conflicts on the platinum belt, and indeed elsewhere, it is crucial to uncover the local and regional historical processes that shaped the power structure of specific parcels of rural land and resources. In so doing, it is necessary to move beyond the simplistic perceptions of homogenous 'tribes' and 'traditional communities' who share common interests. Understanding the ongoing rural struggles along the platinum belt must begin with a greater appreciation of specific historical contexts and socio-political dynamics that shaped the local structure of power. Only then can we begin to fruitfully analyse some of the evolving, complex, political and socio-economic shifts that arise with rural-based platinum mining expansion in South Africa.

Therefore, a shift towards recognition, not only of different layers of rights but also of the historical character of power and the amounts of power that individuals, families and other social units have over land, is essential.

References

Beinart, W. 2014. 'Verwoerd, Zuma and the chiefs'. *Land and Accountability Research Centre* website: http://www.customcontested.co.za/verwoerd-zuma-chiefs/, accessed 21 August 2014.

Bergh, J. S. 2005. '"We must never forget where we come from": The Bafokeng and their land in the 19th century Transvaal'. *History in Africa*, 32, 95–115.

Bergh, J. & Feinberg, H. M. 2004. 'Trusteeship and black land ownership in the Transvaal during the nineteenth and twentieth centuries'. *African Historical Review,* 36 (1), 170–193.

Boone, C. 2017. 'Legal empowerment of the poor through property rights reform: Tensions and trade-offs of land registration and titling in sub-Saharan Africa'. *WIDER Working Paper* 37. Helsinki: UNU-WIDER.

Breutz P. L. 1953. *The Tribes of Rustenburg and the Pilanesberg Districts.* Pretoria: Government Printer.

Breutz, P. L. 1989. *A History of the Batswana and Origin of Bophuthatswana: A handbook of a survey of the tribes of the Batswana, Southern Ndebele, Qwa Qwa and Botswana.* Margate: Thumbprint.

Buthelezi, M. & Yeni, S. 2016. 'Traditional leadership in democratic South Africa: Pitfalls and prospects'. *Nelson Mandela Foundation* website: https://www.nelsonmandela.org/uploads/files/Land__law_and_leadership_-_paper_1.pdf, accessed 21 December 2016.

Capps, G. 2010. 'Tribal-landed property: The political economy of the Bafokeng chieftaincy, South Africa, 1837–1994'. PhD thesis. London: London School of Economics.

Capps, G. 2012. 'A bourgeois reform with social justice? The contradictions of the Minerals Development Bill and black economic empowerment in the South African platinum mining industry'. *Review of African Political Economy*, 39 (132), 315–333.

Chimhowu, A. & Woodhouse, P. 2006. 'Customary vs private property rights? Dynamics and trajectories of vernacular land markets in Sub-Saharan Africa'. *Journal of Agrarian Change*, 6 (3), 346–371.

City Press. 2012. 'Madonsela to probe tribes' lost millions'. Editorial, http://www.citypress.co./news/madonsela-to-probe-tribes-lost-millions-20120211/, accessed 22 August 2014.

Claassens, A. 2011. 'Resurgence of tribal levies: A double taxation for the rural poor'. *South African Crime Quarterly*, 35, 11–16.

Claassens, A. & Matlala, B. 2014. 'Platinum, poverty and princes in post-apartheid South Africa: New laws, old repertoires'. *New South African Review*, 4, 113–135.

Comaroff, J. L. & Comaroff, J. 2009. *Ethnicity, Inc. The Zulu Kingdom awaits you*. Chicago: University of Chicago Press.

Delius, P. & Chaskalson, M. 1997. 'A historical investigation into the underlying rights of land registered as state owned'. Report commissioned by the Tenure Reform Core Group. Pretoria: Department of Land Affairs.

Grischow, J. D. 2008. 'Rural "community", chiefs and social capital: The case of Southern Ghana'. *Journal of Agrarian Change*, 8 (1), 64–93.

Krämer, M. 2016. 'Neither despotic nor civil: The legitimacy of chieftaincy in its relationship with the ANC and the state in KwaZulu-Natal (South Africa)'. *The Journal of Modern African Studies*, 54 (1), 117–143.

Lund, C. 2008. *Local Politics and the Dynamics of Property in Africa*. Cambridge: Cambridge University Press.

Makgala, C. J. 2009. *History of Bakgatla-baga-Kgafela in Botswana and South Africa*. Pretoria: Crink.

Mamdani, M. 1996. *Citizen and Subject: Contemporary Africa and the legacy of late colonialism*. Princeton: Princeton University Press.

Manson, A. & Mbenga, B. 2012. 'Bophuthatswana and the North-West province: From pan-Tswanaism to mineral-based ethnic assertiveness'. *South African Historical Journal*, 64 (1), 96–116.

Mbenga, B. K. 1996. 'The Bakgatla-Baga-Kgafela in the Pilanesberg district of the Western Transvaal from 1899 to 1931'. PhD thesis. Pretoria: University of South Africa.

Mbenga, B. & Morton, F. 1997. 'The missionary as land broker: Henri Gonin, Saulspoort 269 and the Bakgatla of Rustenburg district, 1862–1922'. *South African Historical Journal*, 36 (1), 145–167.

Mnwana, S. 2014a. '"Mineral wealth – in the name of morafe?" Community control in South Africa's platinum valley'. *Development Southern Africa*, 31 (6), 826–884.

Mnwana, S. 2014b. 'Chief's justice? Mining, accountability and the law in the Bakgatla-ba-Kgafela traditional authority area, North West Province'. *South African Crime Quarterly*, 49, 21–29.

Mnwana, S. 2015a. 'Mining and "community" struggles on the platinum belt: A case of Sefikile village in the North West Province, South Africa'. *The Extractive Industries and Society*, 2 (3), 500–508.

Mnwana, S. 2015b. 'Democracy, development and chieftaincy along South Africa's "Platinum Highway": Some emerging issues'. *Journal of Contemporary African Studies*, 33 (4), 510–529.

Mnwana, S. 2016. 'Custom and fractured "community": Mining, property disputes and law on the platinum belt, South Africa'. *Third World Thematics: A TWQ Journal*, 1 (2), 218–234.

Mnwana, S. & Capps, G. 2015. '"No chief ever bought a piece of land!"

Struggles over property, community and mining in the Bakgatla-ba-Kgafela traditional authority area, North-West Province'. Working Paper 3. Johannesburg: Society Work and Development Institute, University of the Witwatersrand.

Morton, F. 1992. 'Slave-raiding and slavery in the Western Transvaal after the Sand River Convention'. *African Economic History*, No. 20, 99–118.

Morton, F. 1995. 'Land, cattle and ethnicity: Creating Linchwe's BaKgatla, 1875–1920'. *South African Historical Journal*, 33 (1), 131–154.

Morton, F. 1998. 'Cattleholders, evangelists, and socioeconomic transformation among the baKgatla of Rustenburg District, 1863–1898'. *South African Historical Journal*, 38 (1), 79–98.

Morton, F. 2005. 'Female inboekelinge in the South African Republic, 1850–1880'. *Slavery & Abolition*, 26 (2), 199–215.

Ntsebeza, L. 2005. *Democracy Compromised: Chiefs and the politics of the land in South Africa*. Leiden: Brill.

Peters, P. E. 2004. 'Inequality and social conflict over land in Africa'. *Journal of Agrarian Change*, 4 (3), 269–314.

Schapera I. 1942. 'A short history of the BaKgatla-bagaKgafêla of the Bechuanaland Protectorate'. *Communications*: Issue 3. Cape Town: School of African Studies, University of Cape Town.

Schapera, I. & Comaroff, J. L. 1991. *The Tswana* (revised edition). London: International African Institute.

Van Kessel, I. & Oomen, B. 1997. '"One chief, one vote": The revival of traditional authorities in post-apartheid South Africa'. *African Affairs*, 96 (385), 565–568.

World Bank. 1989. *Sub-Saharan Africa: From crisis to sustainable growth*. Washington DC: World Bank.

Document sources from the South African National Archives:
Deeds Register RAK 3017
NA: PTD, Vol. 0, Ref. 1442/1956
NTS 3541 478/308
NTS 3541 478/308
NTS, 254, 1137/16/F596
NTS, Vol. 3514, Ref. 323/308
NTS, Vol. 3514, Ref. 323/308 Letter from 'The Secretary of Native Affairs', 1 June 1926.

North West Provincial Archives
File 191, 6/4/2

Notes

1   The Open Society Foundation for South Africa funded part of this research through the Mineral Wealth and Politics of Distribution research project (Project number: OSF-SA 03629). We previously received funding from the Ford Foundation under the Mining and Rural Transformation in Southern Africa (MARTISA) project at SWOP, Wits university.

2   See *Tongoane and Others v Minister for Agriculture and Land Affairs and Others* (CCT 100/09) [2010] ZACC 10 (11 May 2010).

3   I use the term 'tribe' with caution, not to suggest that Africans in the Bakgatla area are members of a homogeneous tribal unit. I use it to portray the way African groups were depicted in colonial historiographies.

4   The period roughly from 1881 to the late 1890s was marked by colonial treaties (the Pretoria Convention of 1881 and the London Convention of 1884) between the English and the Boer/Afrikaner settler communities that gave effect to gradual (albeit contested) Boer self-rule in the former Transvaal Republic.

5   The Natives Land Act No. 27 of 1913 and the Native Trust and Land Act No. 18 of 1936

6   See: NTS, Volume: 3541, Reference: 478/308 [PNA]; NTS, Volume: 254, Reference: 1137/16/F. 596, 534/16/F. 596

7   For details on the involvement of Bakgatla chiefs in colonial land purchases see among others, Pretoria National Archives NTS, Volume: 35/77, Reference: 754/308; Native Land Commission Proceedings in Pilanesberg, 1906 – NLC, Volume, C27, Reference: 13; NTS, Volume: 6853, Reference: 54/319-56/319 and NTS, Reference: 254/139/55s.

8   See: Pretoria National Archives, NA, MHG, Ref. 2243/41

9   Ibid.

10 See also: Pretoria National Archives, PTD, Vol. 0, Ref. 1442/1956

SIX

Traditional leadership, violation of land rights and resistance from below in Makhasaneni village, KwaZulu-Natal

SITHANDIWE YENI

Introduction

In 2011, the mining company Jindal Africa arrived unannounced to the village of Makhasaneni to establish whether the area had sufficient iron ore to justify mining. In the process, the villagers say, family graves, water streams and ploughing fields were destroyed, and some livestock died from drinking chemically contaminated water. The villagers were outraged and resisted the company's plans. Five years later, in 2016, Jindal withdrew the application for a mining licence and the villagers celebrated. The process, however, was bumpy, characterised by coercion, intimidation, divisions and resistance.

Rural resistance is not new. Govan Mbeki (1964) described peasant uprisings in Pondoland, Zululand, Basutoland and Sekhukhuneland between 1946 and 1962. These struggles were, in essence, about land and the roles of traditional leaders. Ntsebeza (2005) adds that control over land was the main issue in rural struggles, right up to the dismantling of apartheid in 1994. Even in post-apartheid South Africa, attempts by the government to secure the land rights of people in the former homelands have not been successful. Instead, contradictory laws that give power over land to traditional leaders have been proposed and passed (Claassens, 2008).

Using the case of Makhasaneni, a village in northern KwaZulu-Natal near Melmoth, this chapter explores how people living in 'communal' areas have campaigned to protect their land rights, when opportunities for profit accumulation have led to traditional leaders abusing their power. It demonstrates both the violation of land rights by traditional leaders and the resistance of villagers. I argue that while rural citizens may show little or no interest in the accountability of traditional leaders in advisory or ceremonial roles in their community, when their land rights are threatened they do demand accountability and resist. Through 'everyday forms of resistance' (Scott, 2008) characterised by subtle sabotage, avoidance and passive noncompliance, rural citizens expose the limitations of traditional leaders in land governance and question their role in advancing the interests of citizens. In response to this push-back from citizens, some traditional leaders have used coercion and divisive tactics in an attempt to weaken resistance.

Research for this chapter was conducted between March and December 2015. Over this period, I was working with the Land and Accountability Research Centre (LARC) to investigate land rights violations and resistance in Makhasaneni. I visited the community again between January and July 2016. I conducted semi-structured interviews with members of Makhasaneni Community Committee, the local headmen, officials at the provincial office of the Department of Cooperative Governance and Traditional Affairs (COGTA) and lawyers representing the community. Attempts to meet with the chief were not successful.[1] In addition, I used participant observation, attending workshops and community meetings with the people of Makhasaneni.

In this chapter, I contextualise communal land rights in KwaZulu-Natal (KZN), where land is held by the Ingonyama Trust, and consider the impact of related laws. I pay attention to the two post-apartheid laws that were passed in the Parliament of South Africa to protect the rights of people living in communal land, i.e. the Ingonyama Trust Act No. 3KZ of 1994 and the Interim Protection of Informal Land Rights Act No. 31 of 1996 (IPILRA). I then assess the roles of traditional leaders today and explore how they have positioned themselves in recent large-scale land investments in rural areas, particularly areas where mining takes place. The chapter looks closely at the case of Makhasaneni village, with a focus on the history of the area, livelihood strategies, the arrival of Jindal, how the community resisted and the push-back from the traditional authorities.

Communal land rights and the role of the Ingonyama Trust in KwaZulu-Natal

The factors that enable land rights violations in current-day rural South Africa can be explained by the way land is held and the nature of relationships between ordinary citizens and traditional leaders, especially in light of the discovery of minerals. Unpacking communal land rights, the government's attempts to secure land tenure through land reform and the role of traditional leaders in mining help us locate some of the underlying causes of land rights violations.

Communal land rights in context

The majority of black people who live in communal areas in the former bantustans have insecure land rights (Claassens, 2008). This is despite laws that have been passed by Parliament to ensure security of tenure for people living in communal areas. While there are laws that seek to protect their land rights, the government has also proposed contradictory laws that concentrate power with traditional leaders, rendering the rights of ordinary citizens insecure. Some of the reasons for the contradictions are located in the history of colonial rule (Weinberg, 2015).

Before recapping what colonial rule entailed with regards to land in rural areas, it is crucial to unpack what communal land rights are. Cousins and Claassens (2004) describe the concept 'communal' with reference to the extent of community control over who can or cannot be allocated land for residential and cropping purposes. The groups of people that make up the particular community are often interested in maintaining identity and coherence and securing their land-based livelihoods (Cousins & Claassens, 2004). While colonial interpretations of communal tenure tried to vest the decision-making powers over land to one individual (the chief), in practice the administration of communal land tends to be more socially inclusive (Weinberg, 2015). Social inclusivity means individuals and families have relative rights to some land, be it agricultural or residential. They negotiate access and control over common resources, such as rivers, mountains and grazing land, which are shared by the larger community beyond the individual or family household (Cousins, 2008).

In some situations, decisions about land allocations are made by one family. At other times, decision-making may include neighbours. There are also situations in which the chief and headman play a crucial role in making decisions about land, after discussion with the relevant individuals or families. As observed by Alcock and Hornby (2004) in KwaZulu-Natal, in cases where the chief or headman made the decisions about land, it was never their decision alone. This shows that communal land tenure, as it is understood and practised by people living in communal areas, is much broader than the way in which colonial governments defined it, namely centred around the control of chiefs (Weinberg, 2015). Private property ownership, where individuals or institutions hold exclusive title deeds to a particular registered and surveyed piece of land, are in contrast to customary law notions of tenure.

The ways in which communal land tenure arrangements are understood, particularly by the state today, were influenced by a range of colonial and apartheid measures, largely characterised by land dispossession and insecure land rights for rural citizens. As explained by Weinberg (2015), both the British and Dutch colonial governments did not recognise indigenous systems of land as property rights. This is evidenced in infamous laws such as the 1913 Natives Land Act, which dispossessed black people of their land and rendered their rights to land insecure, and the 1927 Native Administration Act, which distorted customary law by viewing it from the perspective of common law (thus centring ownership to an individual (a chief) which gave traditional leaders power over land that they never had before). It is the same interpretation of communal land tenure that continues to confuse the discussions around laws and policies that seek to provide security of tenure in communal areas today. But not only that, the unclear role of traditional leaders in democratic South Africa (Ntsebeza, 2004), coupled with the rise in large-scale land investments, particularly in the countryside, is driving revaluation of land ownership (Borras et al., 2011) and contributing to confusion on communal tenure. I will elaborate on this later in the chapter.

In KwaZulu-Natal, communal land is held under the Ingonyama Trust, a state institution established during the dying days of apartheid in 1994, under the Ingonyama Trust Act. King Goodwill Zwelithini is the sole trustee of the trust, which is managed by the Ingonyama Trust Board. The mandate of the Trust is to hold land for the benefit and social wellbeing of the communities living on the land (see Ingonyama Trust Board, 2018). The land thus does not belong to the trust or to the king. People living on this land have strong protection under the Ingonyama Trust Act of 1994, which stipulates that 'the Ingonyama shall not encumber, pledge, lease, alienate or otherwise dispose of any of the said land or any interest or real right in the land, unless he has obtained the prior written consent of the traditional authority or community authority concerned'. This obliges the Trust not to enter into any land agreements, such as leases, that would marginalise people living on that land. In theory, communal land rights are protected. However, it is not always the case in practice, as I will show later in the chapter.

Land reform, policy and the legislative set-up

In an attempt to secure the land rights of people living in communal areas, the democratic government of South Africa has embarked on a land reform programme. Out of the three pillars of land reform – restitution, redistribution and tenure reform – the last, which seeks to give security of tenure to people living in communal areas, has remained the most neglected (Hall, 2009). Instead, the government has focused on transferring private ownership of land to traditional authorities, who would presumably hold the land on behalf of the people living on it. This position, according to Ntsebeza (2004), was initially welcomed by the KwaZulu-Natal House of Traditional Leaders, and later by their counterparts in the Eastern Cape, suggesting that land belongs to traditional authorities and the title deed should be in their name.

Before exploring the different laws, it is worth rehearsing what the Constitution of South Africa says about land tenure, as it relates to people living in communal areas. Section 25(6) of the Constitution stipulates that 'a person or community whose tenure of land is legally insecure as a result of past racially discriminatory laws or practices is entitled, to the extent provided by an Act of parliament, either to tenure which is legally secure or to comparable redress'. According to Section 25(9) of the Constitution, 'Parliament must enact the legislation referred to in subsection (6)' (Constitution of the Republic of South Africa, 1996). In the view of researcher Aninka Claassens (2008), the Constitution recognises the existing differences between practices and occupation on the land, including vulnerability due to past discriminatory laws and practices. But has parliament enacted such legislation?

The answer is not a simple yes or no, because of the contradictory nature of laws that have been passed to date. On the one hand, there are laws that aim to protect the rights of people living in communal areas such as the Ingonyama Trust Act (outlined above) and the Interim Protection of Informal Land Rights Act (IPILRA) of 1996. The latter was passed by Parliament to provide protection for people living in communal areas (former bantustans), most of whom were affected by forced removals and do not have documents to prove their land rights. Informal rights to land include the right to use, live on, or access the land. This implies that IPILRA protects people's rights to their household fields, plots and common natural resources, such as grazing land and rivers. While IPILRA was meant to be a temporary law while Parliament passed another permanent law, this has not been the case and IPILRA is renewed by Parliament every year.

On the other hand, alongside IPILRA and the Ingonyama Trust Act, Parliament has passed laws that give powers to traditional leaders and threaten the rights of ordinary people living in communal land. Claassens (2008) makes reference to the Communal Land Rights Act of 1994. The core of the act was the transfer of title deeds from the government to the community. It authorised traditional councils to represent rural communities as land administrators and to allocate land in communal areas. The Act was strongly challenged by land rights institutions and activists for denying security of tenure to millions of people living in communal land (Claassens, 2008).

Another example is the proposed Communal Land Tenure Policy of September 2014 (CLTP), which would inform the Communal Land Tenure Bill of 2017, and proposes transferring land in the former bantustans to traditional councils. Through this bill the Department of Rural Development and Land Reform (DRDLR) further suggests that traditional councils obtain title deeds for this land, while individuals and families occupying the land would get institutional use rights to parts of the land.

Scholars, land rights activists and civil society organisations have argued that transferring land to traditional leaders would render the rights of those living in communal areas insecure, thus defeating the purpose of tenure reform (Weinberg, 2015). Instead, as Cousins and Claassens (2008) suggest, tenure reform should focus on strengthening existing rights and land administration mechanisms that are derived from social relations under living customary law, which is not static but stems from people's experiences and practices.

Alongside the absence of tenure reform policies that give security of tenure to people living in communal areas, we have observed a growing influx of investors, such as mining companies, acquiring land while dispossessing villagers of their land and displacing land-based livelihoods. I return to this form of land dispossession and how it has been contested and resisted in Makhasaneni later in the chapter.

Traditional leaders and mining deals in KwaZulu-Natal

Researcher Lungisile Ntsebeza (2005) raises questions about the role of traditional leaders in a democracy and suggests that this has been the most challenging task of the South African government post-1994. During colonial and apartheid periods, traditional leaders' roles combined land administration with local government functions and, similar to the colonial-apartheid architects, they were authoritarian and undemocratic. For this reason, traditional leaders were not popular among many (Ntsebeza, 2005). Research and analysis show that some traditional leaders still display such characteristics today. Ntsebeza (2005) argues that in present-day South Africa, the legitimacy of traditional authorities is closely associated with their control of the land-allocation process. This is reflected in some of the laws explained above, but also in the narratives of both the former president of South Africa, Jacob Zuma, and the Zulu monarch, King Goodwill Zwelithini.

Speaking at the opening of the House of Traditional Leaders in 2014, then president Zuma encouraged traditional leaders to get the best lawyers and to embark on land claims on behalf of their communities (South African Press Association, 2014). In 2017, the former president told the same House that land was a central issue for traditional leaders (Zuma, 2017). The Zulu king has come out publicly to praise the potential role of mining in the development of rural areas. Addressing rural residents from mining-affected areas in the province in 2015, the he said traditional leaders should drive mining initiatives and that mining companies should train them (Harper, 2015). All of this is said to be done for the benefit of people living in communal areas. However, in reality, some rural people are further marginalised, as the case of Makhasaneni will demonstrate.

The Case of Makhasaneni

I conducted research in Makhasaneni between March and December 2015, with occasional visits in 2016. Through structured interviews, focus groups and observations, I established how the discovery of iron ore in this village led to the violation of people's land rights, displacement of livelihoods and conflict between the villagers and traditional leaders, leading to the mining company withdrawing its operations.

Background

In an interview, the 97-year-old local headman Mr Jaconia Dludla explained that as a young boy during the 1930s, his family and neighbours were forcibly removed from their homes in eMagogogweni near Melmoth by the colonial government to make way for tree plantations. They were dumped in Makhasaneni village. In 1998, when the South African government opened the call for people to lodge land claims under the land restitution programme, many members of Makhasaneni did so. Mr Dludla has been a headman of Makhasaneni under the leadership of Chief Thandazani Zulu of Entembeni Traditional Council for about 15 years. While reflecting on the painful experience of being forcibly removed, he speaks fondly of his current home, Makhasaneni, and promises that he will not be forcibly removed again. Mr Dludla further explains that Makhasaneni is home to approximately 600 households, which combine land-based livelihood strategies, such as crop production, livestock keeping (cattle, goats and chickens), medicinal plants and water harvesting, with remittances, social grants, informal business and wage employment in the nearby sugarcane farms. Most of the residents are descendants of people who, like Mr Dudla, were forcibly removed from the nearby farms around Melmoth. As a traditional leader, farmer and elder, Mr Dludla sees himself as a local historian who knows the area like the back of his hand. He knows where the village boundaries start and end, and which household belongs to whom in Makhasaneni. When there are disputes over crop fields, or damages caused by unaccompanied cattle or goats, he is the first port of call, and sees it as his duty to try and resolve conflict between families. While the people of Makhasaneni know of their chief, it is Mr Dludla they have a closer relationship with, and they understand his role as it pertains to the day-to-day social relationships in Makhasaneni.

As is the case in most communal areas, land in Makhasaneni is accessed and managed under communal tenure arrangements and the land rights of people are recognised and protected by the Constitution, IPILRA and the Ingonyama Trust Act.

I came to Makhasaneni in March 2015 after hearing about the community struggle to stop a mining company that had started prospecting in the area. I sought to establish how the mining company had obtained access to land in Makhasaneni, why and how people were resisting and what the outcomes of their actions were. In the sub-sections that follow I provide a detailed account of events in this regard.

The arrival of Jindal Africa (Pty) Ltd and the violation of land rights

Jindal arrived in Makhasaneni in November 2011 and began prospecting in people's fields, without consulting the community or the people who depended on the produce grown on the fields, which were destroyed in the process. Explaining what happened, community member Mama Rita Ndlela put it this way: 'I saw cars arriving and people started drilling in my crop field. We were told they were building a mine.' Land rights activist Mr Mbhekiseni Mavuso added: 'They were called geologists. They said there is wealth underneath and we will all be evicted.'

Jindal sought to establish whether the area had sufficiently high levels of iron ore to justify mining. After the prospecting began, a number of cattle and goats died from poisoned water. Ancient family graves were damaged, crop fields were destroyed and water streams became poisonous and ultimately ran dry. In the interview with Mr

Mavuso, who has been one of the key community activists fighting against the establishment of a mine in Makhasaneni, he explained that those families whose fields and family graves were destroyed went to Mr Dludla to report and seek answers.

To everyone's surprise, Mr Dludla knew nothing about Jindal, as the chief never mentioned it to him. Contrary to what the law requires, nobody was consulted prior to the arrival of Jindal. In the view of Claassens (2000), in most cases people who live on communal land with no clear, legally enforceable rights to the land, are often ignored when it comes to decision-making processes pertaining to the land. This leads to decisions being taken that violate their land rights or even dispossess them of the land, which they may have occupied for an extended period of time.

Dludla explained that, as a member of the traditional council, and the local leader of Makhasaneni, he is the interface between the community and the chief, and should be informed of business activities pertaining to his area of jurisdiction. A community meeting was convened and a decision was taken to pause the operations of the mine while seeking clarity from the chief. The headman then convened another community meeting, inviting the chief to come and explain the activities of Jindal on their land. The meeting was held in December 2011, during summer holidays when those family members who worked in places far away from Makhasaneni would also be present.

At the meeting, the members of the community confronted their chief, Mr Zulu, about the matter and he admitted to having given permission to Jindal Africa to conduct prospecting activities. The chief apologised for his actions, including not consulting with the community. However, he insisted that Jindal be given a chance to continue with the prospecting activities.

His actions were a clear disregard of IPILRA and the Ingonyama Trust Act, which stipulate that people should give prior written consent for such activities to take place on their land. Starting from the arrival of Jindal up until the community meeting with the chief, one would assume the chief was deliberate in his efforts to bypass the headman and the community in making the decision to give Jindal permission to access the land. His actions did not serve the interests of the community, but of the mining company and most likely himself. In attesting to this, Claassens (2000) suggests that tensions over land use arise when there are opportunities for investment on the land. Questions arise as to whether or not people want the investment and how the benefits should be distributed within the community. The benefits from this type of investment have often not been paid to communities directly affected, but predominantly to the chief (Claassens, 2000).

The weeks and months that followed the Makhasaneni community's meeting with the chief saw the establishment of the Makhasaneni Community Committee (MCC), the arrival of the chief's brothers, intimidation of activists, intervening of lawyers and, ultimately, the withdrawal of the mining licence application by Jindal.

Resistance and accountability from below: The establishment and functioning of the Makhasaneni Community Committee (MCC)

The MCC was established in early 2012 by concerned members of the community after the arrival of Jindal. Initially, the committee was made up of 30 members, with two members from each of the 15 wards that make up Makhasaneni. The idea behind this set-up was for all wards to be equally represented in the committee. By 2015, the number had dropped by half, as some members were expelled, while others voluntarily left when they could no longer serve the interests of the community. When asked in one of the committee meetings why they did not recruit new representatives to replace those expelled, members pointed out that no new members volunteered to join the committee. The secretary of the committee explained that being a member of the committee had become risky at that time, as there were negative rumours about the committee being against the chief. He thought this might explain why people chose to be bystanders, with the hope that they would also benefit should the committee win the fight. The committee would be the first stop in Makhasaneni for anyone who wanted to discuss any matters pertaining to Jindal. Before elaborating on the experiences of the committee, I will explore the reasons why people in Makhasaneni were opposed to mining in their area.

By resisting mining, what exactly was being protected?

The community members of Makhasaneni were outraged by people coming from elsewhere to impose a mine upon them. The headman explained that they didn't want a mine in Makhasaneni because their goats and cows died from contaminated water due to drilling during prospecting. This is how he expressed his sentiments: 'Firstly, we saw no use in welcoming something that brings us death, and, secondly, people would be moved from here to an unknown place. And they would take people from the graves and bury them elsewhere, and that worried all of us, and this is how we view the mine.' From the headman's explanation, one gathers that, to people of Makhasaneni, mining is a form of destruction that displaces their land-based livelihoods and disturbs deceased family members in their graves. Land in this case belongs both to the living and the deceased and this, the people of Makhasaneni believe, should be respected at all times. Respect for the deceased means not removing them from their graves. For the activists like Mavuso, graves represent hope and strength for the remaining family members, and he sees it as his responsibility to ensure that his father, who was buried in his homestead next to the crop fields, remains there eternally. Mavuso said that in his dying days, his father told him that he depended on Mavuso to ensure that he would not be moved from his grave because of mining.

At the committee meeting I attended in May 2015, one member explained that they visited a village near Mtubatuba, where there was already an established mine, and asked if people were happy with the mine. They said 'no', because the mine had polluted their water and relocated them without compensation. They had also lost their livestock and crop fields, as well as the houses they had built over the years. Instead, the mining company built them smaller houses that were cracking and dangerous to live in. They were promised jobs, but most of the community members were still unemployed. All these reasons persuaded community members to reject mining in Makhasaneni.

Another member of the committee, Mr Dumisani Skhakhane, explained that when the mining company arrived, community members were told they would be moved from their place, which frightened them. He asked 'who would agree to leave such a wealthy place? This area is our beacon. Our mothers produce tons of maize, legumes, sweet potatoes. All kinds of foods are found here. Now if we move, where will our cattle graze?' For these reasons, it is clear that members of the MCC were holding on to their means of social reproduction and identification with the land. Moving them to make way for mining would be similar to the forced removals the likes of which Mr Dludla experienced when the colonial government made way for tree plantations – 'a second round of dispossession', as Claassens and Boyle (2015) put it.

Accountability: Meaning and practice

'We are not saying we do not want the chief, we just want him to be accountable to us on matters relating to our land', one member of the MCC said in an interview. But what does accountability mean in Makhasaneni?

When the committee was established, its position opposing Jindal was clear. So, members who changed their position in support of the mine would be expelled unreservedly. Following the community meeting, in which the chief was confronted, the headman reported to the committee that the chief told his traditional council in a meeting that he was bullied and intimidated in Makhasaneni. The headman felt he was no longer welcome in the traditional council and proposed that the people of Makhasaneni should apologise so as to clear the air. The committee agreed as they did not want relations to sour. They wanted the discussions between themselves, Jindal and the chief to be transparent and conducted in good spirit.

In my view, the chief had already demonstrated his abuse of power when he did not consult the community at the start. To claim that he was intimidated by the community seems to have been a tactic to manipulate the situation, shift the blame to the community and absolve himself of responsibility. The committee, however, remained optimistic and believed a democratic process was still possible.

The headman then scheduled a community meeting with the chief.[2] The chief proposed to come in August 2012 to accept the apology. He came with the mining company staff members, his brothers (the princes or *abantwana* as they are called in Makhasaneni) and members of his traditional council. In his speech to accept the apology, the chief said people should accept the mine, as it was going to bring lots of jobs, especially for women. People applauded. Then one of his delegation proposed that people should vote by a show of hands in favour of or against the mine. In a community that has certain ideas about chiefs, where the line between respect and fear is sometimes blurry, it is problematic, however, to suggest that voting should be done by a show of hands.

Out of the total number of people present, 55 said 'yes' while 15 said 'no'. Reflecting on what transpired on this day, one committee member suggested that, after having been in trouble for confronting the chief about Jindal's unexpected arrival, they were scared to challenge him again. It should also be noted that while the meeting was in Makhasaneni, not all who attended the meeting and voted were from Makhasaneni. There was no space provided for people to ask questions, no information on what exactly Jindal was planning to do, how, for how long and with what outcomes. While IPILRA and the Ingonyama Trust Act do not stipulate the exact procedure for consultation processes and producing written consent, voting by a show of hands from random community members who did not represent the number of households in Makhasaneni was far from the notion of accountability. In the view of one committee member, that entire process was a way to sell out the community.

At this meeting, one of the brothers of the chief announced that he was representing the committee of *abantwana* in Ntembeni, and was going to establish a trust to be in charge of the mine. He also said that the pending land claims on 40 commercial farms around

Melmoth should be withdrawn, and the trust would take over and lodge one consolidated land claim on behalf of everyone. Two people from Makhasaneni should be elected to be part of the trust, he said, and added that the trust would also be in charge of the mine.

Members of Makhasaneni were shocked to learn of this committee of *abantwana* and the plans they already had in mind, not only about the mine but also the pending land claims. No solid decisions were taken at this meeting about the establishment of the trust. However, the seed was planted.

Later, during a focus group meeting with the MCC,[3] I asked who the brothers were, if they had been known to the community, if they lived in Makhasaneni and what their function was. Mama Ngidi responded, saying Chief Zulu and Headman Dludla were the only traditional leaders known to the people of Makhasaneni. With the arrival of Jindal, the community of Makhasaneni came to know of the brothers of the chief. 'We started discussing this issue of the mine with our chief, whom we knew, and suddenly *abantwana* appeared, claiming to be the chief's committee. They want to do whatever they want in our place. When we tell them we are not happy about what Jindal wants to do in Makhasaneni, they tell us the land belongs to them,' Mama Ngidi explained. Another member of the committee, Sithembiso Dubazane, added that 'we have a problem with chieftaincy because they told us as the people of Makhasaneni, we have no right to the land, the land belongs to the Zulu Kingdom.' To claim that the people of Makhasaneni had no right to their land is not only in contravention of the law, but reveals the lack of accountability of some traditional leaders to the citizens whose interests they claim to advance.

Strategies and tactics of resistance

The members of the Makhasaneni community were clear about one thing, and that is that they were not going to allow the traditional leaders to abuse their power and have residents evicted from their homes against their will. While mining is often seen by the state as development, in Makhasaneni it is viewed as destruction as it implies demolishing homes, polluting water and displacing livelihoods. It was for these reasons that the people resisted.

A brief context

I sat in about eight meetings with the MCC between May and November 2015 in which they discussed various strategies and tactics for protecting their land. These meetings took between two and three hours and never started before the headman arrived. The headman would begin by giving announcements or raising any issues that had emanated from weekly meetings with the chief and other members of the traditional council. The chair of the meeting would then open the floor to all the members for comments and questions. If there had been other meetings or tasks that the members participated in, they would also get a chance to share. At the top of the agenda was always the question of Jindal. The members would debate, agree and disagree on certain points until they found common ground, allocated tasks and responsibilities and then closed. I was fascinated by the diverse nature of the group. There were young and old members, women and men, some came in their smart shirts, while others came barefooted with worn-out jeans. Despite their gender and/or class differences, these people were driven by one common goal: to stop the mine from taking their land away from them. My appreciation for Mavuso was great. He was well spoken, bilingual (he speaks Zulu and English), understood the law and could explain it in the simplest ways to the committee. He understood the weaknesses of the traditional council, as he was previously a member. While the people of Makhasaneni in general, and the committee in particular, appreciated him and spoke highly of his role as a thinker in their struggle, he never took decisions unilaterally.

So what were some of these strategies and tactics?

The day after the meeting in which people voted in favour of the mine by show of hands, Jindal made their way back to Makhasaneni.

Following the meeting the previous afternoon, which had left members of the MCC disheartened, the committee had met and agreed to stop Jindal cars from entering. Two committee members, Mavuso and Dubazane, were up early and waited on the street. Indeed, they stopped the car and pleaded with the people not to resume work until at least there was a memorandum of agreement. Jindal understood that there were already tensions in the area due to lack of consultation. Given that they wanted to work in a politically stable environment, it mattered to them, to a certain extent, to cooperate with the people of Makhasaneni. They agreed and proposed that the committee draft a memorandum, stipulating their terms and conditions. Some of the conditions were: 80 per cent of the employees should come from Makhasaneni, Jindal must show them where they were planning to dig before beginning to do so, R5,000 should be paid for each hole to the relevant family and the community's water should not be used in the process of prospecting.

About a month later, a meeting was then called with the mining representatives. They came in their numbers to 'accept' the agreement. The agreement was signed. The mine then started drilling exploration holes around November 2012. Soon after, disputes between Jindal and the MCC began again, and Jindal was stopped from operating. The cause of the dispute was that the committee had found out that Jindal was paying R2,500 per hole to the chief. Jindal refused to stop operating, saying the chair of the committee had granted permission. Following this, the community called a special meeting, where they decided to expel the chair. The chair of the committee was no longer serving their interest, and the committee suspected that he had received a bribe from Jindal. While the dispute between the MCC and Jindal continued, Jindal workers went on strike as they had not been paid. Meanwhile, people in Makhasaneni discovered that their livestock had died due to drinking contaminated water and that community water had been used – in contravention of the conditions put forward by the committee in the memorandum of understanding. Another meeting was called by Jindal to try and resolve the matter, and the committee told them that they demanded compensation for damages (to graves, water and livestock). Jindal reported the committee to the chief and opened a case against the MCC. The MCC, in turn, instructed Jindal to stop working until the case was resolved. At this point, the committee had also discovered that Jindal's prospecting licence would soon expire, so the hope was to delay their work until such time.

About two months down the line a community meeting was called by the traditional council to address the charges and the halting of Jindal's work. *Abantwana* were present and told the members of the MCC that they had no right to stop the mine or charge them for any damages.

Jindal then invited Dubazane and Mavuso (of the MCC) to a meeting in Durban, again to seek suitable solutions to the problem.[4] Jindal wanted to be given a chance to complete the prospecting, so that they could continue the process of obtaining a full mining licence. By this time, the committee had decided to revert to their original position to oppose any and all mining on their land. They were no longer interested in the negotiations and no longer felt intimidated by the traditional council. During the meeting in Durban, *abantwana* asked if Dubazane and Mavuso had intimidated the chief in the first community meeting in which the chief had admitted to having given Jindal access to their land. Before they could answer, one of *abantwana* ordered them to go and tell the people of Makhasaneni that they had no right to stop the mining, since they were not educated.

It is interesting that *abantwana* had ostensibly assumed the duties of the chief, who was not part of this meeting. In fact, according to Mavuso, *abantwana* had also overtaken the Jindal negotiations, and their style was intimidating, arrogant and undermining of the people of Makhasaneni.

Abantwana then asked Dubazane and Mavuso to select five people to be part of a steering committee for the Jindal mining project. They refused and said they would first go back to Makhasaneni and consult the committee. Again, the meeting ended on a bad note. According to Mavuso, while this was happening the chief was arrested for other crimes and distanced himself from the mining issue. In the weeks that followed, one of the *abantwana* was appointed by Jindal as the capacity building officer, as was a former employee of COGTA. According to members of the MCC, this was the beginning of 'a war'.[5]

Push-back from *abantwana*: Intimidation of activists

Abantwana started a campaign against activists using the newspaper *Bayede*[6] to write stories that discredited Mavuso's actions, calling him a spy that was out to dethrone the king (Yeni, 2015). Mavuso saw this as a way to divide the community of Makhasaneni and turn members against him, shifting the focus from the actions of the traditional council onto the activists. Mavuso expressed his regard for the king, stating clearly that his primary objective was to protect the land rights of the Makhasaneni people and that his actions were not aimed at dethroning him. 'Land is everything to us, we are trying to show not only the chief, even the king, that we are the land owners here,' he explained in an interview.

In the space of one month, there were four *Bayede*[7] articles about Mavuso. He was warned that there were rumours that people were out to kill him. The targeting of key activists was a recognisable tactic for clamping down on the rural anti-mining activists, as was the case with the killing of the chairperson of the Amadiba Crisis Committee in Xolobeni in 2016.[8] Discussing the issue of intimidation in July 2015 in an interview with one member of the MCC who asked to remain anonymous, she explained that she received a call from a relative who was a hitman, who claimed to have been bought to kill seven of the MCC members: Mavuso was top of the list. The hitman did not know that his relative was among the seven as the instruction given was 'including the three women' and the names were not provided. The hitman did not proceed with the task. The MCC member added that 'we are not scared of dying, we even sleep with doors unlocked. If they kill us, it will be known that we died for fighting the mine. We do not want the mine.'

In an interview, Mavuso added that 'those who raise questions and attempt to resist face the risk of death. Our traditional leaders claim ownership of our land. What should we do? Should we run away?

Does all the land we live on belong to the chiefs? Do we not have ownership rights to this land? How are we going to fight this form of development?'

The last questions raised by this community member are very well answered in both IPILRA and the Ingonyama Trust Act, which recognise people living on the land as the rightful owners, as the Constitution requires. However, their experience with the arrival of Jindal raised doubts and suggests that land rights are only protected when there are no business opportunities on the land.

It was around February 2015, as articles started to appear in *Bayede*, that I started to work with the community of Makhasaneni. The Land and Accountability Research Centre (LARC) went to Makhasaneni at the request of a few members of the committee, who had previously attended a LARC workshop on land rights. LARC could provide lawyers to look into issues of intimidation and violation of rights, which would help stop Jindal from obtaining a mining licence. The community committee requested that we in LARC link them with journalists who would write about their experiences, as more exposure provided them with a form of security. During this time, their story was published in *Mail & Guardian* (Timse, 2016) and *City Press*. The appointed lawyers wrote to *Bayede* and demanded that they publish an article to apologise to Mavuso for putting his life at risk. Even though *Bayede* never published such an article, they did stop publishing untrue stories about Mavuso.

Abantwana persisted in their attempts to bring the mine to Makhasaneni. The headman shared with LARC that *abantwana* had visited his home in his absence, demanded that his wife accept a letter on his behalf and threatened to assault their daughter, who was also a member of the committee. The wife refused to accept the letter. Mavuso went into hiding for three weeks as the threats to kill him increased. In an interview with Dubazane in July 2015, he explained that he was confronted by one of *abantwana* who told him he was not scared of the people of Makhasaneni and he would do the killing himself. The last attempt by *abantwana* to assume control, and further the mining project, was done through COGTA.

In August 2015, COGTA visited Makhasaneni together with

abantwana and the full membership of the traditional council, except the chief who by then had distanced himself from the matter for quite some time. The purpose of the visit was to redefine boundaries in the area. A few weeks before, the headman was informed about the visit and so convened a community meeting to inform people. I was also informed by the committee members, who requested that I investigate COGTA's intentions. In my interview with the official from COGTA, he explained that their mandate was to create a database of all the village wards and their headmen, and store the boundaries in their GPS. The actual identification of boundaries was the work of the traditional leaders. The members of MCC saw this as yet another attempt by *abantwana* to take their land. In redefining the boundaries, *abantwana* – working through the traditional council – would deliberately push Mr Dludla out and put a different headman in charge of that particular piece of land that they were targeting for mining.

On 20 August 2015, the day that COGTA arrived, community members gathered on the hill called Kwesezulu. They expected the meeting to take place on that hill, but when COGTA and the members of traditional council, including *abantwana,* arrived, they gathered at a different spot. A few members of the traditional council drove up the hill and requested that the headman come down with them as COGTA and *abantwana* were ready to start with the meeting. The crowd shouted 'no', saying COGTA and *abantwana* must come up if they wanted to meet the headman. One community member said that they were not going to allow their headman to be separated from them. The members of the traditional council accepted that the headman was not going to come and left. Mr Dludla remained the headman of Makhasaneni.

Conclusion

The case of Makhasaneni demonstrates the problems that are created by the ongoing lack of clarity about the roles of traditional leaders broadly, and traditional leaders' control of land in particular. By resisting mining on their land, the people of Makhasaneni challenged unaccountable traditional leaders and the dominant profit-driven development model that is advanced and supported by the state. It is neoliberal in nature and characterised by land dispossession, the displacement of land-based livelihoods and the inability to absorb the labour of those dispossessed. The MCC have nicknamed this mode of development 'tsunami', because as soon as it arrives they have to flee. It approaches in a wave of destruction. They go to sleep peacefully and wake up to mining construction on their fields and grazing land. Mavuso said they were aware that certain government officials, mining companies and chiefs collude together without care for the physical, social and environmental wellbeing of the people. This raises serious questions about how we think about land reform and rural development going forward.

In June 2016, the community of Makhasaneni discovered that Jindal had withdrawn its application for a mining licence. In a letter to their stakeholders, they gave the global decline in the price of iron ore as the reason for their withdrawal. The villagers, however, believe it was due to their sustained efforts to drive the mining company off their land. While this was a victory for the people of Makhasaneni, the struggle for recognition of land rights continues. Until the parliament of South Africa enacts a law to give them security of tenure on communal land, people living in the former homelands remain vulnerable. Until their rights to the land they occupy are recognised, they will remain under threat.

References

Alcock, R. & Hornby, D. 2004. 'Traditional land matters: A look into land administration in tribal areas in KwaZulu-Natal'. Legal Entity Assessment Project Pietermaritzburg. Report for the *Legal Entity Assessment Project*, https://sarpn.org/documents/d0000835/AFRA_Traditional_land_2004.pdf, accessed 6 August 2018.

Borras, S. M., Hall, R., Scoones, I., White, B. & Wolford, W. 2011. 'Towards a better understanding of global land grabbing: An editorial introduction'. *The Journal of Peasant Studies*, 38 (2), 209–216.

Claassens, A. 2000. 'Land rights and local decision-making processes: Proposals for tenure reform', in

Constitution of the Republic of South Africa. 1996, https://www.gov.za/documents/constitution-republic-south-africa-1996

Cousins, B. (ed.) *At the Crossroads: Land and agrarian reform in South Africa into the 21st Century*. Cape Town: PLAAS, University of the Western Cape.

Claassens, A. 2008. 'Power, accountability and apartheid borders: The impact of recent laws on struggles over land rights', in Claassens, A. (ed.) *Land, Power and Custom: Controversies generated by South Africa's Communal Land Rights Act*. Athens: Ohio University Press, pp. 262–292.

Claassens, A. & Boyle, B. 2015. 'A promise betrayed: Policies and practice renew the rural dispossession of land, rights and prospects'. *Governance of Africa's Resources Programme*: Policy Briefing 124. *SAIIA* website: http://www.saiia.org.za/research/a-promise-betrayed-policies-and-practice-renew-the-rural-dispossession-of-land-rights-and-prospects/, accessed 6 August 2018.

Cousins, B. 2008. 'Characterising "communal" tenure: Nested systems and flexible boundaries', in Claassens, A. (ed.) *Land, Power and Custom: Controversies generated by South Africa's Communal Land Rights Act*. Athens: Ohio University Press, pp. 109–137.

Cousins, B. & Claassens, A. 2004. 'Communal land rights, democracy and traditional leaders in post-apartheid South Africa', in Evers, S., Spierenberg, M. & Wells, H. (eds.) *Securing Land and Resource Rights in Africa: Pan-African perspectives*. Leiden: Brill, pp. 139–154.

Hall, R. 2009. 'Land reform for what?' in Hall, R. (ed.) *Another Countryside? Policy options for land and agrarian reform in South Africa*. Cape Town: PLAAS, University of the Western Cape, pp. 22–60.

Harper, P. 26 August 2015. 'Amakhosi must drive mining initiatives on tribal land – King Zwelithini', *News24*, http://www.news24.com/SouthAfrica/News/Amakhosi-must-drive-mining-initiatives-on-tribal-land-King-Zwelithini-20150826, accessed 3 August 2018.

Ingonyama Trust Act of No. 3KZ of 1994. 24 April 1994, http://www.ingonyamatrust.org.za/wp-content/uploads/2015/10/Ingonyama-Trust-Act-as-amended.pdf, accessed 25 November 2018.

Ingonyama Trust Board. 2018. Ingonyama Trust website: www.ingonyamatrust.org.za, accessed 3 August 2018.

Mbeki, G. 1964. *South Africa: The peasants' revolt*. Baltimore: Penguin Books.

Ntsebeza, L. 2004. 'Democratic decentralisation and traditional authority: Dilemmas of land administration in rural South Africa'. *The European*

Journal of Development Research, 16 (1), 71–89.

Ntsebeza, L. 2005. *Democracy Compromised: Chiefs and the politics of the land in South Africa.* Leiden: Brill.

Scott, J. C. 2008. *Weapons of the Weak: Everyday forms of peasant resistance.* New Haven: Yale University Press.

South African Press Association. 27 February 2014. '"Land reform laws are biased" says Zuma'. *Mail & Guardian,* https://mg.co.za/article/2014-02-27-land-reform-laws-are-biased-says-zuma, accessed 3 August 2018.

Timse, T. 2016. 'Choose between mining and bloodshed'. *Mail & Guardian,* https://mg.co.za/article/2016-05-03-choose-between-mining-and-bloodshed, accessed 3 August 2018.

Weinberg, T. 2015. 'The contested status of "communal land tenure" in South Africa'. *Rural Status Report,* 3. PLAAS: University of the Western Cape.

Yeni, S. 25 August 2015. '*Bayede* newspaper, traditional leaders and mining deals in KwaZulu-Natal'. *Land and Accountability Research Centre* website: http://www.customcontested.co.za/bayede-newspaper-traditional-leaders-and-mining-deals-in-kwazulu-natal/, accessed 3 August 2018.

Zuma, J. 3 March 2017. 'Annual official opening: National house of traditional leaders'. *South African Government* website: https://www.gov.za/speeches/annual-official-opening-national-house-traditional-leaders-3-mar-2017-0000, accessed 6 August 2018.

Endnotes

1   I did speak with him briefly on the phone, during which he said he preferred not to be interviewed.
2   Interview with Mbhekiseni Mavuso
3   Focus group meeting in Makhasaneni primary school hall, 30 April 2015
4   Interview with Mavuso, in Cape Town 2017. I met with him as I was writing this chapter and needed him to remind me of some of the events that had taken place, which I did not have in my field notes.
5   The term 'war' here was used figuratively to express that the conflict had got tougher, but it was not implying a war in the sense of delegating the army.
6   *Bayede* describes itself on its website (www.bayedenews.com) as a 'weekly isiNguni publication targeting a niche market, interested in a critical approach to policy formulation and implementation, politics, cultural heritage, current affairs, and rural and economic development'.

It targets people living in rural KwaZulu-Natal, but it is also available in the big cities of South Africa.

7 *Bayede* newspaper between February and April 2015 focused extensively on publishing stories pertaining to mining and traditional leaders in KwaZulu-Natal. This included stories about Makhasaneni and Mavuso.

8 The Amadiba Crisis Committee (ACC) was formed in 2007 by villagers of Xolobeni in Pondoland to fight the mining of titanium in their area.

SECTION THREE
Leadership and Legitimacy

This [Traditional and Khoi-San Leadership] Bill says there are traditional leaders who have a geographic area and a territory where they rule and then there are KhoiSan senior leaders who are in charge of branches [...] Five in Manenberg, 10 in Bonteheuwel, and in Vredendal there are a few [...] You have no authority over any geographic territory but the king of the Zulus have! The king of the Xhosas have! The king of the Tswanas have and this government is playing with the people. They rejected the homeland system: Transkei, Bophuthatswana, Venda, Ciskei, KaNgwane, KwaNdebele, Gazankulu, KwaZulu, they rejected independent homelands, but they kept the geographic boundaries and made the chiefs the big boys there [...] We [the KhoiSan] are a first nation, but we are third-class citizens [...]

– MR MARAIS, HIGH-LEVEL PANEL WESTERN CAPE PUBLIC HEARINGS, 5–6 DECEMBER 2016, P. 82

We have the National Traditional House of Leadership, Provincial House of Leadership, and 80% of those who represent us in that leadership are illegal chiefs because SA has not gone and said people were changed and made chief by a certain [apartheid] government.

– KGOMOTSO KHUNOU, HIGH-LEVEL PANEL NORTH WEST PUBLIC HEARINGS, 1–2 MARCH 2017, P. 93

That House of Traditional Leaders is not a house of traditional leaders, it is a house of senior traditional leaders. And senior traditional leaders are those who have been recognised as senior traditional leaders. We've got lots of traditional leaders who are not recognised even when in their birth right [says] they are traditional leaders who were supposed to sit in that house.

– SHIRAMI SHIRINDA, HIGH-LEVEL PANEL LIMPOPO PUBLIC HEARINGS, 14–15 MARCH 2017, P. 22

This set of chapters asks 'who leads?'. How do traditional leaders gain and maintain legitimacy? And what determines their appointment? Sindiso Mnisi Weeks's chapter critiques the South African government's focus on senior traditional leaders (i.e. chiefs), arguing that the bulk of everyday traditional leadership is in fact carried out by headmen and other lower-level tribal authorities. This has not only compromised the efficacy of lower-level leaders, but also those they represent (mostly women). Indeed, Mnisi Weeks's chapter parallels the experiences of women and headmen, arguing that apartheid distortions of customary law stripped both of their power, thereby eroding bottom-up, decentralised leadership. Fani Ncapayi also reflects on people's everyday attachments to lower-level traditional leaders. Ncapayi describes struggles over the appointment of headmen by senior traditional leaders in the Cala region of Eastern Cape, where headmen have historically been elected by residents. The contradictions within post-apartheid law play a central role in the narrative harnessed both by senior traditional leaders in Cala and by the popular movements opposing them.

Questions of legitimacy are similarly central to Tlhabane Motaung's chapter, which describes a century-old chieftaincy dispute in the Hammanskraal region. The chapter is, on the surface, a story about the role of British colonialism, and later the bantustan system, in shaping the course of this chieftaincy dispute. However, it is also about how the dispute has factored in ordinary people's claims to identity and belonging. This leads to the final chapter of the section: William Ellis's contribution explores how the institution of 'traditional leadership' has been mobilised by some contemporary KhoiSan communities as a tool of recognition and a means of making claims on the state. Although history demonstrates a fluid, and largely contingent, set of leadership practices among the KhoiSan, South Africa's new democracy has, ironically, necessitated that some KhoiSan groups assume more fixed forms of 'tradition' in order to reap the benefits of liberation and restitution policies. Amid rallying calls for 'decolonisation', these KhoiSan activists have sought to privilege the political power of 'indigeneity'. Theirs is a recent story of how traditional leadership has been recast and re-imagined – as it has been many times before – to respond to the exigencies of the moment. Motaung's chapter therefore calls on us to ask what South Africa will make of traditional leadership as its democracy matures.

SEVEN

The violence of the harmony model

Common narratives between women and lower-level traditional leaders

SINDISO MNISI WEEKS

This chapter is dedicated to 'Nduna Mshushisi' and to the many women who must live with material insecurity and everyday violence.

Introduction

Political and policy discussion about traditional leadership in South Africa often focuses on senior traditional leaders (formerly referred to as 'chiefs') and kings or queens. However, the bulk of the leadership in rural areas is carried out by headmen, with the everyday support of other lower-level traditional leaders such as those formerly known as 'tribal policemen'. Since the completion of a number of extensive studies on the full traditional governance system, carried out in the early to mid-20th century, the lower strata of the traditional governance system have lost some popularity as a scholarly enterprise, leaving a lacuna in the literature. This lacuna has allowed public discourse to fall back on platitudes about and caricatures of traditional authority that are out of keeping with reality.

Public mischaracterisations of traditional courts, and how they function, have been rhetorically presented as reclamations of pre-colonial conceptions of traditional institutions. Ironically, however, this rhetoric is in fact predominantly formed of colonial and apartheid distortions of traditional leadership. These faulty stereotypes therefore ignore the paradoxes produced and presented by the historical and present-day political economy of rural South Africa. For example, Christine Mhongo and Debbie Budlender (2013) show evidence of a steady decline in marriage rates over the last half-century,[1] which has important consequences for the patriarchal assumptions on which traditional leadership and dispute processes are based. These over-romanticised notions of traditional governance are not innocuous. Rather, these notions are highly political and have tangible consequences for people's lives – to the point of affecting whether people (both ordinary rural residents and those in traditional leadership) live or die. The gendered nature and consequences of these over-romanticised notions – particularly for women – are especially troubling.

This chapter fills part of the lacuna in scholarly and public knowledge of the reality of lower-level leadership and courts in rural South Africa following the end of apartheid.[2] It is based on empirical data, painstakingly recorded over a period of 11 months, about what headmen do on a day-to-day basis, observations of traditional courts at various levels in Msinga, KwaZulu-Natal (see Mnisi Weeks, 2018; Mnisi Weeks, 2016; Mnisi Weeks, 2015a; Mnisi Weeks, 2012) and participant observation in Mbuzini, Mpumalanga (see Mnisi Weeks, 2015b; Mnisi Weeks, 2011; Mnisi Weeks & Claassens, 2011). The chapter argues that national, provincial and local government policies that focus on senior traditional leaders as the primary means of regulating customary law and providing justice and security for its adherents is misguided. Furthermore, such an emphasis in policy making can serve to undermine both the interests of the ordinary people these leaders purportedly represent (the majority of whom are women), and also the role and efficacy of leaders (the majority of whom are men) operating at lower levels in the customary system.

The argument offered in this chapter might first present as an account of the lived realities of rural[3] women, subject to traditional leadership. It describes the disconnect between these women's experiences, on the one hand, and the laws that seek to regulate the institutions that govern them, on the other. Yet, with closer attention, there is a second layer of argument being presented here. The chapter demonstrates how the same lived realities of women in rural areas that are ignored by legislation, affect and shape the ability of headmen to carry out their responsibilities, especially in the realm of local dispute resolution. Hence, this chapter shows that the sources of vulnerability for women that are ignored by government similarly render the headmen vulnerable and undermine their ability to assist the government in keeping the areas under their leadership justly administered and secure.

The chapter makes this argument, systematically, through several key points:

- Rural people's existences are dependent on access to power, and women have little of it with which to negotiate their security.
- Apartheid distorted customary law, firstly by stripping women of any power they had under pre-colonial customary law, thus making women more vulnerable than they had been pre-colonially. Secondly, it stripped away much territorially based, bottom-up and decentralised customary power from headmen, thus leaving them with less authority than they had pre-colonially.
- The security of people living under customary law is highly embedded in and contingent on the reciprocal relationships that make up customary communities[4] and the rights enjoyed within them. Hence, for women, the loss of power with which to negotiate has resulted in the tremendous absence of security for them; so too has the coincidence of headmen's loss of authority at the same time as the severe degradation of the social fabric in customary communities, due to socioeconomic disadvantages, resulted in tremendous loss of security for headmen.

- The solution to this double challenge is *not*, as South African lawmakers seem to assume, the centralisation of power in senior traditional leaders. Legislation like the Traditional Leadership and Governance Framework Act No. 41 of 2003 (TLGFA), Communal Land Rights Act No. 11 of 2004 (before it was struck down) and the Traditional Courts Bill B15-2008/B1-2012 (and, now, the TCB B1-2017) Act change the balance of power in favour of senior traditional leaders (who are predominantly men), making it even more difficult for women to negotiate physical, social and material security. Fatefully, while strengthening the position of senior traditional leaders, these laws simultaneously weaken the position of lower-level traditional leaders and make it more difficult for them (along with women) to negotiate greater human security for themselves and their communities.

Each of these points is addressed in detail below, with brief narratives used to illustrate key arguments.

The argument advanced is ultimately that the legislation impacts on the power balance crucial for changes that would enhance women's and headmen's security on the ground. But so far, the South African government has failed to recognise the damage it is doing to even lower-level traditional leaders. Perhaps this failure is due to the fact that the debate has so far been presented as one between traditional leaders and ordinary rural people, when the reality defies such oversimplification. The chapter therefore ends with the proposal that government's response should be based on an approach that may seem counter-intuitive at first, but is the only solution that is consistent with preserving the integrity of rural communities and their cultures. The government should foreground the decentralisation of traditional leadership in order to strengthen the everyday social relations within which customary norms and the maintenance of social order are negotiated in very localised spaces.

Power: Women have little with which to negotiate their security

A middle-aged woman, MaNovalo,[5] was repeatedly tormented by her husband, Cijimpi, who would brandish his gun whenever he was drunk, which was not infrequently, and threaten her with it. When her husband used his firearm to threaten a neighbour for harbouring her, the neighbour took the matter to the local dispute management council. The council's decision was insipid: they insisted that Cijimpi should have gathered the family council to help resolve the root issue of his affair with another woman, and would do better to move MaNovalo back to her natal home than shoot at her. The council then concluded by asking that Cijimpi stop harassing his wife while simultaneously instructing MaNovalo to extend respect and patience toward Cijimpi in his affair. MaNovalo, on the other hand, was resolute: she would not leave to another woman the home for which she had worked so hard, even if it meant that her daughter was being visibly traumatised by the ongoing abuse. MaNovalo tearfully accepted the real risk that she herself would leave her home in a body bag.[6]

The first case made by this chapter is that rural women's existences are largely determined by unequal power relations; in this context women have very little power with which to negotiate their security (physical, social and material). The following problems reported by women living in rural areas are well-documented by scholarship on women's vulnerability and insecurity under customary law (Claassens & Ngubane, 2008; Mnisi Weeks, 2011; Weinberg, 2013; Mnisi Weeks, 2013; Thornberry, 2016). Women are often evicted from their marital homes when their marriages fail or when they are widowed (Himonga, 2005; Venter & Nel, 2005; Higgins et al.; 2006). Divorced or widowed women who return to their birth homes when marriages end are often made unwelcome and evicted by their brothers. Unmarried sisters are often evicted from their birth homes by their married brothers after their parents die, as sons assert that they alone should inherit the land, even when the father may have chosen a daughter to be responsible for the family home (Mbatha,

2002; Kingwill, 2008; Mnisi Weeks & Claassens, 2011). Married women are not treated as people with rights to land, which is seen rather as the property of the husband and his birth family. Wives are therefore often not consulted on decisions regarding land use or transactions, and women are still treated as minors in their families and communities (Budlender et al., 2011; Mnisi Weeks, 2015).

Furthermore, women, especially single women, struggle to access residential land because 'traditionally' residential sites in patrilineal areas are allocated only to men (Cousins, 2011). Women are often excluded from traditional institutions, such as traditional and village council meetings, where key decisions about land rights are taken – including the decision that women are not to be represented in traditional councils and courts and are not allowed to address meetings. In fact, women are often denigrated or ignored when trying to speak in these forums. Men generally dominate the traditional courts that decide family and land disputes, and these courts are perceived to favour men over women (Curran & Bonthuys, 2005).

One should not draw the conclusion from this evidence that women are powerless or without authority – indeed, in many respects they hold relatively powerful socio-cultural roles (see, for example, Griffiths, 1998; Redding, 2004). Yet, largely as a consequence of the interventions of formal law, women have less authoritative power in relation to men in the more structured aspects of their status (McClendon, 1995). It is this limited negotiating power that negatively affects their ability to negotiate security for themselves in their often-precarious circumstances (Whitehead & Tsikata, 2003; Mnisi Weeks, 2015). The next two sections discuss how this power asymmetry came into being and how, in practice, it disadvantages women in and through day-to-day outcomes.

Apartheid distorted customary law and stripped women and headmen of power and authority

Women and headmen are most unlikely allies, and there are certainly limits to their commonalities. However, I can show that apartheid affected their positions in similar ways, albeit to differing degrees. As men and traditional authorities, headmen were regarded by the apartheid government as being superior to women. Nonetheless, apartheid distorted customary law to strip headmen of their authority and power, as well as women. In the case of women, this was achieved by making them perpetual minors and ever subject to the authority of the men in their lives. For headmen, this was achieved by fixing 'tribal' boundaries, inverting the 'bottom-up' nature of the power in customary communities (Okoth-Ogendo, 2008) and centralising power in senior traditional leaders.

Distorted customary law, limited power for women

Make Musha's fiancé, Myeni, had called her to the area in which he worked, where the two got married and acquired a house. When Myeni died, it turned out that he had another wife in the rural areas who he had married before his marriage to Make Musha. In order to claim some of the death benefits through her, Myeni's family resurrected the old wife, Make Mdala, and chased away the new one saying that the man already had a wife. When they went to the Magistrate's Court and Make Musha produced a marriage certificate, the deceased's family turned against the first wife, Make Mdala, who did not have written proof of her marriage, and asked her who had married her and Myeni. In the back and forth, Make Mdala's fate seemed dependent on the interventions of others – Myeni, his family, and the law – thus demonstrating the limits to her power as a consequence of having married Myeni prior to black women's liberation from the perpetual minority status accorded them under apartheid law.[7]

In this section, I show that women's relative disempowerment was not always a fixture of customary law. Pre-colonially, traditional communities were both patriarchal and matriarchal (Mamdani, 1996; Claassens, 2013). This did not necessarily mean that women were equal (Guy, 1990). But, within the context of the delicate balance between those two political poles (matriarchy and patriarchy), women had some power with which to exercise agency and control over their lives and thus also negotiate their security. For instance, women were able to select their own spouses or draw on customary law to extract themselves from undesirable marriages (Comaroff & Roberts, 1977; McClendon, 1995; Mamdani, 1996). With the distortion of the principles of customary law by colonial and apartheid governments, women lost this negotiating power, which has had devastating long-term consequences for their security.

Readers are probably familiar with this history but, for the sake of completeness, I will summarise it briefly here. The Native Administration Act No. 38 of 1927 (NAA), section 11(3)(b), as inserted by the Native Administration Amendment Act No. 21 of 1943, laid down a new 'customary' law: 'a native woman who is a partner in a customary union and who is living with her husband shall be deemed to be a minor and her husband shall be deemed to be her guardian'. Women (and young people) were disproportionately disadvantaged by a system that privileged 'the adult male members of the tribe', as exemplified by section 3(1) of the NAA, under which men were the only ones who could participate in local decision making.

This is not mentioning laws such as the infamous and pervasive KwaZulu Act 16 on the Code of Zulu Law and Natal Code of Zulu Law.[8] In very similar wording, their respective sections 20 prescribed that:

> The family head is the *owner of all family property* in *his* family home. *He has charge, custody and control of the property* attaching to the houses of his several wives and may *in his discretion* use the same for his personal wants and necessities, or for general family purposes or for the entertainment of visitors. *He may use, exchange, loan or otherwise alienate or deal with such property* for the benefit of or in the interests of the house to which it attaches, but should *he* use property attaching to one house for the benefit or on behalf of any other house in the family home an *obligation rests upon such other house* to return the same or its equivalent in value (emphasis added).[9]

Section 22 of the Natal Code went on to say that '[t]he *inmates* of a family home irrespective of sex or age shall in respect of all family matters be *under the control of and owe obedience to* the family head'.

Of course, historians, social anthropologists and legal ethnographers have shown how (especially in Tswana society) in lived reality, customary norms tended to follow traditional practice which meant that, as demonstrated by John Comaroff and Simon Roberts (1981), women and men negotiated their way around the formal restrictions, despite the overarching colonial legal system. Similarly, Ann Griffiths (1997) shows how fluid the lived reality and the practice of justice under customary law were. And, as seen in this chapter, women were important agents in sustaining and exploiting the negotiability and fluidity of customary law.

In other words, to the extent that (i) formal laws allowed, (ii) distortions of power had not set in too deeply and (iii) the state was absent, people in traditional communities continued to practice customary law and customary relationships as they saw fit, and according to norms that they determined. Yet what they saw as fitting was profoundly shaped by the social and political economy of colonialism, and then apartheid (McClendon, 1995; Hunter, 2005).

While in their negotiations, women even used the new colonial structures to their advantage to the extent possible. Women turned to these external forums for leverage against decisions they deemed problematic in their own traditional settings but felt otherwise powerless to avoid. This is itself a sign of the multifaceted impact of the state's direct and indirect force in these communities.

The Constitutional Court has had opportunity to consider the falsifications of customary law represented in the NAA and has made the following statements on the subject:

> In our pre-colonial past ... women, who had a great influence in the family, held a place of pride and respect within the family. Their influence was subtle although not lightly overridden. Their consent was indispensable to all crucial family decisions. Ownership of family property was never exclusive but resided in the collective and was meant to serve the familial good

(*Gumede (born Shange) v President of the Republic of South Africa and Others* 2009 (3) SA 152 (CC), at para 18).

First, it must be acknowledged that even in idyllic pre-colonial communities, group interests were framed in favour of men and often to the grave disadvantage of women and children (*Mayelane v Ngwenyama and Another* 2013 (4) SA 415 (CC), at para 71).

Hence the Court concluded that while customary law must be accorded the respect it deserves, there remains a need to ensure that it develops in accordance with the framework of the Constitution. Such development should take account of the vulnerability of women and ensure that their right to equality is robustly protected. Yet, any development of customary law must take as its starting point the recognition that customary law was fundamentally altered by a colonial government that sought to exploit it to enforce its own indirect rule.

Distorted customary law, limited authority for headmen

Landzela was the apparent heir to the headmanship of his ward, but elected not to take it up. The reason Landzela's aunts (one biological and the other by affinity) gave for supporting his rejection of the office was the preservation of his life. It was repeatedly said that the young man's father, Nduna Cala, had died because of the position; there were allegedly people who were not happy about Nduna Cala being in the position and resorted to supernatural means to remove him. In the estimation of Landzela's aunts, for a job that did not even pay, it just was not worth it for him to risk his life. Nonetheless, they as well as others acknowledged that it is one's duty to serve when one is called by the chieftainship, bukhosi, to do so. Landzela was therefore living with the tension of having violated an acknowledged cultural and social duty on the grounds of what he and his family perceived as a matter of his survival. At the same time, some people in positions of authority acknowledged the internal tensions surrounding not just the headmanship but bukhosi as well. Groups within the community – like the 'civics' (young people, mostly male, leading the rural resistance in the latter days of apartheid) – were reputed not to wish to be under a chief. Most striking was the explanation given for why the chiefs themselves were not rendered perpetually insecure by this internal resistance; namely, that it had been made evident to these factions that government supports the 'chiefs'. It was broadly understood then that most of the senior traditional leadership's extant power is assigned by govenment.[10]

The argument advanced in this section is that, much like women's roles under customary law were distorted by the dominant legal system, so too were headmen's, which resulted in the undermining and limiting of headmen's customary authority. The NAA was in fact based on preceding legislation passed by the then Transvaal government, Law 4 of 1885, which distorted the authority of headmen by ignoring the lower-level customary dispute resolution forums led by headmen. In fact, legislators considered several cases that revolved around whether or not headmen played a role in the traditional judicial process. Relying upon the Western conception of a court as a forum governed by a single individual in his or her capacity as judge, Law 4 of 1885 recognised only chiefs as being entitled to having courts, and to make decisions in those courts. However, cases were brought to the colonial courts in which people argued for recognition of the fact that headmen were empowered to resolve disputes in their own forums and also to participate in chiefs' forums.

For instance, in the 1923 case of *Makapan v Khope* (1926: 555, 561) decided under Law 4 of 1885, the Appellate Division of the Supreme Court observed that the headman's court was 'recognised by members of the tribe as having authority to hear and decide disputes', but was not recognised by the legislature and, hence, the court found that in terms of the legislation, the chief 'alone' constituted 'a court of justice'.

It is important to observe as the subtext for such decisions that the courts' conclusion that the 'native chiefs' ruled like despots formed the basis of its rationalisation that 'the Governor-General', as the 'Supreme Chief', was in terms of Law 4 of 1885 permitted to expel native men from their land because '[t]he Government today has the power the old chiefs exercised' (*Mokhatle and Others v Union Government*, 1926: 77). This was the decision delivered three years after *Makapan* (1912), by the same Appellate court in *Mokhatle and Others v Union Government*, where the court implied that the 'native mind' was not particularly suited to democratic process, and it was thus appropriate for the chief to have full discretion to determine such matters, and others need not be consulted (*Mokhatle and Others v Union Government*, 1926: 79).

Following on from Law 4 of 1885, the NAA recognised and regulated traditional courts as forums primarily – if not exclusively – constituted by 'chiefs' (that is, senior traditional leaders). This description of traditional courts can be seen from the titles of the relevant sections of the NAA, namely, 'Settlement of civil disputes by native chiefs' (section 12) and 'Powers of chiefs to try certain offences' (section 20). In terms of the legislation, senior traditional leaders were made both legislators and adjudicators. It was only in 1929 that the NAA's sections 12 and 20 were amended in order to recognise headmen's courts as forums below the level of chiefs' courts.

With respect to traditional governance, the apartheid administration used principles laid down in the NAA to both extend and alter the authoritative power of senior traditional leaders. Furthermore, the systematic preference of 'chiefs' over headmen has continued in the legal system until today. According to section 2 of the Traditional Leadership and Governance Framework Act No. 41 of 2003 (TLGFA): '(1) A community may be recognised as a *traditional community* if it (a) is *subject to* a system of *traditional leadership in terms of* that community's customs; and (b) observes a system of customary law' (emphasis added). Yet, section 28(3) titled, 'transitional measures', says that 'any "tribe" that, immediately before the commencement of this Act, had been established and was still recognised as such is *deemed* to be a *traditional community* contemplated in section 2 ...' (emphasis added).

In terms of the NAA, 'chiefs' (and subsequently headmen too) were empowered to settle disputes that arose in the areas under their jurisdiction – that is, within the territories over which they had state-sanctioned 'control'. The 'chiefs' (and later headmen) themselves had to satisfy two criteria: first, they had to be formally recognised or appointed by the state and, second, they had to acquire specific authorisation for deciding civil matters, with this permission having to be written in order for 'chiefs' (and later headmen) to legitimately hear criminal cases.

Under section 28(1) of the TLGFA, '(a)ny traditional leader who was *appointed* as such in terms of applicable provincial legislation and was *still recognised* as a traditional leader immediately before the commencement of this Act, is *deemed* to have been recognised as such in terms of section 9 or 11, subject to a decision of the Commission in terms of section 26' (emphasis added). Furthermore, in terms of section 28(4): 'any tribal authority that, immediately before the commencement of this Act, had been *established* and was *still recognised* as such, is *deemed* to be a *traditional council* ...' (emphasis added).

Under apartheid, those communities that were acephalous (literally, 'without a head', and so meaning having no 'chief', king or queen) were not recognised, and therefore could not own land, because they could not become a 'tribe' or have a 'tribal authority' without the construct of a 'chief'. The effect of the legislation cited above is that these same communities are not recognised as traditional communities under the TLGFA. Some such communities were claimants in the Constitutional Court challenge to the Communal Land Rights Act No. 11 of 2004, *Tongoane v National Minister for Agriculture and Land Affairs* 2010 (6) SA 214 (CC). Under the apartheid legislation, there was only one exception for acephalous communities; 'community authorities' were the only (rarely used) model available under the Bantu Authorities Act No. 68 of 1951 for recognising black communities that did not have a 'chief' or exist as a tribe under the NAA.

The 'transitional measures' in section 28 are still in effect 15 years after the TLGFA came into being and, under this section, 'community authorities' are presumed to have all been disestablished in terms of the TLGFA. Hence, there is no provision for acephalous communities.

Besides that, communities in the Eastern Cape that customarily elected their headmen (as opposed to having their headmen appointed by the Royal House or senior traditional leader) have no provision for doing so under either the TLGFA or the Eastern Cape Traditional Leadership and Governance Act of 2005. This is an issue that the Amahlathi community was the first to challenge in court (but not in the numerous provincial and national government commissions constituted to investigate disputes over traditional authority and land). The Amahlathi won their challenge in an order of the Bhisho High Court dated 27 June 2017.

It is evident therefore that apartheid distorted customary law and stripped women of power and headmen of authority. The significance of this distortion of customary law is immense and can be seen through the practical consequences described in the next section.

Hidden in the shadows of 'harmonious' community: Contingency and contestation[11]

The third major point is that the reason women's and headmen's security declines with their loss of power and authority, respectively, is that for both, their security is highly embedded in and contingent on the reciprocal relationships that make up customary communities and their normative frameworks. Moreover, what is presented in South African policy and legislative discourse as an uncontentious relationship between 'senior traditional leaders' and their 'subjects' is rarely that (Mamdani, 1996; Oomen, 2005; Comaroff & Comaroff, 2009; Mnisi Weeks, 2018). In fact, as this section goes on to show, senior traditional leaders are typically engaged in negotiations to protect and enhance their own 'roles and status' (Comaroff & Comaroff, 2009). Making themselves sound more authoritative than they are under existing customary law, or were under pre-colonial norms, aids their endeavours to extend and entrench their powers in and through formal law.

The context in which women and headmen (actually, all people living in customary communities) negotiate for greater rights under customary law is worth describing in some detail here. This context is one where the law comprises a range of rights and duties and the rule that prevails is negotiated on a case-by-case basis, depending on the needs of the people involved in a particular real-life scenario. This is what scholars (Mbatha, 2002; Himonga, 2005; Bennett, 2008; Claassens & Mnisi, 2009; Mnisi Weeks & Claassens, 2011; Cousins, 2011) and the Constitutional Court refer to as 'living customary law'.

This point has been demonstrated by John Comaroff and Simon Roberts in their work, *Rules and Processes* (1981). In essence, they show that living customary law (in their study, Tswana '*mekgwa le melao*') is made up of a 'normative repertoire', which is a variegated set of norms drawn from a general, undifferentiated repertoire. This means that there is a multitude of norms that exist at different levels of specificity and generality; these norms may even contradict one another but the contradictions are resolved by interpreting some norms figuratively (that is, elevating the norms to the metaphorical or symbolic level as opposed to enforcing them literally). This determination – that is, the differentiation of an otherwise 'undifferentiated repertoire of norms' – is made on the basis of each particular situation (Comaroff & Roberts, 1981).

There are obviously certain norms that enjoy wide social acceptance, and these are typically complied with and regarded as obligatory, but this may change over time as the community's lived reality and demands shift. Thus, the specific weight of most norms is meaningfully determined only in relation to the situation in which the norms are invoked. This means that a particular – even widely held – norm does not *necessarily* determine the outcome of dispute. Of course there are some non-negotiable norms, but these are not determined by any individual but rather are typically evident in practice. Yet it is also true that while norms are generally negotiable and offer some room for manoeuvre to the authorities overseeing dispute resolution, norms are not *completely* non-determinant of outcomes. This is one of the fundamental tensions that must be resolved with the flexibility inherent in the nature of living customary law (Comaroff & Roberts, 1981).

This fundamental negotiability of the norms constituting living customary law is achieved through what the authors describe as the 'paradigm of argument', which they explain operates as follows in the context of cases under Tswana *'mekgwa le melao'*. The process of resolving a dispute is sometimes devoted primarily to debate over precisely the question of competing norms. Disputing parties, and the authorities managing the dispute, organise their utterances (their statements in their argument) with reference to referential principles (the various norms available for them to select from). Disputes are seldom decided by the prescriptive application of norms alone. Rather, the parties will contrive a 'paradigm of argument' that offers a coherent picture of relevant events and actions, in relation to one or more implicit or explicit normative referents (Comaroff & Roberts, 1981).

The 'paradigm' the parties formulate is case specific, not fixed or predetermined. The complainant will establish the paradigm by ordering the facts around normative referents that may or may not be made explicit. In fact, an individual will not typically refer to norms explicitly, except in the anticipation that his or her opponent will question the characterisation of the dispute offered; the individual will try to erode his or her opponent's paradigm in advance. The other party may then either stay within the paradigm that was established by the complainant – thus, arguing the circumstances of the case – or the respondent may choose to present a competing paradigm while accepting the presented facts. In the latter case, an explicit reference to norms seems necessary because the respondent is imposing a different paradigm on the case, and so attempting to assert control over or change the terms on which the debate is proceeding (Comaroff & Roberts, 1981).

It is evident from this account that the power to negotiate is an essential factor in any party being able to win a dispute under living customary law, and in influencing the ways in which living customary law develops in and through the pronouncements made during dispute resolution (see, for example, Mnisi Weeks, 2011). The necessity of the power to negotiate becomes even more evident when one considers the options the dispute resolution forums are given when presented with competing 'paradigms of argument' (Comaroff & Roberts, 1981) and, hence, presented with competing norms.

In such situations, the authority responsible for resolving the dispute and/or the senior men who are observing the case may (a) accept the paradigm agreed to by the parties (if such agreement exists), (b) choose between the competing ones presented by the parties or (c) impose a completely new paradigm on the disputed issues (Comaroff & Roberts, 1981). If the authority goes with option (b) or (c), then he will most often refer to rules explicitly (though usually indirectly, even then) because they are seeking to legitimise the distinction and justify the finding. The dispute resolution authority may also distinguish the issues and thus apply two or more frames to the case (Comaroff & Roberts, 1981).

Under Tswana *'mekgwa le melao'* (Comaroff & Roberts, 1981), legislative pronouncements can sometimes customarily become part of the normative repertoire of the governed communities when they are endorsed by the traditional authority. However, the legitimacy and execution of these pronouncements depend on their:

- reflecting public opinion,
- being delivered by an authority considered legitimate, and
- being of utility to individuals in the circumstances in which they might be raised (Comaroff & Roberts, 1981).

This is fundamentally different from the claim of their being determinative merely at the sovereign's say-so – the latter being the way in which state law is deemed authoritative.

It is therefore significant when customary authorities speak of their legislative rules as 'determinative', in order to advance their claims to institutional legitimacy. This is because the argument that their legislative pronouncements are unconditionally authoritative gives more law-making authority than they have under living customary law, and when they succeed at having it enacted in state legislation it is extremely difficult to overcome. These claims to authority are therefore usually made at the expense of the authority of ordinary rural people to create and observe living customary law based on their values, choices and evolving practices. Again, this is a fundamental disruption of the delicate power balance that is essential to living customary law, and makes living customary law the effective legal system that it can be when it is honoured in its true essence as described above.[12]

Entwined power and the vulnerability of women

Make Mdala's case was brought by her birth family to the traditional council as a claim against her in-laws for reimbursement of the cows that had lobola'd (that is, paid bridewealth for) Make Mdala's child. The grounds for the claim were articulated as being that Make Mdala had not been lobola'd and yet the deceased's family had made her wear inzilo *(the mourning outfit) for the deceased and taken her through* kumeketa *(the terminal marriage ceremony). The deceased's family objected and said Make Mdala should lobola herself with the money she was earning from her husband's death (through the formal inheritance process of the Magistrate's Court). At the traditional council, the deceased's, Myeni's, family lost the case because, as it was pronounced, a woman does not wear mourning clothes when she has not yet been lobola'd. Moreover, the traditional council said Make Mdala had moved into the marital home as a wife-to-be with permission from her husband's family; she had then not been lobola'd even though she had birthed a (girl) child who was married and lobola'd. The child's (paternal) grandparents had taken the lobolo cows and enjoyed them but the child's mother had not been lobola'd. As one female member of the council definitively pronounced, 'The cows [that had lobola'd Make Mdala's daughter] were supposed to go and lobola [the girl's] mother – this is what the traditional law requires.'[13]*

The case presented in this section is that the balance of power in traditional communities is delicate. Women's security, in particular, is vulnerable to the shifts in this delicate balance because of the fragility and contingency of women's control over the security and strength of their relationships. That is, women's security declines with their loss of power to negotiate, because women's security is highly embedded in and contingent on the reciprocal relationships that make up customary communities and rights under the normative frameworks that prevail in these groups.

How do we apply the understanding articulated above of the nature of living customary law to women's ability to ensure their livelihoods and their general security within their local communities? The argument has previously been made that women extend their security in their local contexts partly by mobilising 'rights' (both customary and constitutional) (Claassens & Mnisi, 2009) as part of their 'paradigms of argument' (Comaroff & Roberts, 1981). They thereby emphasise the aspects of living customary law that accommodate and address their particular needs as experienced within a particular, contemporary context. In this way, women may also explicitly or implicitly develop the applicability of both living customary law and constitutional rights to their lives (Claassens & Ngubane, 2008; Claassens & Mnisi, 2009; Mnisi Weeks & Claassens, 2011).

Thus, when women mobilise 'human rights' they typically do so in relational ways that emphasise that autonomy is achieved through positive relationships that strengthen them, rather than in the individualist sense in which human rights are typically conceived of in the West (Mamdani, 1990; Nedelsky 1993; Lacey, 2004; Nyamu-Musembi, 2005). Hence, using rights as part of their 'paradigms of argument' within customary law is a coherent approach for them because customary law tends to emphasise relationships over individuals and interdependence over independence (Claassens & Ngubane, 2008; Claassens & Mnisi, 2009; Mnisi Weeks & Claassens, 2011). Yet, at the end of the day, women are only able to negotiate their security effectively in these terms – that is, introduce and defend 'paradigms of argument' that draw on values within customary law that support their wellbeing and security and that of their children and families – if they have the power (recognised as legitimate) with which to do so (McClendon, 1995; Curren & Bonthuys, 2005; Claassens & Mnisi, 2009; Mnisi Weeks, 2016).

As discussed in greater detail below, one observes a difference in rates of participation between lower-level and higher-level vernacular dispute management forums (Mnisi Weeks, 2015a; Mnisi Weeks,

2018). This coincides with the observation made as early as the mid-20th century that increasing formalisation of the forums results in increased alienation from the forums within the community (Hailey, 1953). Hence, the role of ordinary members of the vernacular grouping (customary community) diminishes the higher up one goes in the forum system (Mnisi Weeks, 2015a; Mnisi Weeks, 2018).

As shown, at least in part, initially colonial law deliberately engineered this formalisation in order to centralise authority in the 'chief' (and, to a much lesser degree, the 'chief's council'). Interestingly, what has resulted is a gaping chasm between the processes in the headmen's and the senior traditional leaders' forums (Mnisi Weeks, 2015a; Mnisi Weeks, 2018). One manifestation of this difference is that women have a little bit more ability to participate effectively in the headmen's forums (Mnisi Weeks, 2018). Of course, the membership of vernacular dispute management forums (or traditional courts) is mainly male and a man, who is the key authority figure for the social unit that the forum serves, typically chairs each forum (Mnisi Weeks, 2016; Mnisi Weeks, 2018). In this sense, these forums retain their patriarchal nature and women are still substantially excluded from this process, resulting in their voices not being well represented in the development of the normative repertoire in their communities.

Nonetheless, lower forums typically allow greater independent female involvement due to the forums' less formal Constitution and procedure, though the forums vary in how much female participation they each allow (Mnisi Weeks, 2016; Mnisi Weeks, 2018). Ultimately, these highly significant dimensions of dispute management suggest that interpersonal and professional relationships premised on social trust are critical to the vernacular dispute management system's strengths and weaknesses. They also suggest that such important matters as how much say women have in the development of local norms should not be left to the whims of individual traditional leaders or to the culture of female non-participation that develops in each sub-community, but should be firmly directed by law and policy (Mnisi Weeks, 2015a; Mnisi Weeks, 2016; Mnisi Weeks, 2018).

Entwined authority and the vulnerability of headmen

Nduna Mshushisi presented as very confident and was regarded as authoritative even by other headmen in his traditional community, some of whom consulted him on how they should settle their own confounding matters at times. In disputes before the chief's council, Nduna Mshushisi was often the foremost interrogator. With his powerful voice and above-average height, he cast such an authoritative shadow over proceedings that one might have mistaken him for the chief headman. Or one might have mistaken him for umshushisi *(prosecutor), which is how one chief headman had described the role that the chief headman is required to play in dispute proceedings. Suffice it to say, Nduna Mshushisi was strong. Yet, that did not make him invulnerable. During the 11 months of my team's data collection, he reported the least dispute management incidents of all six headmen concerning whom we were collecting data daily, and most of the matters were minor. Yet two key conflicts that Nduna Mshushisi had managed and did report to us were ones that dealt with intense violence. After the period of our data collection, our NGO partner informed us that, on 13 February 2016, Nduna Mshushisi had been assassinated in broad daylight. According to our NGO partner's annual report, 'he was the third induna [in his traditional community] to be killed in six months, a tally that makes it difficult to find a replacement for the job'.[14]*

To illustrate how headmen's authority and vulnerability are entwined in practice, I delve deeply into the example of headmen in Msinga. The composition of vernacular dispute management forums there and the restraint with which the local headmen conduct themselves must be read against the historical background of traditional male roles in Zulu communities. It is well known that precolonial Zulu society was patriarchal and, moreover, that men were also ranked according to a hierarchy based primarily on age, in terms of which older men received greater respect than those who were younger (Guy, 1990; Hunter, 2005; Carton & Morrell, 2012).

As Benedict Carton and Robert Morrell (2012) describe, emphasis was placed on patriarchal honour and morality – specifically, 'household honour' entailing 'patience, sobriety and wisdom'. Responsibility to relatives and peers was prized because agrarian Zulu society depended on mutual support within and between households for its survival and health (Carton & Morrell, 2012: 41–42). Carton and Morrell explain that 'guiding idioms of the Zulu kingdom promoted subsistence – not 'man slaying' – with one particular metaphor, *isbuko sikababa*, inspiring herd boys (the proto-stick fighters) 'to mirror' the 'gravitas' of their fathers who oversaw homestead production' (Carton & Morrell, 2012: 41). These authors conclude that, in terms of precolonial ideals, 'all people, young and old, were expected first to uphold life-affirming heroic and house-holder traditions that preserved domestic security' (Carton & Morrell; 2012: 42).

As these and other authors such as Mark Hunter (2005) observe, with time 'man slaying' (Carton & Morrell, 2012: 41–42) has come to acquire prominence in Zulu communities' dominant conceptions of masculinity. This change co-occurred with two dynamics that manifested almost concurrently. On the one hand, African men were co-opted by the state as it sought to tighten control over women and their sexuality. On the other hand, the changing economy and forced labour migration made it ever more difficult for men to maintain a strong household as required by the Zulu masculine ideal (Hunter, 2005: 394). These factors, along with men's participation in urbanisation due to the circumstances they found themselves in, did not render obsolete traditional beliefs about manhood, which revolved around the centrality of marriage and the establishment of a homestead. However, they did contribute to the development of male practices that presented competing conceptions of masculinity (Hunter, 2005: 397).

The restraint shown by headmen as they approach their role must be understood against this background. The headmen approach their roles both in practice and in speech in ways that hearken back to the traditional values that undergirded Zulu society until the mid-20th century, during which time the headmen were born and raised in the area. Indeed, the headmen came of age before the crisis of Zulu masculinity hit its peak in the 1980s (Hunter, 2005). They therefore approach their role as that of safeguarding the legacy with which their grandfathers entrusted them.

The challenge is that things have changed more than they are able or willing to recognise and accept (Campbell, 1992; Hunter, 2005; Mnisi Weeks, 2018). Their approach therefore rubs against the reality and demands of the historical moment, which presents a social context that is vastly different from the context in which their grandfathers lived. Nonetheless, the headmen fail to fully confront this challenge and largely behave as though they can take for granted that those in their charge more than notionally share their beliefs about Zulu gender identity – especially masculinity (Mnisi Weeks, 2015a; Mnisi Weeks, 2018). As the headmen attempt to realise the historical vision of Zulu society given to them by their forefathers, using 'time-tested' methods to perform their role, they are falling further and further out of step with the increasingly challenging contemporary circumstances (Mnisi Weeks, 2015a; Mnisi Weeks, 2018).

The result is a tension between the headmen and their sons' generation that mirrors the tension described by scholars between fathers and sons today (Campbell, 1992; Mchunu, 2007). In brief, fathers largely committed to the ways of old (and, likewise, committed to traditional governance institutions) experience alienation (Marx, 1988; Mészáros, 1970) from having been emasculated by the unemployment and poverty that resulted from the oppressive systems of colonialism and apartheid (Campbell, 1992; Hunter, 2005; Mchunu, 2007). They may self-medicate with alcohol, and sometimes seek comfort in multiple sexual partners or relieve their frustration and try to reclaim their agency through violence. Their sons – many illegitimate or raised by their mothers alone – emerge ambivalent about tradition as they too are demoralised by unemployment and lack faith in institutions. They therefore also widely engage in alcohol abuse, extramarital sex, violence and crime (Campbell, 1992; Hunter, 2005; Mchunu, 2007; Mentjes, 2017; Mnisi Weeks, 2018).

Even though they share the experience of alienation due to political economic causes, there is tension between older and younger men in this context (alienation from each other). Specifically, the older men feel unable to control or even reach the younger generation who they experience as undisciplined. The younger generation feel misunderstood, abandoned and let down by the same older generation who would impose what they perceive as failed notions of masculinity, tradition and order. These younger men also reject the structures that would seek to control – and from their perspective, further repress – them (Campbell, 1992; Hunter, 2005; Mchunu, 2007; Smith, 2015; Mnisi Weeks, 2018).

Symbolising the traditional systems of constraint and the attempts of the older generation to control the younger generation, the headmen are, in many ways, located at the centre of the divide between younger and older men (Mnisi Weeks, 2018). Indeed, the striking symbolism of the generational division in the midst of which the headmen stand is made palpable when one of the young male perpetrators who assassinated a headman shouts the words, '*Babulaleni bonke, bayizinja!*' ('Kill them all, they are dogs!'). This was the case in 2016 when Nduna Mshushisi was killed – reportedly the third headman in six months to be murdered (Mnisi Weeks, 2018).[15]

The fundamental point here is that the internal cultural disparities – shaped by history – between the headmen and the people they serve indicate the necessity for the headmen to re-evaluate their propensity to cater to the 'traditional ideal' of what gender identities should look like in Msinga. Such re-evaluation would hopefully result in a reform of how the headmen carry out their function of leading dispute management in customary communities.

Summary

In essence, then, for both women and headmen, their power or authority and vulnerability are entwined. Women's security is embedded in and contingent on the reciprocal relationships and rights within customary communities. Arguably, to a significant extent, headmen's security is also embedded in and contingent on the reciprocal relationships and rights within customary communities.

Evidently, in contexts such as these, relationships are the seedbed of both security and vulnerability. For women, the power they possess or have access to is the key determinant of whether their relationships will yield security or vulnerability. The moral authority the headmen possess, which is based on personal affiliation and the strength of the gendered and generational relations within their communities, is essential to the amount of security they are able to ensure for themselves and others. For both women and headmen, outcomes of their negotiations for security are also contingent upon broader socio-economic factors such as social fabric and social trust, which in turn are significantly determined or affected by political economy.

Customary law legislation passed by pre- and post-1994 governments changed the balance of power in favour of male minorities and particularly senior traditional leaders, which does not bode well for rural women and lower-level traditional leaders. If the law were to accept that the dream of harmony is a rarity and its projection highly political (Gluckmann, 1955; Bohannan, 1957; Nader, 1960; Gulliver, 1963; Gibbs, 1963; Aubert, 1969; Abel, 1982; Schweitzer, 1996; Nader, 1996; 1991; 1990), and furthermore that negotiation is the more common and persistent reality, then it would have to embrace the reality that power is central to the nature of customary law, justice and security. Likewise, if the South African legislature were to account for the discrepancies between what it espouses and what it does in practice (or what it says it aspires to achieve and what it actually accomplishes), it would then also have to acknowledge that the interests that serve senior traditional leaders often fail to serve not just ordinary people but also lower-level traditional leaders such as headmen. This reality demands that the government reorients its attention and alliance and makes provision for a redistribution of power and a reorientation of authority in rural communities from top-down to bottom-up (Okoth-Ogendo, 2008).

Put differently, what if the government were to stop legislating on the basis of the illusory presumption that traditional communities are simplistically harmonious and peaceful, with only *minor* conflicts for which reconciliation is sought? What if government were to acknowledge that, at least in some rural communities, the political economy of the last centuries has led to *severe* ruptures in the social fabric? On the wall of one Msinga home I took a photograph of a plaque displayed that says:

Kubi okwenza kimi;
Ungeke uthole lutho;
Udlala ngesikhathi sakho,
Muntu wakithi.[16]

It roughly translates as follows:

It is terrible, what you are doing to me;
You will not get anything (out of it),
You are wasting your time,
My friend/relative.

What if hidden in the shadows of 'harmonious' rural communities are contestation and serious contingencies that need to be given voice if healthy social conditions are ever to be achieved?

Laws change the balance of power within which women and (head)men negotiate unavoidable changes

When the family of the deceased (Myeni), took his first wife, Make Mdala, to the Magistrate's Court – hoping to receive some death benefits through her – and Make Musha produced a marriage certificate, the deceased's family turned against Make Mdala, who did not have written proof of her marriage, and asked her who had married her and Myeni. With the Recognition of Customary Marriages Act 120 of 1998 in place, Make Mdala was able to receive her due. When her family brought a customary challenge against deceased Myeni's family, the latter objected, saying that Make Mdala should lobola herself with the money she was earning from her husband's death. Evidently, the laws of inheritance were having a significant influence on social interactions in this case and impacting on Make

Mdala's ability to negotiate her material and social security.[17]

This section details the ways in which legislation passed by the post-1994 government of South Africa has affected the ways in which women and headmen navigate the changes that are taking place in their communities. Study participants in Mbuzini who recognised tensions surrounding the roles of senior and lower-level traditional leaders and the internal resistance traditional leadership faced in their community were asked why 'chiefs' themselves were not rendered perpetually insecure by these tensions. The explanation they gave was that it had been made evident to the factions that oppose *bukhosi* (royalty) that government supports *emakhosi* (chiefs/senior traditional leaders). According to these interlocutors, all members of their traditional community generally understood that government power is behind senior traditional leaders.

The overarching political parameters that are enacted in law alter the balance of power that determines how women and men negotiate their norms under living customary law and negotiate changes in their social and material existences (Oomen, 2005; Mnisi Weeks & Claassens, 2011). In most cases, women come out as the losers under these laws. This impact is clearly shown by two laws that the government either enacted (the Communal Land Rights Act No. 11 of 2004, which was struck down in 2010 as unconstitutional by the Constitutional Court) or attempted to pass but met with public resistance (the Traditional Courts Bill B18-2008/B1-2012). These overarching political and legal parameters also delineate the possibilities for headmen to carry out their charge of leading dispute management and limit the prospects of their success.

Women stood to lose under the Communal Land Rights Act (CLRA) in several ways. With radically declining marriage rates in rural areas, single women make up large (and growing) numbers of rural women (Claassens & Ngubane, 2008; Mhongo & Budlender 2013; Claassens, 2013). Yet, they would have been excluded from benefitting in terms of registration of land under the CLRA, which only referred to married women. Furthermore, even though married women were provided for under the CLRA, it was only in the context of joint registration of property with their husbands, which would mean that even property that the women had on their own would have to be shared with their husbands. This would potentially have had negative consequences for these women's pre-marital children as well (see Mnisi Weeks, 2015b). Women also would not necessarily have been guaranteed a part in decision-making bodies that determined customary land rights under the CLRA since this was not specifically mandated.

Women stood to lose under the Traditional Courts Bill B18-2008/B1-2012 (TCB 2008/2012), and may still do in certain instances under the Traditional Courts Bill B1-2017 (TCB 2017), in the following ways: women were not assured of membership of traditional courts under the TCB 2008/2012 and, now that the Portfolio Committee on Justice and Correctional Services has mandated the Department of Justice and Correctional Services to remove the requirement in the TCB 2017 that women be included as members of traditional courts, there may not even be the single 'token' woman that might otherwise have been included in some courts.[18]

Women were not guaranteed self-representation (or attendance) in courts in the TCB 2008/2012. Regardless of the problems mentioned earlier faced by women in mourning, such as evictions, the TCB 2008/2012 said that husbands could represent wives just as wives could represent husbands 'according to customary law' (clause 9(3)(b)). In other words, men could continue representing women, even in inheritance, and since women have never been permitted to represent men in traditional courts this was a false comparison. Clause 9(2)(a)(i) paid lip service to formal equality but the TCB 2008/2012 as a whole entrenched unequal power relations. The TCB 2008/2012 would therefore have silenced women's voices even where they were beginning to be heard. Moreover, issues affecting women's land rights were not excluded from traditional court jurisdiction (e.g. land matters or succession) under the TCB 2008/2012. The TCB 2017 allows for traditional courts to provide 'advice relating to customary law practices in respect of ... (v) succession and inheritance'. However, it is not clear what the parameters for 'advice' are. Without these parameters, it is difficult for women to assess the il/legality of the traditional courts' conduct in a given succession or inheritance dispute, on which the traditional court has provided 'advice'.

More insidious still, the TCB 2017 is based on the fallacious harmony model (Nader, 1990) – thus assuming voluntariness, consensus and reconciliation within communities that I have shown are not always of that default description. This is in many ways an improvement on the TCB 2008/2012, which largely awarded vernacular dispute management forums similar powers to state courts, but provided nowhere near the same degree of requirements for accountability and safeguards to which the state courts are subject. However, the 2017 bill does not abandon the misguided idea of traditional communities as simplistically harmonious and peaceful, which means that it does not provide for traditional communities' true needs; on the contrary, it denies many of them, especially the security needs of women and headmen. Furthermore, directions given to the Department of Justice by the Portfolio Committee in August 2018 will result in the removal of measures of accountability in the TCB 2017.[19]

Under the TCB 2008/2012, lower courts would not have been recognised – only the courts sitting at the level of 'traditional community', and hence 'chief's courts' (Mnisi Weeks, 2012). Headmen would only have been permitted to 'preside' over that court in the senior traditional leader's absence, and to do so at the bidding of the senior traditional leader and with written permission from the then minister of Justice and Constitutional Development. The TCB 2017 attempts to remedy this by allowing headmen to have their own courts, but it still centralises the 'convening' of traditional courts and prescribes that the 'delegation' of power or authority for decision making is to devolve downwards from the senior traditional leader. It does this by assuming that government will issue credentials.

Presumably to occur under the TLGFA, this credentialing would continue the legacy of apartheid 'tribal leaders' and 'tribal authorities' by relying on section 28. This now-permanent, though still allegedly 'transitional', set of provisions allows the institutions that were invented and/or distorted by apartheid to continue and to pass power and authority downwards to lower institutions like the headmen. In practical terms, this means that lower-level courts could not be established independently of an existing, recognised 'traditional community' with a formally recognised 'senior traditional leader' presiding over it. In other words, vernacular dispute management forums could not come into being – or be recognised as having done so – (a) if they evolved organically, from the bottom up, in the absence of 'delegation' of authority to manage disputes from the 'senior traditional leader'; or (b) if they developed and functioned in an acephalous customary community.

Furthermore, this grounding of the TCB 2017 on the TLGFA's section 28 amounts to the formalisation of these informal forums. I described above how increased formalisation had a negative impact on the participation of ordinary people, and especially women. Unfortunately, the TCB 2017 would not improve or address this as it is a rather technical document reliant on formalistic procedures and judicial and legal criteria for legitimacy. Additionally, the Portfolio Committee's decision in August 2018 to have 'traditional courts' in the TCB 2017 be recognised as 'courts' under section 166(e) of the Constitution further formalises these forums which are, in reality, mediated spaces for negotiation. More disconcerting still, in late 2018, the TLGFA is expected to be replaced by the Traditional and Khoi-San Leadership Bill (B23-2015) (TKLB), which is even more deeply entrenched in the colonial and apartheid imagination of traditional leadership, further centralising power in traditional communities in senior traditional leaders.

The TCB 2017 assumes jurisdictions based on fixed apartheid boundaries which have similar foundations to 'tribal authorities'. With respect to the re-perpetuation of external 'traditional community' boundaries fixed by the apartheid government in particular, the TLGFA (and, building on it, the TCB 2017) further undermine the authority of headmen and their ability to resolve disputes. This is because much of the conflict that arises locally is due to the fixity and location of these boundaries, which go against the grain of customary communities. The TKLB would not provide any relief here. Moreover, the Portfolio Committee's August 2018 decision to do away with allowing people to opt out of 'traditional court' jurisdiction in the TCB 2017 will only exacerbate local conflict (see Mnisi Weeks, 2015a).

These laws – that is, laws such as the TLGFA (and TKLB), CLRA and TCB – entrench the shifts brought about by apartheid distortions and impositions (as discussed earlier in this chapter). The legislation does this at the expense of the possibility of shifting the balance of power more in favour of women, and enabling bottom-up authority to be imparted to headmen as fitting, both of which would be a corrective for the distortions introduced by colonialism and apartheid. The same laws fail at their stated task of giving effect to the living customary law. As I have described, this law is highly adaptable by nature, and can therefore enable women, subject to a very delicate balance of power, to ensure greater security and potentially allow headmen to respond appropriately to the complex demands of their work in the present age.

Conclusion: Lessons for government regulation

As Ben Cousins and others (2011: 58, 68–69) argue and conclude:

- wider social dynamics in favour of women's equality can have a significant impact on women's ability to negotiate greater equality locally under living customary law,
- women's representation on local traditional decision-making bodies can do the same, and
- space for women to speak, and for their voices to be taken seriously, within local institutions is an important factor in women's ability to achieve greater security under traditional leadership and living customary law.

The argument I have advanced in this chapter is that power lies at the foundation of all three of these preconditions. The wider social dynamics and political symbolism of law can send the signal that women are supported in their local struggles for greater equality and security. Women's representation in local bodies allows women greater roles, power and voice with which to speak in the debates on living customary law, and how it should evolve to respond to changing local needs. This form of legitimacy and power then opens up greater space for women, situated both inside the traditional institutions and outside of them, to be taken seriously when they speak about their circumstances and needs. Power is therefore at the core of everything that affects women's security in traditional communities.

As shown, the laws passed by South Africa's democratic government undermine the power that women had under customary law. These laws also undermine the power women had been able to acquire through the Constitution's equality clause, which had temporarily made clear that government supported women's equality. These laws shift power dynamics in rural areas so that women are no longer able to use the flexibility and negotiability of living customary law to negotiate greater security for themselves where they are situated. They therefore return women to the disempowerment, disenfranchisement and dispossession they suffered under colonialism and apartheid. By also ignoring women's realities – such as the extent to which marriage rates have declined and are continuing to do so – these laws put women's existences and those of their children and families at risk. In fact, they threaten women's livelihoods directly.

The provisions pertaining to women in laws such as the CLRA and the TCB exemplify the ways in which the law fails to provide for women's need for equality and security. Even when the democratic government's laws on traditional leadership and customary law do try to give a small boost to women's equality – as in the one third quota for traditional councils enunciated by the TLGFA – these provisions are not implemented and are therefore rendered ineffectual.

Changes in legislation, and in implementation, are necessary to address women's side of the equation. These changes include government ensuring women's equal representation in decision-making bodies in traditional communities. I spoke to one young woman and her friend in Mbuzini. Although they had never been inside *libandla* (the chief's council), she was pleased that there are women there to represent her. She noted that:

> there are people chosen to come and listen to cases here and otherwise we don't come. And now they have women too. Before, anyone could come and listen and women could come

but they could not answer; but now they can listen and answer, and share their views. This helps because if I, being a woman, come into a problem that leads to my appearing here, it may reach a point where I feel intimidated to raise it with only men and, even if I can see that they are oppressing me, I might not be able to say that they are oppressing me, but if there are women there, I, being a woman, gain strength to declare my problem.[20]

Similarly, government should ensure that women – who make up 59 per cent of people living under traditional leadership (Mhongo & Budlender, 2013) – are always robustly consulted in the making of laws for customary communities. Women have not been consulted in the past.

Gender matters are *power* matters. The fact is that, as the Constitutional Court said in *Tongoane v National Minister for Agriculture and Land Affairs* 2010 (6) SA 214 (CC), when government passes legislation regarding customary law, it can safely assume that it is *not* intervening in a vacuum.

> The field that CLARA[21] now seeks to cover is not unoccupied. There is at present a system of law that regulates the use, occupation and administration of communal land. This system also regulates the powers and functions of traditional leaders in relation to communal land. It is this system which CLARA will repeal, replace or amend ... CLARA replaces the living indigenous law regime which regulates the occupation, use and administration of communal land. It replaces both the institutions that regulated these matters and their corresponding rules. CLARA also gives traditional councils new wide-ranging powers and functions (see paragraphs 79 and 96).

It is clear, therefore, that the government can assume that it is disturbing whatever power balance is in place right now. Thus the question is always: which constituencies will government engender with power through its laws, and to what degree?

Laws meant to govern traditional communities should be tailored to the reality of the political economy of rural areas wherein women are not just (or even primarily) wives, and headmen are caught in the crosshairs of the generational tensions between older and younger men in their communities. Not only that, it is clear that the casual aggregation of 'traditional leaders' in policy discussions creates the false impression that 'senior traditional leaders' and lower-level 'traditional leaders' like headmen have identical interests. This chapter has rather argued that the headmen's interests are more accurately seen as aligned with those of women and other ordinary members of their communities who are marginalised members of rural society.

The legislative agenda developed by the South African government is an indictment of its lack of commitment to women's full equality. It shows how the government is complicit in perpetuating conditions that deprive women of full and equal citizenship. As this chapter has argued, the government can be said to have similarly failed to show commitment to the equality of headmen. Furthermore, it is not just that the disregard the government shows for women and headmen is similar, but that the source thereof is largely the same and, hence, the forms of neglect shown by the government to both groups are deeply entwined and mutually reinforcing. The proposal here is essentially that the government is looking in the wrong place for solutions to the problems of people living in rural areas. It assumes that the solution is to centralise and formalise power and authority in senior traditional leaders through legislation (Oomen, 2005), but the solution appears to lie elsewhere entirely.

In order to address the issues I have described above, the government – rather than blindly assuming communal harmony exists – should aim to strengthen relationships in customary communities by empowering vulnerable parties to enable effective negotiation. Government should also permit dispute management authority to come into being independently of the existence or formal recognition of a 'senior traditional leader' in law. Again, it is worth noting that such recognition of the bottom-up authority of customary communities and traditional leaders would effectively undo the legacy of colonial decisions like that in *Makapan v Khope* (1912).

Furthermore, my suggestion is that the government can achieve these changes by means of strengthening, firstly, the power of ordinary people (especially women) and, secondly, the ability of headmen to draw upon the bottom-up authority of lower-level traditional institutions (that is, the authority imparted by their constituents). Such interventions would better allow both women and headmen to negotiate greater security within the context of their respective interpersonal and social relationships. Taking this approach requires passing and implementing laws that place women in influential positions, such as traditional councils, and jettisoning the apartheid model of customary communities that is based on externally fixed boundaries and centralised models of traditional leadership concentrated in 'senior traditional leaders'.

References

Abel, R. L. 1982. 'The contradictions of informal justice'. *The Politics of Informal Justice (1st Edition)*. Cambridge: Cambridge University Press, pp. 267–320.

Aubert, C. 1969. *Sociology of Law*. London: Penguin.

Bennett, T. 2008. 'Official vs living customary law: Dilemmas of description and recognition', in Claassens, A. & Cousins, B. (eds.) *Land, Power and Custom: Controversies generated by South Africa's Communal Land Rights Act*. Cape Town: UCT Press, pp. 138–153.

Bohannan, P. 1957. *Judgement and Justice Among the Tiv*. London: Oxford University Press, pp. 491–503.

Budlender, D., Mgweba, S., Motsepe, K. & Williams, L. 2011. 'Women, land and customary law'. *Centre for Law and Society* website: www.cls.uct.ac.za/usr/lrg/downloads/Women_and_Land.pdf, accessed 24 July 2018.

Campbell, C. 1992. 'Learning to kill? Masculinity, the family and violence in Natal'. *Journal of Southern African Studies*, 18 (3), 614–628.

Carton, B. & Morrell, R. 2012. 'Zulu masculinities, warrior culture and stick fighting: Reassessing male violence and virtue in South Africa'. *Journal of Southern African Studies*, 38 (1), 31–53.

Claassens, A. 2013. 'Recent changes in women's land rights and contested customary law in South Africa'. *Journal of Agrarian Change,* 13 (1), 71–92.

Claassens, A. & Mnisi, S. 2009. 'Rural women redefining land rights in the context of living customary law'. *South African Journal on Human Rights*, 25 (3), 491–516.

Claassens, A. & Ngubane, S. 2008. 'Women, land and power: The impact of the Communal Land Rights Act', in Claassens, A. & Cousins, B. (eds.) *Land, Power and Custom: Controversies generated by South Africa's Communal Land Rights Act*. Cape Town: UCT Press, pp. 154–183.

Clegg, J. 1981. 'Ukubuyisa isidumbu – "bringing back the body": An examination into the ideology of vengeance in the Msinga and Mpofana rural locations (1882–1944)', in Bonner, P. (ed.) *Working Papers in Southern African Studies*: Vol. 2. Johannesburg: Ravan Press, pp. 164–198.

Comaroff, J. L. & Comaroff, J. 2009. *Ethnicity Inc*. Chicago: University of Chicago Press.

Comaroff, J. & Roberts, S. 1977. 'Marriage and extra-marital sexuality: The dialectic of legal change among the Kgatla'. *Journal of African Law*, 21 (1), 97–123.

Comaroff, J. & Roberts, S. 1981. *Rules and Processes: The cultural logic of dispute in an African context*. Chicago: University of Chicago Press.

Comaroff, J. L. & Roberts, S. A. 1986. *Rules and Processes*. Chicago: University of Chicago Press.

Communal Land Rights Act No. 11 of 2004. 20 July 2004, http://www.saflii. org/za/legis/num_act/clra2004207.pdf.

Cousins, B. 2011. 'Imithetho yomhlaba yaseMsinga: The living law of land in Msinga, KwaZulu-Natal'. *Research Report-PLAAS*, 43. UWC website: https://repository.uwc.ac.za/bitstream/handle/10566/390/Cousins LandMsinga2011.pdf?sequence=1&isAllowed=y, accessed 15 September 2018.

Curran, E. & Bonthuys, E. 2005. 'Customary law and domestic violence in rural South African communities'. *South African Journal on Human Rights*, 21 (4), 607–635.

Gibbs, J. L. 1963. 'The Kpelle moot: A therapeutic model for the informal settlement of disputes'. *Africa*, 33 (1), 1–11.

Gluckman, M. 1955. 'The peace in the feud'. *Past & Present*, 8, 1–14.

Griffiths, A.M. 1997. *In The Shadow of Marriage: Gender and justice in an African community*. Chicago: University of Chicago Press.

Griffiths, A. 1998. 'Reconfiguring law: An ethnographic perspective from Botswana'. *Law & Social Inquiry*, 23 (3), 587–620.

Gulliver, P. H. 1963. *Social Control in an African Society: A study of the Arusha: Agricultural Masai of Northern Tanganyika*. New York: New York University Press.

Gumede (born Shange) v President of the Republic of South Africa and Others 2009 (3) SA 152 (CC).

Guy, J. 1990. 'Gender oppression in southern Africa's pre-capitalist societies', in Walker, C. (ed.) *Women and Gender in Southern Africa to 1945*. Claremont: David Philip Publishers, pp. 33–48.

Hailey, W. M. 1953. *Native Administration in the British African Territories: The high commission territories: Basutoland, the Bechuanaland protectorate and Swaziland*: Part V. London: Her Majesty's Stationery Office.

Higgins, T. E., Fenrich, J. & Tanzer, Z. 2006. 'Gender equality and customary marriage: Bargaining in the shadow of post-apartheid'. *Fordham International Law Journal Legal Pluralism*, 30 (6) 1, 1653–1708.

Himonga, C. 2005. 'The advancement of African women's rights in the first decade of democracy in South Africa: The reform of the customary law of marriage and succession'. *Acta Juridica*, 1, 82–107.

Hunter, M. 2005. 'Cultural politics and masculinities: Multiple-partners in historical perspective in KwaZulu-Natal'. *Culture, Health & Sexuality*, 7 (3), 209–223.

Kingwill, R. 2008. 'Custom-building freehold title: The impact of family values on historical ownership in the Eastern Cape', in Claassens, A. & Cousins, B. (eds.) *Land, Power and Custom: Controversies generated by South Africa's Communal Land Rights Act*. Cape Town: UCT Press, pp. 184–208.

KwaZulu Act on the Code of Zulu Law No. 16 of 1985.

Lacey, N. 2004. *Feminist Legal Theories and the Rights of Women*: No. XII/2. Oxford: Oxford University Press, pp. 13–56.

Makapan v Khope 1923 AD 551.

Mamdani, M. 1990. 'The social basis of constitutionalism in Africa'. *The Journal of Modern African Studies*, 28 (3), 359–374.

Mamdani, M. 1996. *Citizen and Subject: Contemporary Africa and the legacy of late colonialism*. Princeton: Princeton University Press.

Marx, K. 1988. *Economic and Philosophical Manuscripts of 1844*. New York: Prometheus Books.

Mayelane v Ngwenyama and Another 2013 (4) SA 415 (CC).

Mbatha, L. 2002. 'Reforming the customary law of succession'. *South African Journal on Human Rights*, 18, 259–286.

McClendon, T. V. 1995. 'Tradition and domestic struggle in the courtroom: Customary law and the control of women in segregation-era Natal'. *The International Journal of African Historical Studies*, 28 (3), 527–561.

Mchunu, M. R. 2007. 'Culture change, Zulu masculinity and intergenerational conflict in the context of civil war in Pietermaritzburg (1987–1991)', in Shefer, T., Ratele, K., Strebel, A., Shabalala, N. & Buikema, R. (eds.) *From Boys to Men: Social constructions of masculinity in contemporary society*. Cape Town: University of Cape Town Press, pp. 225–240.

Meintjes, L. 2017. *Dust of the Zulu: Ngoma aesthetics after apartheid*. Durham: Duke University Press.

Mészáros, I. 1970. *Marx's Theory of Alienation*. London: The Merlin Press.

Mhongo, C. & Budlender, D. 2013. 'Declining rates of marriage in South Africa: What do the numbers and analysts say?' *Acta Juridica*, 1, 181–196.

Mnisi Weeks, S. 2011. 'Securing women's property inheritance in the context of plurality: Negotiations of law and authority in Mbuzini customary courts and beyond'. *Acta Juridica*, 1, 140–173.

Mnisi Weeks, S. 2012. 'Regulating vernacular dispute resolution forums: Controversy concerning the process, substance and implications of South Africa's Traditional Courts Bill'. *Oxford University Commonwealth Law Journal*, 12 (1), 133–155.

Mnisi Weeks, S. 2013. 'Women's eviction in Msinga: The uncertainties of seeking justice'. *Acta Juridica*, 1, 118–142.

Mnisi Weeks, S. 2015a. 'Access to justice? Dispute management processes in Msinga, KwaZulu-Natal, South Africa.' *New York Law School Law Review*, 60, 227–249.

Mnisi Weeks, S. 2015b. 'Customary succession and the development of customary law: The Bhe legacy: Part III: Reflections on themes in Justice Langa's judgments'. *Acta Juridica*, 1, 215–255.

Mnisi Weeks, S. 2016. 'Women seeking justice at the intersections between vernacular and state laws and courts in rural KwaZulu-Natal, South Africa', in Klug, H. & Merry, S. E. (eds.) *The New Legal Realism Vol. 2: Studying law globally*. Cambridge: Cambridge University Press, pp. 113–141.

Mnisi Weeks, S. 2018. *Access to Justice and Human Security: Cultural contradictions in rural South Africa*. Abingdon: Routledge.

Mnisi Weeks, S. & Claassens, A. 2011. 'Tensions between vernacular values that prioritise basic needs and state versions of customary law that contradict them: We love these fields that feed us, but not at the expense of a person'. *Stellenbosch Law Review*, 22 (3), 823–844.

Mokhatle and Others v Union Government (Minister of Native Affairs) 1926 AD 71.

Nader, L. 1969. 'The Zapotec of Oaxaca'. *Handbook of Middle American Indians (Vol. 7 & 8): Ethnology*. Austin: University of Texas Press, pp. 329–359.

Nader, L. 1990. *Harmony Ideology: Justice and control in a Zapotec mountain village*. Stanford: Stanford University Press.

Nader, L. 1991. 'Harmony models and the construction of law', in Black, P. et al. (eds.) *Reformulating Dispute Resolution*. Sydney: Wakeview Press, pp. 41–59.

Nader, L. 1996. 'Coercive harmony: The political economy of legal models'. *Kroeber Anthropological Society Papers*, 80, 1–13.

Natal Code of Zulu Law, published in Proclamation R151 of 1987, GG No. 10966. 3 September 1987, https://www.ncbi.nlm.nih.gov/pubmed/12289657.

Native Administration Act No. 38 of 1927. 30 June 1927, http://uir.unisa.ac.za/bitstream/handle/10500/6648/ZKM_C3_69.pdf?sequence=1, accessed 28 November 2018.

Nedelsky, J. 1993. 'Reconceiving rights as relationship'. *Review of Constitutional Studies*, 1 (1), 1–26.

Nyamu-Musembi, C. 2002. 'Are local norms and practices fences or pathways? The example of women's property rights', in An-Naim, A. (ed.) *Cultural Transformation and Human Rights in Africa*. London/New York: Zed Books, pp. 126–150.

Nyamu-Musembi, C. 2005. 'Towards an actor-oriented perspective on human rights', in Kabeer, N. (ed.) *Inclusive Citizenship: Meanings and expressions*. London/ New York: Zed Books, pp. 31–50.

Okoth-Ogendo, H. W. 2008. 'The nature of land rights under indigenous law in Africa', in Claassens, A. & Cousins, B. (eds.) *Land, Power and Custom: Controversies generated by South Africa's Communal Land Rights Act*. Cape Town: UCT Press, pp. 95–109.

Oomen, B. 2005. *Chiefs in South Africa: Law, culture, and power in the post-apartheid era*. New York: Springer.

Recognition of Customary Marriages Act No. 120 of 1998. 15 November 2000, http://www.lawlibrary.co.za/professionalupdate/2012/03/justice college_recognitionofcustomarymarriages.pdf.

Redding, S. 2004. 'Death in the family: Domestic violence, witchcraft accusations and political militancy in Transkei, South Africa, 1904–1965'. *Journal of South African Studies*, 30 (3), 519–538.

Schweitzer, M. 1996. 'Harmony ideology works at the mill', in Wolfe, A. & Yang, H. (eds.) *Anthropological Contributions to Conflict Resolution*. Athens/London: The University of Georgia Press, pp. 119–131.

Smith, N. R. 2015. 'Rejecting rights: Vigilantism and violence in post-apartheid South Africa', *African Affairs*, 114 (456), 341–360.

Thornberry, E. 2016. 'Ukuthwala, forced marriage, and the idea of custom in South Africa's Eastern Cape', in Bunting, A., Lawrance, B. N. & Roberts, R. L. (eds.) *Marriage by Force? Contestation over consent and coercion*.

Athens: Ohio University Press, pp. 137–159.

Tongoane v National Minister for Agriculture and Land Affairs 2010 (6) SA 214 (CC).

Traditional and Khoi San Leadership Bill B23-2015. 18 September 2016, http://www.cogta.gov.za/cgta_2016/wp-content/uploads/2016/06/TRADITIONAL-AND-KHOI-SAN-LEADERSHIP-BILL.pdf.

Traditional Courts Bill B18-2008/B1-2012. 13 December 2011, http://www.justice.gov.za/legislation/bills/2012-b01tradcourts.pdf.

Traditional Courts Bill B1-2017. 9 December 2016, http://www.justice.gov.za/legislation/bills/2017-TraditionalCourtsBill.pdf.

Traditional Leadership and Governance Framework Act No. 41 of 2003. 11 December 2003, http://www.cogta.gov.za/cgta_2016/wp-content/uploads/2016/06/TLGFA-Traditional-Leadership-and-Governance-Framework-Act-2003-Act-No-41-of-2003.pdf

Venter, T. & Nel, J. 2005. 'African customary law of intestate succession and gender (in) equality'. *Tydskrif vir die Suid-Afrikaanse Reg*, 1, 86–105.

Walker, C. 2009. 'Elusive equality: Women, property rights and land reform in South Africa'. *South African Journal on Human Rights*, 25 (3), 467–490.

Weinberg, T. 2013. 'Contesting customary law in the Eastern Cape: Gender, place and land tenure'. *Acta Juridica*, 1, 100–117.

Whitehead, A. & Tsikata, D. 2003. 'Policy discourses on women's land rights in sub–Saharan Africa: The implications of the return to the customary'. *Journal of Agrarian Change*, 3 (1–2), 67–112.

Yngstrom, I. 2002. 'Women, wives and land rights in Africa: Situating gender beyond the household in the debate over land policy and changing tenure systems'. *Oxford Development Studies*, 30 (1), 21–40.

Notes

1 Also see Walker (2009), according to whom, in 2004, female-headed households made up 44 per cent of rural households.

2 This article is based on empirical research that formed part of a study I completed in Msinga, KwaZulu-Natal for the Rural Women's Action-Research Project while I was a senior researcher in the Centre for Law and Society at the University of Cape Town. The study was conducted between October 2009 and June 2015, with the bulk of data collected between March 2011 and January 2012 (inclusive). Data collection took the form of daily recording of headmen's activities and day-to-day work, observation of traditional dispute management processes such as

dispute hearings that the headmen participated in managing, follow-up interviews with parties to these disputes and traditional authorities, as well as focus groups with the members of the traditional councils and groups of local men and women. Preliminary interviews and observations were conducted from October 2009 to February 2011, and follow-up interviews, focus groups and report-back sessions were conducted from February 2012 to June 2015. The statements made about Mbuzini, in Mpumalanga, and its members are drawn from data collected over a period of eight months in which I conducted ethnographic research by participant observation within this rural, Swati-speaking South African community that is situated close to the Swaziland and Mozambican borders. This research was initially published as Sindiso Mnisi, *The Interface between Living Customary Law(s) of Succession and South African State Law* (2010) (PhD dissertation, University of Oxford) but has since featured in multiple other academic publications.

3   Primarily, in Mbuzini in Mpumalanga and Msinga in KwaZulu-Natal. However, based on the work of other scholars cited herein, I argue that the analysis largely extends to other areas as well.

4   The concept of community is difficult to define, partly because it is very contested. As shown in this chapter, the South African government defines customary communities in terms of their having a formally recognised traditional leader and externally defined boundaries. However, there is plenty of literature that shows that customary definitions of community are fluid, nested and overlapping (Cousins, 2011; Okoth-Ogendo, 2008). As I have argued elsewhere, I am of the view that customary communities should self-identify on a case-by-case basis, as demanded by the circumstances as the members of the self-defined community see it (Mnisi Weeks, 2018; Mnisi Weeks & Claassens, 2011).

5   The names of all participants in the study have been changed to protect their privacy.

6   Interview with MaNovalo, Msinga, KwaZulu-Natal in July 2011

7   Interview with Make Khansela, Mbuzini, Mpumalanga in September 2007

8   Hereinafter, Natal Code. Published in Proclamation R151 of 1987, GG No. 10966

9   KwaZulu Act on the Code of Zulu Law 16 of 1985

10 Interviews with Ndvuna Tigodzi and Ndvunankulu, Mbuzini, Mpumalanga in August and September 2007

11 Refer to Laura Nader's extensive evaluation of how 'harmony' is a fiction that is exploited by both oppressive (colonial) governments and oppressed groups to advance their own political, and coercive, ends. See

Nader, L. 1990. *Harmony Ideology: Justice and control in a Zapotec mountain village.* Stanford: Stanford University Press; Nader, L. 1991. 'Harmony models and the construction of law', in Black, P. et al. (eds.) *Reformulating Dispute Resolution.* Sydney: Wakeview Press, pp. 41–59; Nader, L. 1996. 'Coercive harmony: The political economy of legal models'. *Kroeber Anthropological Society Papers,* 80, 1–13.

12 For further discussion of this subject, see Comaroff and Roberts (1981, especially at 80–83, 180).

13 Interview with Make Khansela, Mbuzini, Mpumalanga in September 2007

14 From fieldwork conducted in Msinga, March 2011–January 2012, and report from Mdukathsani Rural Development Trust annual report, 2015 (accessible at www.mdukatshani.com/ resources/Annual%20report%20 for%20Mrdp%202015%20final.pdf)

15 Refer again to the Mdukathsani Rural Development Trust annual report, 2015

16 No attribution was given.

17 Interview with Make Khansela, Mbuzini, Mpumalanga in September 2007

18 More can be found on this decision: 'Traditional Courts Bill: Deliberations – Justice and Correctional Services', 21 August 2018 at https://pmg.org. za/committee-meeting/26863/.

19 Refer to the Portfolio Committee on Justice and Correctional Services' deliberations above.

20 Informal interview with anonymous young women in September 2007

21 The Communal Land Rights Act No. 11 of 2004

EIGHT

Chieftaincy succession disputes among the AmaNdebele-a-Moletlane in Hammanskraal, 1962 to 1994

TLHABANE MOKHINE MOTAUNG

Multiple chieftaincy succession disputes characterised the AmaNdebele-a-Moletlane community in the Majaneng area, Hammanskraal, between 1962 and 1994. This chapter explores the historical roots of the disputes through oral interviews with both political and cultural brokers in the community. It also builds on some archival materials from the Bophuthatswana regime, during the bantustan era. It argues that the roots of this regime stretch back to the British system of indirect rule, pioneered by Lord Frederick Lugard in the 1800s, and later recalibrated into the bantustan system by the apartheid regime after it took power in 1948.

The bantustan system was established in the 1970s within the framework of colonial and apartheid laws. Under this system, chiefs were appointed and deposed to ensure allegiance and weed out rebelliousness; often the authorities were less concerned about the effects of their approach to succession issues in the affected chieftaincy. Colonialism, apartheid and their progeny, the bantustan system, saw Africans as differentiated by language, culture and custom, therefore naturally belonging to separate political units or chieftaincies. The ongoing succession dispute in the AmaNdebele-a-Moletlane chieftaincy can be seen as largely a product of the insidious effects of indirect rule in the form of the Bophuthatswana bantustan.

This chapter will also look at preceding research into the chieftaincy dispute in this community, for comparative purposes. To this end, it will focus on the findings of Sarah Godsell, whose work has considerable thematic overlaps with the current study.

The origins of the AmaNdebele-a-Moletlane (of Majaneng, Hammanskraal)

According to tradition, the AmaNdebele-a-Moletlane originated in Moletlane, Zebediela, in what is today known as the Limpopo province. Their founder was Lebelo Seroto (Kekana). Lebelo was the younger brother of the reigning chief of AmaNdebele of Zebediela, Numungebe (Mamokebe), according to the then Department of Native Affairs government ethnologist Dr NJ Van Warmelo (1944). Because of his fluency in the Dutch language, Lebelo was said to be the middleman between the chieftaincy and the Voortrekkers, between whom relations were cordial. The Voortrekkers had arrived in the Zebediela area in the 1840s and 1850s. Van Warmelo (1944) reports that his informants mentioned the name Lebese (Sotho-ised version of Louis Trichardt); this was probably a reference to the leader, or at least one of the leaders, of the Voortrekkers.

It is not clear how Lebelo came to master the Dutch language. However, the most plausible inference is that he would have lived among native speakers for some time, developing basic Dutch. The ability to speak Dutch afforded him some social capital in his community. With time, Lebelo's influential position as the chieftaincy representative and interpreter in the dealings with the Voortrekkers aroused either jealousy or fears of a threat to the position of the chief among some of the influential members of the royal court (Van

Warmelo, 1944). Fears of Lebelo becoming a threat to the throne suggest that chieftaincy usurpation would have been par for the course among the AmaNdebele in particular, and pre-colonial African chieftaincies in general. In fact, in tracing the historical origins of the Transvaal AmaNdebele, Lekgoathi (2009) points out a chiefly dispute among brothers, Ndzudza and Manala, following the death of their father, Bulongo. Following this brotherly rivalry for chieftainship, the Ndebele of the Transvaal split into two groupings (Manala Ndebele and Ndzudza Ndebele) named after the two brothers (Lekgoathi, 2009).

Fears of Lebelo's usurpation of the chiefship of Numungebe led to a conspiracy among the chieftaincy councillors to eliminate him. Generally, oral tradition agrees that Lebelo's brother, Numungebe, never fell for this scheme against his brother, despite goading to that effect by his councillors.[1] However, beyond this point in the narrative, contradictions and divergences begin to emerge. Some informants from the Marokolong[2] side of the dispute could only say that Lebelo fled Zebediela following a dispute about chiefship, without further explaining the historical circumstances and context of the fight (Marokolong Royal Family, 2017). From Zebediela he is said to have sought refuge in Moutse, where he became chief. For his side, Molato Kekana, Lebelo's father and one of the pretenders to the throne of the AmaNdebele-a-Moletlane, submits that the successor of Bulongo[3] (one of the earliest ancestors in the Transvaal Ndebele genealogy), whom he does not mention by name, was advised to escape, following the succession dispute over chiefship.

Together with his group and his son, Lebelo ran to Wallmannsthal, where he become a pastor (Kekana, Makera, 2017). Molato Kekana maintains that Lebelo was not a chief. He argues that the chieftaincy began with his son, Johannes Mokonyama Kekana, after the purchase of Leeukraal farm in 1916. Yet another version is given by former chieftainess Esther Kekana, who was shafted from power after 14 years on the throne following the death of her husband, Hans Kekana, who had ruled until his untimely death in a car accident in 1962. Esther Kekana holds that Lebelo returned educated from Kimberly, where he had been a migrant worker. His brothers felt upstaged by his education status and feared that he would use it to take over chiefship. So Lebelo fled with a section of his supporters to a place called Uitvlug, in Moutse, East of Hammanskraal (Kekana, E., 2017).

All three versions of the historical conditions under which a section of the AmaNdebele peeled off from their parent community in Zebediela, and the identity of the individual who led them, differ in important respects. This tangled web of contradictions in the oral tradition flags the innate weakness of oral sources and the need to cross-reference with written sources for purposes of verification. Neither oral sources nor written sources seem adequate or reliable on their own, particularly regarding the historical account that dates back more than a century. For instance, Esther Kekana's version seems to confuse Lebelo's life with that of his son, Johannes Tane Kekana, who lies at the heart of the historical conflict over legitimacy of chiefly succession among the AmaNdebele-a-Moletlane, about which this chapter is concerned. Johannes Tane Kekana is the one historical figure who is said by some accounts to have worked in Cape Town for the acquisition of guns (*dithunyeng*) (Van Warmelo, 1944; Godsell, 2015).

Van Warmelo's (1944) version is that after many dealings between the Voortrekkers and the Zebediela AmaNdebele, in which Lebelo was messenger, the Voortrekkers warmed to him as a result of his good service and began asking for him instead of the chief every time they came to deal with the chieftaincy. This, Van Warmelo says, led to the suspicion that Lebelo might have harboured ambitions to stage a palace coup against his brother, Nomungebe. According to this version, the chief was informed of this ominous possibility, but decided not to act on it, except privately to advise his brother to leave (Van Warmelo, 1944). This Lebelo did, one day after the chief and a section of his people had left to honour an invitation for a social occasion in Mogano (Valtyn), in Mokopane.

Van Warmelo says that Lebelo headed south, to a place called Nokanapedi (Moutse), where he was given refuge by Europeans and where his people lived side by side with the Kgatla people (Van Warmelo, 1944). In Nokanapedi, Lebelo recognised the suzerainty of Sekoti, regent for Maubane, chief of the Kgatla ba Motsha, then living on the Tshwane (Aapies R) on Boschplaats 507 (Van Warmelo, 1944: 16). After moving on to a few other places, Lebelo ended up at a farm owned by a Schoeman, in Mmamotlhabane, Haakdoornfontein 492, where he would later die (Van Warmelo 1944: 16). Lebelo may have converted to the Christian faith at Nokanapedi, as the Europeans who gave him and his people refuge had set up a Christian missionary station and would have probably made conversion to their faith a precondition for staying there. In any case, converting a chief would have been tantamount to converting his subjects, figuratively killing many birds with one stone.

According to Van Warmelo, Johannes Tane, the first-born son of Lebelo, led the chieftaincy to Wallmannsthal, where he found different chiefdoms settled, including the Manala Ndebele. The farm initially belonged to a white man whom the various communities living there nicknamed *phoko*. Later, the farm was purchased by the mission, with whom relations with the Johannes Tane chieftaincy would later sour, forcing the latter to move on with his community to their current location in Leeuwkraal 396 (Van Warmelo 1944: 16). According to Van Warmelo (1944: 15), '[a]fter the Anglo-Boer war, the Native Commissioner King gave him [Johannes Tane] a plan whereby to acquire the farm, and in 1911 they began paying for it'.

The purchase of farms Leeukraal 396 and Tweefontein

The farm Leeukraal 396 is divided into four villages, namely Majaneng (the capital village), Marokolong, where the opposing faction is based, Suurman (also known as Tweefontein) and Ramotse. According to claims of some of the informants in this study, the initial jurisdiction of their chiefdom stretches as far as areas of modern-day Arcadia in Pretoria and Hartebeespoort in the North West province (Kekana, M., 2017). In fact, the Marokolong faction insists on this version of the purchase and, based on this scale of the putative land ownership, sees itself more as a paramountcy than chieftaincy. They accuse the Majaneng faction of selling out to Mangope of Bophuthatswana under chieftainess Esther Kekana, by confining their chieftaincy to the four wards mentioned above (Marokolong Royal Family, 2017). Interestingly, Molato Kekana – also from the Marokolong faction, but who is at odds with the rest of the faction (and is therefore a sub-set) over chiefship on the grounds that the rightful heir forfeited his turn when he turned it down – also agrees that the initial jurisdiction is far wider than the Majaneng faction is claiming (Marokolong Royal Family, 2017).

Correspondence (dated 21 October 1996) from the Commission on Restitution of Land Rights,[4] stemming from the land claims of this community or factions within it, contradicts the key claim made by Molato Kekana (i.e. 15 September 2017, Roodepoort), and other informants, about the scale of the historical ownership of land belonging to AmaNdebele-a-Moletlane. According to the correspondences of Emma Mashinini (9 June 1999), the Regional Land Claims Commissioner, '... the Commission concluded by asserting that claimants were never dispossessed of their rights in land and that their claims on the other eighty-one (81) farms or portions thereof could not meet the requirements of the Restitution of Land Rights Act, 1994 (Act No. 22 of 1994 as amended)'.[5]

The farm, according to the Department of Rural Development and Land Reform[6] (post-apartheid) was purchased by Johannes Kekana. Only when one starts to probe further as to the identity of Johannes Kekana do matters become hazy. The Majaneng faction claims the buyer was Johannes Tane Kekana, while the Marokolong one says it was Johannes Mokonyama Kekana. The Majaneng faction is backed up by the version of Dr van Warmelo. Yet it should be borne in mind that Van Warmelo seems to have consulted only with the Majaneng faction during his ethnographic study, which would explain the similarity of their versions. The Deed of Transfer only has the English first name 'Johannes', complicating matters further. The letter to a Mr Geoff Budlender, Director-General in the Ministry of Land Affairs and Agriculture, by Emma Mashinini, Regional Land Claims Commissioner: Gauteng and North-West, dated 4 May 1999, states:

In terms of the information at our disposal (i.e. Deed of

Transfer No. T7775/1916 date 23rd October 1916) the Ndebele tribe under Chief Johannes Kekana bought a certain portion called 'Michelstraak' of the freehold farm Leeukraal No. 396 (now Leeuwkraal 92-JR), in extent, two thousand six-hundred and seventy-eight (2678) morgen and seventy-three (73) square roods. The said portion was bought for the total sum of 5356.00 (five thousand three hundred and fifty-six pounds) and was later held in trust for the tribe. But other portions such as 1 and 4 of the farm Leeukraal 92-JR are STATE OWNED or registered as STATE LAND meaning that they do not form part of the Kekana domain or Tribal Authority.

A Majaneng District memo, dated 15 December 1987, purportedly replying to a Bishop ME Kekana's protest to the recognition of the Johannes Tane Kekana's chiefly lineage, and signed off by the Bophuthatswana chief ethnologist IM Selebogo claims that: '[T]he available records in the deeds office indicate that the farm Leeukraal no. 396 was bought and registered in the name of Johannes Jan Kekana, but not Johannes Mangonyama Jakkals.' On the other hand, Jacob Leka Kekana of Kekana Gardens, a splinter family lineage from the Marokolong faction, and paternal uncle to Molato Kekana, claims that: 'Chief Johannes (Mokonyama) Kekana – Son of Chief Lebelo's tribal Queen, also ruled the tribe in Moutse till he died and was also buried in Moutse. His death occurred after his purchase of the farms Leeukraal, Tweefontein and Vyeboschlaafte' (Kekana, L. 1994).

All these contradictory statements make it all too murky to understand which of the two 'Johannesses', Tane or Mokonyama, bought the land and was therefore the legitimate heir to Lebelo. The cloud of confusion hanging over the identity of the individual who purchased land in this chieftaincy further confounds the question of the true and legitimate heir to the throne of AmaNdebele-a-Moletlane. This confusion about the chiefly lineage and land purchase is steeped in a history that goes back just over a century and continues to confound this chieftaincy. The dissipation of this confusion is contingent on decoding the two individuals named 'Johannes' at the centre of the matter, as well as their individual roles in this history.

The emergence of the two factions

While the bare bones of this storyline are more or less shared among different factions and individuals, the parting of ways starts with the chiefly status of the sons of Lebelo, Johannes Tane Kekana and Johannes Mokonyama Kekana. What lies at the heart of the dispute about this history is who is the rightful heir to the throne of Lebelo. Once again, oral tradition on its own turns out to be inadequate given the inherent shortcomings of oral sources, yet oral tradition is the only source available since the AmaNdebele-a-Moletlane, like many of their African counterparts, were a pre-literate society (Tosh, 1984: 116).

The current ruling faction is generally known as the Majaneng group, and the rival faction, the Marokolong group. The Majaneng narrative contends that Johannes Tane, Lebelo's first-born son by his first wife, is the legitimate heir to the throne under the customary law of primogeniture. In customary parlance this (i.e. Johannes Tane's) ruling lineage would be called the senior or ruling house. The Majaneng version differs completely from the Marokolong version in the account of how Johannes Tane Kekana came into the picture. The Majaneng version simply states that he was the first-born son of Lebelo. He purportedly headed off to Cape Town to work in order to afford guns (Marokolong Faction, 2017). He came back a Christian convert who was redirected to Uitvlug, to which his father had fled. The Majaneng faction never mentioned the fact that Johannes Tane Kekana was brought by missionaries to the Kekana royal family.

The Majaneng faction's narrative seems to have gone down in history as the authoritative version, as shown by much historiography of this chieftaincy. Van Warmelo, the chief government ethnologist from 1930 to 1969, recorded the history of the AmaNdebele-a-Moletlane, and to all intents and purposes interviewed only informants from the Majaneng faction. His approach is baffling, given his awareness about the murky waters of chiefship. He stated as much when he '…maintained that when a dispute arose the waters were so muddied by tendentious local factions that the truth was impossible to ascertain' (Hammond-Tooke, 1997: 113).

Van Warmelo was apparently the first scholar to record the history of this community and therefore elevated their version to become the subject of historiography. Subsequent studies and official investigations of the chiefly succession dispute in this chieftaincy tend to take for granted Van Warmelo's historical record without question and as such may be unwittingly perpetuating the predominance of the written (Majaneng) version. Ethnographic studies that succeed in covering all sides of the disputed narrative may help to minimise bias resulting from unequal access to the historical record. Jeff Peires (1981: 34) noted this when he states that '[i]n oral societies more than in literate ones, it is the victors who record history, particularly if the losers become reconciled to their defeat. Genealogies, for instance, are not so much accurate chronicles of genetic relationships as indexes of relative political standing.'

This does not mean that there has not been some awareness of the historical depth of the chiefly succession dispute in this community.[7] Although, prior to 1994, there were three government-instituted commissions of inquiry into the chiefly succession dispute in this chieftaincy – one by the apartheid state and two by the Bophuthatswana regime – none of them concerned themselves with the historical origins of this dispute, which is variously said to go back to 1914 or 1916 (see Matabane, 1990; Marokolong Faction, 2017).

Van Warmelo may have done pioneering work in recording the history of this chieftaincy, but his work is not necessarily free of the intrinsic defects of oral history, and Van Warmelo himself was not so much occupied with a critical approach as a simple recording of this history (Lekgoathi, 2009: 53–67). Van Warmelo's approach is even more vulnerable of being susceptible to the subjective perspectives of his researchers and informants in 'the co-production of cultural knowledge' (Lekgoathi, 2009: 53–67). Lekgoathi (2009) has argued that '… Van Warmelo's writings and interpretations of the Ndebele history and society were fundamentally shaped by local informants' perspectives, which were themselves products of old traditions that had been recast in the context of contemporary struggles and changes occurring in early twentieth-century South Africa'.

In terms of Lekgoathi's critique, it is plausible that the canonical version of the AmaNdebele-a-Moletlane's history (the Majaneng version) is but the tendentious history of the victors; victors in the sense of being the only faction in the conflict to tell their side of the story. This is worth keeping in mind, given that both the local informants and the researchers themselves are invariably drawn from the ruling segment, who would have had access to both the history of the community and modern education. Jacob Leka Kekana confirms as much when he tells researcher Sarah Godsell that 'Van Warmelo ... consulted only one of the Kekana family: the branch that has achieved recognition through prolonged interaction with Europeans' (Godsell, 2015: 88).

Godsell's research is not aimed at confirming one side of the historical conflict over chiefly succession. In her own words: '... the purpose of this thesis is not to establish which group is legitimate. My intention is to examine the narratives and ways of belonging created in relation to power structures that administered this space' (Godsell, 2015: 79). Despite Godsell's stated intention of avoiding it, the bias towards the Majaneng faction emerges again, at least by default, in her PhD thesis.

Godsell used oral interviews to explore the nature and history of the chieftaincy disputes among the AmaNdebele-a-Moletlane. In the process, she came up with a raft of findings that relate to the chieftaincy, gender issues and customs, directing her attention to the two primary groupings that constitute the community of AmaNdebele-a-Moletlane.

However, Godsell's research appears to confuse the identity of the correct groupings in this dispute. From the viewpoint of Majaneng, she was right to have interviewed Esther Kekana, a former chieftainess and one of the prominent protagonists in the dispute. Yet Godsell misidentified the second group. She suggests that the second group is from Kekana Gardens. In fact, Kekana Gardens is a subset, to use Godsell's useful terminology, which falls under the second main group and rival to the Majaneng group: the Marokolong group. To detect the main defect in Godsell's conceptualisation of the two groups, it helps to cite her summary of the dispute in her own words. Godsell (2015: 80) states:

These two primary groups (with different subsets within them) have been contesting the leadership of the AmaNdebele-a-Moletlane for over 60 years. The contestations have run through apartheid, bantustan, and post-1994 administrations. To provide a very rough sketch, the dispute centres on two things: first, which wife of the common ancestor Lebelo Seroto was the royal wife, and so whose children would continue the lineage. Johannes Tane was the heir linked to the now Majaneng group. Johannes Mokonyama was linked to the now Kekana Gardens group. Second, but linked to this, was who was the paramount chief when the land (discussed below) was bought; Karel Seroto, son of Johannes Tane, so linked to Majaneng, or Johannes Mokonyama himself, which links the land purchase to Kekana Gardens.

Godsell did not interview the Marokolong group. It may be that she has confused the naming, meaning she has mislabelled the main group as Kekana Gardens instead of Marokolong, under which the former falls. It is true that Jacob Leka Kekana, who is based in Kekana Gardens and whom Godsell had interviewed, is one of the claimants to the throne of the AmaNdebele-a-Moletlane, along with Mavis Kekana (Esther Kekana's daughter), Richard Vonk Kekana (of Marokolong), Molato Kekana (Leka Kekana's nephew, Kekana Gardens) and the current incumbent, Cornelius Kgomotso Kekana (Majaneng). However, before focusing on Jacob Leka Kekana, it is worth noting that Kekana Gardens itself was established in 2002 as the offshoot of Marokolong, and so chiefly claimants from there are the Marokolong sub-group.

Kekana Gardens and Jacob Leka Kekana

In order to understand the central fault in Godsell's research findings, one must first give a synopsis of Jacob Leka Kekana's history, and the origins of the Kekana Gardens. These findings emerged during an interview (Marokolong Faction, 2017) with the prominent actors within the Marokolong camp. These include members of the royal family and clan as well as the individual the Marokolong faction believes to be the paramount chief-in-waiting, Richard Vonk Kekana, who, in keeping with cultural dictates, spoke to this researcher through his spokesman and adviser, Simon Makau Kekana.

This account holds that Kekana Gardens was established by Abram Sombalane Kekana, who is a close kin member of the royal family from the Marokolong lineage. Before marriage, Abram Sombalane Kekana had a girlfriend with whom he had two sons, Zebediela Simon Kekana and his younger brother, Jacob Leka Kekana. This was a girlfriend and not a wife. In terms of the Kekana or Northern Ndebele culture, an individual becomes eligible for the chiefship throne if he was born of a chief and a *timamollo* (or candle wife), or otherwise under exceptional circumstances, such as when he is a son of the reigning chief's brother or uncle and by default happens to be the next in line in the absence of qualifying individuals ahead of him. Jacob Leka Kekana's mother was neither a princess nor married, let alone being a *timamollo* (Marokolong Royal Family, 2017). Of course, as John Comaroff (1974:37) points out, there are 'a number of discontinuities between the ideal and the actual patterns [...] disputes do arise over succession to office; [...] chiefs vary considerably in the power they wield; and [...] may gain or lose legitimacy during their careers'. As we shall see later, though, Abram Sombalane Kekana's descendants' claim to chiefship arise out of unusual circumstances, where the acknowledged legitimate heir passed up his turn. Godsell did interview Leka Kekana, yet she did not reach out to the rest of the Marokolong village faction for their side of the story.

However, while Leka Kekana's version of chiefly lineage seems designed to suit his claims in this historical period, closer scrutiny shows that matters are more complex than that, and Leka may have a case after all. Firstly, Molato Kekana, one of the claimants to the chieftaincy and the son of Zebediela Kekana (i.e. Jacob Leka Kekana's brother) states (2017) that the chieftaincy shifted to his lineage after Vonk Kekana, whom he acknowledges as the initial, legitimate heir, turned down the chiefship in 1992.

Molato argues that according to Ndebele custom, once an heir passes up his chieftaincy turn, it cannot be reinvoked later.

Molato's grandfather, Abram Sombalane Kekana, who is the brother of Richard Vonk Kekana, who forfeited his chiefly turn, drew up 'A Royal Family Tree of Descent' under the rubric of the Kekana Royal Executive Council. This body, also known informally as 'The Ruling Cabinet', had constituted itself as the traditional authority of Marokolong. In this family tree, the chiefly lineage is depicted as starting from Mokonyama, the son of the founder Lebelo, followed by William Makera Kekana, followed by himself, Abram Sombalane Kekana, then his sons Zebediela Simon, Jacob Leka and later Stuurman Kekana (the son of his customary wife). In other words, the contention that the chiefly lineage within the Marokolong faction belongs to the Kekana Gardens lineage was started by Abraham Sombalane Kekana, the father of Jacob Leka Kekana. According to this account, Molato's claim that, by rebuffing his turn, Richard Vonk Kekana irretrievably lost chiefship is backed up by the events pertaining to chieftainess Esther Kekana's court appeal after her deposition. In his judgment, Judge Moll states that Agrippa Kekana, the younger brother of Esther Kekana's late husband, Chief Hans Kekana, forfeited his turn to assume chiefship after turning it down in a letter from 17 December 1976.[8] In like manner, the Kekana Garden lineage based its claim to chiefship on Richard Vonk Kekana's refusal to take his turn, even though he tried to make amends by reclaiming it later on.

The rival historical narrative as told by the Marokolong faction more or less echoes the Majaneng version, except when it comes to the status of Johannes Tane. The Marokolong faction's main issue with the Majaneng faction is that the Majaneng faction was not the chiefly lineage, but rather a regent lineage. They claim that it all started in 1914, when the rightful chief, called Karel Seroto Kekana, was forced to go and fight in the First World War, following an instruction from the colonial government which reasoned that because he was a chief he had to fight for his people. Karel Seroto Kekana left for war and would eventually die on the ship *SS Mendi*. In the meantime, an acting chief had to be appointed, and this is how, as the story goes, the Johannes Tane lineage came to assume the throne.

Karel Seroto Kekana was then replaced by Karel Mmatshetlha

Kekana as acting chief. Karel Mmatshetlha Kekana hailed from the lineage of Johannes Tane Kekana.The Marokolong faction claim that Johannes Tane Kekana was brought to the Kekana family by the missionaries, who claimed that he was a long-lost son of Lebelo Kekana, who had gone to Cape Town to work for guns (Marokolong Faction, 2017).

Yet this narrative has some factual inconsistencies. Firstly, no one knows how the missionaries met Johannes Tane Kekana, since he is said to have gone to Cape Town for work. Oral tradition tends to be muddled when it comes to chronology. This garbled narrative by informants who are themselves of royal descent resonates with Lekgoathi's argument about '... old traditions that had been recast in the context of contemporary struggles ...' (Lekgoathi, 2009: 53–67). For instance, it is not clear how the missionaries know about Johannes Tane's family, given that he had been working in Cape Town and therefore would probably never have made his acquaintance with local missionaries, who would have had to know enough about his background to take him to his father's chiefdom. Equally, it is just not comprehensible that no one knew about his existence when he was the first-born son of Lebelo Kekana.

For his part, Van Warmelo says that Johannes Tane, who died in May 1916, left for Cape Town and when he returned found that his father, Lebelo, had left the Moletlane chieftaincy following the advice from his brother. He was redirected to Ga Mantsubuko, at his father's chiefdom, only to find that his father had already died two years before and the chiefship was in the hands of a headman. The chiefdom had also absorbed people other than the Ndebele from Moletlane, which enlarged it considerably. Then some among the chiefdom refused to be ruled by Johannes Tane on account of his education and so split from the chieftaincy, moving to Leeuwkloof, further east (Van Warmelo, 1944: 17). Dr van Warmelo says the splinter group later rejoined the mother chieftaincy.

While the Majaneng faction sees their chiefship as historically legitimate, the Marokolong version depicts them as usurpers of the chieftaincy of the AmaNdebele-a-Moletlane. This is how the second royal kraal (which is informal) in Marokolong came into the picture.

It was into these historically toxic conditions of chronic rancour over the chieftaincy that the Bophuthatswana regime, set up under the bantustan system and headed up by Lucas Manyane Mangope, emerged. Bophuthatswana would play no insignificant role in further roiling the already disturbed waters.

Succession disputes during the bantustan era: The politics of bantustan system and gender

The Bophuthatswana bantustan came into being within the context of the wider bantustan system. This was set up with successive pieces of legislation: first came the apartheid state's promulgation of the Bantu Authorities Act No. 68 of 1951, which was followed by the 1959 Promotion of Bantu Self-Government Act No. 46, which in turn paved the way for the establishment of the Bophuthatswana homeland for Tswana-speaking people in 1961. From being a self-governing territory, Bophuthatswana was granted independence in 1977. There is a thread connecting these two acts (Bantu Authorities and Bantu Self-Government Act), especially the former Act, with the 1927 Native Administration Act No. 38. This Act was promulgated by British colonial authorities to be the bedrock of the colonial strategy of indirect rule, which would turn the institution of chieftaincy into a tool of colonialism.

Conceptually, the difference between the 1927 Native Administration Act and the 1951 Bantu Authorities Act was that the former designated customary law for the 'natives' as a category and civic rule for settler society. In comparison, the latter Act was intent on breaking down the monolithic 'natives' category into clusters of minorities, each with its own traditions, customs and chieftaincy (Myers, 2008). Some scholars have argued that the bantustan system was born out of the apartheid state's need to further refine the concept of indirect rule in order to deal with increasing resistance to apartheid in the 1950s and 1960s, when militant African nationalism led by both the African National Congress (ANC) and its breakaway, the Pan African Congress (PAC), was rapidly gaining ground (Myers, 2008).

The Natives Land Act (No. 27 of 1913) had corralled Africans into reserves, partly to pander to the political sentiment of emerging Afrikaner agricultural capital, and partly for the forced proletarianisation of Africans, designed to meet the needs of growing industry, especially mining (O'Meara, 1983). Growing industrialisation did not only provide 'detribalising' conditions for the rapidly urbanising Africans; in the decades to come, it also created ideal conditions for political mobilisation against increasing racial oppression. This modernising impulse by the subject population posed an existential threat to the colonial mode of domination and had to be reworked to respond to the exigencies of the historical period.

Therefore, thinking up new strategies to meet the challenges of its times head on, the apartheid state set up the 1950–54 Tomlinson Commission 'to conduct an exhaustive inquiry into, and to report upon, a comprehensive scheme for the rehabilitation of the Native areas, with a view to developing within them a social structure, in keeping with the culture of the Native, based on effective socio-economic planning' (Myers, 2008: 32). The Tomlinson Commission's findings saw ethnic identity among Africans as the linchpin of the future of South Africa, arguing that '… the Bantu peoples … do not constitute a homogeneous people, but form separate national units on the basis of language and culture' (Myers, 2008: 32).

Along with the influence of Van Warmelo's ethnological texts, the depiction of Africans as clusters of ethnic groups provided the rationale for 'territorial homeland and separate system of political representation' (Myers, 2008: 32). The bantustan system was therefore the recalibration of indirect rule, based on the ethnic fragmentation of indigenous populations, as per findings of ethnographers such as Van Warmelo and the Tomlinson Commission itself. The Tswana territorial authority was constituted to incorporate the Odi-Moretele district, which is made up mostly of non-Tswana (including the AmaNdebele-a-Moletlane community).

Yet the depiction of Africans as clusters of ethnic groups is both embedded in, and consistent with, the intrinsic logic of indirect rule. The Native Affairs Act No. 23 of 1920 had already provided a legal framework for this. It had created the statutory basis upon which

African chiefs could be turned into servants of the state, whereupon a white governor-general was made the supreme chief of all natives. In effect, the governor-general had the powers to define who was, and who was not, the chief; he could depose and appoint at will in keeping with the interests of the colonial system. Gone were the days when a system of indigenous political authority determined chieftaincy succession. The Bantu Authorities Act of 1951, which envisaged the subordination of chieftaincy to the bantustan authorities, served two purposes: firstly, it increased the powers of the chiefs and, secondly, it cemented the apartheid state's control over them. William Beinart contends that 'in this way, the state hoped to secure a conservative, or reactionary, rural hierarchy which would help to defuse broader national struggles. Modern chieftaincy, in short, has been seen as a creation of, and creature of, the state' (Beinart, 1995: 177).

Consequently, the emergence of the Bophuthatswana bantustan compounded the historical feuds among AmaNdebele-a-Moletlane, thereby entrenching a deep legacy of bitterness among all the claimants, individuals and groups. One of Mangope's blatant interventions was to prevail on the chieftaincy to change their name from AmaNdbele-a-Moletlane to AmaNdebele-a-Lebelo, on the grounds that they would not be confused with their ancestral chieftaincy, from which they had splintered. However, members of the Marokolong faction resisted, choosing to continue going by the initial name to preserve their historical identity (Marokolong Royal Family, 2017). Between 1977, when Bophuthatswana gained 'independence', and its dis-solution in 1993, no less than 10 individuals had been appointed chief (or acting chiefs) and deposed, as the regime saw fit (save for those who died in office). Mangope is also on record as making many important decisions about who was to become chief or acting chief. Consequently, the chiefly succession dispute within the Majaneng group cannot be understood without taking cognisance of external interference by the government of Bophuthatswana.

What sharply defined the pernicious role of the Mangope regime in this community was its unilateral imposition of decisions regarding the imposition and deposition of chiefs. As provided for in the 1951 Native Authorities Act, it was the logic of indirect rule to imbue the bantustan political leadership with unquestioned powers to appoint and remove chiefs as they deemed fit. Equally, ethnic particularism was inherent in this Act and it did not take long before its manifestations surfaced as the Bophuthatswana bantustan took shape. This arbitrary power over chiefs preceded the bantustans. Citing figures in the Native Affairs Department, Myers shows that the number of chiefs increased '… from 384 in 1936, to 466 in 1945, and 701 in 1947' (Myers, 2008: 17). Although this was at a national level, it shows the arbitrary appointment or creation of chiefs, even where none existed before. The Bophuthatswana government enjoyed the same arbitrary powers provided by the 1951 Bantu Authorities Act. As a 'state' with questionable credentials, but nevertheless powerful authority, it seemed set to assert itself in whatever manner it deemed fit, as in this instance (Kekana, E., 2017).

In keeping with the ethnic particularism inherent in the notion of bantustans, Bophuthatswana under Chief Lucas Manyane Mangope, who was to remain its leader throughout its existence as a chief minister and later president, asserted its ethnic character shortly after its establishment. All non-Tswana people were to bear the brunt of its founding ethnic philosophy, and the AmaNdebele people would be no exception.

The climate of ethnic chauvinism emerged in the early 1960s. Among its various manifestations was the removal of the non-Tswana people from a certain area in Ga-Rankuwa earmarked for the building of the Medical University of South Africa (Lekgoathi, 2003). Subsequent to that, the non-Tswana communities across Bophuthatswana were to be subjected to systematic discrimination when government came up with the philosophy of *popagano* (welding together of a people), which it rolled in through its education system (Lekgoathi, 2003). According to Lekgoathi (2003), *popagano* was meant to help advance the goal of Tswana-isation of the entire homeland. The philosophy of *popagano* was therefore an inherently exclusionary approach that would trample on the human rights of all non-Tswana people, irrespective of their historical ties to the territories now falling under Bophuthatswana.

The Bophuthatswana education philosophy *popagano* was aimed at socialising the young into a single ethnic and cultural identity, by imbuing them with ethnic consciousness through the medium of instruction of the Setswana language. This unilateral policy would cover all learners within Bophuthatswana territory, including the non-Tswana communities such as the northern Sotho and northern Ndebele people, who had until then received education through their mother tongues. *Popagano* was to have a toxic impact on the AmaNdebele-a-Moletlane under the chiefship of Esther Kekana. 'The new change', according to Lekgoathi (2003: 53–76), 'affected, among others, eight schools belonging to the Kekana-Ndebele or AmaNdebele-a-Moletlane community at Majaneng (Leeuwkraal) near Hammanskraal in the Odi-Moretele district'. That most of the people in this district were non-Tswana did not make matters any easier. Until then, this community had used northern Sotho as the medium of instruction in the education of their children, as the northern Ndebele community had largely been culturally assimilated into the northern Sotho people over the years, possibly even before they splintered from the Zebediela AmaNdebele back in the 1800s (Lekgoathi, 2003).

During this time, the chieftaincy was under Esther Kekana, who had succeeded her late husband in 1963 after he perished in a car accident in 1962. Esther Kekana ascended the throne prior to the onset of Bophuthatswana, at the time when the chieftaincy was still under the jurisdiction of central government in Pretoria. Protesting the imposition of Tswana on the AmaNdebele-a-Moletlane, chieftainess Kekana closed seven schools for about three years (Kekana, E., 2017). She tried without success to secede through the route of joining forces with the Ndebele nationalist organisation called Northern AmaNdebele National Organisation (NANO).

NANO was furiously agitating for a separate homeland for the northern AmaNdebele people. This impulse can be understood as a product of the ethnic mentality generated by the Tomlinson Commission, which atomised Africans into ethnic minorities. They advocated the need for separate development for the Transvaal AmaNdebele, not unlike that of other 'tribal groups'. In this spirit, the northern AmaNdebele, who were aggrieved at being left out when the southern Ndebele were offered the Kwa-Ndebele bantustan, were keeping up the fight for officially recognised space. Chieftainess Kekana found resonance with this organisation yet, ironically, tried to affiliate her chiefly jurisdiction to the Lebowa homeland, from which NANO was striving to break away. After failing, she tried the newly formed Kwa-Ndebele homeland, which was set aside for the southern Ndebele people, still to no avail. Her defiance turned her into the foe of the Mangope regime and led to her forfeiting some of the privileges of the office of chiefship, starting with the rescinding of the purchase of a car (Lekgoathi, 2003). As she continued to dig in, Mangope finally dethroned her, replacing her with a pliable individual in the person of Nathaniel Sello Kekana (Lekgoathi, 2003).

However, Esther Kekana refused to blink. Instead she approached the Supreme Court of South Africa in a case in which Mangope was the first respondent, her replacement, Sello Nathaniel Kekana, the second respondent and the minister of Bantu Administration and Development the third respondent. The matter sat on 1 June 1977.[9]

However, Esther Kekana lost this case on the grounds of her gender, which, according to the judgment, was out of step with customary law as per the findings of the Holt Commission of Inquiry, instituted by the South African government before Bophuthatswana gained independence.[10] From this point onwards in the history of this chieftaincy, the Mangope regime was to be entangled with the royal affairs of the AmaNdebele-a-Moletlane, especially as they pertained to the appointment and deposing of chiefs.

The removal of Esther Kekana from office coincided with a confluence of processes within this community itself. As Lekgoathi (2006: 109) shows:

[T]he ousting was relatively easy to execute because of the ongoing split within the Majaneng community over chieftainship. There was a 'small band of rebels' who claimed that the community wanted a man to rule it. The chief minister used this to his advantage and replaced the chieftainess with Mr Nathaniel Kekana, one of the contenders who appeared to be amenable to the policies of Bophuthatswana.

A section of the AmaNdebele-a-Moletlane was dead set against the chiefship of Esther Kekana (see below) primarily because her line of descent (i.e. the ruling house) was deemed to be ruling on the basis of regency, historically speaking. Based in Marokolong, this section went by the name 'the ruling cabinet'. Simon Makau Kekana, one of the elders of the Kekana ruling clan from the Marokolong faction, explains that the reason for the adoption of the name 'ruling cabinet' was to distinguish themselves from the Majaneng faction, to avoid confusion in the public mind as to who came from which side (Kekana, V., Marokolong Faction, 2017).

The two sides interestingly have contradicting narratives about the role played by Mangope in the ongoing fight. The Marokolong side, the main rival to the ruling house, depicts Esther Kekana as a sell-out who let in Mangope and therefore compromised the independence of their chieftaincy (Kekana, V., 2017). The fact that she worked for the Bophuthatswana government in the capital city, Mmabatho, did not endear her to some of her people, providing her detractors with ammunition against her. For instance, the Marokolong faction believes that '… Esther Kekana was collaborating with Mangope and she has even worked for him based in Mmabatho while she was the leader of the AmaNdebele people. Our people felt that she could not represent us while she had chosen to live in Mafikeng' (Kekana, V., 2017). Esther saw nothing wrong with the position, contending that '[t]hrough chiefly experience, the Bophuthatswana government appointed me to the House of Traditional Leaders. I was in Mafikeng for 10 years, the laws kept changing' (Kekana, E., 2017).

While ambiguity seems an apt term for Esther Kekana's relationship with the Mangope regime, it may nevertheless serve the purpose of her detractors to use that relationship against her, as seems to be the case now. In fact, they hold that Esther Kekana's embracing of the Mangope regime was what froze relations, in addition to the question of gender and the refusal to acknowledge their ownership of the land and the chieftaincy of Leeukraal (Marokolong Faction, 2017).

On the other hand, Esther Kekana tells of a rather hostile attitude from Mangope towards her because she refused to give in to his regime's philosophy of *popagano* and the imposition of Tswana as a medium of instruction. For her, the fall-out with the Mangope regime could be ascribed to her refusal to accept Tswana-isation. While the Marokolong section accuses her of collaboration with the Mangope regime, she denies the accusation, instead depicting herself as having been on the frontline in the resistance to cultural imposition. She maintains that deposition was ultimately the price she had to pay. Esther Kekana (2017) insists that:

Along with chiefs like Pilane and Maselwane, I was in opposition to Mangope's government in Mafikeng, so he never supported me. That is the reason he pushed me out of my acting position. So, when he forced seTswana on us and we reacted by closing down schools, lowered the flag etc., he said fine go on and find yourselves a land in Lebowa because this is Bophuthatswana.

From the preceding excerpt, Esther Kekana presents herself as the victim of the Mangope regime, which removed her from her rightful position as chief following her husband's death. On the other hand, the Marokolong faction has a totally different version of events. On this issue, the Marokolong faction (2017) argues that:

Mangope found Esther Kekana in power. But Esther Kekana had issues with the elders of the clan and community because they would not be ruled by a woman in terms of their culture [...] Mangope used Esther Kekana for his own political ends. Mangope used Esther as a pawn and she could not see that. For instance, there are many houses in this neighbourhood which Esther razed down. Initially when Esther took over chieftainship there were no serious issues. Issues between her and the community were started with the onset of Bophuthatswana when Mangope started changing things through Esther Kekana. This pitted her against her own people. She sold them out to the Batswana or to government.

While Esther Kekana's version shows her pitted against Mangope for the sake of her people's interests, the Marokolong section has a different take. It is also advisable in a case like this to remember that both Esther Kekana and the Marokolong faction have been at daggers since the late 1960s when Marokolong arrived into the chieftaincy from Uitvlug or Moutse without formally announcing themselves, as they thought themselves the true ruling house, accountable to no one. This resulted in the chieftainess, Esther Kekana, tearing down their houses (Kekana, V., Marokolong Faction, 2017).

Against the background of this hostile history, the Marokolong faction members credit themselves with removing the chieftainess from the throne, not Mangope. They contend that:

> It is the AmaNdebele not Mangope. So, the two main issues that ejected Esther Kekana from power were her gender and her apparent collaboration with the Mangope government. During this court case Mangope supported Esther Kekana. Esther Kekana once lived and worked in Mafikeng for a long time (Kekana, V., 2017).

However, the judgment that upheld Mangope's decision to depose Esther Kekana defies the Marokolong claim that their faction was the one that removed her from the chieftaincy. Interestingly, as the judgment shows, Mangope dethroned Esther Kekana in terms of Section 2(8) of the Bantu Administration Act No. 38 of 1927, read with Section 21 and item 27 of the Bantu Homelands Constitution Act No. 21 of 1971. Two conclusions can be drawn about the removal of Esther Kekana.

The first is that oral history can be fluid to suit the historical circumstances of particular political interests, as the Marokolong claim shows. While the ongoing chiefly feud between them and the Majaneng faction did provide background context to the removing of Esther Kekana, the Marokolong faction alone cannot be credited with her removal as the court case shows. Secondly, the contention that the British colonial system of indirect rule, as institutionalised by the 1927 Native Administration Act, provided the impulse for the later apartheid Acts such as the 1951 Bantu Authorities Act is vindicated in this judgment that enabled the Mangope regime to dethrone Esther Kekana.

Both Lekgoathi and Godsell show that at some point the Mangope regime lost patience with Esther Kekana and schemed to remove her from office (Lekgoathi, 2006: 109; Godsell, 2015: 98). This conclusion is corroborated by the fact that it was only after a long, drawn-out if volatile relationship that the Mangope regime suddenly found her regency could not be permitted under cultural norms. The Bantu Authorities Act of 1951, as well as the Bophuthatswana Traditional Authorities Act of 1978, empowered the bantustans to subject chiefs to their will. It was because of these unchecked powers that the Mangope regime deposed chiefs such as Chief SK Mankuroana of Taung, Chief Marcus Mathibe of Bahwaduba, Chief RD Mabe of Batlhako ba Matutu in Mankwe, Chief DK Manimane of Bakwena ba Modimosana and many more.

This exercise of arbitrary power by the Bophuthatswana government was therefore not just confined to the case of the AmaNdebele-a-Moletlane. Rather it was extended to all the chieftaincies falling under Bophuthatswana. Billy Mokgabodi, the most senior royal councillor, confirms that Esther Kekana did enjoy significant support (Mokgabudi, 2017). As Godsell shows in her study, Esther Kekana was a popular figure during her reign, at least from the side of Majaneng (Godsell, 2015: 98). She even earned the nickname '*Mmabatho*' (mother of the people), as a *Drum* magazine article of 1970 reported (Godsell, 2015: 79). It is also true that when Mangope started imposing unpopular policies, this put Esther Kekana under strain. Matters reached a head on the Marokolong side, where she enjoyed less legitimacy and had already crossed swords with the elders over many demands she refused to meet (Marokolong Faction, 2017).

Over the years, Esther Kekana has taken multiple sides in the succession dispute. In fact, as will be shown below, she at some point ended up fighting against the Marokolong faction (for reasons set out), the Majaneng faction (when she could not agree with them on the succession plan based on gender considerations) and the Mangope regime (for resisting imposition of policies). Her narrative about being deposed by Mangope is given credibility by Billy Mokgabudi, the elder within the Majaneng faction. He sees the trouble beginning with the onset of Bophuthatswana, when Mangope rammed policies down their throats. According to Billy Mokgabudi (2017):

> The trouble started then. The reigning chief was Esther
> Kekana for 13 years. After the death of her husband in 1962,
> she took charge. All this peace was disrupted by Mangope
> when he started to make claims over our land. Esther put
> up resistance but Mangope was joined by so-called 'ruling
> cabinet' from Mamelodi. This ruling cabinet was established
> by Abram Kekana's daughter. She mobilised broadly among the
> AmaNdebele community against the gender of Esther. But all
> of them ended up nowhere.

Mokgabudi thus identifies the combination of hostility from the
Mangope regime and the rival faction combining to dethrone
Esther Kekana, as playing a part in her deposition, with no internal
squabbling within the Majaneng faction itself playing any part. Yet
this line of thought is contradicted by the opinion of Stella Kekana,
one of the elder women (aunties, *kgadi*) within the Majaneng royal
council. For her, Mangope had nothing to do with Esther Kekana's
removal from office. She insists that 'Mangope did not cause any
troubles in this chiefdom. It is just that he found the situation already
conflicted. Some elders within the clan mobilised, including those
living outside the chiefdom, to remove Esther' (Kekana, E., 2017).

Stella Kekana and Billy Mokgabudi are of the same generation
and cultural status within the chieftaincy. They witnessed the same
historical events, probably sat in the same royal council meetings, yet
have different interpretations of the role of Mangope.

Contrary to Stella Kekana's representations, documentary evidence from the Mangope regime consistently shows Mangope's hand
in the royal affairs of the AmaNdebele-a-Moletlane. Again, in the
1986 document called 'Recognition and Appointment of Acting Chief
Mbofane Thomas Kekana: Majaneng District Moretele', which sets
out the reasons for the appointment of the acting chief, Mbofane
Thomas Kekana, the Bophuthatswana government contends that it
had been a mistake to appoint Esther Kekana a regent in the first
place. In this connection, the document states that:

[T]herefore the recognition and appointment of the great wife Nchadi Esther Kekana was contrary to the principle of primogeniture which provides that the first-born and eldest son of the deceased chief shall succeed to the hereditary office of chieftaincy.

The argument is based on the interpretation of Ndebele principle of primogeniture. According to the principle of primogeniture, the eldest son is eligible for succession to hereditary office of chieftaincy (provided the mother is also candle wife) (Kekana, M., 2017). Mokgabudi's citation seems to evoke the innate weakness of oral history, which tends to conflate personal feelings with objective analysis. Mokgabudi says that Mangope was joined by the so-called 'ruling cabinet' in dislodging Esther Kekana from power. Yet we know that the Marokolong faction, of which the 'ruling cabinet' was part, did not see eye-to-eye with the Mangope regime from the beginning. Their interest in her deposition may have coincided with Mangope's, but there is no evidence to imply collaboration.

As will be shown later, the Marokolong faction blames Mangope for ignoring a court order from the South African jurisdiction instructing Nathaniel Sello Kekana to step down after a period of six months. During this period he would serve as Acting Chief (as an olive branch to the Majaneng faction), after which the Marokolong faction would reclaim 'their' chieftaincy forever. Had the Mangope regime honoured this judgment, according to the Marokolong faction, the age-old chiefly feud would have been solved once and for all. Their explanation is that Mangope ignored this judgment as a form of revenge against them for their vociferous opposition to his policies (Marokolong Faction, 2017). Be that as it may, when Mangope deposed Esther Kekana he did not cite the Marokolong conflict, which centred less on gender and more on the historical illegitimacy of the Majaneng faction. Instead, Mangope leaned to culture, citing chieftainess Kekana's gender and primogeniture as the key issues. The gender issue comes up repeatedly in the documentation of the Bophuthatswana government, especially as a matter for customary law, commissions of inquiry and legal processes (*Kekana vs Mangope,*

Kekana & Ministry of Bantu Administration & Development, 1977; Mophatlhana, 1986).

Despite the apparently untenable situation Esther Kekana was entrapped in, the care-taker administrators of Marokolong insist that had she thrown in her lot with the whole community, Mangope would not have made any headway in his impositions. '[I]f she teamed with the AmaNdebele community, Mangope would have failed in his mission. Esther is accused of conceding to Bophuthatswana. The four wards (villages) closed down schools' (Marokolong Faction, 2017). This statement appears not to accord with the historical evidence that shows Esther Kekana to have been in the forefront of fighting against the imposition of Tswana-isation policies (Lekgoathi, 2006; Godsell, 2015).

What makes matters worse for an observer of these historical processes is the mass of contradictions that emerge every time a historical occurrence is interpreted. The caretaker administrators of Marokolong persist in their belief that Esther Kekana was not deposed by Mangope, but by her subjects, by which they mean themselves, the Marokolong section. Among these contradictions are also clashing points among people who are in the same camp, as is the case with Stella Kekana, from Majaneng. From her viewpoint, Esther Kekana was not deposed by Mangope. In fact, for her Mangope had nothing to do with local politics. She simply believes that Ester Kekana ended up working for the Bophuthatswana government until she was deposed by a section of the Kekana clan, just when her eldest daughter Mavis was about to take over. She insists that '[i]t was not Mangope who removed Esther from office. Mangope did not have any problem that we know of. The family insisted that the AmaNdebele are not ruled by women' (Kekana, S., 2017).

As stated elsewhere, the Mangope regime removed Esther Kekana from chiefship, following the recommendations of the Holt Commission, instituted in February 1976.[11] As Esther Kekana submits, she challenged the decision in a court, apparently with the assistance of the community, but lost (Kekana, E., 2017).

Complicating the process leading up to Esther Kekana's deposition is that the Majaneng faction largely supported her (except for the tiny section that always demurred on account of her gender), and the Marokolong section supported her removal, driven by their long-term feud with the Majaneng section. Indeed, Stella Kekana does not seem to differentiate between the internal Majaneng group that objected to Esther Kekana's gender without disputing the legitimacy of the chiefship of their faction, and the Marokolong faction, which was dead set against her primarily because of the question about the historical legitimacy of the Majaneng group, though her gender may also have troubled them.

Divisions within the Majaneng faction

Given the ethnic politics of the Bophuthatswana regime, Esther Kekana's gender played no small part in the continued fragmentation of the Majaneng grouping as the issue of chieftaincy continued to be a source of discord. As the descendants of Johannes Tane Kekana, there are no reports of divisions with the Majaneng faction until the death of chief Hans Kekana in 1962. Hans Kekana's death, however, precipitated protracted internal strife over who is the legitimate heir to the throne, given that he died without sons. This contention should be understood within the broader context of the Majaneng faction, which sees itself as the legitimate ruling house (Kekana, E., 2017). By April 1994 – some 42 years after the death of Hans Kekana – when the democratic government came into power and the bantustan system was dissolved, this issue was still an area of discord within the Majaneng faction. For its part, the Bophuthatswana government had been entangled with and implicated in the ongoing chiefly succession dispute within this section of the AmaNdebele (Mokgabudi, 2017). It had also instituted commissions of inquiry and had countless meetings in which Mangope himself took part (Bophuthatswana Office of the President, 1988).

Go tsena mo tlung/seyantlo

The principle of *go tsena mo tlung* (literal meaning, 'to enter the house') or *seyantlo* (literally, 'the one who goes into the house') also does not seem to have been applied in the case of Esther Kekana, according to her. Practised by both royalty and commoners alike, *seyantlo* was a common cultural tradition among different African cultural communities. Linguistic evidence suggests the existence of widely shared, common socio-cultural concepts that governed the processes of chiefly succession across many cultural communities. We know for a fact, for instance, that '*Ukungena/Go tsena mo tlung*', was a near-universal practice. Comaroff explains that '[a]ccording to this prescription, any man who dies without an heir should have one raised in his name. This is to be undertaken by a younger brother or close agnate, who cohabits with the wife of the dead man' (Comaroff, 1974: 39). Interestingly, the term '*go tsena mo tlung*' is Tswana (and may have had Pedi and southern Sotho variants), and *Ukungena* falls under the Nguni languages, which means it may be Zulu, Swati and Xhosa, all at once. It would seem reasonable to conclude that both among the Sotho and Nguni groupings it was a common practice to fill a vacuum in terms of chieftaincy succession by letting a brother or other agnate partner with the widow of the male relative who died childless.

Popoti Kekana (2017) concedes that, at some point in history, this practice was in use among AmaNdebele: '... we do. If a woman is married and cannot bear children they normally fetch her sister for this purpose. This practice used to be done before, but now it has fallen off.' If the practice was still enforced, Esther Kekana would have married her late husband's surviving brother, Agrippa Kekana. She did not. Some blame her for this, while she blames the Kekana royal family for failing to make this arrangement for her. In her own words, she was prepared to have an arranged second husband so as to retain chiefship within Hans Kekana's homestead.

From the Majaneng faction viewpoint, some think that Esther Kekana spurned Agrippa Kekana, her late husband's brother, because he was disabled and not classy enough for her. Molato Kekana seems to be among those who subscribe to this view. He holds (Kekana, M., 2017) that:

> Esther was supposed to mate with one [of the] male relatives in the clan to have a successor; she did not and chose an outsider because of status. The brother to her husband was probably not classy enough for her. She was already used to classy life. Her son with Motsepe happened after the death of Hans.

Meanwhile, the Marokolong faction contradicts Lekgoathi's claim that Mangope replaced Esther Kekana with Nathaniel Sello Kekana (Marokolong Faction, 2017). According to them, Mangope 'forwarded Agrippa Lepheng Kekana to succeed Esther Kekana; the AmaNdebele community were eyeing Nathaniel Sello (NS) Kekana. NS Kekana was in Alexandra Township and the community went to fetch him to replace Hans Kekana after the removal of Esther Kekana' (Marokolong Faction, 2017).

They claim that Mangope removed NS Kekana because he was not sure of his allegiance and pliability and instead imposed Agrippa Lepheng Kekana on them, the late chief Hans Kekana's brother. However, Agrippa Lepheng Kekana turned out to be an embarrassing choice, since he was a borderline alcoholic and generally indolent (Marokolong Royal Family, 2017). Consequently, Mangope removed him and replaced him with Thomas Mpofane Kekana as Acting Chief. Then he removed Thomas Mpofane Kekana and replaced him with Agrippa Lepheng Kekana for the second time. All these decisions Mangope made unilaterally (Marokolong Royal Family, 2017).

Lepheng died of his alcoholic habits. His wife, Tshidi Rose Kekana, acted as Chief a short while, in place of Lepheng's minor son, Silas Tlhabaki Kekana. Then came allegations against Silas Tlhabaki Kekana, namely that he was illegitimate because he was fathered elsewhere. Silas Tlhabaki Kekana was also disapproved of because of associations with the Mangope government, according to the Marokolong Faction (Marokolong Faction, 2017). Reports say he was a drunk, dissolute and his behaviour bordered on criminal. Yet, if Silas Tlhabaki Kekana was ever co-opted by the Mangope regime, the relationship did not last long. He penned a letter in 1993 titled 'My Grievances as Chief of AmaNdebele-Ba-Lebelo', in which he laments that:

> [I]t is with sore-heart that I grieve as Chief of Amandebele-Ba-Lebelo. Since my installation as Chief of the said tribe, I never had peace of mind to do my job as expected. I've been interrupted all the time when I tried to settle down to my job and this is attributed to the state of Bophuthatswana Republic since my installation in 1990 (Kekana, S., 1993).

Silas Tlhabaki Kekana was knocked down and killed by a car. He died without a son. Subsequently, Agrippa's son, Cornelius Kgomotso Kekana, was installed as Chief, acting for the House of Silas Tlhabaki Kekana.

The future of the AmaNdbele-a-Moletlane

Cornelius Kekana is still (September 2018) the acting chief of the AmaNdebele-a-Moletlane, amidst the ongoing vortex of controversy about which house the legitimate chiefship belongs to. Stella Makatu thinks the community is keen on Mavis Kekana, the daughter of the late Hans Kekana, even though Mavis's old age is an impediment to bearing children. If this were not an inhibitor, Stella Makatu suggests, Mavis would be paired with one of the men from the Kekana royal clan for procreation and therefore solve the problem (Kekana, S., 2017). She also wishes for Cornelius to ask for Mavis's endorsement with a view to sharing the spoils of office of chiefship, so as to give his office legitimacy. She believes because Cornelius's wife is not from the royal house, his succession is already problematic since, if he were to die, he would have no legitimate successor.

Esther Kekana is not sanguine about the future. She believes that '… if it were not for jealousy, these people know that they have the duty to resuscitate this house (i.e. Chief Hans Kekana's House), but in actuality they are killing it. When you ask them as to who they want, they have no clue' (Kekana, E., 2017).

Molato Kekana has set his sights beyond the chiefship and jurisdiction of the current incumbent. His ambition is to once again restore all the areas the Marokolong faction believes historically belong to AmaNdebele-a-Moletlane (Kekana, M. 2017). This he is pursuing despite the findings against the claim, cited earlier.

From the viewpoint of Marokolong, Molato Kekana, who believes himself the paramount chief-in-waiting, is locked in legal battle (at the time of writing, September 2018) with the Gauteng provincial government over the issuance of a certificate of chiefship. He believes the reason for not receiving the certificate is political and that 'individuals with economic interests in our areas are the ones holding up the process. When our matter comes up, it is stalled. Each time we approach the provincial government, we see different people' (Kekana, M., 2017).

Like Molato Kekana, Richard Vonk Kekana is awaiting a certificate from Gauteng provincial government, which will recognise him as the legitimate (paramount) chief of AmaNdebele-a-Moletlane. His concern is that the youth have taken up this struggle and at times keep them (elders) in the dark about developments. It would seem the current generation of the AmaNdebele-a-Motlane have also hurled themselves into this ongoing chiefly saga. He also insists that '[w]hat is for sure is that the current incumbent must be removed. We are only awaiting the legal process and the obtaining of the certificate. Then we will appoint Richard Vonk Kekana to his rightful place' (Marokolong Faction, 2017). Richard Vonk Kekana also alleges that Mavis Kekana has forged documents purporting that the clan support her chiefship. He continues that:

[O]n being asked what we thought about the fraud we assured them that we wanted to challenge them legally. One of us whose signature was genuine reported that the Kekana clan was once called to a meeting in which they were asked to support the claim of Mavis Kekana to the chieftaincy. Many were so incensed that they even left the meeting. Those who remained behind were invited to lunch and plied with alcohol and then a paper was circulated which we were asked to sign without full explanation. Even the one that signed also denounced the resolution (Kekana, V., 2017).

All these claimants are determined to stake a claim on the chiefship of the AmaNdebele-a-Moletlane, each convinced of the legitimacy of their claim, based on the same meta-history of this community.

Conclusion and implications of the findings

This chapter has established the historical conditions responsible for the ongoing chieftaincy succession dispute among the AmaNdebele-a-Moletlane in Hammanskraal, between 1962 and 1994. However detailed the findings presented are, space constraints still prevent full coverage of the entire historical process, spanning a period of 32 years. The mapping of the processes also illustrates how scholarship and divergent, even conflicting, findings tend to complicate and confuse definitive historiography. Hopefully, the current study advances the process of identifying the underpinnings of this dispute.

While it cannot be said that pre-colonial chiefly succession was trouble free, or that there is a direct causal link between indirect rule and chiefly succession disputes within the AmaNdebele-a-Moletlane, colonial rule manifested in the 1928 Native Administration Act and later, through the 1951 Bantu Authorities Act, provided conditions conducive to the perpetuation of chiefly succession disputes. Within the framework of these laws, the bantustan system and the Bophuthatswana regime intervened in the internal affairs of this chieftaincy in a way that proved insidious in the long term.

According to the Marokolong version, the roots of the chieftaincy succession dispute among AmaNdebele-a-Moletlane go back to the early 20th century, but became more pronounced after the death of Chief Hans Kekana in 1962.

Historiography does not seem to have approached the study of this community with even-handedness as far as both factions are concerned. The ethnological studies of Van Warmelo provided the authoritative background on the main narrative of this history. Yet Van Warmelo does not seem to have consulted both sides to the conflict. Critiques of oral sources and other historians have demonstrated the intrinsic bias of both the researchers and the informants, the latter invariably being linked to the ruling elites and therefore recasting history to suit the needs of the moment. The narrative of the AmaNdebele-a-Moletlane seems to have suffered the same fate.

Overall, one can submit that oral sources on the history of this community from both the Majaneng and Marokolong sides have not been entirely impartial or fully informed. Their narratives are garbled, facts and chronologies are incorrect and the personal feelings of informants interfere with even what is generally known or acknowledged from both sides. This, however, does not mean that all oral sources on this history are suspect. Oral sources have over time yielded considerable historical content on this chieftaincy and other areas of historical research.

By covering both sides of the conflict, this chapter attempts to bring out the underlying issues at the core of chieftaincy succession. Many attempts to get to the roots of the historical origins of the chiefly dispute of the AmaNdebele-a-Moletlane scuff the issue by confining their focus to the early 1960s, after the demise of Chief Hans Kekana. Inevitably, this only scrapes the surface of the dispute in that it restricts the focus to one side only, while providing the illusion that the fissures within that one side are the main scope of the issue.

When open hostilities emerged, it turned out that it was not a straightforward matter of a dispute between the Marokolong and the Majaneng sides; there were also internal conflicts within each faction which further complicated the conflict. The Majaneng faction was divided along the lines of gender as Esther Kekana bore the brunt of customary law that saw her turfed out of the position of acting chiefship. The ousting of Esther Kekana took place within the context of the Bophuthatswana bantustan ethnic policies, which were in turn the culmination of the colonial and apartheid systems of indirect rule. The bantustan concept was ethnic in orientation, which resulted in the chieftaincy of the AmaNdebele-a-Moletlane being subjected to continued harassment and arbitrariness.

The Mangope regime used the prevailing climate of hostility within this community to its own advantage; it rewarded those who towed the line and punished those who rebelled against it, without seeking to address the root causes of the chiefly succession dispute. The regime also took it for granted that the legitimate lineage of chieftainship resided in the line of Johannes Tane Kekana, as has historically been the case.

This chapter does not cover the period since April 1994, when the bantustan system was dissolved. Even though commissions of inquiry were instituted to consider the question of chiefly succession disputes, the post-1994 period does not appear to have brought justice to the issue of the AmaNdebele-a-Moletlana. As the pre-1994 era overflowed into the post-1994 one, there are historical continuities that blur the boundary between the two periods. In fact, the conflict may have been exacerbated by the various findings of the post-1994 government's commissions of inquiry. During its time, the Mangope regime seems to have taken for granted much of the historical record handed down from the time of Van Warmelo; it appears that the democratic dispensation has been doing the same and has not explored the historical roots of the chieftaincy succession dispute.

Overall, this study has found that it is not possible to fully understand the ongoing, entangled chieftaincy succession dispute among AmaNdebele-a-Moletlane without taking account of the framework of the bantustan system and the environment created by a history of indirect rule. While the origins of the dispute cannot be directly ascribed to the Bophuthatswana bantustan, the hypothesis argued here is that British colonial policies which distorted or misunderstood indigenous political and cultural systems, served to both worsen and perpetuate the division.

The 1951 Bantu Authorities Act propped up the bantustan system and the wider apartheid system that underpinned it. However, the Act also compromised the institution of chieftaincy, rendering it unstable. Thus, the institution of chieftaincy came to be based on misapprehension, fabrications and wilful distortion for self-preservation, and so was refigured into an institution contingent on external forces and historical conditions. This intervention into the nature and character of chieftaincy proved insidious for the AmaNdebele-a-Moletlane in the Hammanskraal area.

References

Beinart, W. 1995. 'Chieftaincy and the concept of articulation: South Africa circa 1900–50', in Beinart, W. & Dubow, S. (eds.) *Segregation and Apartheid in Twentieth-Century South Africa*. London: Routledge.

Bophuthatswana Office of the President. 1988. 'Commission of Inquiry Report about the AmaNdebele-a-Moletlane Tribal Authority'. Report 6/4/2, 1988. Northwest Provincial Archives, Mafikeng.

Comaroff, J. L. 1974. 'Chiefship in a South African homeland: A case study of the chiefdom of Bophuthatswana'. *Journal of Southern African Studies*, 1 (1), 36–51.

Esterhilder Nchadi Kekana vs Lucas Manyane Mangope & Nathaniel Sello Kekana, The Minister of Bantu Administration and Development. 1 June 1977. Supreme Court of South Africa.

Godsell, S. 2015. 'Blurred borders of belonging, Hammanskraal histories 1942–2000'. PhD thesis. Johannesburg: University of the Witwatersrand.

Hammond-Tooke, D. 1997. *Imperfect Interpreters: South Africa's Anthropologists 1920–1990*. Johannesburg: Wits University Press.

Kekana, Esther (former chieftainess). 14 September 2017. Interview with author, Majaneng, Hammanskraal.

Kekana, Leka. 22 March 1994. Memorandum of Agreement. Kekana Royal Executive Council. North West Provincial Archives, Mafikeng.

Kekana, Setlaboswana & Kekana, Popoti. 16 October 2017. Interview with author, Rathoke.

Kekana, Silas Tlhabaki. 28 September 1993. 'My Grievance as chief of AmaNdebele-Ba-Lebelo'. Letter. North West Provincial Archives, Mafikeng.

Kekana, Stella. 20 October 2017. Interview with author, Majaneng, Hammanskraal.

Ketlano, Molato. 15 September 2017. Interview with author, Roodepoort.

Lekgoathi, S. P. 2003. 'Chiefs, migrants and North Ndebele ethnicity in the context of surrounding homeland politics, 1965–1978'. *African Studies*, 62 (1), 54–75.

Lekgoathi, S. P. 2009. 'Colonial' experts, local interlocutors, informants and the making of an archive on the Transvaal, Ndebele, 1930–1989'. *The Journal of African History*, 50 (1), 61–80.

Majaneng District Memo. 15 December 1987. 'Recognition and appointment of chief Karel Seroto Kekana'. North West Provincial Archives, Mafikeng.

Marokolong Faction: Kekana, Vonk (Paramount Chief of Leeukraal), Kekana, Simon (his senior uncle) & Kekana, Makera (Royal Family member). 24 October 2017. Interview with author, Marokolong, Hammanskraal.

Marokolong Royal Family: Kekana, Stuurman; Kekana, Jakalas & Kekana, Makera, 20 October 2017. Interview with author, Hammanskraal.

Matabane, Mrs. Secretary to the President (Mangope). 15 May 1990. 'Amandebele Tribe. Moretele'. Letter. North West Provincial Archives, Mafikeng.

Miller, J. 1999. 'History and Africa/Africa and history.' *The American Historical Review*, 104 (1), 1–32.

Mokgabudi, B. 19 October 2017. Interview with author, Majaneng, Hammanskraal.

Mophatlhana, A. 17 September 1986. 'Reconstitution and appointment of acting Chief Mbofane Thomas Kekana'. Majaneng District, Moretele. Memorandum. North West Provincial Archives, Mafikeng.

Myers, J. C. 2008. *Indirect Rule in South Africa*. Rochester: University of Rochester Press.

O'Meara, D. 1983. *Volkskapitalisme; Class Capital and Ideology in the Development of Afrikaner Nationalism 1934–1948*. Cambridge: Cambridge University Press.

Peires, J. 1981. *The House of Phalo: A history of the Xhosa people in the days of their independence*. Berkeley: University of California Press.

Prins, G. 1992. 'Oral history', in Burke, P. (ed.) *New Perspectives on Historical Writing*. University Park: Penn State University Press.

Tosh, J. 1984. *The Pursuit of History,* 2nd Edition. London/New York: Longman.

Van Warmelo, N. J. 1935. 'A preliminary survey of the Bantu Tribes of South Africa'. *Ethnological Publications*, 5. Pretoria: Government Printer, pp. 43–61.

Van Warmelo, N. J. 1944. 'The Ndebele of J Kekana'. *Ethnological Publications*, 18. Pretoria: Government Printer, p. 12.

Notes

1   It is useful to distinguish between 'oral history' and 'oral tradition'. The former refers to '… oral evidence specific to the life experiences of the informant. Such evidence does not pass from generation to generation …', while the latter denotes 'oral testimony transmitted verbally from generation to the next, or more' (Prins, 1992: 120).

2   The Marokolong faction is one of the two main factions (along with Majaneng faction) fighting over the chieftaincy succession of the AmaNdebele-a-Moletlane in Hammanskraal.

3   Genealogically, Bulongo is one of the early ancestors of the Transvaal Ndebele people. Yangalala, one of his three sons, fathered Maboyaboya, from whom descended Mamokebe and Lebelo Seroto. It is thus not possible for Bulongo to have been part of the palace intrigue during Lebelo's generation as alleged by Molato Kekana.

4   Letter to Leka Jacob Kekana, of the Kekana Royal Executive Council, by Emma Mashinini, Regional Claims Commissioner: Gauteng, Mpumalanga, North West and Northern Province, 21 October 1996

5   Letter from Emma Mashinini, Regional Land Claims Commissioner of Gauteng and North-West, to Geoff Budlender, Director-General Land Affairs and Agriculture, 9 June 1999

6   Letter by Emma Mashinini, Regional Land Claims Commissioner: Gauteng and North West, 4 May 1999. This letter was intended for Mr Geoff Budlender, Director-General of Land Affairs and Agriculture, under the title: Response to Queries Raised by the Kekana Royal Executive Council in their Letter Dated 27th May 1999 Regarding the Non-Acceptance of their Land Claims on the Farms Leeuwkraal 92 JR and Eighty-One Others in Districts of Hammanskraal, Pretoria, Moretele 1, Warmbad in Gauteng, North West and Northern Province.

7   For instance, the Mangope regime has always referred to this dispute, even though it has often dismissed the Marokolong faction's claim as false. See, for example, the findings of the Commission of Inquiry, AmaNdebele Tribal Authority, 'Bophuthatswana Office of the President', 6/4/2, p. 2.

8   *Esterhilde Nchadi Kekana vs Lucas Manyane Mangobe, Nathaniel Sello Kekena, the Minister of Bantu Administration & Development.* 1 June 1977. Supreme Court of South Africa (Transvaal Provincial Division).

9   *Esterhilde Nchadi Kekana vs Lucas Manyane Mangobe, Nathaniel Sello Kekena, the Minister of Bantu Administration & Development.* 1 June 1977. Supreme Court of South Africa (Transvaal Provincial Division).

10 *Esterhilde Nchadi Kekana vs Lucas Manyane Mangobe, Nathaniel Sello Kekena, the Minister of Bantu Administration & Development.* 1 June 1977. Supreme Court of South Africa (Transvaal Provincial Division).

11 *Esterhilde Nchadi Kekana vs Lucas Manyane Mangobe, Nathaniel Sello Kekena, The Minister of Bantu Administration and Development.* 1st June 1977. Supreme Court of South Africa (Transvaal Provincial Division).

NINE

Emerging rural struggles against unelected traditional authorities and the role of the courts

Lessons from rural villages of the Eastern Cape

FANI NCAPAYI

Introduction

In seeking to realise the more radical vision [...], perhaps most problematic is the road to this future agrarian economy. As noted earlier, neither a land movement nor a radicalising state presently exists in South Africa. Historical and global evidence, including the example of Zimbabwe, strongly suggest that massive rural mobilisation is required in order to push through any meaningful rural change (Hendricks et al., 2013: 357).

A s this quotation argues, there is a view that South Africa needs to chart a 'radical vision' that is based on an agrarian economy with equitable access to productive land for rural residents with land-based livelihoods. More importantly for our purposes is the argument that 'massive rural mobilisation is required' for the attainment of the 'radical vision'. But in his chapter, 'South Africa's countryside: prospects for change from below', Ntsebeza (2013b: 153–4) concludes that 'rurally-oriented social movements' are still weak and 'would remain weak at least for some time'. Ntsebeza bases his conclusion on the lack of a clear indication from social movements of how to attain the radical vision, and their heavy dependence on external funding (Ntsebeza, 2013b: 153–154).

This chapter reflects on emerging rural struggles over leadership, land and other resources, and the possibilities for rural mobilisation in South Africa's countryside, similar to the Mpondo Revolts and the Mnxe Tshisa-tshisa campaign in the 1960s (Ntsebeza, 2011). Since 2013, there has been a mushrooming of rural struggles[1] across the Eastern Cape for the democratisation of rural governance. Civil society organisations in the form of rural people's organisations and non-governmental organisations (NGOs) played an important role in the struggles and mobilisation of rural people. In Cala Reserve, this followed attempts by Chief Gecelo and the KwaGcina Traditional Council (KTC) to impose an unelected headman in the village. The imposition of unelected traditional authorities has triggered a growing demand for the democratisation of governance in rural areas. The struggle of the residents of Cala Reserve, despite their reliance on the legal system, has snowballed as news of their battle spread to other rural areas across the Eastern Cape. This followed a challenge in the High Court by the residents of Cala Reserve against the imposition of the unelected headman by Chief Gecelo and his traditional council in 2013. The residents opposed the imposition because it conflicted with the longstanding practice of residents electing their headmen. On the other hand, the chief believed that it was his sole prerogative to decide, without consultation with the residents, who the headman of the village should be. Not only did the residents successfully challenge the imposition, they also used the judgment to encourage other communities to stand up against the chiefs' undemocratic tendencies. Thus, the High Court judgment became a mobilising tool in other rural communities in Ngcobo, Lady Frere, Cofimvaba, Indwe, Centane, Whittlesea, Stutterheim, Berlin and Peddie. This marks a groundswell in these rural villages of demands for the right of residents to elect their local leaders.

This chapter argues that while it is true that there are presently no strong rurally oriented social movements in South Africa, the emerging rural struggles discussed above raise the possibility of the development of just such a rurally oriented social movement to lead the transformation of the countryside. Although the case started in Cala Reserve and was largely pursued through the High Court, the judgment became an organising instrument, whose ramifications go well beyond Cala Reserve, reverberating throughout the whole province. Indeed, during a Provincial Conference in June 2016, which was co-hosted by the Eastern Cape House of Traditional Leaders (ECHTL), the South African Local Government Association (SALGA) and Mrs Serobe, the founder of the Women's Investment Portfolio Holdings (WHIPHOLD),[2] demands were made by community representatives from across the Eastern Cape, starting from communities such as Prudhoe around Peddie, in the west, to Caguba in Port St John's in the east. The community representatives demanded elected and accountable leaders in their areas.[3] The successful High Court challenge to the legitimacy of Chief Maqoma by the Amahlathi Crisis Committee, representing eight communities next to Stutterheim, is another example.[4] Furthermore, in November 2017, submissions were made by 22 rural communities in the Western Cape to the senior chief in Qamata about the undemocratic and abusive behaviour of traditional authorities, illustrating the reverberations of these rural struggles.[5]

The next section discusses the origins of the current rural struggles, highlighting processes leading to the emergence of the struggle to democratise rural governance. Following on from that, consideration is given to the response of members of a group called the Planning Committee (PC) to the imposition of an unelected headman in Cala Reserve, including the decision to pursue the legal route. The PC consists of representatives from the six sub-villages of Cala Reserve established to support the outgoing headman. The paper ends with discussion of, and concluding remarks about, the wider significance of such moments and the possible ramifications for future challenges to traditional authorities.

The genesis of rural struggles to democratise governance

The genesis of the current rural struggles is the 'landmark judgment' by the High Court in Bhisho on 18 August 2015 (Rickard, 2015). As is explained later, the judgment appears to have opened the floodgates by enabling rural residents to challenge the legitimacy of traditional authorities in many rural areas of the Eastern Cape. The judgment by a full bench of High Court judges followed an appeal against an earlier judgment by the lower division of the High Court by the local chief (Chief Gecelo of the KTC), the premier of the Eastern Cape, the Member of the Executive Committee (MEC) for the Department of Cooperative Governance and Traditional Affairs (COGTA) and the Eastern Cape House of Traditional Leaders (ECHTL). This appeal was the reason for the second judgment of the full bench of the High Court.

It was collaboration between the provincial government and traditional authorities, rather than an election, that led to the imposition of a headman in Cala Reserve on 27 March 2013. The imposed headman replaced Mr Jongilizwe Hamilton Fani, who had retired at the end of February 2013. Since the colonial period in the late 19th century, headmen in Cala Reserve had been elected. Mr Fani's election to headmanship in 1979 was the last in the area. According to Ntsebeza (2013), there is a list of elected headmen in Cala Reserve,[6] beginning with Duncan Makhohliso (Mfengu), followed by Boy Nophothe (Mpondomise), Mahlamvana Guata, Velile Guata and Sthukuthezi Guata (amaGcina). As can be seen from the list, all the headmen, except the Guatas from the amaGcina clan, came from different families. Even the Guata members assumed leadership through election. Thus, Cala Reserve, together with the 20 other villages in the former Xhalanga magisterial district, had an established tradition of elected headmen.[7]

The Transkei Authorities Act No. 4 of 1965 prescribed that registered voters, who happened to be only men in whose name land was registered, were consulted in the selection of headmen. Yet, in practice, elderly men and women also participated in electing their headmen. These residents would participate from the identification of candidates, who were given time to canvass support before the actual elections. On the day of the elections, the candidates were put in front of voters, who were asked to queue behind the candidate of their choice (see Ntsebeza, 2013a). The residents of Cala Reserve reported similar processes in their area.[8] Thus, the election process of headmen was transparent and democratic in so far as it was conducted publicly and allowed the participation of elderly men and women.

According to Cala Reserve elder Mr Jongilizwe Tasana, the impending retirement of Mr Fani sparked polarised discussions in Cala Reserve from the outset.[9] Mr Tasana is not just one of the few elders in the community, but is also one of the councillors and a close confidante of Mr Jongilizwe Fani. The discussions revolved around the headman's replacement and the process for this. Some residents were concerned about whether there would be adherence to the tradition of electing a headman, while others were not. Nonetheless, the discussions divided the residents between those who wanted an elected headman, in line with their custom, and those who wanted an umGcina[10] (of the chief's family) as leader of the village.

The indifference of some residents about whether the tradition of electing headmen would be followed or not stems from their different interests. Some residents saw the vacancy of headmanship in Cala Reserve as an opportunity for their family members. Instead of pulling together, the discussions rekindled historical social divisions between the *bona fides* or *iinzalelwane* (i.e. born and bred in the area) and the outsiders also referred to as *amalose*. *Amalose* consist mainly of former farm workers who are viewed as *omabhulwini*[11] or outsiders in the community. Some *bona fides* reject the leadership of people considered as *omabhulwini*. The candidate headman – Gideon

Sitwayi – was regarded as an outsider even though he had lived in the village since the 1950s. He had also been headman Fani's right-hand man and even acted as headman when the former's health failed, according to the court papers.[12]

The character of the person chosen to lead the village was of particular concern for Mr Tasana.[13] Sharing his views with the author at the beginning of February 2013, Mr Tasana pointed out that the residents may take 'ill-considered decisions by choosing someone who is not useful to the community' (*izigqibo ezingenangqiqo, sithathe umntu ongeyonzuzo kulelali*). Mr Tasana made clear his preference for Mr Gideon Sitwayi, not only because he was already a sub-headman and the deputy of headman Fani, but also because he was a well-mannered person. Other residents were equally concerned about the headman's retirement. One of these was Mr Mcebisi Ntamo, a community leader in the area who echoed Mr Tasana's views.[14] On 26 February 2013, Mr Mcebisi Ntamo reported on a community meeting that took place in Cala Reserve the previous day.[15] The meeting was called by members of the local PC[16] who decided to be pro-active and not allow the KTC members to dictate terms to the community. Participants in the meeting selected Mr Gideon Sitwayi as the new headman. All except one of the participants at the meeting chose Mr Sitwayi as the future leader. The dissenter was a member of the Guata family, who, according to Mr Ntamo, indicated that he would prefer the new headman to come from his family. The member reasoned that the headmanship should revert to his family because as far as he was concerned, headman Fani held the position on behalf of the family.

Although at the meeting in which Mr Sitwayi was selected as headman everyone was allowed to express views about the replacement of Mr Fani, no other names were proposed for the vacancy besides the name of Mr Sitwayi. The residents present in the meeting were allowed to discuss at length the issue of the replacement of Mr Fani and no one objected to the identification of Mr Gideon Sitwayi as the replacement.

Participants in the meeting later mandated the incumbent headman, the late Mr Penrose Ntamo (a brother of Mcebsis Ntamo), and one of Mr Fani's sub-headmen, to report the community's decision to the KTC. However, the community decision did not sit well with the council members (i.e. councillors of the chief) who severely criticised Mr Fani when he and Mr Penrose Ntamo delivered the report. The first to register his disapproval was the secretary of the council who angrily told the delegates that the community acted illegally by not involving the traditional council when holding the meeting to choose the new headman. Nonetheless, the secretary promised the delegates that the council members would discuss the report in their meeting scheduled for 4 March 2013. The secretary's unhappiness was just a prelude to what was to follow.[17]

The council's hostile attitude towards the decision of the Cala Reserve residents should be seen in the context of a long struggle that rural residents, in various parts of South Africa, have mounted from the 1940s. Examples include the rural struggles in Sekhukhune in the 1940s, Witzieshoek/Zeerust in the 1950s, Mpondoland in the late 1950s to early 1960s and in Xhalanga in the late 1960s (see Redding, 2009; Ntsebeza, 2011; Badat, 2012). The denial by the apartheid government of the rights of rural people to democracy and equality accounts for the resistance (Ntsebeza, 2011: 2). Fierce opposition to traditional authorities from rural residents in the 1980s to early 1990s, led by the South African National Civic Organisation (SANCO), weakened and even led to the collapse of some structures of traditional authority, especially in the Ciskei (Manona, 1997; Wotshela, 2009). The formation of the ANC-aligned Congress of Traditional Leaders of South Africa (Contralesa), in 1987, marked traditional authorities' resurgence (Ntsebeza, 2004). Contralesa gained implicit recognition in the new South African Constitution of 1996, which called for legislation to ensure the recognition of traditional leaders. One such piece of legislation is the Traditional Leadership and Governance Framework Act (TLGFA) No. 41 of 2003 which, among other things, calls for the transformation of tribal authorities into traditional councils.

In Xhalanga, rural resistance led to the burning down of the houses of opponents and supporters of tribal authorities in two villages – Mnxe and Tsengiwe – in the 1960s (Ntsebeza, 2004). Four tribal authorities were eventually established in Xhalanga in 1957, despite fierce opposition.[18] The KwaGcina Tribal Authority (now the KTC), under Chief Gecelo, is one of the traditional councils with six administrative areas – Cala Reserve, Manzimdaka, Mbenge, Hota-Mbeula, Nyalasa and Qhiba. As in other rural areas, traditional authorities were under tremendous pressure in Xhalanga in the late 1980s to early 1990s. In 1991, the headman of Mnxe was removed and replaced with an elected headman (Ntsebeza, 2005). The number of unelected headmen grew in Xhalanga from 2007, following the promulgation of the provincial Traditional Leadership and Governance Act No. 4 in 2005. Traditional authorities believe the provincial act empowers them to select headmen without consulting communities.

The KTC members were furious about the developments in Cala Reserve, according to two text messages from Mr Zwelakhe Moni, who worked for the local NGO – Cala University Students Association (CALUSA).[19] He wrote:

> Things are getting tough regarding the election of the new headman (in Cala Reserve). It seems there are people in the traditional council who are opposed to the elected new headman. (*Izinto zifuna ukubanzima malunga nosibonda omtsha. Ingathi kukho abantu abayiphikisayo enqileni.*)[20]

Zwelakhe's second message was even more revealing of the attitude of the amaGcina royal family.

> I am presently accompanying members of Cala Reserve to deliver a letter to the traditional council about the election of the new headman. My sense is that there are headmen (from the six administrative areas that are under the council) who disapprove of the election of the new headman, especially those from the amaGcina clan. These headmen allege that Mr Fani acted out of line in allowing the election of the headman to take place.[21]

Zwelakhe further reported that the headmen in the traditional council harshly criticised headman Fani for allowing the community meeting to take place. This was despite the fact that headman Fani had explained that the meeting was called by the PC and it was the right of the community to meet if they wanted to. According to Zwelakhe, members of the traditional council would hear none of that.[22] The KTC members viewed the developments as thwarting their intentions of installing their close relative.

Mr Fani's report in the meeting of the PC on 10 March 2013 confirmed Zwelakhe's report. He said: 'the KTC members attacked me for allowing the community to elect my replacement' (*iNqila indihlasele kakhulu ngokuvumela ukuba umzi wonyule umntu ozakuthatha iintambo kum*). Thus, the council had rejected the community decision. In the process of rejecting Mr Sitwayi's name, members of the council questioned the authenticity of the attendance register on the grounds that there were no signatures against the names of participants in the community meeting. The council members ended their attack on Mr Fani by informing him that they would come to the community on 11 March to handle the process of replacing the headman. They also warned him that they would come with the police to maintain law and order during the community meeting.[23]

The hostile reaction from the KTC members shows their disrespect for the views of local people and how keen the members were on imposing their views on the residents. The reaction also confirms the criticism about traditional authorities' lack of accountability to the people they lead (Hendricks & Ntsebeza, 1999; Ntsebeza, 1999; 2005; Jara, 2011).

In the same meeting, PC members discussed preparations for the impending visit by members of the council. The behaviour of the council members hardened the attitude of the PC. Mrs Nomvuzo Nophothe's views, which were expressed in the same meeting, aptly capture the mood of PC members. She pointed out that, '[w]e are in a struggle that needs us to constantly meet to strategise. Therefore, we should not waste time arguing about the attendance register. We need to think about how we engage in this struggle (*Sisedabini, masihlale singqubana, sibonisana ngalomba. Akuzukusinceda ukuba sibesixoxa nge-register. Intoekufanele siyenze kukucinga ukuba elidabi sililwanjani na)'.*[24] The reference to the attendance register relates to the query by members of the council about the authenticity of participants in the community meeting that had selected the new headman. In appreciation of Nomvuzo's challenge, PC members resolved to meet weekly to review developments and to plan their actions. They honoured this resolution, and from 2013 up to the present day the council has met weekly.

It also transpired in the meeting that the visit of the KTC delegation planned for 10 March had been postponed indefinitely. Although members of the PC suspected that the postponement was a ploy by the council to confuse the community and to disrupt the leadership, they decided to continue with the meeting in order to strategise. They also decided to notify the community about the postponement of the meeting at a community meeting, which they would hold on the 13 March 2013 (Ncapayi, 2013).

The agenda of the community meeting on 13 March, which was attended by 20 community members, had two items: report on the meeting of the KTC and report on land allocations in Cala Reserve. Headman Fani reported his hostile reception by members of the council. In view of the report, participants in the meeting concluded that the council members had adopted a confrontational approach. The discussions then focused on how to deal with the situation. It was agreed that the KTC delegation should not be allowed to have a separate meeting with the PC. Instead, the delegation should meet with the community. The aim was to avoid confusion and suspicions that members of the PC had been bought over by the council delegation.[25]

The meeting of the council delegates with Cala Reserve residents eventually materialised on 27 March 2013. From the outset, Chief Gecelo and his traditional council showed unwillingness to be held accountable. They unsuccessfully tried to block residents in the meeting from discussing the issue of the headmanship. After the formalities, the chairperson of the meeting – Mr Jentile (a member of the council) – remarked that they did not intend to have a discussion, but came to introduce the person the royal family had chosen as the headman of Cala Reserve.

Indeed, when the chief spoke, he reiterated Mr Jentile's remarks that they came not to answer questions, but to announce the new headman of the area. He continued, saying 'the man with spectacles in this house should stand up for the people to see him (*indoda eneglass aph' endlwini mayiphakame abantu bayibone*)'.[26] To the surprise of the residents, the person who stood up was Mr Ndodenkulu Yolelo, a taxi owner who had, until recently, mostly been based in Cape Town. Like the chief, he is an umGcina. The chief then asked whether the nominee accepted the nomination to be headman. When the person responded in the positive, the chief exclaimed: 'I am done with what I came for (*ndiyigqibile ke into ebendizokuyenza*).'[27] Thereafter, the chief sat down without explaining what had happened to the name of the headman the residents had selected and submitted to the council.

After a moment of silence, as if people were still digesting what they had just heard, the hands of residents abruptly shot up. Participants wanted to comment on or ask questions about the events they had just witnessed. The chairperson unsuccessfully attempted to block discussions by once more reminding the residents that his delegation was not there to respond to questions. He further indicated that he was rushing somewhere. Eventually, he reluctantly allowed questions and comments, after people started grumbling.[28] One of the participants wanted to know whether the council delegation intended to disregard the views of residents concerning the name of the person they preferred as the new headman. Another asked whether or not democracy applied to rural areas.

As in other communities, the views of the residents in the meeting were not unanimous. Some residents took a different view to the majority of the residents. For instance, an elderly woman asked: 'Why are you questioning decisions of the chief? I am really surprised at the lack of respect for the chief that I'm witnessing here (*Kutheni niyixambulisa kangaka nje inkosi? Noko ndiyothuka yilento ndiyibonayo yokungahlonitshwa kwenkosi*).' Another participant, Mr Madoda Nophothe, demanded that the residents should stop the questions 'which are a waste of people's time'. He further pleaded with the residents to accept what the delegation had decided. He almost did not finish his point as people shouted him down. Amid grumblings, Mr Mcebisi Ntamo furiously shouted: '[J]ust leave the meeting and do not stop us if you have no questions. Don't decide for us.' The tension in the room rose as other residents pointed out that there was no protocol that prevented people from asking the chief questions.[29] In response, Mr Jentile (of the traditional council) explained that things had changed with regard to the election of headmen by communities. According to him, 'that practice has stopped since the new law, which instructs that the royal family elects the headmen'. In other words, he suggested that it was the prerogative of the chief to decide who the headman of Cala Reserve should be. He further pointed out that the community could only object to the chief's choice if there was evidence that the nominee was a criminal or a rapist. The headman of Mbhenge – Headman Gecelo – concluded the discussion by arrogantly remarking that, 'whether you like it or not, it is the royal family that decides on the headmen (*nokuba niyathanda okanye anithandi na, yiroyal family ethatha izigqibo ngokubekwa kweenkosana*)'.[30] Thereafter, the chairperson requested that the delegation be released as some of them had already indicated that they had other commitments. He advised those who were unhappy to write to the traditional council, stating the reasons for their unhappiness.

This section has shown how traditional authorities rode roughshod over the residents and disregarded the views of the community regarding ascension to the position of headman. The traditional authorities disregarded the community's expressed wish to have a headman of their choice, something which is a standing practice in the community. The actions of traditional authorities, which confirm Ntsebeza's (2005; 2013) argument that traditional authorities are unelected and thus undemocratic, left the residents of Cala Reserve very unhappy. Their unhappiness triggered a struggle that spread like a prairie fire from one village to another across the province. The rapid spread of this struggle is evidenced in the number of communities that approached CALUSA[31] for assistance, as well as in the views expressed by residents in various Transkei and Ciskei communities visited by the author and by representatives of the Legal Resources Centre following the High Court judgment.

The response of the PC and other structures to the imposition of an unelected headman

This section focuses on the response of the PC leaders, structures of Siyazakha Land and Development Forum and CALUSA members to the imposition of the unelected headman in Cala Reserve. Siyazakha is a local rural people's organisation that was formed in 2007 to act as a voice for rural people in the Sakhisizwe Local Municipality and other neighbouring municipalities. Cala is one of the two towns under the Sakhisizwe Local Municipality. Although not registered, Siyazakha has a Constitution and an elected leadership. Siyazakha is part of a national rural movement called Inyanda National Land Movement. CALUSA is a non-governmental organisation with seven staff members and works with rural communities in Sakhisizwe, Emalahleni, Ngcobo, Intsika Yethu and Enoch Mgijima local municipalities. It focuses on land and agrarian issues, democratisation of governance and youth development. Underpinning the programmes is research that is aimed at building Siyazakha as a rural movement. Siyazakha is at the forefront of the struggle to democratise rural governance.

As will be seen below, the PC organised local meetings and kept the struggle alive through a range of activities, including approaching its lawyers. Siyazakha encouraged its members to actively support the struggle of Cala Reserve. For instance, Siyazakha included a discussion about the struggle in its workshops to update its members and to encourage its members' participation in the struggle. CALUSA members supported the residents of Cala Reserve by documenting the processes, providing transport, linking the PC members with the traditional council and the Regional Traditional Council in Qamata and facilitating communication with the provincial government (the Premier's Office, the Department of Cooperative Governance and Traditional Affairs) and the Legal Resources Centre (LRC). CALUSA members, including the author, also raised awareness in communities through workshops and inputs in meetings.

Soon after the meeting of the KTC members, the agitated local leaders (members of the PC) briefly met and resolved to take further steps regarding the issue of headmanship in their community. The resolve of the leaders to pursue the matter is captured by Mr Mcebisi Ntamo's remark that, 'it is now time for cowards to move backwards (*Ngoku kufuneka amagwala ayekulonina*)'.[32] The remark is indicative of the determination of the PC members not to give up the fight to defend the democratic rights of the community. Thus, after the events at the meeting of the KTC delegation with the residents of Cala Reserve, the PC members decided to challenge the imposition of an unelected headman. Importantly, the decision to challenge the imposition of an unelected headman marked the beginning of the struggle for the democratisation of rural governance in Cala Reserve.

A number of actions were identified to take the struggle forward. The first one was a meeting with representatives of CALUSA on 2 April to formulate a response to the developments.[33] In the meeting, PC members also handed in a formal request for support from CALUSA, which was accepted by CALUSA.[34] Members of the KTC were also informed that the author would lead CALUSA's work relating to this matter. Flowing from discussions in the meeting, the agreement was to mount the struggle on three fronts; namely engaging and putting pressure on the chief and the council members to reverse their decision; exerting pressure on the premier and the Member of the Executive Council (MEC) of COGTA to intervene; and mounting a legal challenge.[35]

Regarding putting pressure on the chief and KTC members, the council members and Chief Gecelo were bombarded with a flurry of letters. The first of the letters was written to the council on 2 April 2013. In the letter, the PC members sought to persuade the council members to reconsider their stance with regard to the community views about Mr Yolelo (the council's elected headman). Copies of the letters were also sent to the MEC for COGTA and to the Premier's Office, as the institutions responsible for traditional authorities. Although traditional authorities operate under COGTA, it is the premier that accepts and endorses the names of new headmen and chiefs. Letters were also sent to the Regional Traditional Council in Qamata, which is the regional structure in Western Thembuland that the KTC and chiefs account to. It was only the Premier's Office that responded and indicated that the matter had been referred to COGTA for consideration.

Furthermore, CALUSA members advised the PC leaders to ensure that residents were mobilised around the headmanship issue. The aim was to ensure that the struggle did not become the concern of PC leaders only. In line with this, Siyazakha had to be approached for support.[36] Indeed, Siyazakha did support the struggle by teaming up with PC leaders to organise a protest march to Chief Gecelo's place, where a petition was handed over in early November 2013.[37] Representatives from groups in the villages of Sifonondile, Mnxe and Luphaphasi also participated in the march, as members of Siyazakha. The presence of Siyazakha members in the march showed its support for the struggle. Two weeks after the march, Chief Gecelo and his council responded by indicating that the Regional Traditional Council would respond on their behalf. However, the chief's response did not impress the PC members and CALUSA because the regional structure had already been unsuccessfully lobbied to intervene in the issue, and it was clear that the Regional Traditional Council supported Chief Gecelo's actions (Ncapayi, 2013).

In addition to the march, PC members conducted door-to-door visits in the community to explain what the struggle was about. During the door-to-door visits, the PC members also collected signatures from the residents to demonstrate community support for the struggle. Copies of the forms were also sent to residents who were migrant workers in urban centres such as Johannesburg and Cape Town. These efforts solicited about 390 signatures of local residents and migrant workers who pledged their support for the struggle.[38] Migrant workers constituted about 30 per cent of the signatories, while the rest were local residents. Cala Reserve has 435 households and the majority of the signatures were those of location community members. Moreover, the PC members organised regular community meetings in December, starting from 2013, to brief locals and migrant workers about developments in the village.[39] Some of the migrants even pledged financial support to assist with the payment of transport costs incurred when PC members attended the High Court in Bhisho. The holding of meetings in December has since become an annual occurrence, when the migrant workers are around (see CALUSA Annual Report, 2014). The rural-urban linkage shows that the struggle is not localised/parochial, but has urban linkages and support, similar to the rural resistance of the 1960s (see Ntsebeza, 2004). This shows the active interest migrant workers took in developments in their rural areas.

The legal route and the spread of the campaign beyond the Sakhisizwe Local Municipality

When lobbying the traditional authorities and the government did not yield results, the PC and CALUSA resolved to take the struggle to the courts as the next phase of the strategy. Working with CALUSA, PC members approached the Legal Resources Centre (LRC) to mount a legal challenge in the High Court in Bhisho (CALUSA, 2013; 2014). As is already known, the legal challenge led to two High Court judgments in Bhisho (Case No, 169/14). The first judgment, by Acting Judge Nhlangulela in the lower division of the High Court, in October 2014 found the premier of the Eastern Cape to have erred in recognising the nomination of Mr Ndodenkulu Yolelo as the headman of Cala Reserve. The judge reasoned that the recognition disregarded the customary practice of not only the village, but also of the entire former Xhalanga magisterial district. According to the judge:

> [The] respondents could pitch their argument no higher than the contention that the Governance Act places the identification of a headman in the hands of the Royal Family only. I have already found that the statement is wrong to the extent that the Royal Family and the Premier failed to take into account the applicable customary law in the Cala Reserve Community as proven in the doctoral thesis of Professor Ntsebeza. In the light of this failure, I find the respondents acted in breach of section 18 of the Governance Act ... Consequently, the applicants must succeed.

This emphatic judgment notwithstanding, the Premier's Office, the MEC for COGTA, the Eastern Cape House of Traditional leaders (ECHTL) and the KTC royal family appealed. This was immediately after the judgment was handed down. The involvement of the provincial government in the appeal was surprising to the civil society organisations considering that all provincial political leaders are elected. This shows that politicians are prepared to sacrifice the democratic rights of rural residents to keep traditional authorities on their side.

Nonetheless, from the beginning of 2014 the judgment became an organising tool for CALUSA and PC members. CALUSA members, working with Siyazakha, attempted to ensure that the struggle was not confined to Cala Reserve. In a message communicated to rural residents through local community radio – Vukani Community Radio – we from CALUSA and representatives of the PC pointed out that the judgment meant that rural residents can challenge the imposition of headmen in their areas. The responses of listeners to the radio presentations gave an indication of the number of communities with similar challenges. Thus, a coordinating structure called the Democratisation Task Team (DTT), consisting of three representatives from each of these villages: Cala Reserve, Indwana, Mnxe, Sifonondile and Tsengiwe, was established. These are administrative areas in which residents experienced governance problems caused by their headmen. For instance, the representatives highlighted that some headmen refused to append signatures when required for the initiation of boys, used vulgar language against residents and threatened residents physically.[40]

There were fears that the struggle would be isolated or marginalised. This is reflected in the internal documents of CALUSA and the discussions of the author with various members of CALUSA.[41] The members of CALUSA, including Professor Ntsebeza, the NGO's board member, also realised that the court process had to take place in conjunction with the mobilisation of rural residents. Workshops, seminars, dialogues, as well as electronic and print media, became the tools to spread the message and to mobilise rural residents. Workshops involving members of the DTT and the leadership of Siyazakha were used to discuss the experiences of rural residents in relation to rural governance and the legislation that impacts on it.

Although participants were representatives mostly from the rural villages of Sakhisizwe, Emalahleni and Engcobo municipalities, one of the workshops also included representatives of Ilizwi Lamafama from the Amathole District Municipality; the Rural People's Movement and the Unemployed People's Movement from the Sarah Baartman District Municipality, and Makukhanye in the Nelson Mandela Bay Metropolitan Municipality. The first two workshops, which preceded the High Court judgment in October 2014, sensitised participants about the legislation related to traditional authorities, while the third workshop, held after the conclusion of the court case, discussed the implications of the judgment (CALUSA Report, 2014).

After the first judgment, CALUSA and members of the PC established links with rural communities in other parts of the Eastern Cape. In April 2014, CALUSA accepted an invitation to a seminar organised by the Border Rural Committee (BRC), an NGO with offices in East London, and Ntinga Ntaba kaNdoda, a social movement operating in the villages of Keiskammahoek. As will be seen later, both organisations work with rural communities and organised rural residents to hold regular pickets during sessions of the Cala Reserve court case in support of CALUSA and Siyazakha. The seminar discussed the implications of the High Court judgment. Members of the Vulamasango Singene campaign[42] and representatives of rural communities where Ntinga Ntaba kaNdoda operates also attended the event. In his presentation to the seminar, the author not only updated participants, but also discussed implications of the judgment for residents in areas under traditional authorities (BRC, 2015). When the BRC and Ntinga members heard that traditional authorities and political leaders had appealed the judgment, they resolved to support the struggle of the residents of Cala Reserve. In line with the resolution, participants in the seminar were encouraged to picket outside the High Court on the dates that the case was heard. Indeed, there were pickets outside the High Court whenever the case was heard. To keep the picketers informed, there were briefings to representatives of communities experiencing governance issues by the author and the representative of the LRC about the case after each court sitting.

Information on the struggle was also shared through newspaper articles.[43] In an opinion piece in the *Daily Dispatch* (Ncapayi, 2014), the author warned that rural people were being denied their democratic right to elect and be elected into decision-making structures in rural areas. Since this is a provincial newspaper that serves people in urban and rural communities across the Eastern Cape, the information was widely distributed in the Chris Hani District Municipality. Information was also shared through Vukani Community Radio and there were weekly radio presentations to update members of the public about the struggle and the progress of the case. It is not possible to gauge the impact of these efforts on the public, but phone calls and public comments during the presentations on Thursday evenings showed the interest the public took in the struggle for the democratisation of rural governance. Most of the people who commented expressed support for the struggle.

The Full Bench of the High Court heard the appeal in August 2015. In their appeal, the advocate for the appellants argued that:

> while the royal family is granted the power to decide a person who qualifies to be appointed with regard to customary law, there is no requirement that the royal family must take into account the popular views of the community and no community consultation is envisaged in section 18 of the Governance Act.

The royal family referred to in the above quotation are family members of Chief Gecelo. Moreover, as the extract shows, the premier, the MEC for COGTA and traditional authorities do not see it as necessary to consult rural residents about the determination of local leaders. However, the Full Bench judges disagreed that rural residents do not have to be consulted. To the judges: '[T]he facts set out in Professor Ntsebeza's affidavit establish a practice of long duration. That practice, judging from the community of the Cala Reserve's response to the retirement of Fani, is the current practice.' The judges further argued that the election of headmen (pp. 17–18):

> ... is a reasonable practice in that is not in conflict with legislation or the Constitution. Indeed, it is a practice that is in

consonant with the value of democratic governance, aimed at achieving accountability, responsiveness and openness, that is one of the Constitution's founding values. It is also consistent with various fundamental rights, such as the right to dignity, the right to freedom of opinion, the right to freedom of association and the right to make political choices.

Thus, the judges delivered what has become a 'landmark judgement' by dismissing the appeal on 18 August 2015 (see Rickard, 2015).

Once more, the conclusion of the court case was followed by a flurry of newspaper articles, which not only informed the public, but also helped to mobilise rural residents. Commenting on the judgment, Wilmien Wicomb of the Legal Resources Centre wrote: '(B)eing able to vote for our leaders is what it means to live in a democracy. Yet the Eastern Cape government tried to block a rural community from electing their leader' (see Rickard, 2015). In another opinion article (Ncapayi, 2015) the author encouraged rural residents to use the judgment as an opportunity to claim their democratic right to elect their local leaders.

The judgment of the Full Bench and the newspaper articles triggered reactions from various rural communities as well as from civil society organisations across the province. These responses led to the development of a campaign locally and provincially to democratise rural governance. Locally, there was more demand from various rural residents to CALUSA to assist residents to deal mostly with unelected headmen, non-transparent land allocations and undemocratic decisions about who should be sub-headmen, following the second High Court victory. Thus, Siyazakha and CALUSA resolved to broaden the DTT by incorporating representatives from communities with similar governance challenges who had also shown interest in being part of the campaign. Consequently, the DTT's members increased from five to 12 communities that came from the Emalahleni, Engcobo and Sakhisizwe municipalities.[44] Moreover, the judgment was translated into isiXhosa and its copies circulated in Cala Reserve. The youth of Siyazakha also had to be involved in popularising the court judgment by circulating and explaining it to the households beyond Cala Reserve (CALUSA, 2014; 2015).

In addition, Siyazakha and CALUSA initiated discussions with members of the DTT on what it means to have democratised rural communities. Workshops were then organised in 2015 and 2016 to clarify the matter. Each workshop had between 60 and 70 participants from areas such as Bengu, Guba Hoek, Machubeni, Mbinzana and Mgwalana in Lady Frere (Emalahleni Municipality); Qhumanco and Beyele (Engcobo Municipality); and Cala Reserve, Draaifontein, Indwana, Mnxe and Mthingwevu in Cala (Sakhisizwe Municipality). The experiences of African states such as Guinea-Bissau and Mozambique, which established liberated zones during their struggles for liberation, were shared with participants in the workshops. In the context of Guinea-Bissau, the liberated zones, which were areas that were won over by the liberation forces from colonial rule, saw the establishment of alternative socio-economic and political systems to mark the break with the colonial past (Chabal, 1983; Davidson, 1984). According to Chabal (1983: 107), village committees were set up in the liberated zones as part of their political re-organisation. The committees served as the 'political and administrative nerve centres' of the liberated zones. Economic reconstruction of the liberated zones was also undertaken. This involved dismantling the colonial agricultural model of export-oriented agriculture. Production of cash crops, for instance, was done away with in favour of production of food. Such information was shared with participants in the workshops. Consequently, the participants agreed in the workshops that democratised communities should have democratically elected leaders; have leaders that are accountable to the residents rather than those above them; have leaders that respect the residents they lead, and have residents that actively participate in development as well as in decision-making processes (CALUSA, 2015).

At the same time, there were regular presentations by various leaders of the DTT on Vukani Community Radio on the democratisation of rural governance. These initiatives popularised the struggle for democratisation of rural governance. The radio presentations reached other rural communities in the Chris Hani District Municipality. For instance, during the radio presentations there were telephone calls from people in Whittlesea who indicated that they also had serious problems of governance in their areas (CALUSA, 2015). When following up the calls, it emerged that more than 12 communities in Whittlesea had governance-related problems. Giyose's (2015: 13) research with members of the people's organisation, Sikhulule Bawo, in Qhumanco and Beyele, paints Chief Mgudlwa as a dictatorial leader who treats the residents as servants and does not allow them 'any free will'. The demands of rural residents were clearly articulated in a meeting of community representatives from more than 21 communities across Western Thembuland – that is communities under the Qamata Regional Traditional Council. The meeting was held in Qamata with Dalimvula Matanzima, the senior chief of Western Thembuland, and his councillors. The representatives demanded the withdrawal of unelected headmen in their communities. Additionally, they complained about the ill treatment of rural residents by headmen and some chiefs. For instance, some representatives complained that some traditional authorities abused them. In other instances, the residents alleged that some traditional authorities denied them services such as permits for circumcision of their children and papers for deaths. The residents of Xonxa complained that their headmen blocked development processes led by a local committee that was elected by the residents. As can be seen, it was and continues to be the dictatorial tendencies of the chiefs that are at the centre of the struggles in these rural communities.[45]

As local leaders, headmen are responsible for land administration and allocations, cases of civil nature, signing of affidavits for residents who die at home and witnessing for residents who apply for social grants (Act 41, 2003). Headmen are also expected to hold regular community meetings to report and discuss issues with their residents. Moreover, headmen account to the traditional councils at weekly meetings of these councils. Thus, headmen attend weekly meetings of the traditional council they are under. The chief, as the head of the traditional council, is expected to hold monthly meetings with residents in villages under his jurisdiction. Some of the meetings are supposed to keep rural residents abreast of developments, including policy changes.[46]

Reliance on the legal process as opposed to community mobilisation

The story of growing mobilisation beyond Cala Reserve also has a downside. PC members have been relying on the legal system. This contributed to the failure of PC leaders to sustain the mobilisation of residents. Legal processes take time, and the longer the legal process took, the more the imposed headman was able to entrench himself in the community by allocating land to residents sympathetic to him and allegedly giving them preference when job opportunities arose (see CALUSA, 2016).

Pursuance of the legal route without social mobilisation is problematic. As Gloppen (2005) points out:

> [L]itigation on its own has limited potential to change the situation on the ground, but creates opportunities for other actors. With a 'receptive apparatus' in place litigation seems to be effective in bringing out facts that can be used for advocacy purposes, fed into social and political discourses and directly inform policy processes.

The inability of the elderly PC members to win the youth over to their cause also turned out to be one of the challenges of the campaign. The imposed headman promised job opportunities to the youth, and this swayed the youth to the headman's side. The position of the headman was further boosted by the continued support the government departments and the local municipality gave to him. For instance, government departments such as those dealing with agriculture and social development, as well as the police and the municipality, recognised him as the leader of Cala Reserve. With regard to the coronation ceremony of Mr Yolelo, the mayor of the Sakhisizwe local municipality advised Chief Gecelo to disregard papers from the lawyers warning him against going ahead with the ceremony. So, government institutions supported Mr Yolelo. Government departments and the municipality deliberately supported the headman – and this meant that, as political deployees, these government officials also ensured political support for the ruling party.

On the opposing side, PC members were unable to counter the support government departments and the local municipality gave to Mr Yolelo. In the absence of a convincing counter programme, the elderly PC members in effect allowed a section of the residents to believe that Mr Yolelo's appointment was final and official. As a consequence, the support base of the PC dwindled and the meetings it organised were gradually restricted to meetings among themselves as PC members. Accordingly, the struggle in Cala Reserve began to wane, even though the flames that had been fanned in other parts of the Eastern Cape continued blowing.

Spreading the struggle provincially

The rural struggles from 2013 to 2017 have to be understood in relation to rural struggles of the 1950s and early 1960s. Mostly coordinated by the Transkei Organised Bodies (TOB), the rural struggles of the late 1950s and early 1960s were in response to the introduction of the betterment schemes of the 1940s and the Bantu Authorities Act (Ntsebeza, 2011: 21). Political activists such as the ANC-linked Govan Mbeki and the All-African Convention-linked (AAC) IB Tabata moved around the Eastern Cape, mobilising rural residents to resist implementation of the policies (Ntsebeza, 2011: 21). Although the three collaborating organisations – Border Rural Committee (BRC), CALUSA and Ntinga Ntaba kaNdoda – support the current struggles, there is no similar coordinating structure for the struggles. Development activists from the Border Rural Committee (BRC), CALUSA and Ntinga Ntaba kaNdoda led the rural mobilisation provincially. In 2017, the Inyanda National Land Movement adopted a national position supportive of the struggles. It is too early, however, to assess whether it is in a position to coordinate the struggles. Without an independent and self-funded local organisation, the campaign runs the risk of collapsing as soon as support from the externally funded collaborating organisations run out of funds.

Nonetheless, the members of these three organisations – BRC,

CALUSA and Ntinga Ntaba kaNdoda – made an effort to link up with other NGOs, rural movements and communities with similar concerns. The collaboration culminated in a decision to elevate the rural democratisation campaign to a provincial campaign. A series of provincial workshops and seminars that brought together more than 30 rural organisations were held across the province from 2015 to 2017, with the Cala Reserve case being the point of reference (CALUSA, 2015). As already indicated, BRC and Ntinga Ntaba kaNdoda co-hosted the first seminar in East London on 9 April 2015, involving community representatives from various villages in Keiskammahoek, Stutterheim and Cala Reserve, as well as representatives of the Vulamasango Singene campaign (BRC, 2015). Professor Luvuyo Wotshela from the University of Fort Hare, Ms Wicomb from the Cape Town office of the Legal Resources Centre and the author made presentations. It also emerged in the seminar that there was contestation of power between local headmen in various communities such as Amahlathi in the Stutterheim area, Ncerhana in Centane, Dwesa-Cwebe in Willowvale and Xolobeni in Mbizana.

Additionally, the three organisations visited various communities under the Mnquma, Buffalo City, Raymond Mhlaba, Ngqushwa, Enoch Mgijima, Ngcobo, Emalahleni and Sakhisizwe local municipalities. The visits also confirmed that rural residents in these communities wanted to have a voice in who leads and how land and natural resources in their communities are managed. Rural residents complained about unilateral decisions by some headmen in land allocation, even to people from outside the village, and the refusal of some headmen to account for money collected from the sale of natural resources (e.g. crush stone, sand, firewood, etc.).[47]

The visits to various communities caught the attention of traditional authorities who initiated discussions with representatives of civil society organisations immediately after the visits. The deputy chairperson of the Eastern Cape House of Traditional Leaders (ECHTL), Mr Zolile Burns-Ncamashe, initiated talks with the three organisations (BRC, Ntinga Ntaba kaNdoda and CALUSA) who brought community representatives along. Two meetings were held between Mr Burns-Ncamashe and the civil society organisations towards the end of 2015 and early 2016. According to Mr Burns-Ncamashe, the exploratory talks aimed at opening dialogue between the ECHTL, the organisations and the communities they worked with. As he put it, 'there is a need to talk so that we speak with one voice when making policy proposals as people of the Eastern Cape'.[48] He invited the organisations to a roundtable organised by the ECHTL in December 2015. When reviewing the meetings with Burns-Ncamashe, representatives of civil society organisations in the Eastern Cape agreed that the meeting was an attempt by traditional authorities to ensure that they influenced and controlled the developments in rural areas. Nevertheless, representatives of community structures in the meeting, and the three organisations, resolved to attend the roundtable to put forward the views of rural residents.

This marked the beginning of a more coordinated approach to the rural struggles, at least at the level of the three collaborating organisations. The organisations jointly mobilised the communities and supported representatives of the affected communities to raise their issues in the roundtable. Furthermore, the organisations mobilised the community representatives to participate in the Provincial Conference on Communal Land Tenure organised by the ECHTL, the South African Local Government Association (SALGA) and the Women's Investment Portfolio Holdings Limited (WIPHOLD) in June 2016 (Jara, 2016; see also CALUSA, 2015). Moreover, it was organised for community representatives to attend public hearings on the Traditional and Khoi-San Leadership Bill in Mthatha, East London, Graaff-Reinet, Port Elizabeth and Kokstad towards the end of 2016 and the beginning of 2017.

Land ownership and control, as well as the election of headmen featured prominently in discussions during the roundtable, conference and public hearings. Traditional authorities argued against the establishment of Communal Property Associations (CPAs) as democratic landholding entities. Instead, they vociferously called for the registration of rural land in their names (Jara, 2016). Chief Mwelo Nonkonyana, for instance, warned the Conference that 'such structures (CPAs) will never be allowed in the land of amaBhala'.[49] On the other hand, community representatives fearlessly argued for the registration of land in their names or through structures decided by the residents (see Jara, 2016). Nolundi Zitha of Ntinga Ntaba kaNdoda informed traditional leaders in the Conference that 'we want our land registered in our names or in the names of structures elected by communities, such as CPAs. In our community we do not recognise traditional leaders. The South African National Civic Organisation (SANCO) is our governing structure'. The sentiments expressed by communities about rural governance, land ownership and control were echoed in the community and district workshops that the three organisations organised in 2016 and 2017 to discuss the Traditional and Khoi-San Leadership Bill. The above community views are in line with Claassens's (2014) argument that decision-making over land should be vested in 'small social units such as families, clans and user communities' (see also Mafeje, 2002). According to Mafeje (2002), chiefs were never holders of community land, which was the prerogative of households, clans or communities.

Towards a conclusion

This chapter has reflected on the contemporary struggles of rural residents who want their voices heard. Using a combination of social mobilisation and the legal system (the High Court in particular), what started out as a local struggle in Cala Reserve has spread into a provincial campaign; it mushroomed in communities in various parts of the Eastern Cape where residents, with the support of civil society organisations, are taking up the struggle to democratise rural governance. As Claassens (2014: 1) puts it, there is widespread 'contestation concerning the content of chiefly power over communal land …' Indeed, the struggle is about the democratisation of governance, which includes ownership and control of land in rural areas. The struggle manifests as demands for space in decision-making by rural residents. Primarily, residents are demanding that they should have a say in who their leaders should be, but also about the governance of land and other natural resources in rural communities. However, while there are demands by rural residents to have a voice in choosing their leaders, there is no indication of the term of office for the elected leaders or whether it should be fixed as for municipal councillors or indefinite.

Two issues come to the fore in this chapter regarding provincial mobilisation for the democratisation of rural governance. The first is the utilisation of the legal judgment as a springboard for civil society organisations and rural residents to mobilise for rural governance to be more democratic. This means the courts are also useful instruments for mobilising rural societies to fight for democratic change. Secondly, civil society organisations played a role in coordinating rural struggles locally and provincially. The interventions have managed not only to bring together rural residents, but have also enabled rural residents to express themselves on decisions about leadership, the ownership of land and the governance of such land and other resources in rural areas. The concern of rural residents about the land and other resources challenges the view of some scholars, such as Manona (1997) and Bernstein (2005), that rural residents are less interested in productive land than in land for housing, or jobs in urban areas.

And, as shown earlier, the struggle was started by the members of the PC in Cala Reserve who organised local people to challenge the imposition of an unelected headman. Although it had limited success in organising at the local level, the PC-led struggle served as an inspiration to other communities. Rural residents gained confidence when they witnessed the way in which PC members challenged traditional authorities, something that is very rare if not unheard of. The mushrooming of communities that took up the challenge was due to the realisation that it is possible to challenge the power of traditional authorities, as the PC's actions and the Cala Reserve court case clearly demonstrated.

At the same time, the experience of Cala Reserve shows that, indeed, the legal system on its own has limitations. The participating civil society organisations are mindful that the strategy has not worked well in Cala Reserve where local leaders relied too heavily on the legal system rather than on mobilising the residents. As Gloppen (2005) warns, legal processes have to be accompanied by social mobilisation and local struggles to achieve the intended goal, which in this case is an elected local leader that also ensures the participation of rural residents in decision-making. Heywood (2009) concurs with this view and shows that, in the context of the Treatment Action Campaign's struggle for access to medicines for HIV-positive people, a combination of mobilisation, awareness-raising and litigation was the key to the success of the struggle. However, in the bigger picture of the democratisation of rural governance campaign, the Cala Reserve case, despite its reliance on the legal system, proved to be a useful organising tool and serves as inspiration to other rural residents that are faced with similar governance challenges.

The government and some traditional authorities have reluctantly acceded to the demands for the voices of rural residents to be heard on the need to have elected headmen, and on the governance of land and other natural resources. The Regional Traditional Council in Qamata and the four traditional councils in the former Xhalanga magisterial district have acknowledged this fact. As such, four headmen have since been elected in Indwana, Manzimahle, Tsengiwe and Mnxe. These are concrete outcomes of the campaign.

However, the outcomes of the current campaign still have limitations in relation to the election of headmen by local people, and the campaign does not affect all levels of traditional authorities. The upper levels remain unchanged and the campaign runs the risk of being undermined as elected headmen still operate within the undemocratic institution of traditional authorities. In addition, the existing close relationship between the institution of traditional authority and the ruling party – the ANC – means that there is no real inclination from the ANC to transform the institution. The pieces of legislation the ANC-led government seeks to pass such as the Traditional and Khoi-San Leadership Bill, Traditional Courts Bill and the Communal Land Tenure Bill, which seek to strengthen the power of traditional authorities, confirm the attitude of the ruling party towards the institution of traditional authority. Thus, unless the campaign's approach is to democratise governance at all levels of traditional authority, it runs the risk of being undermined both by some traditional authorities and by the government.

Closely linked to the above, the sustainability of the current rural struggles is highly questionable at two levels. Besides the coordinating role played by the NGOs, an independent coordinating structure – constituted by the affected people – is yet to emerge. As Ntsebeza eloquently puts it, leadership of the affected people in their struggles is important as a driving force. Additionally, inability of the affected people to fund their struggles makes it impossible for them to establish a self-funded, coordinating structure. Instead, the struggles are dependent on other organisations for funding. Thus, the affected communities are unable to run a sustained campaign without external financial and human resources support.

References

Badat, S. 2012. *The Forgotten People: Political banishment under apartheid*. Johannesburg: Jacana.

Bernstein, A. 2005. *Land Reform in South Africa: A 21st-Century Perspective*. Johannesburg: Centre for Development Enterprise.

Border Rural Committee. 2014. 'Annual report of the Border Rural Committee'. Unpublished.

Border Rural Committee. 2015. 'Six-monthly report: January to June 2015'. *Border Rural Committee* website: www.brc21.co.za/sites/default/files/.../6-monthly%202015%2001%20-%2006.pdf, accessed 14 May 2017.

Cala University Students Association (CALUSA). 2013, 2014, 2015. Annual Reports. Unpublished.

CALUSA. 2016. 'Director's Overview of 2016'. Unpublished.

Chabal, P. 1983. *Amilcar Cabral: Revolutionary leadership and people's war*. London: Cambridge University Press.

Claassens, A. 2014. 'Communal land, property rights and traditional leadership'. *WISER* website: https://wiser.wits.ac.za/system/files/documents/Claassens2014.pdf, accessed 25 May 2017.

Davidson, B. 1984. *No Fist Is Big Enough to Hide the Sky: The liberation of Guinea-Bissau and Cape Verde*. London: Zed Books.

Giyose, M. P. 2015. 'Research report on profiling of Qhumanco and Beyele'. Commissioned by CALUSA. Unpublished.

Gloppen, S. December 2005. 'Public interest litigation, social rights and social policy'. *New Frontiers of Social Policy Conference*. Arusha.

Hendricks, F., Ntsebeza, L. & Helliker, K. 2013. 'Colonial pasts and democratic futures in South Africa', in Hendricks, F., Ntsebeza, L. & Helliker, K. (eds.) *The Promise of Land: Undoing a century of dispossession in South Africa.* Johannesburg: Jacana Media, pp. 341–358.

Hendricks, F. & Ntsebeza, L. 1999. 'Chiefs and rural local government in post-apartheid South Africa'. *African Journal of Political Science*, 4 (1), 99–126.

Heywood, M. 2009. 'South Africa's Treatment Action Campaign: Combining law and social mobilization to realise the right to health.' *Journal of Human Rights Practice*, 1 (1), 14–36.

Jara, M. 2011. 'Changing landscapes of democracy, rural governance, traditional power and degraded commons in a former apartheid homeland'. *Indiana University* website: https://dlc.dlib.indiana.edu/dlc/bitstream/handle/10535/7206/687.pdf?sequence=1, accessed 29 December 2016.

Jara, M. 2016. 'Reflections on the Provincial Communal Land Tenure Summit'. Eastern Cape. Unpublished.

Mafeje, A. 2002. 'Democratic governance and new democracy for the future in Africa: Agenda for the future'. *African Forum for Envisioning Africa Conference*, 26–29 April 2002. Nairobi.

Manona, C. 1997. 'The collapse of the "tribal authority" system and the rise of civic associations', in De Wet, C. & Whisson, M. (eds.) *From Reserves to Region: Apartheid and social change in the Kieskamahoek District of (Former) Ciskei, 1950–1960*. Grahamstown: Institute of Social and Economic Research, Rhodes University, pp. 49–68.

Ncapayi, F. 2013. 'Record of processes regarding the replacement of Headman Fani in Cala Reserve'. Sakhisizwe Local Municipality. Cala Reserve File, CALUSA offices. Unpublished.

Ncapayi, F. 2 July 2014. 'Rural South Africans not part of new democracy'. *Daily Dispatch,* https://www.dispatchlive.co.za/news/opinion/2014-07-02-rural-south-africans-not-part-of-new-democracy/, accessed 6 August 2018.

Ncapayi, F. 5 May 2015. 'Seize opportunity to get full rights in rural areas'. *Daily Dispatch*, https://www.dispatchlive.co.za/news/2015-05-05-seize-opportunity-to-get-full-rights-in-rural-areas/, accessed 6 August 2018.

Ntsebeza, L. 1999. 'Democratisation and traditional authorities in the new South Africa'. *Comparative Studies of South Asia, Africa and the Middle East*, XIX (1), 83–93.

Ntsebeza, L. 2004. 'Rural governance and citizenship in post-1994 South Africa: Democracy compromised?' *USAID* website: https://rmportal.net/library/content/ntzebeza_paper.pdf/view?searchterm=institutions, accessed 23 March 2018.

Ntsebeza, L. 2005. *Democracy Compromised: Chiefs and the politics of land in South Africa*. Leiden: Brill.

Ntsebeza, L. 2011. 'Resistance in the countryside: The Mpondo revolts contextualised', in Kepe T. & Ntsebeza, L. (eds.) *Rural Resistance in South Africa: The Mpondo revolts after fifty years*. Leiden: Brill, pp. 21–43.

Ntsebeza, L. 2013a. 'Headmanship in post-1994 South Africa with specific reference to the Tsengiwe administrative area in the Eastern Cape'. Report commissioned by the Legal Resources Centre. Unpublished.

Ntsebeza, L. 2013b. 'South Africa's countryside: Prospects for change from below', in Hendricks, F., Ntsebeza, L. & Helliker, K. (eds.) *The Promise of Land: Undoing a century of dispossession in South Africa*. Johannesburg: Jacana Media, pp. 130–158.

Ntsebeza, L. 2014. Supporting affidavit in the High Court of South Africa. Bhisho, Eastern Cape. Case 169/14.

Redding, S. 2009. 'Sorcery and sovereignty: Taxation, power and rebellion in South Africa, 1880-1963'. *American Historical Review*, 114 (4), 1203–1204.

Rickard, C. 25 August 2015. 'People's rights upheld in landmark Cala ruling'. *Daily Dispatch*, http://www.customcontested.co.za/peoples-rights-upheld-in-landmark-cala-ruling/, accessed 3 August 2018.

Wicomb, W. 2014. 'Supplementary affidavit in the High Court of South Africa'. Bhisho, Eastern Cape. Case 169/14.

Wotshela, L. 2009. 'Land redistribution politics in the Eastern Cape midlands: The case of the Lukhanji municipality, 1995–2006'. *Scielo* website: www.scielo.org.za>scielo, accessed 29 March 2018.

Notes

1 The struggles have also erupted in Prudhoe (Peddie area), Tshabo (Berlin), Amahlathi (Stutterheim), 12 villages of Whittlesea, Beyele and Qhumanco (Ngcobo), Xonxa, Bengu (Lady Frere) and Guba (Lady Frere), Manzimahle, Tsengiwe and Mnxe (Xhalanga) and Ncerhana (Centane).

2 WHIPHOLD is a company aimed at empowering that was formed in the early 1990s.

3 The author was part of a delegation of rural organisations participating in the conference.

4 See article entitled 'Xhosa community asks court to confirm they have no chief' in *Sunday Times Live* (25/6/2017), accessed 29 March 2018.

5 The author was personally involved in the meeting, accompanying the

delegation from Cala.

6 It has not been possible to find out why the area is called Cala Reserve.

7 Unfortunately, it has not been possible to determine the dates at which the various headmen were in power.

8 Founding affidavit of Penrose Ntamo, 26 May 2014

9 He expressed these views on several occasions during conversations with the author, which started at the beginning of 2013.

10 UmGcina is the clan name of one of the Nguni groups.

11 *Umabhulwini* is a derogatory term referring to a person from white-claimed farms who were also called *amalose* (loose people) because they had no land and later became labour tenants of the local landholders (see Ntsebeza, 2005; Ncapayi, 2013).

12 See also Founding Affidavit of Penrose Ntamo for the High Court Case, page 11

13 He expressed these views on several occasions when he had conversations with the author from the beginning of 2013.

14 Conversation of the author with Mr Ntamo and Mrs Nomvuzo Nophothe on 10 February 2013

15 Notes of the author, 28 February 2013

16 The PC is a local committee that worked closely with headman Fani to plan developments in the area.

17 Conversation with Mr Penrose Ntamo in Cala Reserve

18 See Ntsebeza Supporting Affidavit to the Bhisho High Court in 2015.

19 CALUSA (Cala University Students Association) is a locally based NGO, which has been in existence since 1983. The NGO works with rural communities on issues of land access, land use and rural governance.

20 The author received two SMS messages from Mr Zwelakhe Moni on 27 February regarding the reaction of the traditional council to the Cala Reserve delegation.

21 Zwelakhe Moni, 27 February 2013

22 Meeting the author had with Mr Moni on 28 February 2013

23 Notes of the author who was a participant observer in the meeting, which was held in headman Fani's homestead.

24 Notes of the author who was a participant observer in the meeting, which was held in headman Fani's homestead.

25 Notes of the author who was a participant observer in the meeting, which was held in headman Fani's homestead.

26 Notes of the author who was a participant observer in the meeting, which was held in headman Fani's homestead.

27 Notes of the author who was a participant observer in the meeting, which was held in headman Fani's homestead.

28 Undated notes of Nomvuzo Nophothe. Cala Reserve File, CALUSA office
29 Author's observations and personal notes. See also notes of Nomvuzo Nophothe
30 Personal notes the author took in the meeting
31 CALUSA was formed in 1983 by Lungisile Ntsebeza, Meluxolo Silinga and Bambo Qongqo, local political activists who wanted to contribute in the field of education, in Cala and the former Xhalanga magisterial district.
32 Author's observations and notes. As a member of CALUSA, the author also led the programme for the democratisation of rural governance of the NGO.
33 The author was part of the delegation from CALUSA.
34 See copy of the letter dated 2 April 2013
35 Notes of the author in the meeting
36 Siyazakha Land and Development Forum is a conglomeration of local development initiatives such as agricultural projects, land reform groups and other local community development initiatives.
37 Author's notes about the meeting he also chaired
38 Answering Affidavit of Penrose Ntamo, 2014
39 Personal notes of the author as a participant-observer in the struggle
40 Written submissions by community representatives in a meeting with traditional authorities in Qamata, November 2016
41 See CALUSA operational plan for 2014
42 The Vulamasango Singene campaign is a rural movement of betterment-planning land claimants in the Eastern Cape, which works with BRC.
43 See also Legal Resources Centre. 'Cala Reserve: What does this judgment mean for rural democracy and governance?', http://lrc.org.za/lrcarchive/other-news/3439-cala-reserve-what-does-this-judgment-mean-for-rural-democracy-and-governance, accessed 14 May 2017.
44 See CALUSA reports from 2015 onwards
45 Verbal account of Siphiwo Liwani and Nonceba Ntlonze, staff members of CALUSA who accompanied members of Siyazakha Land and Development Forum, 17 November 2017
46 Chief Gwazinamba Matanzima pointed some of this out during the meeting that he and his council had with the PC and CALUSA representatives in Qamata in 2013.
47 Notes of the author who was part of the delegation that visited the communities in October 2015
48 The second meeting between Mr Zolile Burns-Ncamashe and the three organisations with the community representatives was on 15 June 2016,

in the International Convention Centre, East London.

49 The author was an active participant in the Provincial Conference on Communal Tenure in East London.

TEN

Situational chiefs

Notes on traditional leadership amidst calls for KhoiSan¹ recognition after 1994

WILLIAM ELLIS

The !Kung [San] are a people without a state; they have no overriding authority to settle disputes, maintain order and keep people in line. Whatever order there is has to come from the hearts and goodwill of the people themselves (Lee, 1979). Differences in influences exist, but only to the degree permitted by those who are influenced (Lenski & Lenski, 1982).

Introduction

This chapter is about how contemporary KhoiSan communities have mobilised 'traditional leadership' in order to gain recognition and make claims on the post-apartheid state. Although the historical record reflects a dynamic, varied and largely ad-hoc form of leadership among the KhoiSan, in a contemporary context, some KhoiSan communities have participated in recreating 'authentic' leadership in order to reclaim their humanity in democratic South

Africa. Ironically, this has sometimes entailed drawing on apartheid and colonial constructions of 'authenticity'.

The question of KhoiSan genetics and the debate about autochthony are part of a discourse that seeks to establish an authenticity among KhoiSan activists, who readily draw on scientific studies of KhoiSan groups to help bolster their claims to identity and land.

The archaeology and physical anthropology of the KhoiSan were key episodes in the history of racial studies in South Africa, and held the interest of such famous scientists as Raymond Dart, Robert Broom and later Phillip Tobias (Dubow, 1996). Tobias, professor of physical anthropology, would spend a career testing and disproving racialised theories about the KhoiSan. These debates about the linkages of race, culture, language and biology continued to plague KhoiSan research until Jenkins and Tobias (1977) suggested a clarification of the terrain, namely that KhoiSan be subject to a threefold distinction of biology, linguistics and socio-cultural constructs in distinctive ecologies. Although a thorough critique of this paradigm has yet to be delivered, the threefold distinction remains the basis for many conceptions of KhoiSan identity into the present. The critique of this paradigm is for another paper, but let us at least comment briefly on the three aspects mentioned above.

First is the belief that KhoiSan is a physical type that is, or at least has been in the past, distinct from other African forms. The early work in this regard was done almost exclusively through the study of skeletal remains, serological studies, photography and the production of plaster and fibreglass moulds. With the discovery of DNA, many of the early studies were disputed by Tobias[2] himself and new possibilities opened up. Tobias was widely regarded as an expert in physical anthropology and studied KhoiSan and hominid fossils from South Africa. His pronouncements on racial studies of KhoiSan people thus held a certain weight. Two sets of findings stand out: the discovery of so-called KhoiSan genes and the discovery of the mitochondrial Eve. There are at least some genes that are specifically KhoiSan and these are deployed by activists to prove their KhoiSan heritage. The mitochondrial Eve is claimed to be a woman who lived along the southern tip of Africa about 100,000 years ago. Some scholars of KhoiSan society claim that the theory of the mitochondrial Eve suggests that KhoiSan people belong to the oldest genetically distinct human population. They are thus representatives of the earliest anatomically modern human population (Schuster et al., 2010). In concert, these two scientific findings are used by KhoiSan activists to claim land in southern Africa and also to stake their claim as autochthonous peoples (i.e. original inhabitants).

The status of the KhoiSan as autochthonous is only rarely disputed, but there are some who attach less importance to claims to autochthony: many in Africa refuse to designate any one group as worthy of special recognition and thereby deny them potential advantages over other populations (Kuper et al., 2003; Pelican, 2009). Arguments are usually for the general democratic rights of all peoples in a country and the distinction between autochthony and allochthony (that which was not originally part of a habitat) is given no credence (see Wilmsen, 2002). In South Africa, the arguments for autochthony sit even more uncomfortably because they are seen as having their origins in ideologies that helped create the racial character of apartheid. Arguments about autochthony were used to divide the country into two halves: the west belonging historically to the KhoiSan and coloured and the east to the Bantu-speaking peoples. This so-called Eiselen[3] line would underwrite policies such as the infamous Coloured Labour Preference Area Policy in the old Cape Province. Many thinkers are against the argument for autochthony, suggesting that we are all Africans and that the attempt to distinguish between these two remnants of racist ideologies developed under apartheid is counter-productive (Pelican, 2009; Geschiere, 2009).

Nonetheless, the view still exists that the KhoiSan were, in the past, a separate cultural, political and economic entity that existed prior to the arrival of other groups like the Bantu-speaking iron-age farmers and the European merchant capitalists of the 17th century. This KhoiSan entity is further understood to be the 'people' that have had the longest history of habitation in southern Africa. Roughly 2,000 years ago, some San groups were assimilated first into the agricultural economy of the Bantu-speaking colonisers, and later into the European agricultural settler economy (Smith et al., 2000). It is not difficult to see how this academic view of the history and peopling of southern Africa sparks a nostalgia for a return to KhoiSan culture, and how it is very easily mobilised towards specific political ends, such as a coloured or 'Brown' nationalism. I return to this issue later in the chapter, especially as some, but not all, KhoiSan activists have mobilised around the issue of coloured nationalism.

The second distinctive aspect to mention is the linguistic diversity of the KhoiSan. In total, there are at least 20 different linguistic groups and dialects found throughout southern Africa that are grouped as 'KhoiSan languages'. Linguists who specialise in South African Khoi (SAK) languages categorise them into three main groups: Khoe, Ju and Tuu (Du Plessis, 2009). The 30 or so specialists on SAK disagree on matters of exact classification of these languages (Du Plessis, from comm 4 August 2018). In this chapter I will choose to speak about a linguistic community as a group of people that speak the same language or one or other dialect. The largest of these linguistic communities is the Nama with about 20,000 speakers, the vast majority of whom live in southern Namibia, and about 6,000 in South Africa, concentrated in small geographic locales in the Northern Cape, such as Riemvasmaak and the Richtersveld. The smallest of these language communities, and the most threatened, are the N/u speakers of the southern Kalahari with less than 10 known speakers and very little institutional transmission of the language. Historically, these languages have been under threat and some like Xam have completely died out, existing only as doculects, i.e. they are preserved in written archives and thus still exist as language, even though no active speakers are alive. The attempts to re-teach Nama and other KhoiSan languages to those who claim the identity in the present is a major part of the attempts to revive KhoiSan culture. Furthermore, the language revival grants an authenticity that is today employed in a variety of other contexts, such as film, as evidenced in the film *Krotoa* (2017).

The KhoiSan were the first of the indigenous people of southern Africa to encounter the colonial settlers. They were the first to be dispossessed, and they were the first to resist, with battles recorded as early as the 1510s. In support of the above claim, activists often refer to the Battle of Maitland. This battle was fought in 1510 between the Khoi and Portuguese sailors from the ship, the *D'Almeida*. The Khoi trading party defeated the sailors in a skirmish that saw the Portuguese flee. The KhoiSan were later to be reduced to mere servants, labourers, debt peons, indentured labourers and farm workers (Bredenkamp, 1982; Elphick, 1977; Van der Ross, 1979; Penn, 2005). Their consignment to these labour categories was largely the result of the complete and utter dispossession of their land and the subsequent destruction of their ability to subsist independently of the colonial economy, a process that was complete by the mid-19th century (Ross, 1983).

This sounds no different from what other African colonial subjects endured, except that the KhoiSan suffered a further process of 'dysselection'. McKittrick (2016) suggests that 'dysselection' (in contrast to natural 'selection') is a complete negation of your humanity – a radical alterity or otherness. In the process of dysselection, all familiar signs of human-ness defined by the self are removed: the mother tongue, the name and any institution that defines one as human. Dysselection came to a head in the 1950s in South Africa, when all who still thought of themselves as 'KhoiSan' were re-classified as coloureds. Dysselection is complete when you are granted a name and type not your own, and your absorption into the labour economy of settler capital marks you out for particular labour, like farm work.

It is this dysselection that gives rise to the process of indigenisation in the present. The present-day revival of KhoiSan identity attempts to recreate the authentic lifestyles of the past. It wants to revive all those things that were buried and interred in the previous centuries: the personal name, the language, the dress and institutions whether marriage, religion or leadership. With this perspective, becoming indigenous is not simply an ontological status; rather, it is a process that is entirely contingent on a confluence of forces in the present.

One event that marks the advent of this process more than others is the first National KhoiSan Consultative Conference of 1996 held in Cape Town. This conference brought together large numbers of academics, activists, non-govermental organisations (NGOs), government representatives and, most importantly, members of the

KhoiSan communities across southern Africa. I attended the opening sessions of the conference and, during these sessions, many community activists issued their calls for recognition. Among the calls was an appeal to the then Department of Constitutional Development for an inquiry into the recognition of key institutions and specifically KhoiSan 'traditional leadership'. It is important that, with the exception of the Griqua, KhoiSan communities had neither officially recognised traditional structures nor any leadership structures whatsoever.

Over the next two decades (1996 onwards), this initial call for traditional leaders to be recognised would mature into the Traditional and Khoi-San Leadership Bill (hereinafter TKSLB). During these two decades, the Department of Constitutional Development remained actively engaged with KhoiSan communities in order to develop the particulars of the bill. This bill would propose, among other things, the recognition of legitimated leaders with verifiable traditional communities tied to assigned territories. In other words, the KhoiSan would be brought under the rule of customary governance models, similar to those at play in the former homelands. Yet, as my colleague, Rafael Verbuyst, researcher of the KhoiSan revival, points out in his response to, among others, Claassens (2016): it would be too simplistic, and somewhat disingenuous, to class all KhoiSan claims to land and recognition as a form of KhoiSan apartheid (personal communication, 11 April 2018). He further asks why these claims would be acceptable in the case of, say, chiefs in the former homelands but not from those active in – and advocating for – KhoiSan revival?

This is not to say that systems of tenure and land distribution developed during colonial and apartheid regimes should be allowed to hold force in the present. Many activists and researchers argue that the bill will reproduce problematic laws developed under colonialism and apartheid; that such laws will subject rural residents to undemocratic principles of governance. This is especially so because the bill allows traditional authorities power over land. There are fears that land can be used to further bolster the power of chiefs and to unfairly exclude rural residents from livelihoods (Claassens, 2016). This brings to the fore the point that this legislation, however regressive, has been mobilised by the KhoiSan revival, in a democratic context, for what this community deem to be the ends of justice. In their petitions for recognition and redress in post-1994 South Africa, re-imagining 'traditional' leaders among the KhoiSan has been instrumental.

Questions of 'authenticity'

I will not be suggesting an 'authentic' or 'traditional' form for Khoi or San traditional leadership. The line of enquiry that posits authentic culture is not, in my view, productive. Furthermore, cultural authenticity leads down some dark roads (for more on this see Ellis, 2014). The question of authentic forms, in this case forms and institutions of governance, traps those who might lay claim to such institutions and forms within what has been called a 'cunning of recognition' (Povinelli, 2002). The cunning of recognition reworks and cautions us about the apparent democracy of political recognition by showing how a people seeking rights as citizens can become victims of their claims to culture. Povinelli (2002) shows that the people of the Belyuen community in Australia find that they are suddenly excluded from land claims processes by cultural rules that they themselves had put forward as 'authentic'.

In the case of the Belyuen community, individuals and groups are expected to provide evidence for their cultural authenticity based on a set of rules distilled from some combination of ethnography, customary law, political studies and even archival sources (Povinelli, 2002). Of course, at the moment, something very similar is being asked of the KhoiSan in the TKSLB. Some may end up being disqualified from processes of recognition if they are unable to engage with either ethnographic criterion or principles, or if their own version of their 'culture' contradicts archival evidence. Those who volunteer the identities in question, and who lay claim to the ethnic monikers, fall prey to those official, administrative and bureaucratic disciplines that require lexicon and formality. In other words, to commit culture to rules, types, forms and standard practice is to confine it to history and, especially in South Africa's case, to colonial history. The *capture* (the violence of this word is purposely implied) of traditional leadership on paper, and in law, serves to fossilise what is potentially a very dynamic and creative form.

In various calls for recognition, KhoiSan activists and revivalists have called for a creative institution of leadership and the historical data seems to corroborate this kind of call. The idea of creative leadership is key to the arguments being made in this paper and will be elaborated further on, after I have considered the nature and character of KhoiSan leadership through the lens of some historical and ethnographic data.

The lament of 'weak leadership'

In this chapter, I follow Pierre Clastres (2010) in opening up the question of leadership. For Clastres the heart of the matter is in the question: why should any person subject themselves to the will of another? Or, why do we choose to be led by others? Similarly, in this chapter, I am less interested in distinguishing the Khoi and San politically or as some form of 'tradition'. Rather, I treat the question as one of leadership and governance more broadly.

Clastres (2010) attempted to understand the nature of leadership outside the purview of those forms of headship found in state societies. He remarks that Europeans were often baffled by how little real authority leaders in what he called 'primitive' societies wielded. Clastres's studies of traditional societies in the Amazon – traditional because they were small scale, relatively 'uncontacted' and thus untainted by Western influences – reveal what he believes holds the key to understanding leadership in many non-Western societies, namely the granting of prestige versus the wielding of power. He argued that an individual may be granted prestige in society, but this prestige does not give the holder any special place or rank in society other than being a spokesperson.

Societies would have granted these individuals this particular office, possibly because the holder of the position had some particular qualities, skills or abilities. Yet, as easily as this prestige was granted, so easily could it be taken away. In fact, Clastres (2010) claims that a very simple criterion could lead to the disqualification of the leaders, and that is a failure on the part of the leader to adequately and accurately give voice to the ideas and beliefs of the people they served. Failure to adequately represent could quickly lead to loss of prestige. Overall, Clastres's theory and ethnography of leadership suggests a loosely granted position of prestige that could be momentary, fleeting and easily lost. The leader in one situation or of one moment may, without much ceremony, find that someone else is speaking for the group.

Those who think only in a particularistic fashion may argue that the work of Clastres was done among the Yanomami, a group living in the Amazonian rainforest. These farmers and hunters are, among other things, known most famously for their alleged warlike nature – a role created by Changon's (1968) ethnography, entitled *The Fierce People*. How does one draw on theory from so far away, and how might it be relevant if it emerges in such a specific ethnographic context?

My response is twofold: The first has to do with the nature of theory and ethnography. Da Col and Graeber (2011) remind us that the source of theory is explanation, and that ethnographic exploration, thinking and writing is the raw data of theorisation. It is theory at its most basic. Clastres (2010) does not only want to understand leadership among the Yanomami, nor is he simply trying to understand 'chieftaincy' (his term, not mine). His aim is more global. The aim of the ethnographic enquiry into leadership is to open a broader question of leadership, both in state and stateless societies, in large and small-scale systems, in devolved and centralised political institutions. One last question then remains: can we find the elements of this somewhat plebeian democracy among the KhoiSan in southern Africa? A few pertinent elements must be highlighted from Clastres's work. The aspects of leadership in these non-Western forms that he thinks are pervasive are: their situational nature, the basing of leadership on skill set, the role of the leader as spokesperson and the granting of prestige versus the holding and wielding of power. Application of these characteristics to the KhoiSan will take a historical and ethnographic view.

As with Clastres's European observers in South America, the colonists of southern Africa were equally puzzled at the lack of real influence and power exercised by Khoi leaders. In fact, Abrahams

(1995) reports that in the early 18th century, some European observers were lamenting the disappearance of Khoi chiefs and 'captains'. Some would argue that this is due to the structurally weak nature of the institution (see Elphick, 1977). Perhaps observers wanted to see a strong centralised management of power, as in the systems they were accustomed to in Europe. Abrahams (1995), however, argues that the problem was not that the Khoi had weak leadership. Rather, during contact with the KhoiSan, the settlers wanted to impose their conception of leadership onto KhoiSan society. The European conception of leadership would not only clash with KhoiSan ideas, but would also contribute to the demise of 'traditional' leadership among the Khoi. Furthermore, it is not possible, today, to recover the 'authentic' or 'original' form that leadership took among the KhoiSan prior to colonial encounters with Europeans (Ellis, 2012).

With regard to KhoiSan archaeology, historiography and ethnography there are three instances in the literature in which historians noted visible leadership in KhoiSan societies. Firstly, contact leaders were produced through the colonists' need to find individuals with whom they could negotiate and trade. Secondly, key individuals often organised resistance in various parts of the country in response to the threats to their tenure of the land. And, thirdly, the functions of certain KhoiSan individuals as ritual specialists and rainmakers often gave them prominence in their societies (Prins, 1996; Prins & Lewis, 1992; Ellis, 2012). This special role could have allowed them to gain status in their own groups. It could also be argued that, with the associated material benefits, they might have been a step higher up in the hierarchy of their group.

Some historians have examined travellers' accounts of KhoiSan society and attempted to draw conclusions about San political institutions, including traditional leadership. Smith et al. (2000) are of the opinion that the San did not have chiefs [sic], but that often such leaders were produced under special conditions. These conditions were usually situations of 'contact'; they could be violent encounters with other groups (Nguni or settlers) or passive encounters, such as trade or travel. Penn (1996) argued that in trade, as with the pacification of the indigenous population, the settlers needed 'strong men' with whom to negotiate. Schapera (1930) shared those sentiments about a weak leadership among the KhoiSan. He states 'that these [leaders]', however, were not 'chiefs' who wielded power, but were more like 'leader[s] rather than ruler[s]', since they did 'not exercise any organised control over [their] subjects'. Hence when these 'strong men' were unavailable, Europeans selected individuals they thought exhibited characteristics of a 'chief', and obviously this meant applying European standards of leadership and, if needs be, imposing leadership. Elsewhere Smith (1990) argues that the early colonists had a cultural bias towards hierarchy and that they preferred to deal with individuals rather than collectives. So, the individuals they selected as 'authority figures' might not necessarily have reflected the manner in which KhoiSan society would have been stratified (Abrahams, 1995). In addition, the process the settlers undertook of appointing captains made the issues first 'one of struggle, then of contestation' (Abrahams, 1995: 30). Selection of leaders is thus a matter of a jostling for political power, struggle and then a game of making and asserting interpretations of the exact character of the leadership institutions – hence contestation.

One such contest of meaning has to do with the application of social Darwinist logic to KhoiSan society, specifically a reading of societal evolution that places KhoiSan people on the bottom of evolutionary architecture. The consignment of San to the lowest rung on the social evolutionary scale had a definite impact on European thinking about the nature of political institutions among the San. Societies that were viewed as more advanced had, according to this perspective, a more stratified social formation and therefore had to have a centralised leadership (Humphreys, 1985). Even so, the presence of these leadership positions, whatever their authentic nature may have been, were usually qualified or diminished by colonists. Famed European traveller and naturalist Robert Gordon argued from his observations of KhoiSan society that the San had weak leadership, but that the Khoi had a clearly established institution of 'chiefs'. For the Khoi, he claims, the chiefly office was characterised by patrilineal descent, supported by a class of elders (Gordon, R. as cited in Smith, 1990). Even as he offers up these two very clearly articulated principles, namely age and patrilineality, it seems Gordon shares the scepticisms of his contemporaries about KhoiSan leadership. Gordon thus only mentions some vaguely described form of leadership. This leadership would be treated as somewhat spurious or decided on in the moment. Furthermore, the moment of leadership could be determined as one in which the 'bravest and most dextrous would only take charge where skills are needed' (Gordon R. as cited in Smith, 1996).

While, in principle, the ideas of Gordon (cited above) seem to square with some of this chapter's arguments, there is one aspect that differs fundamentally with other thinkers. Gordon's observations support the view that leadership was situational and that it was influenced by the skill set of the individual. Patrilineality is, however, a disputed aspect of KhoiSan culture. Some sources suggest that the Khoi had a matrilineal descent system – descent traced through the female line (Boonzaier, 1997). Khoi attitudes to aspects such as divorce were rather relaxed, suggesting to some a society that was characterised by some measure of gender parity. Matrilineality, however, is not to suggest an absence of patriarchy, it is just that the Khoi groups that the colonialists encountered were sometimes led by female chiefs. One example is the famous leader of the Hessequa people of the southern Cape, 'Lang Elsie', literally translating as 'tall Elizabeth' (De Jongh, 2016). In the early 20th century, Dorothea Bleek argued that the San had 'no chiefs but rather pay deference to a patriarch' (Bleek D. as cited in Schapera, 1930). Schapera responds to the above quote by qualifying that the person to whom deference is given could also be a woman. In the recreation of this institution in the present, it would serve to recognise that, in the past, Khoi leaders could be female and not simply recreate an institution based on male descent.

Leadership figures among the KhoiSan of the past have often emerged in the terrains of the struggle against colonialism, and the movement of the KhoiSan (San, Khoi, Griqua, Basters) beyond the border of the Cape Colony in search of self-reliance during the late 19th century. In this movement of people, many leaders were produced and I will not rehearse the whole litany of names. A short account may suffice to suggest some of the forms this leadership took. Some of the leaders that were produced were individuals like

Adam Kok III (1811–1875) and Dirk Vilander (ca. 1820–1896), who sought territory outside the Cape Colony, where they often petitioned the British crown to grant them sovereignty. Alas, the desired sovereignty never materialised and much Khoi Baster land would be lost to swindles, dispossession, grazing licences and the like. So, the Griqua and the Vilander Khoi would see how Boer republics (like Stellaland, Goshen and Rooigrond) all around them grew and were given official recognition by the British crown. All the while, those of Khoi descent were never given this kind of recognition of their sovereign or land rights. Beyond this, groups like the Vilander Khoi of the southern Kalahari and the Griqua had to defend their lands against the depredations of European invaders and other Khoi who lived by the commando system. The commando Khoi were those like Kootjie Afrikaner (ca. 1820–1889) who lived by raiding other Khoi and European farms. The commando system was learned from the Dutch colonists who used it effectively against the San. It consisted essentially of groups of armed men on horseback roving and raiding settlements (Penn, 1996). There were also those commando Khoi who fought directly against the colonists, like the many unnamed San leaders who rose to defend their watering holes and hunting territory against European farmers and Khoi Basters (see Saunders, 1977; Broodryk, 1992; Gordon and Sholto-Douglas, 2000).

It is clear, therefore, that many a Khoi leader rose on the colonial frontiers of the late 19th century. The question can be asked of whether or not the leadership positions that were created in response to colonial pressures morphed into more permanent leadership or traditional leadership positions. The answer is twofold: The first set of leaders like Dirk Vilander didn't leave behind a hereditary traditional leadership. Their land tenure and territories were never secured and they simply became colonial subjects (Broodryk, 1992; Ellis, 2012). The Griqua, however, did leave behind a clear hereditary traditional leadership, partly because they were able to secure political recognition (Ross, 1974; Waldman, 2007).

A third category of leader emerged and may be thought of as a version of a contact leader, and that is the ritual specialist. Ritual specialism is a range of activities that hold significance for groups as mechanisms that help to ensure the production and reproduction of a particular social and cosmic order (see Turner, 1967; Van Gennep et al., 2004). The exact nature of the activities and the significance varies greatly from group to group. More so, these activities range from storytelling to healing to religious activities, and may include specialised knowledge like painting and the production of talismans, plus the manufacturing of goods. On occasion, the monopolies individuals had over these ritual activities granted them prestige and material benefits. For instance, we have historical and ethnographic accounts that suggest that the Nguni prized the services of San people as rainmakers (Saunders, 1977; Prins, 1990; 1996; 2009; Prins & Lewis, 1992) and this allowed them to insert themselves into patronage networks with material benefits. Control of patronage networks grant individuals some power vis-à-vis their compatriots. Equally, the historical evidence suggests that particular rock art sites had owners who managed these sites and controlled the material benefits and prestige of them (Woodhouse, 1997).

Individuals involved in traditional medicine and specialists in magic constituted a further set of roles that were often revered, and could translate the practice and knowledge of these arts into prestige. Suffice to say that ritual specialism, if controlled by individuals and families, is easily translated into power prestige and material benefit. Wilmsen (1989) argues that although San society was often understood to be egalitarian, his own fieldwork seemed to contradict this perspective. He documents exactly the process described above and shows how those individuals and families who controlled patronage from outsiders, who controlled the craft trade, who had ritual and religious capital or who controlled hunting rights and key products were able to use this to their own advantage in terms of the management of power and prestige in these groups.

Present-day KhoiSan leadership

At least two of the above factors persist into the present: the contact leaders and the ritual specialists. My own research into the land claim community tracks the historical production of traditional leadership through 'contact' (Ellis, 2012). This is not contact through colonialism and state as such, but sustained contact with ethno-entrepreneurs, researchers and leadership in institutions such as the conservation authority. For instance, the Kruiper family, through a series of interactions with conservation authorities, filmmakers, researchers, lawyers and journalists gain prominence in the land claim community. Dawid Kruiper, who had always been a spokesperson during the land claims process of the 1990s, was eventually elected as the traditional leader. Kruiper was even selected to make a speech at the United Nations Working Group on Indigenous Populations in 1994.

This, however, was not 'traditional' leadership in the generally accepted sense of the term. Rather it is an official title of office in the Khomani San Common Property Association. In this sense, anyone could stand for office after this person's term of office was over. Dawid Kruiper, although generally accepted as a traditional leader, held this as an elected position and not as an inherited position. Moreover, there was no regional Khomani traditional leader for the San in this region. Notwithstanding, the aforementioned ethnographic and archival evidence is not intended to destroy the legitimacy of, or completely occlude the possibility for, the creation of a traditional leadership institution among the San in the southern Kalahari (I return to this point later).

Leadership in the present continues to be influenced by ritual specialism. Again, the Kruiper family serves as a clear example of this (Ellis, 2012; 2014; 2015). Over the last three decades, the Kruiper family have built quite a reputation as healers and diviners adept at producing talismans and apotropaic charms, and producing counter-magic. In the late 1990s, I spoke to some of their clients who had come as far afoot as the Eastern Cape, a distance of about 1,000 kilometres, to seek out the Kruipers' services. This craft was a practice that Dawid Kruiper and several other family members learned from Kruiper's father, Regopstaan, and his grandfather, Makai. The role the Kruipers played as ritual specialists was aided by their close relationship with conservation authorities in the national parks. This connection gave them access to resources that were revered as magical in various communities, such as lion body parts (including hair, fat, nails and hide) and products from a range of other animals, some of which are endangered, like the pangolin. The family's networks were vital in their eventual reverence as ritual specialists and subsequently leaders. So, although there is no real inherited, historical traditional leadership that can be traced in the Kruiper lineage, their family access to this 'ritual capital' contributes to the eventual selection of members of this family as leaders.

The category of ritual specialist can be brought into the present and expanded to include a range of activities that are vital to the leadership question within the KhoiSan revival. A number of prominent figures in the KhoiSan movement have taken it upon themselves to become ritual specialists, or are officially in roles that are akin to ritual specialists. Ritual specialists refer to those who have a key role in the reproduction of the cosmological world of their groups; they are often also religious specialists. The first of these ritual specialists are a number of ordained ministers who have been elevated to, have been appointed to or have assumed key leadership positions. One could think of such key figures as Ds Willa Boesak and his brother Reggie Boesak, and Mario Mahongo of the Platfontein community in the Northern Cape. A second set of figures are those that attempt to reproduce the cosmological world of the Khoi and San by deploying readily available symbols and artefacts associated with KhoiSan identity, and recombining them in a creative process in order to recall or recreate a world that was lost in the colonial encounter. This creative deployment serves as an auratic critique, the critique that recalls the romantic past and continues to mourn it. This process also draws on various naturalistic symbols that recall land dispossession. These ritual specialists don springbok skins, animal skins or clothes with animal prints, and they burn *Helichrysum*,[4] and so recall all the natural resources that the land can bring forth. These are as much rituals of mourning as they are of rebirth. The individuals who lead these rituals are called upon to lead because they are seen as having the knowledge to rediscover the lost world of the KhoiSan by successfully deploying the available symbols. Very little has been written about these ritual specialists in the present-day KhoiSan revival, and the above has been based on a few personal observations in various parts of South Africa.

Authenticity, as a feature of cultural strategies in general, can be used as an auratic recall of an apparently real African past. It is important to note that authenticity is not an actual recoverable state. The past has been so distorted by historical debate, the tainted practice of archiving and romanticisation, that a sentimentalised project of recovery and salvage is not desirable. Such projects of recovery characterise culturalised political strategies in the present, a relevant example being traditional leadership itself (Verbuyst, 2016). We are reminded also that authenticity is largely a modern concern that develops at particular moments in the maturation of industrial capitalism (see Ellis, 2014). With this understanding, the various strategies of deploying authenticity serve not as recovery of genuine or actual historical institutions, but as particularly modern social, cultural and political strategies. As Rassool (2006) has argued elsewhere, those who have studied San people often sought authority by appeals to 'authenticity', for example by calling upon 'voices of authenticity'. These voices of authenticity are often the San themselves and researchers deploy this to authenticate paradigms that are of dubious value and of colonial origin (Tomaselli, 2006; Ellis, 2012; Koot, 2016).

Rassool (2006) raises another problematic aspect of the deployment of authenticity, namely its paternalism, and here I turn to the ethnography again. First, the link between the two concepts, paternalism and authenticity, is made apparent in the 'expectations' that the other be 'present as authentic' (Enwezor, 1997). This call to be present as authentic is a call by the 'powerful Westerners' that 'the other', and that which these Westerners see as 'real culture', be presented to them (Enwezor, 1997). Ironically any 'modernised,' altered or constructed form is taken as fake, ersatz or somehow not real enough to be anything but a reproduction (Enwezor, 1997). These often European audiences demand that the African self be presented as 'authentic'. Then the European serves him or herself up as the curator, advocate and arbiter of this self-same authenticity (Enwezor, 1997).

In fieldwork done from 1999 to 2004 with San communities in the southern Kalahari, I often noted that the San people who were not considered authentic were not treated with the same regard as those who acted out a script that suggested a particular type of 'bushman'. For instance, those San individuals who wanted to farm with livestock were not thought of as 'genuine' San and their livelihood strategies did not enjoy the same importance in NGO agendas. Elsewhere, these tensions of 'authentic' versus 'inauthentic' are well documented as tensions between so-called traditional versus westernised San (Robins, 2001; Ellis, 2012; 2014; 2015). The westernised San often found their own proposals and ideas sidelined in favour of those proposals considered to be more 'authentically' San. Activities considered more authentic were those which promoted cultural tourism, hunting, conservation and language survival, and excluded were livestock farming and associated activities. Paternalism is largely a component in the support for, and promotion of, particular agendas over others.

Earlier on, I mention the Kruipers' ability to control ritual resources because of their networks. The Kruipers are able to display and realise authenticity because they are also successfully able to fit the script of bushman-ness. For instance, the prominence of this family is not a matter of simple hereditary leadership. This leadership is locked into an intergenerational storehouse of family stories, networks of patronage, access to ritual and natural resources, as well as alliances of paternalism that help them to underwrite the script of authenticity. In fact, we must be conscious that these displays of authenticity are exhibiting forms that echo 'colonial fantasies' (Enwezor, 1997).

In closing this leadership sketch, with regard to the Khoi and San, the question of what constitutes an authentic form is pertinent. What is often considered to be the authentic form of leadership, which is a largely hereditary, patrilineal chieftaincy seated within a hierarchical system of governance with a tendency towards centralised management of power, does not in my view come close to reflecting the reality among the KhoiSan, neither in the past nor in the present. Above I have noted, *inter alia*, an apparently weak chieftaincy in historic KhoiSan groupings, where power was somewhat divorced from the office. We are presented with what was a range of 'contact' spokespersons who could just as easily have been selected by outsiders as by insiders. These spokespersons, when selected by the group of which they were members, were not granted any power but rather momentary prestige to speak on behalf of the group. This role could be fulfilled as long as the person expressed the point of view of the society in question. Clastres (2010) suggests that leaders must be those who merely repeat or articulate societies' discourses about themselves. Spokespersons remain key in the politics of the KhoiSan revival and it is from one of these that I want to draw my statement about KhoiSan leadership. Simple selection of a spokesperson as leader is not a means of creating authentic leadership. In his challenge to the TKLB, leader and KhoiSan activist Johnathan Muller instead suggests a form similar to the above. He holds that the first point of accountability and representation is not the 'traditional leader' but rather a structure. In articulating this view, Muller is contesting the clause in the TKSLB that proposes that KhoiSan traditional leaders should receive salaries. His point is simple:

> ... it is said our leaders will be co-opted onto structures and then they are going to receive remuneration. Please I ask you not to be that divisive because we have customary structures. Monies don't go to leaders, money come to structures, structures pay the leaders (Muller, 2015).

Muller's point is simply that we need to consider that in some ways it was fortunate that KhoiSan systems were not drawn into colonial forms of governance, and subsequently into the system of apartheid. Instead, at this moment, we have the opportunity to create a system of governance for those KhoiSan who should want it, that reflects more accurately, and I shudder to say authentically, a system of traditional leadership. The system suggested by Muller is one where the leadership, that is those granted the prestige to lead, are held responsible for those they speak on behalf of. The suggestion is that the present structures proposed for traditional leadership are open to abuse. In this system, where traditional authorities get salaries directly from government structures, structures have no direct mechanism to allow communities to hold leadership accountable. Leaders are only spokespersons who articulate the views and standpoints of the people or structures they represent. If communities so desire, the above system gives them opportunity to withdraw power from the person. Where leadership is inherited, there are very few direct mechanisms that are as powerful and decisive as the act of withholding remuneration.

The final point here is about the exact nature of institutions like traditional leadership, although the relevance of the point is not confined to traditional leadership only. My suggestion above is that we maintain an open approach to these and do not attempt to fossilise these institutions. The validity of this approach is supported by two factors already discussed. The first is the gender inclusiveness of the institution. It is suggested that the KhoiSan were not clearly either matrilineal or patrilineal. Thus, rules about either matrilineal or patrilineal lineage can limit the potential participation of certain groups, such as women, making these institutions rigid and exclusionary. The second factor, the recreation of cosmological and social worlds by ritual specialists, suggests further that there is no fixed authentic culture, but rather that culture has a dynamism that needs to be constantly accommodated. It has often proved elusive to create policy that considers the dynamic nature of culture. This brings us to the second part of the paper that deals more directly with the 'creative' versus the 'authentic' in KhoiSan governance.

Tensions of the authentic versus creative

The argument that there is a tension between the 'authentic' and the 'creative' is best illustrated with reference to two characters in the Khomani San land claim that was lodged in 1995 and resolved in 1999. Much of what follows is based on observations I collected during fieldwork conducted from 1999 until 2003 in the southern Kalahari. In this claim, a group of about 600–800 San descendants, including 25 of the last known speakers of the N/u language, claimed land in what is now the Kgalagadi Transfrontier Park (KTP). In their settlement, the community was given 36,000 hectares of farm land, game animals and a concession in the transfrontier conservation area, along with other cultural rights. The Khomani case was hailed as a great success and a triumph for indigenous or first peoples of southern Africa (Ellis, 2012). However, within a year of the claim being settled, several problems began emerging. One of the problems was the competition for leadership of the group, mainly between the elected traditional leader and the chairman of the Common Property Association or CPA (the actual juristic body through which the land was owned and managed). I have characterised this elsewhere as a clash between democratic governance and tradition. This is a loose application of the critique of traditional leadership offered by Lungisile Ntsebeza (2006).

The elected traditional leader of the Khomani San was the now-deceased Dawid Kruiper (1936–2012), who insisted that his position as elected traditional leader, as well as the leadership role he played in the land claim, afforded him a position of rank. During the first years after the land claim was resolved, he continuously made calls for a separation of land for 'traditional' activities such as hunting, tourism, tourist rituals and the like, from land that was to be used for westernised purposes. Western activities included farming, specifically livestock farming, and residential use. Tourism was considered a traditional activity, largely because tourism encounters were managed to portray performances of what are thought to be 'authentic' Bushmen activities and lifestyles. Kruiper additionally called for the exclusion of those he considered 'westernised' from the farms and the land inside the national park (KTP). His rival took charge of very different aspects of the lives of the claimant community. Petrus Vaalbooi committed his time to the continuous attempts to house many of the San who had moved onto the farmland. At the same time, he promised assistance with healthcare, welfare and pension, as well as transport. Vaalbooi busied himself with the provision of grazing land to those San descendants who were also livestock owners, ensuring that they could occupy land, that they had access to water and that the infrastructure on the farms was in good repair (Ellis, 2012). For Vaalbooi, the agenda was mainly a developmental one.

The two leaders also formed very different alliances with outsiders. Kruiper mostly formed networks with NGOs who supported his cultural agenda. Vaalbooi, however, was a *bricoleur* and could adjust his agenda to suit any audience. His networks ranged from journalists, government officials and international scholars, to NGOs and fellow KhoiSan activists. His style of leadership was much more inclusive and, in fact, creative. At certain points, Kruiper found it difficult to engage with situations of power that required navigation. At these moments, he often withdrew from participation or relied on powerful or influential outsiders to help him assert his agenda. The world of committees and collective decision-making within the CPA was strange terrain for Kruiper. While Vaalbooi navigated this terrain with ease, Kruiper struggled because the group would often reject his call for an exclusive traditional space, reserved for him and his extended family. Sometimes they would stage a 'walk out', leaving community meetings *en masse* to attempt to make their point. Kruiper's position as traditional leader did not grant him any real power, nor did it facilitate the realisation of his vision of a 'traditional' territory where San descendants could revive their language and culture. Vaalbooi, on the other hand, could easily bring about his programmes of development, mostly because he was familiar with political activity, having been involved in regional politics for many years (Ellis, 2012).

In the case of the Khomani San, we can see a traditional leader attempting to push a particular agenda but encountering resistance from his political rivals. In the end, the way things played out suggests that those leaders who were not only more politically savvy but also creative in their engagement with all players, were able to assert political power. Thus, in the short term, the creative triumphed over the authentic.

As an endnote, I may add that at present (mid-2018) the San farms are under administration – a situation that came into effect in 2008.[5] No traditional or other forms of governance could resolve the deep-seated issues in the San community.

KhoiSan dysselection and indigenisation as rebellion

In this final note on the issue of KhoiSan leadership, I want to regard the KhoiSan from yet another far corner of the world. McKittirck

(2016), reading Sylvia Wynter's vast manuscript 'Black Metamorphosis' (unpublished), offers us a fresh view of the idea of 'indigenous'. The first point he makes is that it must be read as a verb not a noun, a 'becoming', not resting place or essence. The reading of indigenous begins by postulating that the black population of the Caribbean is not indigenous, but has become indigenous to that region of the world. All autochthonous peoples have virtually disappeared. African-American slave descendants have stepped in to fill this gap and have in effect become the indigenous people of the region. Wynter asks that without, as she says, 'rehearsing the litany of dehumanising activities', we arrive at the site of, and a process that responds to, this dehumanising (Wynter as cited in McKittirck, 2003). Wynter has named the dehumanising process as dysselection. Dysselection is that which constantly re-minds us of our less than human-ness. The people subject to this process of dehumanising can only respond with rebellion and, in the rebellion, create new humans that affirm their place and history, not as autochthonous but as an allochthonous indigenous people. Wynter therefore argues that what we see in the present as an assertion of 'indigenous' identity, in forms such as music, funerals, fictions and art, are in fact all rebellious forms (Wynter as cited in McKittirck, 2003).

I want to argue here that the KhoiSan, as with many other people the world over, have suffered a process of great dysselection, a literal and continual refusal of their humanity that for some continues into the present. The KhoiSan were, from the first encounters with others, denied their humanity in multiple ways. The insertion of their people into an economic system of unequal value exchange (cattle for trinkets) is well known (Coetzee, 2000). The dysselection continued with the introduction of alcohol, disease and rape, and the subsequent labelling of the KhoiSan as drunkards, indolent and sexually depraved – and all this just in the 17th century. I can continue with other examples: the hunting of San people as vermin, the extermination of the men and the enslavement of women and children. By the mid-1800s, the San found themselves refused in all ways: jailed for hunting, starved, dying of thirst, dispossessed of their land and converted into virtual slaves on white-owned farms. The complete and total dysselection of the KhoiSan in these periods creates inhumane labour practices that many are still not able to escape today. In addition, there was the final negation and stripping of identity – and here McKittrick's (2016) words ring true – in that the KhoiSan cultural practices were threats and that they were 'bereft of their humanity'. An incident that comes to mind is of the loss of KhoiSan languages. Dawid Kruiper notes how he was pinched and his ears twisted by teachers and non-San adults when he spoke Nama as a young boy. Violent practices continued to dysselect for culture after even after land had been lost.

The dysselection of the KhoiSan continues in the present. Many KhoiSan activists argue[6] that there has been little recognition for KhoiSan people in the present and that even in South Africa's new democratic dispensation they continue to be treated as 'coloureds' and thus considered a people without a culture. The apparent lack of culture masks the true loss here: the loss of the land.

McKittrick (2016) suggests the solution to dysselection is to be found in the recreation of humanity. Likewise, if this recreation is in a constant rebellion against dysselection, then the KhoiSan revival must be read as a rebellion too. Thus, the various aspects of the revival are more than just a peaceful recreation of a lost culture. No, the indigenisation, as mapped by Wynter (cited in McKittirck, 2016) and applied to the KhoiSan, is a process of active upheaval, engaged debates and a feverish recreation of not just a culture but a humanity. The activities of some of the KhoiSan activists seem to support this assertion.

In a video made by a colleague, Rafeal Verbuyst, we see several activists gathered outside the Castle of Good Hope in Cape Town in 2014 – a fitting site that many activists hail as the origin of the oppression of KhoiSan people. People who are protesting are not simply standing about peacefully. One of the participants walks on the white lines in the middle of the street. He shouts incoherently but you can tell he is outraged. They chant a litany that includes Nama words, reclaiming those phrases that were denied them at one point in history. They end the protest with a joint act of defiance. The men, about 10 or 12, all urinate against the wall of the castle. The revival is not just a plea for peace, a request for inclusion or a plea for the return of land and culture. The revival is a fervent, openly vulgar rebellion against the Castle.

One of the critiques of those 'traditional' communities advocating for the TKLB is that they are willingly subjecting themselves to a system of rule that has been implicated in the oppression of people under both colonialism and apartheid (Claassens, 2016). Fears that the TKLB will bring new oppression and subjection may be well founded. In some quarters, the regressive ramifications of the TKLB are now generally accepted wisdom. Yet, people who potentially fall under the Khoi-San Bill seem undeterred by this commentary. Why should the people be so resolute in their calls for a system that is viewed as compromised? One has to read it, in part, as a call for political recognition. In other ways, it is a political strategy that this community hopes will deliver the rights of citizenry and the benefits of the post-apartheid era.

In the calls for the creation and recognition of traditional KhoiSan leaders, there are two core issues. The first of these are volunteer kings and chiefs – self-professed traditional leaders, with or without followers, with or without mandates. The second issue is what I am calling 'brown nationalism' – attempts by some to use the category 'KhoiSan' as a national category, in opposition to all other categories in South Africa.

The first issue is one that asks about the authenticity of the leaders that are to be recognised. The bill has a provision that not only requires these leaders to prove that they are not spuriously claiming traditional leadership positions, but also that groups validate their existence by showing that they actually exist as a 'tribe'. The final say on these matters is vested in an expert appointed by the president (Claassens, 2016). It would seem that traditional leadership remains a position that is ultimately created and validated in law, and not in custom or history. In the final analysis, the authenticity of the claims to traditional authority aside, one needs to ask what a spurious king or chief would hope to achieve. The simple dismissal of such persons as culturally dubious displaces an issue that constituents want addressed within the frame of KhoiSan politics of revival. One must be reminded that indigenisation is a process of rebellion. If so, a chief emerges to challenge some aspect of the past but also to engage with the issues of the present. If even spurious claims to chieftaincy are legitimate acts of rebellion, what might the issues be? The unresolved issues of the post-apartheid period, taken here to refer to a state of mind and culture of being rather than being simply temporal, are numerous. Suffice to say that the KhoiSan activists continue to voice an experience akin to the dysselection mentioned earlier. Not that I support the critique voiced by 'brown nationalists', in fact I dispute it vehemently, but some KhoiSan activists claim that at present they are neglected as a political category and that other groups are granted both cultural and land rights that are denied to them. According to this argument, it follows that from the rights to land there are certain knock-on effects. Thus, the recognition of leaders, spurious or not, will help these communities deal with social welfare issues and power issues that still plague their 'people'.

Although not always articulated as such, there is a dangerous subscript of coloured nationalism in some of the KhoiSan revival politics. The political questions raised, and the framing of the debates, are dangerously close to ideas that held sway under apartheid. One of the key debates is about a reading of the history of the peopling of southern Africa. In these terms, the call for political leaders like those that were created under apartheid, with all the accompanying power bases, is a central call issued by certain proponents of the revival. Some are literally suggesting separate territories. Most of these calls fall short of naming the 'swart gevaar'. This approach represents a solidification of the structures and political institutions of apartheid through the mobilisation of key cultural institutions, and the linking of these to physical resources such as land as power base. This of course is true of any group, KhoiSan or not, that continues to live as subjects of chiefs and kings.

On 'brown nationalism', the politics of KhoiSan indigenisation includes a call for the recognition of the KhoiSan as an autochthonous population and the *de facto* first peoples. All other people are considered recent arrivals. Although the term indigenous is used for most of the non-white population, the KhoiSan activists would like to see it applied only to themselves and not to allochthonous settlers. Activists believe that the recognition of 'traditional leaders' should bring with it all the desired effects concerning land.

Conclusions

Lalu (2008) asks us to consider whether we are in fact in the 'post'-apartheid period, and what this post-apartheid might mean. He concludes, among other things, that post-apartheid, as in postcolonial, has never really happened, and is thus a mindset, not a temporal appellation. If anything, post-apartheid, like postcolonial, has meant a solidification of the structures of apartheid. Among some KhoiSan activists, this has led to intense calls for the recognition of what are essentially apartheid ideologies or institutions. Hence, we see the calls for readings of apartheid history to be officially recognised, calls for the granting of customary authority as under apartheid and, lastly, re-inscription of apartheid categories such as 'coloured' but by a different name (KhoiSan). The rulings on all these exceptions have repercussions in the fields of land, minerals and political territory. And across South Africa, the call for the official recognition and legitimacy of traditional authorities is, in part at least, a call for the concretisation of the structures of apartheid, as an exception!

The KhoiSan revival is not monolithic in its response to the ravages of apartheid. I have suggested that the KhoiSan are following various paths in the post-apartheid period, and many of these strategies are creative and active in their reconstruction of a KhoiSan identity. The responses to dysselection have been dignifying to many who assume and claim the KhoiSan moniker, and it would be premature to simply dismiss the entire movement as re-establishing, and attempting to make permanent, the institutions of apartheid. We must accept that some of the traditional and customary positions created by the KhoiSan activists are founded on a philosophy of care for people and kin.

In the final analysis, I have argued that traditional leadership can and does play a role in the lives of people who choose to associate with these institutions of culture. In fact, many of those who have emerged in the KhoiSan revival seem to reflect styles of leadership that are at once situational, and also dynamic and creative. However, I advise caution in the application of these notions and we must always be wary that the professed logic and philosophy of care does not continue to be, or evolve into, a practice of domination.

References

Abrahams, Y. 1995. '"Take me to your leaders": A critique of Kraal and castle'. *Kronos,* 2, 21–35.

Agamben, G. 1998. *Sovereign Power and Bare Life.* Stanford: Stanford University Press.

Boonzaier, E. (1997). *The Cape Herders: A history of the Khoikhoi of Southern Africa.* Cape Town: New Africa Books.

Bredenkamp, H. C. 1982. *Van Veeverskaffers tot Veewagters: Historiese ondersoek na betrekkinge tussen die Khoikhoi en Europeërs aan die Kaap.* Bellville: University of the Western Cape.

Broodryk, M. 1992. 'Die Kaapse noordgrensoorloë, 1868–1879', *Archives Yearbook.* Pretoria: Government Printers.

Changon, N. 1968. *Yanoamo: The fierce people.* New York: Holt, Rinehart & Winston.

Claassens, A. 2016. 'South Africa's traditional leadership proposal: The TKLB is desperate and dangerous'. *Land and Accountability Research Centre* website: http://www.customcontested.co.za/south-africas-traditional-leadership-proposal-tklb-desperate-dangerous/, accessed 7 August 2018.

Clastres, P. 2010. *Archeology of Violence.* Los Angeles: Semiotext(e).

Coetzee, A. 2000. *'n Hele os vir 'n ou broodmes: Grond en die plaasnarratief sedert 1595.* Pretoria: Van Schaik Publishers.

Da Col, G. & Graeber, D. 2011. 'Foreward: The return of ethnographic theory'. *Journal of Ethnographic Theory,* 1 (1), vi–xxxv.

De Jongh, M. 2016. *A Forgotten First People: The Southern Cape Hessequa.* San Francisco: Watermark Press.

Du Plessis, M. 2009. 'A unity hypothesis for the southern African Khoesan languages'. Doctoral dissertation. Cape Town: University of Cape Town.

Dubow, S. 1996. 'Human origins, race typology and the other Raymond Dart'. *African Studies,* 55 (1), 1–30.

Ellis, W. 2012. 'Genealogies and narratives of San authenticities: The Khomani San land claim in the Southern Kalahari'. PhD thesis. Cape Town: University of the Western Cape.

Ellis, W. 2014. 'Simulacral, genealogical, auratic and representational failure: Bushman authenticity as methodological collapse'. *Critical Arts,* 28 (3), 493–520.

Ellis, W. 2015. 'Ons is Boesmans: Commentary on the naming of Bushmen in the southern Kalahari'. *Anthropology Southern Africa,* 38 (1–2), 120–133.

Elphick, R. 1977. *Kraal and Castle.* New Haven: Yale University Press.

Enwezor, O. 1997. 'Reframing the black subject ideology and fantasy in contemporary South African representation'. *Third Text*, 11 (40), 21–40.

Geschiere, P. 2009. *The Perils of Belonging: Autochthony, citizenship, and exclusion in Africa and Europe*. Chicago: University of Chicago Press.

Gordon, R. & Sholto-Douglas, S. 2000. *The Bushman Myth: The making of a Namibian underclass (2nd Edition)*. Boulder: Westview Press.

Hammond-Tooke, W. D. 1997. *Imperfect Interpreters: South Africa's anthropologists, 1920–1990*. Johannesburg: Witwatersrand University Press.

Houlton, T. M. R. & Billings, B. K. 2017. 'Blood, sweat and plaster casts: Reviewing the history, composition, and scientific value of the Raymond A. Dart Collection of African Life and Death Masks'. *HOMO-Journal of Comparative Human Biology*, 68 (5), 362–377.

Humphreys, A. B. 1985. 'A kaleidoscope of values: Changing perspectives on San society'. *Kronos*, 10, 58–66.

Jenkins, T. & Tobias, P. V. 1977. 'Nomenclature of population groups in South Africa'. *African Studies*, 36 (1), 49–55.

Koot, S. P. 2016. 'Contradictions of capitalism in the South African Kalahari: Indigenous Bushmen, their brand and baasskap in tourism'. *Journal of Sustainable Tourism*, 24 (8–9), 1211–1226.

Kuper, A. 2003. 'The return of the native'. *Current Anthropology*, 44 (3), 389–402.

Lalu, P. 2008. 'When was South African history ever postcolonial?' *Kronos*, 34 (1), 267–281.

Lee, R. 1979. *The !Kung San: Men, women and work in a foraging society*. Cambridge: Cambridge University Press.

Lenski, G. & Lenski, J. 1982. *Human Societies: An introduction to macrosociology*. New York: McGrawhill.

McKittrick, K. 2016. 'Rebellion/invention/groove'. *Small Axe*, 20 (149), 79–91.

Muller, J. 15 January 2015. 'Johnathan Muller ... Parliament'. *YouTube*, https://www.youtube.com/watch?v=K2RSBm-F6fE, accessed 20 June 2017.

Ntsebeza, L. 2006. *Democracy Compromised: Chiefs and the politics of the land in South Africa*. Cape Town: HSRC Press.

Pelican, M. 2009. 'Complexities of indigeneity and autochthony: An African example'. *American Ethnologist*, 36 (1), 52–65.

Penn, N. 1996. 'Fated to perish', in Skotnes, P. (ed.) *Miscast: Negotiating the presence of the bushmen*. Cape Town: University of Cape Town Press, pp. 81–92.

Penn, N. 2005. *The Forgotten Frontier: Colonist and Khoisan on the Cape's Northern Frontier in the 18th century*. Cape Town: Juta.

Povinelli, E. A. 2002. *The Cunning of Recognition: Indigenous alterities and the making of Australian multiculturalism.* Durham: Duke University Press.

Prins, F. E. 1990. 'Southern bushmen descendants in the Transkei – rock art and rainmaking'. *South African Journal of Ethnology,* 13 (3), 110–116.

Prins, F. E. 2009. 'Secret San of the Drakensberg and their rock art legacy'. *Critical Arts,* 23 (2), 190–208.

Prins, F. E. 1996. 'Praise to the bushman ancestors of the water: The integration of San-related concepts in the beliefs and ritual of a diviner's training school in Tsolo, Eastern Cape', in Skotnes, P. (ed.) *Miscast: Negotiating the presence of the bushmen.* Cape Town: University of Cape Town Press, pp. 211–223.

Prins, F. E. & Lewis, H. 1992. 'The bushmen as mediators in Nguni Cosmology'. *Ethnology,* 31 (2), 133–147.

Rassool, C. 2006. 'Beyond the cult of "salvation" and "remarkable equality": A new paradigm for the Bleek-Lloyd Collection'. *Kronos,* 32, 244–251.

Robins, S. 2001. 'NGOs, bushmen and double vision: The Khomani San land claim and the cultural politics of community and development in the Kalahari'. *Journal of Southern African Studies,* 27 (4), 833–853.

Ross, R. 1974. 'Griqua government'. *African Studies,* 33 (1), 25–42.

Ross, R. 1983. 'The first two centuries of colonial agriculture in the Cape Colony: A historiographical review'. *Social Dynamics,* 9 (1), 30–49.

Saunders, C. 1977. 'Madolo: A bushman life'. *African Studies* 36 (2), 145–154.

Schapera, I. 1930. *The Khoisan Peoples of South Africa: Bushmen and Hottentots.* London: Routledge.

Schuster, S. C., Miller, W., Ratan, A. (plus 42 scholars). 2010. 'Complete Khoisan and Bantu genomes from Southern Africa'. *Nature,* 463 (7283), 943–947.

Smith, A. B. 1990. 'On becoming herders: Khoi-Khoi and San ethnicity in Southern Africa'. *African Studies,* 49 (2), 51–73.

Smith, A. B. 1996. 'Khoi/San relationships: Marginal differences or ethnicity', in Skotnes, P. (ed.) *Miscast: Negotiating the presence of the Bushmen.* Cape Town: University of Cape Town Press, pp. 249–251.

Smith, A., Malherbe, C., Geunther, M. & Berens, P. 2000. *The Bushmen of Southern Africa: A forager society in transition.* Ohio: Ohio University Press.

Tomaselli, K. G. 2006. 'Negotiating research with communities of practice', in Denzin, N. & Giardina, M. (eds.) *Contesting Empire/Globalizing Dissent: Cultural Studies After 9/11.* Boulder: Paradigm Publishers, pp. 250–263.

Traditional and Khoisan Leadership Bill No. 39220. 18 September 2015, http://www.cogta.gov.za/cgta_2016/wp-content/uploads/2016/06/TRADITIONAL-AND-KHOI-SAN-LEADERSHIP-BILL.pdf, accessed 14 July 2017.

Turner, V. W. 1967. *The Forest of Symbols: Aspects of Ndembu ritual.* Ithaca: Cornell University Press.

Van der Ross, R. E. 1979. *Myths and Attitudes: An inside look at the coloured people.* Cape Town: Tafelberg.

Van Gennep, A., Vizedom, M. & Caffee, G. L. 2004. *The Rites of Passage.* London: Routledge.

Verbuyst, R. 2016. 'Claiming Cape Town: Towards a symbolic interpretation of Khoisan activism and land claims'. *Anthropology Southern Africa*, 39 (2), 83–96.

Waldman, L. 2007. *The Griqua Conundrum: Political and socio-cultural identity in the Northern Cape, South Africa.* Oxford: Peter Lang.

Wilmsen, E. N. 1989. *Land Filled with Flies: A political economy of the Kalahari.* Chicago: University of Chicago press.

Wilmsen, E. N. 2002. 'Mutable identities: Moving beyond ethnicity in Botswana'. *Journal for Southern African Studies*, 28 (4), 825–841.

Woodhouse, H. C. 1997. 'Some palace caves of the bushman chiefs'. *South African Journal of Ethnology* 20 (2), 93–102.

Endnotes

1   As a thought and theory experiment I want to withhold pronouncements of certain identity such as KhoiSan, Khoi or San. Rather I want to treat these forms as cooperative, working together in the defining and reassertion of an identity formation that has its origin in First Nations descent and autochthony. Usually thought of as two distinct groups and sometimes treated as economically, linguistically and politically separate, for our arguments here I will assume the Khoi and San as being the same construct united by a common origin, history of habitation and genetics. Where terms such as San, Khoi, Hottentot, Bushmen are used it should be taken to be the terms used in the texts being referenced. Further, when the term Khoi is used it will be understood as referring to those KhoiSan people who were formerly or presently herders/pastoralists. In the same way, when San is used it will be taken to refer to former hunter gatherers.

2   Philip Tobias Took steered the Wits Kalahari Research Committee from the 1950s to the 1990s and also headed the Wits anatomy department – a position he held until 1990 as well. He participated in various expeditions

to study Bushmen. He was widely regarded as one of the premier physical anthropologists in South Africa if not the world (Houlton & Billings, 2017)

3 Werner Willi Max Eiselen was a professor of *volkekunde* at Stellenbosch University during the 1930s, where he founded, among other things, the Department of Bantu Studies or, as it was known in Afrikaans, Bantoelogie. He was renowned as a linguist and *volkekundige* and served as Government Ethnologist under apartheid. During his term as Government Ethnologist he developed the Eiselen scheme that would call for the removal of all 'so-called' natives from the western parts of South Africa. This scheme would be the foundation of the Coloured Labour Preference Area Policy, an apartheid policy that was first hinted at in the 1950s and implemented slowly over time during the 1960s and 1970s (see Hammond-Tooke, 1997).

4 *Helichryum petiolarum* is one of a number of plant species that are burned at ritual occasions. It is known by a less flattering name, 'Hotnotskooigoed', literally Hottentot bedding in Afrikaans. In Zulu and Xhosa it is known as *imphepho*.

5 The land that had been returned to the Khomani in 1999 had been so badly managed and the community was so rife with conflict that the Department of Land Affairs decided to take over the management of the land and the associated resources.

6 Much of what is recounted here is from first-hand observations during fieldwork.

SECTION FOUR
Opinions from Two Traditional Leaders

In this final section of the book, we hear from traditional leaders themselves. Two senior traditional leaders, both hailing from the Eastern Cape and with many years of experience in traditional governance structures, offer reflections about the evolution of traditional leadership in a democratic South Africa. In contrast to the rest of the book, these are not scholarly chapters, but works of personal reflection. The authors do not state their sources upfront and many of the claims they make are contested (including by other contributors in this book). Indeed, these final chapters remind us just how fiercely contested traditional leadership is, as well as what is at stake for those who hold the institution dear. It is crucially important that readers, policymakers and practitioners understand how traditional leaders themselves understand the history, role and future of their institution. Implicit in the reflections presented by these two traditional leaders are questions related to identity, authenticity, 'postcolonial' society and the very definition of democratic practice.

*Before the colonialists took over the land and imposed their system
of governance, which ironically has been embraced by all democratic
governments in Africa, traditional leaders and their communities
led wars of resistance. They paid supreme sacrifices as many were
brutally killed.*

– NKOSI MWELO NONKONYANA

*Development and service delivery in rural Africa continues to suffer
because politicians do not want to give due recognition to the role of
the institution of traditional leadership. Where there is cooperation
and mutual respect between government and traditional leaders, the
people benefit.*

– NKOSI PHATHEKILE HOLOMISA

ELEVEN

In defence of traditional leadership

NKOSI PHATHEKILE HOLOMISA
(AH! DILIZINTABA)

Twenty-three years into freedom and democracy, South Africa still grapples with the role of traditional leaders in the life and governance of the country's citizens. This in itself is indicative of the fact that when the current constitutional order was negotiated, key elements of our traditions and governance systems had not been fully expressed or taken on board. Unfortunately, this gave the impression that, when the colonial settlers took over the land and control of the lives of the natives, the latter had never had governance systems of their own.

The truth of the matter is that pre-colonial South Africa, like the rest of Africa, did have its own governance systems. The institution of traditional leadership was the epitome of such a system, a system that was underpinned by African laws, which in turn were anchored on customs and traditions adopted and adapted over ages. The Bill of Rights which was embedded in South Africa's original constitutional order was informed by 'ubuntu', a humanitarian philosophy ensuring that citizens look after each other before they promote their own personal interests. Thus, even before democracy, when ubuntu was the overriding principle, we had no orphanages, no old-age homes, no landless or homeless people.

The land was governed by traditional leaders together with counsellors who were trusted to guide leaders in the exercising of their powers. It was incumbent on all to respect the values and mores enshrined in the customs and traditions of the people. The system of justice administration, as well as decision-making in general, was characterised by openness, inclusivity and democratic principles. Of course, in the past, women and the youth were generally not directly involved in these activities, although, with the passage of time, women could become rulers and commanders of armies under certain circumstances.

History tells us that the wars of land dispossession unleashed by the colonial settlers, mainly Dutch and British, upon the natives resulted in the loss of 87 per cent of the land to the settlers. The remaining 13 per cent, which had been successfully defended from marauding bands of European invaders, came to constitute the land over which the nine apartheid homelands were created. Having been dispossessed of most of their land, Africans were able to lead their lives in more or less their own ways in these so-called homelands. Inevitably, under the control and supervision of the colonial and apartheid masters, traditional leaders continued to govern the affairs of their people according to tradition.

Let me also assert that the role of traditional leadership in the fight for freedom and human rights in this country looms large in the background, and cannot be ignored. As a collective, we are certainly proud of luminaries like Nkosi Langalibalele Dube (uMafukuzela), the founder president of the African National Congress (ANC), of the Qadi clan in Zululand; Nkosi Albert Luthuli (uMadlanduna), another ANC president, of amaKholwa in Zululand; King Sabata Dalindyebo (Ah! Jonguhlanga) of the Thembu, who died in exile after joining the ANC, and many others who occupied the moral high ground in defence of the rights of the citizens of this country in years gone by.

Needless to say, the iconic first president of democratic South Africa himself, Nkosi Nelson Rolihlahla Mandela (Ah! Dalibhunga), hails from the royal house of the Thembu. The moral of this story is that in the history of our beloved country, traditional leadership permeates virtually all facets of the development of ordinary people who would otherwise remain at the margins of society economically.

All in all, traditional leaders, in support of the broader struggle for freedom, remained a moral compass and refuge for many South Africans. To this day, they continue to govern the affairs of their people according to tradition. When the apartheid governments failed to provide the requisite resources, traditional leaders mobilised their communities to raise funds for the building of schools, clinics and other social amenities. They approached the corporate world, notably mining companies where most of their people worked, to ask for funds to provide these amenities.

They served as channels, in the manner of present-day municipalities, for public funds to local communities; they ensured infrastructure developments such as roads and bridge-building, as well as the fencing of arable and grazing lands. As administrators of traditional community land, they allocated land for residential, crop cultivation and business purposes. Traditional leaders were automatically members of school and clinic committees and hospital boards. They were responsible for agricultural development and livestock improvement, working closely with all relevant government departments.

Essentially, they were, and still are, the link between government departments and the people – in other words, they were conduits for government services.

The great majority of criminal and civil cases across the whole of South Africa are tried and heard by the Royal Courts of Traditional Leadership, so-called 'traditional courts'. In the conduct of these cases, the parties do not pay legal fees. The proceedings are held in familiar surroundings, in a language they speak and understand, in accordance with laws, customs and traditions they know, and presided over by their own peers, i.e. fellow tribesmen. The main goal is restorative justice, rehabilitation of offenders, reconciliation of the victims with perpetrators, as well as the maintenance of peace in the community. As stated before, the proceedings are inclusive, participatory, democratic, transparent and open.

It is in this context and against this background that Parliament has a duty to consider and process a law giving full and meaningful recognition to these Royal Courts of Traditional Leadership. This is but one example where government and traditional leadership need to come much closer for the benefit of the country as a whole.

The prevalent question when it comes to the role, place, powers, functions and relevance of the institution of traditional leadership tends to be misguided and, at times, even patronising. Those who show sympathy for the institution ask: 'How can we accommodate the institution of traditional leadership in a democratic South Africa?' Had our current political leaders been true to the history and heritage of Their Majesties – such as King Mampuru of the Pedi, Cetshwayo of the Zulu, Nyabela and Mabhena of the Ndebele, Ngungunyana of the Shangaan, Makhado of the Venda, Moshoeshoe of the Sotho, Montshioa of the Tswana, Ngubengcuka of the Thembu, Langalibalele of the Hlubi, Mhlontlo of the Mpondomise, Faku of the Mpondo, Hintsa of the Xhosa, Autshumato of the Khoi, Kok of the Griqua and Le Fleur of the Korana, as well as Queens Modjadji of the Lobedu, Mantantisi of the Tlokwa, Labotsibeni of the Swazi, Nonesi of the Thembu and countless other traditional leaders who led their people in the wars of resistance to colonial invasion – the question from the onset would have been: 'How shall we accommodate the Western way of governance within the original African forms of governance?'

The role and participation of traditional leaders in the decision-making structures of the land, such as legislative bodies, the judiciary and the executive, remain paramount. This is more so in light of the erosion and, in some instances, abolition of African values, systems and cultures, and their replacement by those of the European colonisers.

Irritating as it is, it falls upon us as Africans in general and the descendants of the legendary traditional leaders mentioned above in particular, to explain ourselves in order to justify our existence and relevance. We need to take responsibility and use the platforms and mechanisms provided by our government to confront these matters as custodians of African culture, customs and systems of governance.

The Great Place

My own insight into the institution of traditional leadership stems from the fact that I was born into it. My parents and their forebears were royal. I was destined to succeed my father as traditional leader of my clan, amaHegebe, in accordance with the dictates of our customary law of traditional leadership succession.

At the young age of six, I was taken by my father Nkosi Mathathisa Moses Holomisa (Ah! Jongisizwe) to live at the home of Nkosi Douglas Dywabasini Prince Ndamase (Zwelinzima!) of Mpondoland in Ngqeleni. He was married to one of my father's cousin's sisters, Princess Nozilumko Victoria MaLuSwazi. I had not been told why I had to leave my home to stay at the home of Zwelinzima. Later, I learned from conversations MaLuswazi had with various people that I had been brought to her place to be hidden from my own people, in accordance with traditional practice applicable to royal heirs. It was even later that I learned I was the prospective traditional leader of my clan when those who knew let slip that that was the reason I was there.

The Mampondomiseni Great Place, as the royal homestead was known, was the seat of a great deal of activity, a place full of men and women, young and old, living as members of the family. However, over time, some would leave, while others would join us. It dawned on me that some of them were in a position similar to mine for, as they became adults, they had to go home to take up their duties as traditional leaders of their clans. The women would follow various life paths, including getting married, going to high school, attending college to become teachers or nurses and returning home. The place was a training ground for leaders of the future.

We all learned how to perform our domestic duties as males and females; some chores were strictly for males, while others were for females, yet others still had no gender bias. I learned to look after lambs, kids and calves as a little boy. I had to make sure the calves did not suckle before the cows were milked, otherwise punishment was to follow. I graduated to the level of looking after sheep, goats, cattle and horses. These had to be taken to the veld in the morning and back to the homestead in the afternoon. I had to ensure that they did not stray into people's gardens and mielie fields, otherwise punishment and sanctions were the consequence.

All of these chores we had to perform before and after school. The fact that there were people who were employed to perform them as well did not mean that we were absolved from doing our bit. They were there to assist us while we were otherwise engaged with school work. The idea, I came to learn later, was that as future leaders we should be able to do work that we would require others to do. Assistants were not servants that were required to serve your whims, but were there to assist you when you were not in a position to do the work due to other responsibilities.

Mampondomiseni Great Place was the administrative, legislative, judicial and cultural hub of the tribe falling under Zwelinzima's jurisdiction. On a daily basis, men and women would come with issues requiring the advice or arbitration of the Nkosi. I came to learn a technique that I found to be very effective in resolving the people's issues.

Zwelinzima would listen to a person, ask him or her a variety of questions and, with the answers given, the person would go home thoroughly satisfied with the advice, even though the answers came from himself or herself.

The exercising of traditional authority was done in a layered, systematic way. Those who sought the traditional leader's advice would be advised to first consult the family head, then the head of the clan, the sub-headman of the village, the headman and ultimately the senior traditional leader, if all the other rungs of leadership were unable to resolve the issues. Each of these leaders had at their disposal a council that assisted them where they could not handle a matter by themselves. Resolutions taken would serve as precedents to be used by others finding themselves in similar positions.

The family heads constituted the sub-headmen's council, the sub-headmen the headmen's council, the headmen the senior traditional leader's council, the senior traditional leaders in turn the king's council. Each one of these heads had, in addition, at their disposal, elders knowledgeable about the history and culture of the family, clan and/or tribe. Some of these counsellors would be relatives, such as brothers and uncles. Thus, the head was in a position to be advised and even admonished on how to conduct the affairs falling within his area of jurisdiction.

When I had occasion to sit close by and listen to the proceedings of the councils, mostly at the level of the senior traditional leader's council, I would learn that Zwelinzima would introduce the subject of discussion, outlining its origin, the path it had followed to be finding itself at that particular forum and why it had not been resolved. The matter would then be discussed, debated and argued, with everyone in attendance allowed to participate, until it was time for the Nkosi to pronounce the decision. He never imposed his own views without regard for those of the meeting. This was so even though they would leave the seat of administration stating that it was the Nkosi's decision.

This principle of participatory democracy applied also to the trials of cases – criminal and civil. All the witnesses would be given the opportunity to give their evidence and, while there was an officer designated as the evidence leader, everyone was allowed to examine and cross-examine the witnesses, sometimes to the extent of inadvertently giving evidence themselves. This could be so because, generally, people in the court were familiar with each other's circumstances. Hearsay evidence was allowed, provided it could be corroborated by other witnesses or evidence. The proceedings were conducted in respectful ways, yet within an environment of informality so as to put everyone at ease.

With regard to the question of land, I learned about the manner in which the land of the Mampondomiseni people had been acquired, which was essentially through fights with other tribes who had been living on the land previously. The defeated would either flee, to fight others elsewhere and to settle, or were subjugated by the conquerors and became loyal to the new traditional leader. They had been allowed to have their own sub-headmen and headmen, and to continue to practice their customs.

Harmony thus prevailed. While the land was said to belong to the Nkosi, in practice he dealt with it not as his personal property, but as that of the people. This was so because even if he was the leader, when it was acquired the people were directly involved. Thus, it was regarded as communal land. When an application for a land allotment was made to the traditional leader, the applicant had to first satisfy the sub-headman and the villagers that he was deserving of such allotment by reason of the fact that he had a new family or was about to start one, and was thus expected to build a homestead and to cultivate food for his family's sustenance. Such an allotment became that family's property in perpetuity, unless the community as a whole convinced the senior traditional leader that the head was a criminal or a person who unjustifiably refused to abide by the rules and norms of the community.

Quite often it is asked why traditional leaders get paid salaries by the state, instead of being maintained by the people they lead. From my observation of how the Great Place was viewed by the people of Mampondomiseni, it seemed that in the distant past, the people did maintain the royal family. There were three large mielie fields that belonged to the Great Place. They were all ploughed, planted, cultivated and harvested by the community. Villagers took turns to perform each of the activities necessary for a successful production. I remember it being one of my responsibilities at some stage to record the spans of oxen that came to work in the fields. There was a great deal of enthusiasm on the part of the families as they came to register the presence of the working villagers. For all the work they did, no financial payment was expected. They were doing a job that they considered their civic duty to perform and were satisfied with the meals given to them first in the fields, and later at the Great Place.

It later dawned on me that in times of want, destitute families were able to come and ask for food parcels from the Great Place. Invariably, they would be given food. Those who had some means to pay for the food parcels, but did not have enough money to pay the price demanded by the local white shopkeepers, would be given the parcels at reduced and affordable prices.

The introduction of taxes and other levies on the people by government quite clearly meant that the maintenance of the royal families by the tribe could not be sustained. Their energies had been thereby diverted to filling government coffers. To continue with the traditional practice would amount to double-taxation, and thus oppression. Besides, the taxes were the money that should have been used to service the community and the royal family.

When I returned to my home in Mqanduli at the conclusion of my post-graduate studies, I discovered that the systems that pertained in Mpondoland were a replica of what was in place in the land of amaHegebe. I have had the benefit of a tertiary education including two university degrees that qualified me to be a lawyer, with funds having been collected at the behest of Nkosi Zwelinzima, from amaHegebe. I have thus been exposed to the white man's world, through education and the world of work. Yet I remain unconvinced that there is any inadequacy in the institution of traditional leadership that calls for a diminution of its relevance in modern-day South Africa. On the contrary, if given the necessary resources – such as those at the disposal of state institutions – then the institution is best placed to bring a better life to the people in the countryside.

I became even more convinced of the efficacy of the institution when I led the Congress of Traditional Leaders of South Africa (Contralesa) from 1989 until 2013. The stories I heard from traditional leaders in all the bantustans painted a picture similar to that evident in Nkosi Zwelinzima's Mampondomiseni territory.

Authenticity and legitimacy

While we justifiably raise concerns about the discrediting of traditional leaders under a democratic dispensation, it is also important to acknowledge that in the last 20 years government has enacted laws that have set up the National, Provincial and Local Houses of Traditional Leaders, as well as the traditional councils. These platforms enable traditional leaders to make some contribution to the formulation of policies and laws that shape the future of the people of this land, albeit in an advisory capacity in national, provincial and local spheres of governance. In resolving the question of the role of traditional leaders in a democracy, South Africa must look at the disposition of the founders of the ANC. They set up two Houses –

the Lower House and the House of Chiefs – ostensibly modelled on colonial Britain's parliament, which was and still is composed of the House of Commons, made up of democratically elected Members of Parliament, and a House of Lords occupied by traditional leaders and custodians of British traditions and customs.

The fact of the matter, however, is that this dispensation was in accordance with African tradition. This tradition allowed for counsellors to hold deliberations among themselves over issues pertinent to the nation, at the end of which recommendations would be referred to the traditional leadership for review and possible endorsement.

It should not be forgotten that the whole of South Africa historically belongs to the indigenous people of the land. Those of foreign origin may not be allowed to claim they owe no allegiance to traditional leaders and thus have no obligation to provide for their maintenance. That is arrogance of the first order and a manifestation of deliberate amnesia. If other Africans have forgotten this historical fact, traditional leaders have not. We look at other nations in Europe with traditional leaders being accorded the appropriate status to the extent that some white South Africans regard them as their traditional leaders, and feel nauseated by such racism. All the riches in our oceans, below and above ground, exploited or not, belong to us and our people and, accordingly, traditional leaders deserve recognition as their custodians.

At the heart of this discussion is not only the role of the institution of traditional leadership in a democracy, but also the issue of our identity as Africans. We must be bold if we want to recover our true heritage and cast off imposed colonial architecture. In so doing we need to integrate the Houses of Traditional Leaders and traditional councils into the law-making structures and decision-making bodies of the land. Besides, the law governing the conduct of traditional leaders in democratic South Africa and the Traditional Leadership and Governance Framework Act of 2003 both enjoin all state departments to formulate ways of engaging traditional leaders in the execution of their policies and programmes. A symbiotic relationship between government and the institution of traditional leadership will go a long way towards harmonising relations between the two and forging a sustainable developmental agenda.

In fact, we lose none of the good that comes with the positive elements of European systems and norms; on the contrary we gain by becoming a truly modern and innovative African nation. The wrath of the ancestors will, unfortunately, be visited upon the African house, and not on the European one, if we continue to conduct ourselves as if they never existed. Their descendants are with us.

Let it be known that here I am talking about traditional leaders who serve as such, rather than those who actively conducted themselves as politicians leading the bantustan homelands of the apartheid era. The bulk of ordinary traditional leaders, even as they participated in those homeland parliaments, paid attention to serving their people. Some such traditional leaders actually gave clandestine support to the struggle for liberation by, *inter alia*, giving sanctuary to the freedom fighters who worked in the underground structures of the liberation movement. Some of them ended up in jails such as Robben Island for their fight against the racist regime and its satellites.

The council of the senior traditional leader, having been successively modified by the apartheid and democratic governments to become tribal authorities and traditional councils, should be accorded the necessary resources in the form of human resources, offices and other forms of accommodation, equipment and amenities. This will enhance the institution's capacity to serve the people in the modern day, just as it did in the past. The question should not be asked as to how the institution of traditional leadership can be accommodated in a democratic South Africa, as if it is that institution that is new in this land. Instead, new forms of government, especially at the local government level, should be modified to fit in with the original mode of governance.

This brings us to the matter of resources exploited by developers. Just as communal land belongs to the people as a collective, so too do the natural resources that are embedded in the soil. The royal family, as the first family, is entitled to a *pro rata* share of the proceeds arising from investments in those resources, be it in the form of shares, dividends, profits or royalties. Government and developers/investors have a duty to ensure that the traditional relationship between the people, the land and traditional leaders is not violated. All – the royal family, the people, the investor and the state – should benefit in equitable measure. None must benefit at the expense of the other but, importantly, the traditional leader must not be manipulated, extorted or blackmailed by any of the outside entities in the name of development.

Finally, a note on gender: I had the opportunity to engage traditional leaders of the Southern African Development Community in a series of human rights seminars organised by the Zambian women's organisation, Women for Change. This women's rights organisation was convinced that for the culture of human rights to take root in the region's rural areas, traditional leaders had to be taken on board. To their surprise, Women for Change were lectured by traditional leaders on human rights from an African perspective. They became converts, who went on to champion the cause of traditional leadership.

It needs to be borne in mind that the legitimacy of the incumbents in the institution lies in the customs, cultures and traditions, the norms and moral values of a traditional community. If, for instance, those tenets decree that a woman must inherit a position upon the death of a traditional leader, then let that decree be followed. The same applies for a man. Democracy has opened up the space for men and women to apply for appointment, or campaign to be elected, to all forms of leadership, as opposed to inheriting leadership positions. To open the institution to such norms would serve only to destroy the institution and all that it stands for. At the end of the day, we hold these positions in the name of our ancestors who cast the rules in stone.

Research and the democratic agenda

Academics, scholars and researchers rely on studies conducted by people who do not necessarily have experience of either traditional leaders or the people who are directly affected by the institution of traditional leadership. Others may be people who have some connection with these communal areas, having been born there, but have since gone to stay in the cities in search of better education or employment opportunities. These researchers tend to become aware of the existence of the traditional institution when they come for short holidays or weekend cultural events such as weddings, rites-of-passage, celebrations or for a few days to conduct research on particular aspects of African cultures and traditions. Some of these people are interested in finding ways in which the institution of traditional leadership can be weakened, if not done away with, so that foreign forms of governance, dubbed 'democracy', can replace the institution. Of course, they will not admit that this is their goal, but you will detect it when you note their lamenting of the fact that traditional leadership continues to thrive and to be relevant to traditional communities, despite its association with colonial and apartheid regimes, and the advent of democracy. They wonder why and start picking at the anomalous conduct of a few traditional leaders to conclude that the institution is bad.

Development and service delivery in rural Africa continues to suffer because politicians do not want to give due recognition to the role of the institution of traditional leadership. Where there is cooperation and mutual respect between government and traditional leaders, the people benefit. It is thus incumbent on government to make laws that view the institution as an ally in the cause of good governance, service delivery and human rights, rather than seeing it as an as opponent of progress.

TWELVE

A long walk for traditional leadership in South Africa

NKOSI MWELO NONKONYANA
(ZANEMVULA!)

Introduction

I have been involved in the struggle for the restoration of pride and dignity in the institution of traditional leadership in South Africa from an early stage. It began from about 1975, when I was a student at Jongilizwe College, the college for the sons of traditional leaders in Tsolo, located in what was then the Transkei bantustan.

I then went to the University of Fort Hare and studied law. The degree, which was then known as a Bachelor of Juris, included a course in African law.

To further my studies, I enrolled at the University of South Africa, where I obtained a Bachelor of Laws (LLB), conducting research in African law. My dissertation critically evaluated the then repugnancy clause[1] (see II of Native/African Administration Act No. 38 of 1927).

I was among the traditional leaders instrumental in the formation of a national organisation of traditional leaders known as the Congress of Traditional Leaders of South Africa (Contralesa), having taken over *ubukhosi* (chieftainship) from my late father and mentor Nkosi David Malayipheli Nonkonyana (Bambilizwe!) in 1988.

Institution of traditional leadership

The institution of traditional leadership in South Africa is the only institution that is indigenous, original and entrenched in our beloved country. It encompasses all families, represented by a head of the family, who is more often than not an elderly male person. He has an overall responsibility to ensure that family norms and values are observed by all the members. The members share a common family and clan name although they may have different houses. The family unit is fundamental in the institution, which is why we have influenced current government policy to recognise royal families as basic structures responsible for appointing and disciplining traditional leaders.

Furthermore, disputes between members of the family must be considered first by the family, with the head of the family presiding over such disputes to enhance unity and cohesion within the family, and to instil family values.

The family is entitled to a residential site on which to build a home that should have a yard for family gatherings that is big enough to accommodate a bundle of firewood (*igoqo*) and other necessities for the family, as well as stock kraals (for sheep, goats and cattle).

Together, the families constitute what we term a traditional locality (*isigodi*), which is preferably led by a head of a family who needs to command respect from members of such a community. The person is given a title of being a sub-headman (*usibonda/induna/ibhodi/unozithetyana*) who must pay respect, on behalf of the community concerned, to the head of the various other communities forming a traditional community area (*ilali*). The headman may be a traditional leader junior to a senior traditional leader of the same clan. However, in South Africa, the colonial and apartheid regimes introduced a headmanship system and also established tribal (now traditional) authorities. Included within the areas of jurisdiction of traditional authorities, set by apartheid and colonial administrations, are families from other clans, which gradually regained independence when they claimed to have their own cultural norms and values.

There are heads of clans who have to administer the affairs of their clan, in accordance with the cultural norms and values of the clan concerned. These persons are referred to as senior traditional leaders (*amakhosi/dikgosi/iinkosi/marena*). These senior traditional leaders generally head the traditional authorities envisaged in the Constitution of the Republic of South Africa and are often referred to as 'traditional councils' in national and provincial legislations. In terms of our culture and custom, members of the council that advise the head of a clan are heads of traditional communities within that clan. Also part of the advisory council are selected wise men/women in the community who have been identified as custodians of the culture and customs of the traditional community concerned.

The heads of various clans constitute a kingship/queenship. The king/queen is advised by a council composed of all the heads of the clans and councillors who are selected in accordance with tradition and culture and on the basis of experience and wisdom to advise the king/queen in the execution of his /her duties. The councillors must be persons of good character.

The king/queen, like all other traditional leaders, must uphold the view of his/her council and, in case of divergent views must guide the council to reach decisions by consensus. These decisions are based on general meetings of various clans. The king/queen then pronounces the decision/s of the council and his/her pronouncements are binding and cannot be challenged. Amazulu put this in their language as follows: '*umlomo weNkosi awuqambi manga*', meaning, 'what is said by a royal leader is the whole truth and nothing but the truth'.

Participation of traditional leaders in the struggle for freedom

When the colonialists came to South Africa in 1652, Africans were living happily in the country, enjoying freedom under a traditional leadership system that was based on the will of the people. Under this system, land was administered in the interests of those who were not living (ancestors), those who were living and of future generations to come.

Before the colonialists took over the land and imposed their system of governance, which ironically has been embraced by all democratic governments in Africa, traditional leaders and their communities led wars of resistance. They paid supreme sacrifices as many were brutally killed.

The struggle for freedom was initiated and led by our forebears and the generals in charge of *imikhosi yesizwe* (commandos). When traditional leaders and the people were united, the enemy (colonialists) realised that it could not succeed and had to develop false propaganda. They denounced our institution of traditional leadership, arguing that it was undemocratic. Colonial leaders also promoted a divide and rule policy with respect to traditional communities. Precisely because our forebears fought on tribal lines, Africans were divided, and after some limited successes they were defeated.

Establishment of the liberation movement

Tradition leaders realised the need to be united in order to defeat the apartheid regime. They participated in the formation of a liberation movement, the African National Congress (ANC), that was constituted on 8 January 1912 and that governs South Africa today.

The original constitution of the ANC recognises traditional leaders as the authentic leaders of the people and grants them status as leaders within the ANC. The leaders of the ANC knew that they would lead well, given that they were answerable to royalty, in the same way that political parties in England are answerable to the British monarch.

Participation of traditional leaders in the multiparty negotiating forum

By the early 1990s the apartheid regime had released Nelson Mandela and other political leaders and agreed to hold constitutional talks to bring about freedom in South Africa. This was a result of the intensification of the armed struggle by liberation forces, especially Umkhonto weSizwe (MK) and the Azanian People's Liberation Army (APLA); the mobilisation of masses inside the country determined to make South Africa ungovernable and the condemnation of the apartheid regime by the international community, due in part to the struggles of those in exile.

Strangely enough, traditional leaders were not part of the initial talks in what was known as the Convention for a Democratic South Africa (CODESA). While we were making submissions to the Rev. Mohapi Commission, the talks in both CODESA I and CODESA II collapsed. In our submission to the Mohapi Commission, we made the point that freedom in South Africa was taken away from traditional leadership by violent colonial rule and a racist apartheid regime, and argued that logic dictated that we should be allowed to participate in the talks. Furthermore, we contended that governments would come and go, but the institution of traditional leadership would exist forever. As a direct result of our compelling case, we were admitted to take part in the constitutional negotiating forum known as World Trade Centre talks. After our involvement in the constitutional talks, we were part of a forum that successfully adopted constitutional principles binding on the Constitutional Assembly in drafting and adopting a constitution for the new democratic South Africa.

Traditional leaders participated side by side with the ANC in the constitutional negotiations that brought about a new democratic state. Among the constitutional principles that were agreed upon to guide the Constitutional Assembly were the following:

The institution, status and role of traditional leadership, according to indigenous law, shall be recognised and protected in a constitution' (see Constitutional Principle X111).

At each level of government, there should be democratic representation. This principle should not derogate from the provisions of principle X111 (see Constitutional Principle XV11).

Adoption of the Constitution of the Republic of South Africa

The Constitutional Assembly that was mandated to draft and adopt the final Constitution of South Africa should have been guided by the constitutional principles that were agreed upon at the negotiating forum known as World Trade Centre talks. These talks took place after CODESA I and II, which had not included traditional leaders, had failed.

Traditional leaders of South Africa were not part of the proceedings of the Constitutional Assembly, which considered and adopted the final Constitution on 8 May 1996. Hence, it is not surprising that – with respect – the Assembly failed to make provisions in the Constitution for the powers and functions necessary for the institution of traditional leadership.

Chapter 12 – the shortest chapter – of the Constitution provides for the recognition of traditional leadership in South Africa in the following terms:

CHAPTER 12
Traditional Leaders
Recognition

211 (1) The institution, status and role of traditional leadership, according to customary law, are recognised, subject to the constitution.

(2) A traditional authority that observes a system of customary law may function subject to any applicable legislation and customs, which includes amendments to or repeal of that legislation or customs.

(3) The courts must apply customary law when that law is applicable, subject to the constitution and any legislation that specifically deals with customary law.

Role of traditional leaders

212 (1) National legislation may provide for a role for traditional leadership as an institution at local level on

matters affecting local communities.

(2) To deal with matters relating to traditional leadership, the role of traditional leaders, customary law and customs of communities observing a system of customary law

    (a) National or provincial legislation may provide for establishment of houses of traditional leaders; and

    (b) National legislation may establish a Council [now National House] of Traditional Leaders.

Contralesa, aggrieved by the apparent possibility of the obliteration of the powers and functions of traditional leadership in South Africa, objected to the certification of the Constitution by the Constitutional Court on various grounds, which included the following:

a. Imposition of foreign norms and values at the expense of entrenched African norms and values;

b. Recognition of municipal councils and the extension of their areas of jurisdiction to include traditional communities under the jurisdiction of traditional authorities in South Africa (so called 'wall-to-wall municipal jurisdiction');

c. A Eurocentric constitution that embraces foreign systems of governance that have been inherited from violent and illegitimate colonial and apartheid regimes, which took over from African traditional systems of governance;

d. No express recognition of our traditional courts, despite express recognition of courts established by illegitimate regimes that promoted a foreign Roman Dutch legal system at the expense of an African legal system.

In response to our objections to the certification of the final Constitution, the Constitutional Court, which was composed of justices who obtained legal qualifications and practiced under a foreign Roman Dutch legal system (so called common law of South Africa), held thus:

[197] In our view, therefore, the NT complies with CP X111 by giving express guarantees of the continued existence of

traditional leadership and the survival of an evolving customary law. The institution, status and role of traditional leadership are hereby protected. They are protected by means of entrenchment in the NT and any attempt at interference would be subject to constitutional scrutiny. The CA cannot be faulted for leaving the complicated, varied and ever-developing specifics of how such leadership function in the wider democratic society, and how customary law should develop and be interpreted, to future social evaluation, legislative deliberation and judicial interpretation.

Our attempts to interdict first local government elections

Contralesa instituted a legal action in the Mthatha High Court in the Eastern Cape to interdict the holding of local government elections in traditional communities. The application was dismissed on technicalities, including that Nkosi Gwadiso, who was secretary of Contralesa, had no power to institute the application for and on behalf of the organisation (see *Contralesa vs Minister for Local Government, Eastern Cape and other 1996(2) 57 898(TK)*).

The legal action was based on what traditional leaders believed was an intention, on behalf of the institution of local government, to remove the powers and functions of traditional institutions and bestow them instead on municipalities. This intention was inferred from the fact that local government structures were established in traditional communities, and their powers and functions are clearly set out in the Constitution. We argued without success that there could not be two bulls in one kraal. The traditional institutions were and still are unfairly discriminated against, as government merely provides for them to be advisors in the House of Traditional Leaders and curious onlookers in municipal councils.

Municipal councilors are well resourced and remunerated (more so than traditional leaders). The tension between traditional leaders and municipal councilors has been fueled by this, hence the development of our areas remains a pipe dream.

Engagement with government

The Coalition of Traditional Leaders of South Africa, composed of Contralesa, the National House of Traditional Leaders, Provincial Houses and the Royal Bafokeng Nation, submitted various memoranda to government in 2000. These initiatives culminated in a meeting with President Mbeki on 23 August 2000, during which traditional leaders requested that he respond to them in writing. Indeed he responded on 28 August 2000 and concluded:

> The challenge we are faced with at this moment in time is to find a way of stabilising our system of governance in the rural areas by creating a climate within which the institution of traditional leadership and elected institutions of government can coexist. This is a challenging time, but it is achievable.
>
> In tackling the enormous challenges facing us, government, traditional leaders and other stakeholders must jointly promote the common ideal of nation building in our country. Government is committed to promoting development throughout South Africa. We will, together with you, continue to work out mechanisms which will ensure the attainment of these ideals.

We pursued our discussions with government. On Saturday 30 September 2000, an agreement was reached between the government and ourselves. It was mutually decided that a joint Technical Committee would be created to determine, *inter alia*, whether the establishment of municipalities in traditional authority areas would diminish or obliterate the powers and functions of traditional leadership in South Africa.

The Joint Technical Committee on Traditional Leadership terms of reference were agreed as follows:

1. Will the establishment of new municipalities, immediately after the elections, result in the powers of traditional leaders being diminished in any way? If so, in what way;

2. If the powers of traditional leaders will be diminished, what should be done to remedy the situation?

The Joint Technical Committee was composed of the following members: on the part of government, Messrs. Z. Titus, R. K. Sizani, T. F. Seboka, S. Louw and M. C. Deliwe, and on the part of traditional leaders, Nkosi M. B. Mzimela (now deceased, Morena M. F. Mopeli, Hosi Mhinga, Nkosi P. Holomisa, Nkosi M. Nonkonyana, Messrs. J. Sutherland, S. Phiri, Adv M. Motshekga and Dr M. Ambrosini (now late).

On 4 October 2000, a report of the Joint Technical Committee on Traditional Leadership was submitted at a meeting between ourselves and government. The Committee found that '… the establishment of such municipalities would substantially diminish the local government functions of traditional authorities'.

The report was considered at a meeting between the government and traditional leaders and it was agreed that provision should have been made for the powers and functions of traditional leadership to be upheld in tandem with those granted to municipalities. This would have created a situation in which the two structures could have worked together to improve the quality of life of South Africans in accordance with the principle of cooperative governance provided for in our Constitution of the Republic.

The then deputy president of the Republic of South Africa, Jacob Zuma, was mandated to process the legislation necessary to give effect to the agreement between traditional leaders and government. To date this has not been done, notwithstanding several requests from us.

Contralesa resolved to engage the ruling party (ANC) directly

The ANC established another Joint Task Team under the leadership of Dr Z Mkhize who is presently, in 2018, our minister of Cooperative Governance and Traditional Affairs. The Task Team agreed to address the concerns of traditional leaders and to convene a national conference, which was held at Birchwood Conference Centre and was attended by all stakeholders.

The conference deliberated on the issues affecting the institution of traditional leadership, and agreed once more to address them by amending the Constitution and other legislation to give effect to the resolutions adopted there.

During the debate on the speech delivered by President CM Ramaphosa in March 2018, we reminded him to honour several agreements with traditional leaders and urged him that this should be done before national elections in 2019. Some of members of Contralesa, aggrieved about the apparent breach of the agreement between the organisation and the ANC government, even threatened to form a political party to participate in the elections. To date, no bill has been presented to cabinet and publicised to give effect to our agreement.

It seems unlikely that there is any political will to address our concerns. In fact, government continues to implement the Spatial Planning and Land Use Management Act (SPLUMA) No. 16 of 2013 in our traditional communities, and is dragging its feet to pass the Traditional Courts Bill. Instead, it has prioritised an amendment of the Constitution to enable government to expropriate land, hopefully not the 13 per cent fought for and occupied by traditional communities, without compensation. To add salt to the wound, former president Motlanthe, when addressing the ANC land summit this year, referred to traditional leaders as 'village tin-pot dictators' whose land must be taken away from them and administered by government structures.

Conclusion

It seems to me that the government is playing mind games with traditional leaders, as the necessary re-instatement of the pride and dignity of the institution of traditional leadership in South Africa seems to be perpetually delayed.

Be that as it may, I remain optimistic that the government will realise its mistake of not giving powers and functions to the institution of traditional leaders, and restore these powers to facilitate the promotion of African norms and values.

We hope that South Africa will recognise African systems of

governance and allow these to take their rightful place among systems of governance in the world.

Notes

1 The 'repugnancy' clause is a proviso to the general recognition of customary law, laying down certain requirements with which customary law must comply.

Traditional leadership

South Africa's paradox?

DINEO SKOSANA

Now that traditional leadership has made its unexpected comeback in post-apartheid South Africa, how do we explain the ways in which the institution has kept itself relevant? This book has addressed the different operative modalities of traditional leaders in the current democratic system. The survival tactics that have been employed by traditional leaders range from distortions of the history and identity of the formerly colonised to claims to custodianship of 'African culture', resistance to colonialism and the emancipation of African people and finally to their strategic positioning at the centre of a booming mining economy in the former bantustans. The ANC-led government has also provided conditions hospitable to the survival of traditional leaders through a series of laws (the Traditional Leadership Framework Act of 2003, the Restitution of Land Rights Amendment Act No. 48 of 2003, the Communal Land Rights Act of 2004, the Traditional Courts Bill of 2012, the Restitution of Land Rights Amendment Bill No. 48 of 2014), as well as the Commission on Traditional Leadership Disputes and Claims – colloquially known as the Nhlapo Commission.[1] The strategies and the conditions that make it possible to use such mechanisms point to the past, present and future paradoxes of the post-apartheid state in South Africa.

This book highlights the conflicting binaries of what Richard Sklar (1994) calls 'mixed governments'. In postcolonial Africa, mixed government, '... conserves traditional authority as a political resource without diminishing the authority of the sovereign state' (Sklar, 1994: 2). The chapters illustrated the paradoxes as far as the country's constitutional democracy is concerned: how the contradictions unfold from a legal point of view, as well as how these affect heterogeneous African communities at local levels. Insofar as these paradoxes continue to manifest, the continued salience of traditional leaders appears likely. To draw on a few overarching themes in the book, which reveal the contradictions in South Africa's political system, let us turn to the tensions of a 'modern' constitution that provides for a society whose majority either subscribe to or reject the historically and contemporarily defined traditional identities and the politics thereof.

The 'traditional' in the Constitution

In a country whose traditional identities became synonymous with colonial and apartheid modes of oppression (Kepe & Ntsebeza, 2011; Mamdani, 2013; Gibbs, 2014), it was not expected that traditional leaders would be recognised by Chapter 12 of the Constitution of the Republic of South Africa, 1996. Evidently, in accordance with the spirit of reconciliation during the country's transition, there was no deliberation about what the acknowledgement of traditional leaders in the Constitution would involve. The failure of the government to reflect on this is articulated in Phathekile Holomisa's chapter about the relevance of traditional leadership in democratic South Africa. Very little, if any, consideration was applied to a question like, 'Should all traditional leaders – including those who were historically handpicked, the collaborators whose genealogy was altered by colonial and apartheid administrations and those who resisted oppression in one way or another – be recognised?' Peter Delius captures this in his chapter in this book, in which he observes that South Africa missed a moment to deliberate on these set of questions. He notes that, 'the dramatic transition in the years after 1990 provided an opportunity to fundamentally rethink the nature of chieftainship and its potential role in a constitutional democracy. This was an opportunity that was far from fully exploited' (see page 45).

The incorporation of traditional leaders into the Constitution was not the genesis of the contradictory nature of the state in South Africa; rather it was the formal perpetuation of the paradoxes in the country's supreme law in the new political dispensation. The only limitation, as far as the recognition of traditional leaders is concerned, is reflected in the condition that they be subject to the country's customary law and that both be subservient to the Constitution of the Republic of South Africa, 1996 (Chapter 12: Section 211). The underlying assumption is that being subject to customary law and abiding to the Constitution cleanses traditional leadership of its chequered past and makes it function in harmony with a democracy, when in fact there are further contradictions that arise from this set-up.

Moreover, while bestowing recognition, insufficient consideration has been given to determining which aspects of 'tradition' are to be 'recognised' in the institution of traditional leadership – especially considering all that has been deemed 'traditional': for example, the law of primogeniture, succession laws, patriarchy and fixed ethnic identities were mechanised by colonial and later, apartheid administrations to oppress the black majority in the 'homelands'. The recognition of traditional leaders in the Constitution not only acknowledged some traditional leaders who were accomplices in the oppression of the rural population, but also embraced their construction of the institution, which was based on values that historically subjugated the black majority and are, therefore, contradictory to democracy. In accord with this line of reasoning, Delius once more draws our attention to the worry that, 'a co-opted institution, reconstituted to serve as an instrument of colonial control, and formed by fantasies about primitive and tribal Africa, has served as the primary template for chieftainship in postcolonial South Africa' (see page 45).

In this regard, Sindiso Mnisi Weeks, in chapter 7, illustrates how the laws passed by the democratic government, such as Traditional Leadership and Governance Framework Act No. 41 of 2003

(TLGFA), Communal Land Rights Act No. 11 of 2004 (before it was struck down) and Traditional Courts Bill B15-2008/B1-2012 (and, now, the TCB B1-2017), undermine the power that women were able to acquire through the Constitution's equality clause. Fani Ncapayi, in chapter 9, shows the continuous contestation over the imposed, unelected headman in the Eastern Cape's Cala Reserve. Both chapters flag the tensions between the Constitution and legislative frameworks[2] whose foundations interpret customs in rigid ways, often drawing on notions of customary law that were applied during colonial and apartheid South Africa (Claassens & Cousins, 2008). Ncapayi's chapter illustrates the contradictions in the Constitution, its impact on communities and the resistance thereto, all of which produce a socio-political condition in which communities are 'neither citizens nor subjects' (Ntsebeza, 2005: 295). This is a condition, in other words, in which rural South Africans living under traditional leaders are legally subjected to authoritarian rule and so denied the realisation of the rights enjoyed by urban South Africans (see Claassens, chapter 4, for example).

One of the high-profile people to be caught in the inherent contradictions between the South African Constitution and customary law, is the jailed abaThembu King, Buyelekhaya Dalindyebo. He has been sentenced to 12 years in prison for crimes committed against his 'subjects', including kidnapping, arson and defeating the ends of justice, while applying his notion of customary law in his traditional court (Evans, 2013).

Reflecting on the case, Makhubu (2016) writes that the conviction and sentencing of Dalindyebo 'sparked a debate on social media among some Swazis, particularly lawyers, who were astounded that a king could be jailed. One asked on Facebook: "… how do you reconcile kingship (and the traditional law associated with that institution) with the concept of a republic? Last time I checked, kings operate within kingdoms and a legislative framework that entrenches certain fundamentals inherent in the institution.' The Facebook user in question is correct to point out that in South Africa's pluralistic form of law, traditional leaders operate within a framework of customary law that is recognised in Chapter 8 of the Constitution of the Republic of South Africa, 1996. However, there is not a 'textual connection in the definition of customary law to the communities recognised in section 31(1)' (Nwauche, 2015: 575). The application of African customary law is subject to the Constitution, as well as to any legislation that specifically deals with it (Nwauche, 2015: 575). Claassens, in chapter 4, argues that these legislations, including the Mineral and Petroleum Resources Development Act No. 28 of 2002, fundamentally betray the promise of a unitary, democratic South Africa. The logic of Claassens's argument is that the paradoxes in the legislation pertaining to the Constitution and post-apartheid traditional leadership foster a dual dispossession in which the black majority who were marginalised during colonial and apartheid South Africa continue to be treated unjustly in the new political era. The workings of these conflicting binaries (between 'constitutionality' and 'custom'), sometimes obvious and sometimes inconspicuous, are carefully explored in different parts of this book to show how historical and emerging contradictions in the country's hybrid government system hinder communities' potential to fully enjoy the benefits of being democratic citizens.

The modern and traditional: Sometimes in collaboration but mostly in contestation

The relationship between the traditional and the modern is often discussed as divergent in the linear theory of social change (Gusfield, 1967), when in fact the institutions and processes attributed to both continuously overlap, particularly in the context of South Africa (Skosana, 2013). For example, in her chapter, Skosana has shown that mission schools that sought to civilise the children of chiefs unintentionally bred 'politically conscious militants', who merged traditional and nationalist politics. The post-apartheid overlaps between traditional and elected government institutions were highlighted, for example, when I asked the residents of Magongwa (Mokopane) about their support for traditional leadership in a country that is democratic. Anna Phago, an old resident in Magongwa, replied:

Chieftainship is good to safeguard culture. It is also good in rural areas where the majority are unemployed and uneducated. Parents hardly have money to pay for school fees, water and electricity. However, if it were the municipality which was directly involved we would have problems because they privatise services [...] the existence of chiefs makes it possible to stay in areas for free.[3]

Anna made a point, which I explore later, about how traditional leadership steps in for the failings of local government. The more she elaborated her views, the more she pointed to a fundamental problem about 'mixed governments', namely the 'chiefing' or 'traditionalising' of democracy and, vice versa, the democratisation of chiefs. In other words, government begins to function in ways that are not formal and inclusive of the majority's interests, whereas chiefs begin to be bureaucratic and to operate formally in matters where they would normally be impromptu (which works for some communities). This is a recurring issue highlighted by different chapters in this book.

In another local-level example, during my field work on chieftaincy in Mokopane (Skosana, 2012), one resident in Magongwa, Andries Matshotshwane, mentioned that he supports traditional leadership, but his reasons for doing so were slightly different from others. He said:

Chieftainship should continue to exist. Without chiefs we cannot succeed in instances where we have to deal with the mines. If the mines could only come through local government, then it would be worse. When the government has taken a decision, it is final, but chiefs and headmen are usually accessible and open to negotiation.[4]

Of course, such responses must be contextualised and cannot be generalised. But, in this instance, chiefs were found to be more likely to uphold democratic principles than democratically elected officials.

Indeed, it is noteworthy that those Magongwa residents who spoke against traditional leadership's tendency to be corrupt, authoritarian and irrelevant in a democracy pointed to identical ills in democratic institutions, leaving us with questions about whether South Africa's democracy is fragile because of chieftaincy, or whether the country's democracy might have been fragile anyway, without chieftaincy. Postcolonial societies have had to adapt to a governing system that emerged and developed in a European context.

Chieftaincies: Sites of consumption?

The mechanisms of the global political economy, which foster the interconnectedness of states and operate under the conditions of a global free market, partly explain the convergence of modern and traditional institutions (Comaroff & Comaroff, 2009). Oomen (2005: 6) adds that broader global developments have fragmented nation states and national identities, and the result has been the emergence of alternative politics that operate locally, transnationally and internationally to deal with the challenges of modernity. What became more evident in the post-Cold War era was that all that is 'traditional' would not wither away in the mist of modern capitalist developments. If anything, all that is 'traditional' would be reconfigured to cohabit with modernity.

What we then began to witness in the 21st century in South Africa, amid the workings of the global economy, was the boom of the mining economy in the former bantustans (Capps, 2012a, 2012b; Manson & Mbenga, 2014). Traditional leaders, as noted in Sonwabile Mnwana's chapter and Aninka Claassens's chapter, have positioned themselves at the centre of growing local economies in the former bantustans. It is, therefore, appropriate to conclude that chieftaincies are sites of consumption in post-apartheid South Africa. However, this is not a new trajectory in politics. Traditional leaders have continuously been able to accumulate, at least in the form of offerings from their subjects. This comes with their divine status[5] (Gluckman, 1965). Those who were appendages of colonial and apartheid administrations were also well rewarded by the regimes then in power (Davenport, 1987).

To explain how traditional leaders have crafted their way to the centre of mining economies, Capps (2012a) shares the view that the tribal trust property (a type of black minerals ownership), predominantly found in the late 19th and early 20th centuries in the former Bophuthatswana and the Transvaal, endowed 'tribal authorities' with far greater autonomy over mining activity than their counterparts on state land. In those two regions, land was historically purchased by Africans and subsequently registered to a state official 'in trust' for a recognised 'chief and his tribe' (Mnwana, chapter 5). Although the mineral rights were often severed from tribal trust land after some time, they remained attached in some cases (Capps, 2012a: 71–75).

In post-apartheid South Africa, Capps (2012: 5) writes that:

> The minerals held by the former homeland governments reverted to the (new) national government. The Department of Minerals and Energy ... and all tribal and state land (including ex-South African Development Trust land) was thus unified under the trusteeship of the Minister of Land Affairs. The Lebowa Minerals Trust was exempted from the new pattern of state trusteeship and instead placed under the administration of the (new) Minister of Minerals and Energy in 1996, pending specific legislation for its abolition at a future date (DME 2000).

Capps (2012a: 5) concludes, however, that, 'the platinum industry's juridical control over the mineral resources of the former Lebowa and Bophuthatswana territories would remain untouched, thus, safeguarding the essential condition of an accumulation strategy for chiefs' (in the contemporary environment).

Recently, in October 2018, the Constitutional Court passed a highly significant judgment in favour of the Lesetlheng community in the Bakgatla Ba Kgafela region, where land has historically been held 'in trust'. The judgment, which unsettles the power of traditional leaders over land, is likely to give rise to future contest as the role of traditional leaders in land reform continues to be negotiated, at both national and local level. In the context of gains from local mining economies, as well as the ongoing power of recognised chiefs over land, this book draws attention to what William Ellis, in his chapter, calls 'situational leadership'. His argument acknowledges that the

KhoiSan were historically marginalised and are, therefore, justified in making claims to recognition and legitimacy in the post-apartheid era. However, Ellis also points to the ways in which many of those who have emerged in the KhoiSan revival make claims to traditional leadership in a manner that is dynamic, creative and responsive to a moment that requires situational leadership. His notion of 'situational chiefs' perhaps also explains, in part, the increased relevance of headmen. Sindiso Mnisi Weeks, chapter 7, argues that these headmen carry the everyday burdens of rural communities in South Africa, more so than senior traditional leaders.

To assess the increased claims of 'situational leaders' to 'senior' traditional leadership or headmanship, the Nhlapo Commission, which was established by the Traditional Leadership and Governance Framework Act No. 41 of 2003, lays out guidelines for the recognition of traditional leadership and attempts to cleanse the institution of its chequered past (Buthelezi & Skosana, 2018: 114). However, not only did the Nhlapo Commission enact the ethnological approach of the Bantu Affairs Department when it became embroiled in matters of chieftaincies, the Commission has also perpetuated some of the practices of the apartheid regime by applying rigid genealogical customary rules to determine the rightful incumbents to office (Peires, 2014). Those traditional leaders who convincingly recount their genealogy in accordance with the customary law of succession gain political recognition within a democratic space. In such instances, as we have seen in this book, traditional leadership is a source of political power (Skosana, 2013: 8). By gaining recognition, traditional leaders accrue a stake in the country's democracy, because recognition provides successful traditional claimants with the material and political resources to which only officially recognised leaders can gain access (Buthelezi & Skosana, 2018: 8).

Will traditional leadership eventually become extinct?

Traditional leadership will remain a competing government system for as long as the democratic system is not effectively established in rural parts of South Africa. This is because in some rural communities where local government has not entrenched itself, traditional leadership is an alternative form of government (Oomen, 2003; Williams, 2004). Oomen (2003) observes that, in those instances that traditional leadership was not favoured, in some areas of Sekhukhune for example, it was not because of abhorrent feelings towards the institution, but rather a dislike of a particular style of leadership (see this also in Sithandiwe Yeni's chapter). In those areas of Sekhukhune where there was support for chieftainship, Oomen illustrates that this was largely issue based; the reasons to appeal to chiefs ranged from land allocation and dispute resolution, to their administrative function in initiation schools (Oomen, 2003). In areas where the functions of traditional leaders have been completely replaced by democratic structures, traditional leaders have positioned themselves as influencers of politically binding decisions about who gets to mine their mineral-rich areas and who gets to benefit. Although we cannot make conclusive generalisations, based on the rich case studies presented in this book, it is evident that traditional leaders are here to stay.

Some may ask whether the institution of traditional leadership might self-annihilate, since it has diverted from its conventional founding principle that, *'kgosi ke kgosi ka batho'*, (a chief is the chief through the people). But this is unlikely when legitimation, as in colonial and apartheid South Africa, is awarded by state institutions and consolidated through post-apartheid legislation (including the Traditional Leadership Framework Act of 2003), which have sought to re-establish chiefly authority in rural parts of the country.

In the early days of South Africa's democratic transition, the alliance between the ANC-led government and traditional leaders was explainable by the ruling party's desire to gain the votes in rural constituencies, particularly KwaZulu-Natal, which was the Inkatha Freedom Party (IFP) stronghold (Van Kessel & Oomen, 1997). However, political dynamics in South Africa, and the political behaviour of voters, has since changed. One of the factors changing the political spectrum has been the growth of the Democratic Alliance (DA) and the emergence of the Economic Freedom Fighters (EFF). The EFF has gained the attention of the young electorate in some provinces which were originally an ANC stronghold, including the Limpopo province (The Electoral Commission of South Africa, 2016).

Now that traditional leaders have an equivocal role in the county's electoral system, what else could be keeping them relevant? What if, among other things, it is nostalgia for imagined pre-colonial indigenous systems that has kept chieftaincy relevant? Can traditional leaders partly owe their continued existence to an association with a pre-colonial past that we have been eager to understand and reconnect to? Hence, there have been calls for 'decolonisation' (Mbembe, 2015). Traditional leaders are arguably symbolic of this pre-colonial past, despite this history also representing, at times, the atrocities of the colonial and apartheid governments.

Finally, the chapters in this book illustrate that one of the key reasons that traditional leaders remain relevant in post-apartheid South Africa is because of their historical role in the administration of land. Land and traditional leaders are historically entwined concepts, so much so that even when land is now 'owned' by the state, historically enduring titles such as 'land held in trust', discussed in chapters such as Mnwana's and Claassens's, allow some leaders to continue to sub-divide, and in some instances, sell farms to people in communities. If anything, the beginning of the process of transferring land to the state in the mid-1990s was, to traditional leaders, very ceremonial for the nationalist government and completely meaningless to traditional leaders. Traditional leaders did not see the transfer of land to the state as a paradigm shift – they continued in their respective communities with business as usual. This has given them the confidence to participate in the booming mining economies in the former homelands.

Keep the institution of traditional leadership but resolve the paradoxes?

Africa has always been, and continues to be, a continent of paradoxes. This book has shown these from a South African perspective. The conflicting binaries, such as mixed governments, customary and state governance, as well as the modern and traditional, were perpetuated by colonialism and apartheid, in which traditional leaders were subjected to different kinds of administrative regimes. Taking this past into account, the role of traditional leaders in the country's democracy should not continue to be defined through ad-hoc legislation, passed by the governing elite for the rural poor. This perpetuates the paradoxes that are highlighted throughout this book. To remedy this, perhaps rural residents should be included more substantively in the process of negotiating and crafting the kind of traditional leadership they want, if any. For example, the passing of laws relating to customary law and traditional leaders should be a negotiated process that leaves room for altering or getting rid of the content in a proposed law, when need be. The consultation processes should not be merely a bureaucratic exercise. So far, the notorious laws that provide for traditional leaders and their subjects, such as the Traditional Leadership and Governance Framework Act No. 23 of 2003 and the Communal Land Rights Act No. 11 of 2004, seem as if they would have been passed anyway, because of the pressure of wanting to clarify the role of traditional leaders, despite public outcry (Claassens, 2009). What is a democracy then, if public consultations are a formality and not a part of a substantive negotiation process? If substantive negotiation takes place, then those who would want, for example, to use traditional courts, do so freely. The same applies for subjects who want to use civil courts of justice. Here, the state must make both court systems accessible to any persons and should not subjectify people by confining them to accessing traditional courts only, and therefore making modern justice systems unreachable. By doing so, rural people can choose moments in which they want to be subjects of traditional leaders and other moments in which they wish to enjoy the benefits of being citizens in the republic.

References

Buthelezi, M. & Skosana, D. 2018. 'The salience of chiefs in post-apartheid South Africa: Reflections on the Nhlapo Commission', in Comaroff, J. & Comaroff, J. (eds.) *The Politics of Custom: Chiefs, capital, and culture in contemporary Africa*. Chicago: University of Chicago Press, pp. 100–135.

Capps, G. 2012a. 'Victim of its own success? The platinum mining industry and the apartheid mineral property system in South Africa's political transition'. *Review of African Political Economy*, 39 (131), 63–84.

Capps, G. 2012b. 'A bourgeois reform with social justice? The contradictions of the Minerals Development Bill and black economic empowerment in the South African platinum mining industry'. *Review of African Political Economy*, 39 (132), 315–333.

Claassens, A. 2009. 'The Traditional Courts Bill in the context of other laws dealing with traditional leadership'. University of Cape Town: Working Paper, Centre for Law and Society.

Claassens, A. & Cousins B. 2008. *Land, Power and Customs: Controversies generated by the Communal Land Rights Act*. Cape Town: UCT Press.

Comaroff, J. & Comaroff, J. 2009. *Ethnicity Inc*. Chicago: University of Chicago Press.

Comaroff, J. & Comaroff, J. (eds.). 2018. *The Politics of Custom: Chiefs, capital, and culture in contemporary Africa*, Chicago: University of Chicago Press.

Davenport, T. R. H. 1987. *South Africa: A modern history*. Canada: Toronto University Press.

Evans, S. 18 June 2013. 'Dalindyebo the "tyrant": The court case against the king'. *Mail & Guardian*, https://mg.co.za/article/2013-07-17-dalindyebo-the-tyrant-the-case-against-the-king, accessed 1 September 2018.

Gibbs, T. 2014. *Mandela's Kinsmen: Nationalist elites and apartheid's first Bantustan*. Oxford: James Currey.

Gluckman, M. 1965. *Politics, Law and Ritual in Tribal Society*. London: Transaction Publishers.

Gusfield, J. R. 1967. 'Tradition and modernity: Misplaced polarities in the study of social change'. *American Journal of Sociology*, 72 (4), 351–362.

Kepe, T. & Ntsebeza, L. 2011. *Rural Resistance in South Africa: The Mpondo revolts after fifty years*. Leiden: Brill.

Makhubu, B. 8 January 2016. 'Africa battles to rid itself of absolute kings and mini-monarchs'. *Mail & Guardian*, https://mg.co.za/article/2016-01-07-africa-battles-to-rid-itself-of-absolute-kings-and-mini-monarchs, accessed 1 September 2018.

Mamdani, M. 2013. *Define and Rule: Native as political identity*. Yale: Harvard University Press.

Manson, A. & Mbenga, B. 2014. *Land, Chiefs, Mining: South Africa's North-West Province since 1840*. Johannesburg: Wits University Press.

Mbembe, A. 9 June 2015. 'Decolonizing knowledge and the question of the archive'. Paper presented in Johannesburg: Wits Institute for Social and

Economic Research (WISER).

Mineral and Petroleum Resources Development Act 28 of 2002. 10 October 2002, http://www.eisourcebook.org/cms/South%20Africa%20 Mineral%20&%20Petroleum%20Resources%20Development%20 Act%202002.pdf.

Ntsebeza, L. 2005. *Democracy Compromised: Chiefs and the politics of land in South Africa*. Leiden: Brill.

Nwauche, E. 2015. 'Affiliation to a new customary law in post-apartheid South Africa'. *Potchefstroom Elektroniese Regsblad*, 18 (3), 569–593.

Odendaal, A. 2012. *The Founders: The origins of the ANC and the struggle for democracy in South Africa*. Johannesburg: Jacana Media.

Oomen, B. 2003. 'Walking in the middle of the road: People's perspectives on the legitimacy of traditional leadership in Sekhukhune', in Vaughan, O. (ed.) *Indigenous Political Structures and Governance in Africa*. Ibadan: Sefer Press, pp. 83–131.

Oomen, B. 2005. *Chiefs in South Africa: Law, power and culture in the post-apartheid era*. Oxford: James Currey.

Peires, J. 2014. 'History versus customary law: Commission on traditional leadership: Disputes and claims'. *South African Crime Quarterly*, 49, 7–20.

Sklar, R. 13–15 July 1994. 'The significance of mixed government in Southern African studies: A preliminary assessment'. Delivered at *Democracy: Popular Precedents, Popular Practice and Popular Culture*, University of the Witwatersrand: History Workshop.

Skosana, D. 2012. 'Why are chiefs recognised in South Africa's new democracy? Issues of legitimacy and contestation in local politics: A case study of chiefly and local government in Vaaltyn'. MA thesis, University of the Witwatersrand.

Skosana, D. 2013. 'The interface between tradition and modernity: An outline of the Kekana succession dispute and their encounter with the Platinum Reef resource mine'. *New Contree*, 67, 83–96.

Van Kessel, I. & Oomen, B. 1997. 'One chief, one vote: The revival of traditional authorities in post-apartheid South Africa'. *African Affairs*, 96, 561–585.

Williams, J. 2004. 'Leading from behind: Democratic consolidation and the chieftaincy in South Africa'. *Journal of Modern African Studies*, 42 (1), 113–136.

Notes

1   This is the Commission on Traditional Leadership Disputes and Claims,

established by the Traditional Leadership and Governance Framework Act 41 of 2003 (TLGFA).

2 For example, Restitution of Land Rights Amendment Act No. 48 of 2003, the Communal Land Rights Act No. 11 of 2004, and the Traditional Courts Bill of 2012

3 Phago, M. and community members, interviewed by Dineo Skosana, Magogwa (Mokopane), 14 August 2011

4 Matshotshwane, A. and community members, interviewed by Dineo Skosana, Magogwa (Mokopane), 14 August 2011

5 Gluckman explains how, for example, traditional leaders were often assumed to be pre-ordained by God.

Index

www.ingramcontent.com/pod-product-compliance
Lightning Source LLC
Chambersburg PA
CBHW022131020426
42334CB00015B/852